INTERNATIONAL STUDIES

THIRD EDITION

INTERNATIONAL STUDIES
An Interdisciplinary Approach to Global Issues

Sheldon Anderson
MIAMI UNIVERSITY

Mark Allen Peterson
MIAMI UNIVERSITY

Stanley W. Toops
MIAMI UNIVERSITY

Jeanne A. K. Hey
UNIVERSITY OF NEW ENGLAND

WESTVIEW PRESS

A Member of the Pereus Books Group

Westview Press was founded in 1975 in Boulder, Colorado, by notable publisher and intellectual Fred Praeger. Westview Press continues to publish scholarly titles and high-quality undergraduate- and graduate-level textbooks in core social science disciplines. With books developed, written, and edited with the needs of serious nonfiction readers, professors, and students in mind, Westview Press honors its long history of publishing books that matter.

Find us on the World Wide Web at www.westviewpress.com.

Every effort has been made to secure required permissions for all text, images, maps, and other art reprinted in this volume.

Westview Press books are available at special discounts for bulk purchases in the United States by corporations, institutions, and other organizations. For more information, please contact the Special Markets Department at the Perseus Books Group, 2300 Chestnut Street, Suite 200, Philadelphia, PA 19103, or call (800) 810-4145, ext. 5000, or e-mail special.markets@perseusbooks.com.

Designed by Trish Wilkinson
Set in 11 point Goudy Old Style

Library of Congress Cataloging-in-Publication Data

Anderson, Sheldon R., 1951–
    International studies : an interdisiplinary approach to global issues / Sheldon
Anderson, Mark Allen Peterson, Stanley W. Toops, Jeanne A. K. Hey.—Third Edition.
        pages   cm
    Revised edition of: International studies / Sheldon Anderson . . . [et al.]. 2013.
    Includes bibliographical references and index.
    ISBN 978-0-8133-4932-9 (paperback)—ISBN 978-0-8133-4933-6 (e-book)
1. International relations. 2. Political science. I. Peterson, Mark Allen. II. Toops,
Stanley. III. Hey, Jeanne A. K. IV. Title.
JZ1242.A528 2014
327—dc23   2014008799

10 9 8 7 6 5 4 3 2 1

Contents

v

PART TWO

INTERDISCIPLINARY APPROACHES TO
REGIONAL AND INTERNATIONAL TOPICS

PART THREE

_____

CONTEMPORARY GLOBAL ISSUES

Preface

International studies (ITS) at Miami University and at many other colleges and universities has evolved in recent years from a branch of political science or world languages into a true interdisciplinary approach to current global affairs. Through the vision of Dean Stephen Day and ITS Director William Hazleton in the early 1990s, the ITS program at Miami expanded its curriculum and hired new faculty members with joint appointments in ITS and geography, history, anthropology, and political science. The ITS program now serves hundreds of majors, and over five hundred non-majors take the ITS introductory course every year.

The ITS faculty had difficulty finding suitable readings to accompany the unique interdisciplinary approach of the introductory course. Several years ago we decided to write a text that mirrors the structure of the course and emphasizes an interdisciplinary analysis of issues of regional and global importance. The first half of the course, and the first part of this book, covers the way each discipline—history, geography, anthropology, economics, and political science—contributes to understanding and solving world problems. Part Two examines various regions of the world—North America, Europe, East Asia, South Asia, Africa, the Middle East, and Latin America—while stressing the diversity within the regions and the interconnections among them. Part Three includes essays that analyze contemporary global issues through an interdisciplinary lens. These can be used for discussion coinciding with Part Two of the book.

The authors recognize that the interdisciplinary nature of international studies will draw teachers from various areas of expertise into unfamiliar academic realms. This book is designed to give them a construct with which to teach international studies and an approach to enhance students' understanding of the complexities of the modern world.

This is the third edition of the book. The new edition features up-to-date information on each region of the world, a new chapter on the United States in the global context, new global issues chapters in Part Three, current country statistics, and additional supplementary material. Each chapter is accompanied by a list of recommended readings, films, and websites. There is a glossary of keywords and an appendix that provides a ready reference to country information, such as population, gross national product, and type of government.

The text also comes with an online teacher's manual, including course objectives, syllabi, and assignments that have proven effective in the classroom over many years. Please visit www.internationalstudiescourse.com.

The authors of the text have published extensively in their respective disciplines, and each has a different regional and linguistic expertise. Dr. Sheldon Anderson has written several articles and three books on Cold War history, including a study of Warsaw Pact relations and another on US containment policy. He is fluent in German and Polish. Dr. Anderson is currently working on a study of the history of sport and national identity. He wrote the introduction, the chapters on history, Europe, and Africa, and the essays on Turkey and the "Responsibility to Protect." Dr. Stanley Toops is one of the foremost US geographers of the Uyghur region of northwest China. He is fluent in Chinese and conversant in Uyghur, and he has written articles and chapters on geography, tourism, and population in China and Central Asia. His new work is an atlas of Central Eurasia. Dr. Toops wrote the chapters on geography, East Asia, South Asia, and the essays on BRICS and population. Dr. Mark Allen Peterson has published groundbreaking work on Middle Eastern and South Asian media and globalization. He is fluent in Arabic. Dr. Peterson authored the conclusion and the chapters on anthropology and the Middle East, and contributed to the economics chapter as well as the essays on veiling, international terrorism, and the Arab uprisings. Dr. Jeanne Hey is currently the dean of the College of Arts and Sciences at the University of New England. Dr. Hey authored the politics and Latin America chapters.

The authors owe a debt of gratitude to many people. We would like to thank our colleagues in International Studies at Miami, Melanie Ziegler, Carl Dahlman, Charles Stevens, Kathryn LaFever, Christopher Sarver, and Dilchoda Berdieva for their suggestions on updating the book. Stanley Toops would like to thank Simone Andrus for her contributions to his chapters, and students Daniel Kyale, Kristy Fortman, Adanma Ogboo, Hannah Koonce, Ana Contessa, and Lisa Dershowitz for their work on the maps and tables. Sheldon Anderson would like to thank his family—Kristie, O Maxwell, Lauren, and Mongo—for their patience and support as he worked on this edition of the book. In addition to his coauthors, Mark Allen Peterson would like to thank John Cinnamon, Cameron Hay-Rollins, Linda Marchant, Geoff Owens, Susan Paulson, Dawna Peterson, Douglas Rogers, Daniel Varisco, and Jessica Winegar for their comments on various drafts of chapters, and Lisa Suter for her work on the teacher's manual. Miami University's GIS coordinator, Robbyn Abbitt, edited the maps.

Introduction

Why do international studies? Why take an interdisciplinary approach to global issues? The answers are found in the increasing interdependence of people, nations, and institutions at all levels of human society. Five hundred years ago Europeans explored the Western Hemisphere and broadened their commercial contacts with Africa and Asia, beginning this gradual **globalization** process of bringing regions of the world together. The Industrial Revolution in the nineteenth century and the high-tech revolution in the late twentieth century have brought many of us to the point today where a phone call is possible between someone riding a train in Peru and a climber standing atop Mount Everest. An Indian doctor can read an X-ray for a patient sitting in a physician's office in Topeka. A Russian can buy a car built in South Korea, Germany, Italy, Japan, or the United States. Although most people in the world could not locate Bangladesh on a **map**, the cap they wear might have been made there.

Never before has the world been so integrated. Politics, markets, culture, the media, and information are no longer local but global. The ripple effect of local events on wider regions has grown exponentially in the last century; a century ago events in one part of the world often went unnoticed in another. Today, the proliferation of information through the Internet, cell phones, print media, and television allows people on opposite sides of the globe to experience events simultaneously. What happens on Tokyo's stock exchange has an instantaneous effect on other markets as they open throughout the day. The extent of the destruction of the tsunamis that hit Indonesia in 2004 and Japan in 2011 was known to the world within hours, and faraway countries immediately flew in emergency aid. The effects of terrorist attacks are amplified because the media

1

disseminate the chaos of the moment and engender the fear that follows. Suicide attackers often make videos for posting on the Internet after they have struck, which maximizes the sense that these murderers will stop at nothing to claim innocent people's lives. Beginning in 2011, the so-called Arab Spring of pro-democratic revolts in Tunisia, Egypt, and Libya, among others, was spurred on by Internet and cell phone connections.

The boom in world commerce since World War II is unprecedented. Global currency transactions ballooned from $15 billion daily in 1973 to $4 trillion in 2010. World exports totaled $61 billion in 1950, expanding to $18.3 trillion in 2012. About 25 percent of the world's gross domestic product (GDP) derives from international trade (El-Ojeili and Hayden 2006, 60, 63; TAM 2011; www.wto.org). International financial and business transactions happen instantaneously on electronic networks. The possibility of a default by the Greek government in 2011 sent shock waves through international markets. Millions of foreign workers send money home using secure global-banking services. Products move around the world on airplanes, ships, trains, and long-range trucks, often without human hands touching the containers. On any one day there are about 93,000 airplane departures from approximately 9,000 different airports, and over 65,000 large merchant vessels plying the high seas (InIT 2013; www.marinetraffic.com).

The ramifications of globalization on traditional political, economic, and social relationships are profound. Journalist Thomas Friedman titled one of his books *The Lexus and the Olive Tree* to capture the conflicts in the interconnected world economy. The Lexus represents the boons that a globalized economy offers individuals across the world—the potential for wealth and the products and services coming from all corners of the earth. The olive tree represents the pressures such an economy puts on traditional local societies and communities, including not only low wages and poverty experienced by too many in this modern age, but also the decline of traditional beliefs, practices, and cultures. Even those who seek to conserve old beliefs and values embrace the new technologies. Friedman shows a devout Jew in Israel holding up his cell phone to the Western Wall in Jerusalem so a friend in France can say a prayer at this holy site. Some no doubt feel that the friend should make the trek rather than rely on high tech (Friedman 2000, 29).

This increasing interdependence is usually called globalization, an "intensification of worldwide social relations which link distant localities in such a way that local happenings are shaped by events occurring many miles away and vice versa" (Giddens 1990, 64). Weapons of mass destruction, global climate change, interconnected and fragile trade and financial systems, armed conflict, burgeoning populations, humanitarian crises, and global poverty are among the many international problems that demand the attention of scholars, policymakers, and citizens. Never before has it been so important to find solutions to these problems, and never have these complex issues been harder to grasp. An interdisciplinary approach is essential to fully understanding the historical, geographical, political, cultural, and economic dimensions of these global challenges.

The authors contend that the complexities of the modern age and the interconnectedness of global people, events, and processes is so strong that a break from traditional methods of research and inquiry is required. Foreign-policy makers and educators are becoming increasingly aware of the deficiencies of strict disciplinary approaches to the globalization processes and international affairs today. By *disciplinary* we mean approaches connected to the traditional academic disciplines of history, political science, economics, geography, and anthropology. Instead, international studies offers an integrative, comprehensive, and interdisciplinary approach to issues of global importance.

This book breaks new ground by introducing five disciplines applicable to international studies, and addressing regional and global issues through an interdisciplinary approach. Four of the five disciplines considered here are social sciences, whereas the fifth, history, tends to fall in with the humanities. This is because history does not pretend to be a science. Rather it is the study of past events based on available primary and secondary sources. Professional historians make a good-faith attempt to gather reliable evidence and render the past accurately, but they understand that history is controversial because no two accounts of the past are the same. Historians' interpretations of the past depend on their own biases, the availability of sources, their use of them, and their objectives. Since there is no definitive historical truth, the lessons of history tend to be subjective as well.

Nonetheless, a complete understanding of current international affairs is impossible without knowing the historical context. Historians play a vital role in resolving international conflicts by writing objective historical accounts free of polemic and propaganda. But the advent of the Internet and the rapid flow of information from sources of dubious reliability have created new challenges. Different memories or interpretations of past events are at the heart of many international conflicts. For example, the controversy between the United Nations and Iran over Tehran's quest for nuclear power has its roots in Iran's resentment of British imperialism and US intervention in Iran's domestic affairs during the Cold War. And Japanese-Chinese friction often revolves around the brutal Japanese occupation of China during World War II. At the heart of these tensions is the way historical memory is manipulated to create a national identity. Some Chinese view the Japanese as imperialists, whereas some Japanese remember themselves as progressives and missionaries who brought the benefits of civilization to a supposedly backward people.

Geography's role in international studies is to analyze space, regions, and environments. The physical geographer studies the processes of the natural environment; the human geographer is concerned with human interaction with the physical world. Geographers' evidence includes demographic statistics, climate studies, health records, and communication networks. The map is a special tool that geographers use in their analyses of the earth and people's interaction with it.

Geographic study goes to the heart of such international problems as population density, the spread of disease, water shortages, environmental degradation, border conflicts, population flows, use of space, and transportation networks. Hundreds of millions of migrants annually move from one region to another, millions even making leaps from one continent to another, bringing new customs, expectations, and political agendas. Diseases, blights, and bugs travel on the thousands of ships, airplanes, trains, and automobiles moving around the globe daily. Delicate regional ecologies are subject to alien invaders that hitch rides on long-distance transports. The world waits on edge for invisible strains of flu, drug-resistant tuberculosis, and other deadly diseases transferred on the global highways. Global warming, water and air pollution, soil erosion, and desertification know no political boundaries and are best understood through geography's contribution to an interdisciplinary analysis.

Political science analyzes the power relationships between peoples and the institutions used to mediate their competing interests. Political scientists often employ case studies to identify the variables that explain political behavior, trying to determine if past models are applicable to present cases. Questions of international import are ultimately tied to those who have the power to solve them. Democratic development, international institutions, international relations, and international conflict and conflict resolution are within the purview of political science as it relates to international studies.

Some political scientists have moved from paradigms that seemed to explain international power relationships in the past, such as hegemony and dependence theory, to complex interdependence, which the interdisciplinary approach of international studies seeks to explain. Political relationships are more complicated today because globalization has created greater "power for the powerless" (Havel 1985). For example, international human-rights organizations and the media can disseminate information on a government's political practices that is difficult to control. The Chinese regime is desperately trying to regulate Internet sites that criticize its undemocratic practices. Political scientists are keenly interested in whether China can maintain political repression while participating in a globalized economy.

The global information network can also undermine the power of liberal democratic governments, which can be criticized for the influence of money in politics, the disparity between rich and poor, and racial discrimination. Easy access to information also foments identity politics, which can divide societies into cultural or political groups that oppose each other and make democratic compromise and cooperation nearly impossible. The street protests in Egypt in 2013 attest to the power of the social media to rally supporters. Internet commerce also undermines national legal systems. For example, it is illegal in Germany to sell Adolf Hitler's *Mein Kampf*, but it became one of Amazon.com's top-ten sellers in Germany in 1999 (Friedman 2000, 37).

Anthropology examines global culture: the similarities and differences of human environments, economic systems, ideologies, political systems, and languages. People understand and explain the world in different ways, which helps to explain why people in one society behave differently from those in another. This elusive concept of **culture** is a learned system of meanings through which people orient themselves in the world.

Global cultural transfers put pressure on local customs and traditions, but these transfers, that were once dominated by the richer countries, now go both ways. The world's consumption of McDonald's burgers and Hollywood films is often cited as an example of the effect of globalization on local eating habits and artistic expression, but Indian Bollywood movies, South Korean cars, the low prices of goods from China, and workers moving from one country to another are also causing profound challenges to local cultures. Indians may be eating barbecue, but Texans are eating curry, too. Anthropology urges us to look also at the flip side of globalization—localization—through which people localize the commodities, services, and ideas that enter their communities from outside, transforming them and making them their own.

Although some scholars highlight a "clash of civilizations" (Huntington 1996) that globalization engenders, others argue that the world is actually experiencing an integration of civilizations that brings peoples closer together. Understanding the cultural elements of behavior is an essential component of a broad international studies education. In this increasingly mobile world, cultural clashes, cultural sharing, and cultural changes are happening faster now than ever before.

Economists study the production, distribution, and consumption of goods and services. International economics concerns financial relations, trade regimes, and economic development. Economists deal with the most basic yet most complex problems facing any society. For example, what strategies promote economic growth and provide for basic human needs and economic opportunities? Are there any fundamental economic rights, such as medical care, housing, and food?

One of the hot economic debates in the world today pits globalists against economic nationalists. The globalists, or liberal economists, advocate free and unfettered economic relations between states as a means to increase the wealth and prosperity of all people in all nations. Some even argue that war is less likely between open-market economies because the economic costs to an aggressor are too high. Economic nationalists argue that the world's free-trade regime lowers wages and causes unemployment for workers in developed economies. They also point to the increasing economic disparity between the rich and the poor, both within and between countries. Small businesses in every country struggle to compete against the world's giant corporations, which can often provide cheaper goods and services and consistently meet demand at lower cost to the consumer. But in some industries small businesses may be more nimble at utilizing or inventing productive technologies than bigger corporations.

The second half of the book introduces six regions of the world: North America, Europe, East Asia, South Asia, Africa, the Middle East, and Latin America. Some scholars have criticized the area-studies approach because Westerners arbitrarily constructed these regional labels. For example, if we think of the so-called Middle East as an area comprised mainly of Arab peoples, it also has to include northern Africa as well as southwestern Asia. Iran and Turkey are bookends of the region, but neither of these countries is Arab. Geographically, Russia is both European and Asian, although its cultural and political heritage comes primarily from the West.

The authors are fully aware of the limitations of a regional approach to international affairs. However, even in an era of globalization, thinking about the world in terms of geopolitical regions remains useful for several reasons. First, dividing the world into regions offers a way to manage enormous amounts of information about environments, people, and social relations. Trying to understand international issues in terms of the nearly 200 countries in the world and recognized dependent areas—each with its unique history, environment, economy, and political and cultural systems—is beyond the scope of any scholar or analytical approach. Trying to attend to every country can lead to a failure to see the forest for the trees.

Second, thinking regionally allows us to aggregate information common to groups of peoples and countries in order to see big pictures. Each region exhibits some common political, economic, linguistic, religious, or historical currents. Most Europeans have a Christian heritage, similar cultural norms, and social democratic political systems. Latin Americans are mostly Catholic, speak either Spanish or Portuguese, have similar economic challenges, and have struggled to establish stable democracies. Although Westerners devised most of the world's continental designations and national borders, peoples in these regions have constructed their regional identities as well.

The authors have made conscious efforts to illustrate the diversity within the regions as well as their interconnectedness. There are no walls dividing them, but many bridges linking them together. Globalization along the electronic highway, sea lanes, rails, and roads has blurred old regional categories. Understanding the political, economic, historical, geographic, and cultural differences both within and among these areas is the essence of international studies inquiry.

Thinking about the world regionally can also serve as a useful heuristic device that helps us avoid ethnocentric and region-specific thinking. For example, Americans tend to see issues of global terrorism through the lens of Islamic terrorism, because this has become particularly important to US national security. By making a point of looking at international issues in terms of every region, we discover terrorism in Latin America, Asia, and Africa. Terrorism is certainly not a Muslim or Middle Eastern activity, although too much of the Western press might arrive at that conclusion. Al Qaeda is not representative of mainstream society in any Muslim region of the world. That said, terrorist organizations are at the top of the global agenda because of their responsibility for the September 11, 2001, attacks in the United States, as well as for the urban bombings in Madrid in 2004 and London in 2005. Islamic anger has also been blamed for the murder of Dutch filmmaker Theo van Gogh for allegedly defaming Islam, and for widespread (and sometimes violent) demonstrations throughout the Islamic world in reaction to a Danish newspaper's printing of satirical cartoons of the prophet Muhammad. Neither van Gogh's murder nor the demonstrations were terrorism, and it is important not to conflate al Qaeda's activities with those of troubled individuals or groups expressing their anger. Yet there is evidence that the thinking behind September 11 and these other activities are similar and rooted in Islamic anger at perceived Western imperialism.

Globalization creates a new context within which terrorism—a centuries-old political tool—occurs in the modern world. Indeed, globalization creates a new context within which all political activity operates. First, events themselves are publicized instantaneously, repeatedly, and globally. Modern terrorists know that their acts will gain worldwide attention. Second, all political organizations, including terrorist ones, benefit from the Internet's global reach. Personal computers and global networks make fund-raising, recruiting, and disseminating information easier than ever before. Third, and in a different vein, globalization and technology also give terrorists and other groups access to points of view different from their own group's ideology. Finally, law enforcement uses the instruments of globalization to monitor and capture potential terrorists and other criminals.

Scholars, politicians, and ordinary people have desperately searched for answers to the terrorist threat emanating from a tiny minority of the fundamentalist Muslim community, and the larger problem of what one scholar has called the "jihad versus McWorld" conflict (Barber 1992). A geographer might find answers in the demographic explosion of an unemployed, frustrated, and angry younger population. A historian might place terrorism in the continuum of a long history of conflicts between the Middle East and Western imperialists. A political scientist might approach the problem through the lens of the Israeli-Palestinian conflict, illegitimate borders, or the authoritarian regimes and lack of democracy in the Middle East. An economist might emphasize the poverty in the Middle East or the region's frustration with the challenges of modernization and economic development. An anthropologist might ask what kinds of cultural symbols are employed by terrorist organizations to recruit people willing to kill and die for a cause—and why these ideologies attract a relatively small number of people.

International studies, unlike any singular discipline, draws on *all* of these disciplines in an integrated way for answers. Twenty-first-century challenges, such as terrorism, sustainable economic development, poverty, pollution, global warming, AIDS, nuclear proliferation, human rights, and interstate and civil conflicts do not stop at national boundaries or disciplinary categories. The notion that any global challenge can be studied or solved with the lenses and tools of one discipline is outdated. This book aims to help students begin to think in an integrated and critical way, relying on valuable perspectives from many disciplines but moving beyond disciplinary boundaries toward complex explanations and understanding.

References

Barber, Benjamin R. 1992. "Jihad vs. McWorld." *Atlantic Monthly* (March).

CIA (Central Intelligence Agency). 2009. *The World Factbook.* Washington, DC: Central Intelligence Agency. https://www.cia.gov/library/publications/the-world-factbook/index.html.

El-Ojeili, Chamsy, and Patrick Hayden. 2006. *Critical Theories of Globalization.* New York: Palgrave.

Friedman, Thomas. 2000. *The Lexus and the Olive Tree.* New York: Anchor Books.

Giddens, Anthony. 1990. *The Consequences of Modernity.* Stanford, CA: Stanford University Press.

Havel, Václav, et al. 1985. *The Power of the Powerless: Citizens Against the State in Central-Eastern Europe,* edited by John Keane. Armonk, NY: M. E. Sharpe.

Huntington, Samuel P. 1996. *The Clash of Civilizations and the Remaking of the World Order.* New York: Simon & Schuster.

InIT (Institute of Applied Information Technology), Zurich University of Applied Sciences, 2013. www.fiixxy.com.

TAM (Tapestry Asset Management). 2011. "Foreign Exchange Markets." TAM Spotlight April 2011. http://www.tapestryam.com/tam_spotlight.

PART ONE

The Disciplines of International Studies

1

The Past in the Present

Historical Interpretation in International Conflict

Historical inquiry combines all of the disciplines of international studies. Historians use geographical, economic, political, cultural, and any other relevant sources—regardless of their disciplinary category—to create an accurate portrayal of the past. History teaches students to evaluate evidence, consider contradictory interpretations, and construct coherent narratives. History is one of the best ways to understand human experience and the patterns of change within society.

The history profession is divided into several arbitrary and fluid categories. **Political and diplomatic history** is concerned with the study of power and power relationships. It is the oldest historical tradition, often characterized by biographies of significant people. Politics, law, and foreign policy come under the purview of political history.

Political history is central to understanding current international relations. For example, the rapid growth of the Chinese economy under the tutelage of an authoritarian Communist government has foreign-policy makers debating the future of China's role in the world. Some realists argue that every great power in history has flexed its muscles and threatened the interests of other powers. China's political history can provide clues to its likely foreign-policy course.

Economic history involves the study of the exchange of goods and services. Economic historians seek insight into economic trends that might inform future economic and business decisions. Economic problems call for gathering sources relevant to a given question, analyzing their reliability, and interpreting their meaning. For example, if a business wants to expand into a certain market, it must consider the demographic character of the population, the location, the standard of living, and the success or failure of previous business ventures in the area.

Theories of economic development depend on accurate case histories of regions that have experienced economic prosperity. Policies that work in one area, however, may not work in another. Historians of economic development are cognizant that the success of a certain growth strategy depends on factors such as climate, culture, political leadership, infrastructure, and resources.

A subfield of economic history is **labor history**, which focuses on the development of working-class solidarity, and relations between workers, management, and the government. In the context of international studies, globalization has raised new questions about free-market economics and the plight of wage earners.

Broadly defined, **cultural and social history** include the study of music, sports, religion, and art, as well as the history of urban and rural society, immigration, race, family, population, gender, and disease. We depend on historians to provide in-depth understanding of many relevant global issues, such as women's rights, the clash of global and local cultures, the role of religion in regional conflicts, aging populations in the developed world, and the threat of pandemic diseases.

Intellectual historians study the power of ideas to move historical events. **Intellectual history** concentrates on the development and influence of ideologies such as religion, **nationalism, liberalism, Marxism**, and feminism. For example, when Vladimir Ilyich Lenin brought a Marxist revolution to Russia in 1917, the idea of a classless society inspired leftists throughout the world for seventy-five years. The Russian manifestation of that idea, however, was a failure, and the Soviet Union fell apart in 1991. National allegiances proved stronger than class solidarity as the Soviet Empire broke up on national lines.

Historians can provide a long view of current ideological debates in international affairs, such as the advantages and disadvantages of a global liberal economic system, the efficacy of spreading democracy in some regions of the world, and the influence of religion and nationalism on international conflict.

The progress of civilization depends on reliable histories of science and technology. No scientist or engineer works without a thorough grounding in the past. Isaac Newton once said, "If I see farther, it is because I stand on the shoulders of giants" (quoted in Westfall 1993, 643). Technological innovation plays a central role in international affairs. Medical experts debate the causes, prevention, and treatment of disease. For doctors and their patients, accurate clinical studies and reliable interpretations and histories of them are matters of life and death. Doctors want to know family medical history to examine susceptible patients or to make possible diagnoses. Engineers depend on past experience to improve on previous constructs, such as hydroelectric projects, irrigation plans, and transportation systems. For example, careful study of earthquakes in Haiti and Japan, or the collapse of the World Trade Center towers on September 11, 2001, has spawned new construction plans for buildings that can withstand such calamities.

The related field of **environmental history** is devoted to people's interaction with their natural surroundings. This important new field has generated works on the history of such international issues as water usage, farming practices, food distribution and famine, and marine and forest preservation. The debate on global warming centers around evidence of past climate change and whether human activity is contributing to a rise in global temperatures. Climate history provides a base from which to judge the peculiarities of present weather patterns.

WHAT IS HISTORY?

In 2003, author Bill Bryson wrote a thin volume called *A Short History of Nearly Everything*. On the one hand, the irony in Bryson's title is obvious, but on the other there is a commonly held notion that history is everything that has happened in the past. That would be a very long book indeed. The past disappears if no one remembers it or passes it along. History is a written, oral, or visual reconstruction and interpretation of past human endeavors based on available sources.

Students often use the slang phrase "you're history" in the same way they think about history, that it is something over and done with. The historian's task is to revisit the past again and again, scrutinize histories for their veracity, and use new sources of information to verify, add to, or revise them.

There is no agreed-upon record of the past. Historians can come to some consensus on what was a major event and when it took place, such as natural disasters, economic depressions, or wars, but they differ on questions of **causation**, interpretation, and significance. History resembles a criminal trial: detectives compile evidence, and prosecutors use it to reconstruct the crime. Defense lawyers then call witnesses to revise that version of history. The reasonable-doubt standard for conviction always applies to any history.

The word *history* comes from the Latin *historia*, meaning "to inquire." Histories have existed as long as people have reflected on what went on in the past. The first histories were oral and visual. As far as we know, written history is only several thousand years old. Mythical history sought to explain the origins of the world, natural phenomena, and the meaning of life. Parables and morality plays, ostensibly based on real stories, laid down the norms of societal behavior. This early philosophy evolved into the tracts of the major religions—Judaism, Christianity, Islam, Hinduism, and Buddhism.

Historians usually remembered the exploits of major political and religious leaders, such as Alexander the Great of Macedonia in the fourth century BCE or Emperor Charlemagne in the late eighth century CE. Written histories were often tales of war and imperial victories or defeats. Family histories traced the lineage of important historical figures, for example the dynastic succession of ancient Roman or Chinese emperors, or the popes of the Catholic Church. Bureaucracies and legal standards were built on keeping records of past practices.

Until the late twentieth century, political history dominated the profession. From Thucydides's *History of the Peloponnesian War* in the fifth century BCE to Edward Gibbon's late-eighteenth-century *History of the Decline and Fall of the Roman Empire*, most historians studied the political fortunes of the most powerful members of society. Many histories were panegyrics to glorify and justify the rule of the dominant political classes. The history of religion and ideas provided the spiritual and philosophical foundations of temporal power. Historical accuracy played a secondary role to the narrative's didactic purpose.

Influenced by the humanism and rational thinking of Renaissance and Enlightenment scholars, as well as by the rapid technological changes of modern industrial society, some nineteenth-century historians in the West championed a new empirical approach to history. Karl Marx devised a political-economic theory of history based on the "scientific" truth of class conflict. German historian Leopold von Ranke claimed to write history "wie es eigentlich gewesen ist," or history "as it really was." Von

FIGURE 1.1 Karl Marx. SOURCE: Library of Congress.

Ranke and fellow positivists tried to inject the scientific method into the process of writing history. They called for histories based on empirical evidence and historical objectivity. Reference notes cued the reader to the documents used to prove the truth of the history. To reflect this change in the approach to studying history, many history departments shifted from the humanities to the social sciences during the twentieth century.

The Rankean model came under increased fire after World War II when **revisionist history** began to question the "scientific truth" of history. Revisionists claimed, often correctly, that conventional histories about the past were myths intended to foster a sense of national unity and national pride. They revealed that many stories of the past manipulated historical facts and ignored nondominant perspectives. In the United States, revisionists laid bare the lies that the Johnson and Nixon administrations told about the Vietnam War. Civil-rights advocates demanded a truer version of the past to reflect the dismal treatment of minorities in American history. In Europe, historians exposed the brutality of imperial rule, state violence against working classes, and, in light of the Holocaust, Europe's endemic anti-Semitism and fascist tendencies. Historians examine and reexamine new evidence to reframe the past, or to confirm previous accounts.

Today, so-called **postmodernist historians** deny the existence of any objective histories. They argue that the past cannot be recovered and that no narrative can be an accurate reflection of what actually transpired. Like impressionist and expressionist art, they consider history to be a partial and particular depiction of reality as the creator creates it or the audience perceives it. Observed from different angles and distances, and under different kinds of light, the image changes.

Postmodernists emphasize the cultural mediation of historical memory; in some ways, they argue, historical narratives reveal more about the author's beliefs and cultural milieu than history "as it really was." Historians are the filter through which the past is constructed. They bring their own personal, national, or class biases to the trade. They are carried along by the stream of human history, and they influence the cultural context and are influenced by it. Even video and film documentation is dependent on the framing, camera angle, and editing. Scenes can be staged, and in this age of computer imaging, entirely contrived. Because history is merely a representation of the past and is continually shaped and reshaped, postmodernists argue, there can be no objective historical truth.

Professional historians know this, but they still make a good-faith effort to use all relevant sources and write balanced narratives that come as close to the truth about the past as possible. Reliable histories depend on the skill and thoroughness of historians, the cogency of their logic, and conscious subordination of the biases they bring to their work. Sources take good historians where they may not want to go. Writers who start with a premise, fit the sources to prove it, and ignore contrary evidence are more interested in polemical than historical discourse. The resolution of international disputes often depends on histories and historians dedicated to accurate renditions of the past.

HISTORIANS AND THEIR TOOLS

The historian's task is to garner all available relevant sources to construct a plausible story of the past. Historians scour archives, libraries, museums, and other repositories of documents and artifacts. They often gather data through interviews, although the passage of time limits their utility. Journalists are historians too, but short-term deadlines limit their access to relevant evidence. Historians benefit by drawing on a wider range of sources, although the clues to the historian's case are always incomplete.

Historical data are often divided into two somewhat subjective categories. **Primary sources** include artifacts, diaries, letters, memoirs, e-mails, autobiographies, interviews, official documents, visual images, coins, stamps, demographic statistics, economic records, and polls. Primary sources are direct evidence about the past from someone involved in the past event, without an intermediary's interpretation. Theoretically, primary sources are raw objective data that are untainted by bias or the knowledge that historians will use them to construct a history. There is a fine line between primary and secondary sources, however, because it is often difficult to know what motives people had for leaving sources behind. For example, did the minute taker of an important foreign-policy planning session give an honest rendering of the meeting, or did that person intend to exaggerate the wisdom of the participants? Like a prosecuting attorney, the historian must search for other corroborating evidence to find the truth and decide which primary sources are most reliable.

Letters and diaries may seem to be direct and objective links to the past, but the authors often write them knowing that historians will read them later. Autobiographies are also written for posterity; authors are unlikely to provide critical self-examination of their lives. Eyewitness accounts, a staple in the journalist's trade, provide very different pictures of a single event. The historian is well aware of the irony in the witness-stand pledge to "tell the truth, the whole truth, and nothing but the truth." There is no such thing. Taken at face value, statistics appear to be the most objective of all primary sources. But as any sociologist knows, statistics are only as good as the data from which they are derived. And even the most accurate statistics can be skewed to say almost anything.

Secondary sources are oral or written narratives derived from primary sources. The authors of newspaper articles, journal articles, and books gather sources to interpret what happened in the past. The distinction between primary and secondary sources is muddled when a historian writes a history of histories, often called a **historiography**. In that case, previous histories become the author's primary sources.

Historians must make judgments about the reliability of their source material. Both historians and political scientists try to find patterns in the past, but historians are more skeptical about categorizing behaviors into definitive categories and using them to make predictions about the future.

POLITICS, POWER, AND HISTORY

The victors in power struggles have passed down most of recorded history. The politically powerful have greater access to written, oral, and visual media. Histories often glorify political leaders, praise heroic exploits on the battlefield, or emphasize a particular group's cultural and scientific accomplishments. Political agendas filter out dissonant historical evidence. The "triumphal" version of American history includes Christopher Columbus's "discovery" of America (as though no one lived in the Western hemisphere), the unique democratic character of the American form of government (what about the Netherlands, France, or the United Kingdom?), and the "benevolent" US expansion into the American West and abroad (ask Native Americans). This history typically exaggerates the peculiar democratic and righteous character of the American people and downplays the country's slaveholding past, imperialism, and ethnic cleansing of America's native peoples.

The history of the oppressed has always existed, but until recently their stories have been excluded from the dominant cultural discourse. It is only in the last half of the twentieth century that "history from below" has become mainstream. Revisionist histories have become common; now historians study Native Americans, colonized peoples, women, the working classes, and other groups hidden from view in the old political histories of "dead white guys."

Histories of the "defeated" can be just as biased as those of their oppressors, however. Some historians have exaggerated the peace-loving character of Native American or African peoples before Europeans corrupted their cultures. Some Afrocentrists have shaped the historical record to argue that Egyptians and other African peoples were more advanced than the Greeks or Romans, or have downplayed the lively African slave trade before the arrival of European slavers. Some labor historians portray working-class leaders as intelligent, nonviolent, altruistic champions of the people, and factory owners as inherently greedy, inhumane, and exploitative. Victims of oppression do themselves no service by exaggerating their political and cultural achievements and distorting the historical record. No other group will believe myths based on historical falsehoods.

When leaders distort the historical record to suit their political aims, tragedy often results. The French were fully appreciative of American military assistance in World War I, but their military histories stressed the

FIGURE 1.2 Landing of Christopher Columbus in the Caribbean. SOURCE: Library of Congress.

sacrifices and heroism of the French forces for winning the war, and the success of trench warfare in defending Paris. These histories downplayed the role of American soldiers in turning the military balance in favor of the Allies in 1917. Acting upon these false assumptions about why they had won the war, the French built the massive Maginot Line along the French-German border. This costly, sophisticated line of defensive fortifications did not save France from the German onslaught in 1940.

Soviet scholars ran a historical enterprise that was dedicated to "predicting the past." In other words, the past had to be cast in a way that squared with Marx's theory of history as class struggle. Thus peasant revolts were part of an inexorable struggle against the aristocratic classes, and the middle classes were deemed keepers of an inherently oppressive democratic-capitalist system. After his death in 1924, Lenin was permanently encased in a glass mausoleum for all Soviet citizens to view for eternity. Although Marx had focused on classes rather than individuals to explain historical progress, paradoxically there was room for sainthood in "scientific" Soviet history. Russians are now divided about whether to bury Lenin.

The leaders of the Soviet Communist Party could do no wrong; even Soviet leader Nikita Khrushchev's "secret speech" in 1956, in which he exposed Joseph Stalin's crimes, did not result in a serious revision of Soviet history. The system survived by hiding the Party's culpability (Khrushchev included) for the ruthless suppression of any opposition, the collectivization that resulted in mass starvation in the 1930s, and the incarceration and murder of hundreds of thousands of innocent people during the Great Purges. The last Soviet leader, Mikhail Gorbachev, allowed a policy of *glasnost* (openness) in the late 1980s that finally released Russian historians from seventy years of lies and distortions. Once Gorbachev revealed the falsehoods of Soviet history, the system could not survive. The Chinese Communist leadership today knows that they must control their version of the past lest they meet the same fate as the Soviet Union.

Some historians credit nuclear deterrence for keeping the peace between the United States and the Soviet Union during the **Cold War**. There is no evidence in newly released documents from Soviet and US archives, however, that either side contemplated a first strike except in response to a direct conventional military attack on a friend or ally. Will the deterrent principle prevent nuclear powers India and Pakistan from going to war again? If we believe nuclear weapons prevent war, some countries may try to build their own deterrent nuclear arsenal. Nuclear proliferation could be the result. In the age of weapons of mass destruction, the stakes are obviously too high for the public to tolerate the willful use of inaccurate histories to make and justify policy decisions.

HISTORY AND INTERNATIONAL CONFLICTS

The current state of international affairs cannot be understood without a thorough understanding of the way history is constructed. Contradictory versions of the past are at the heart of the most intractable international conflicts today. Collective memories are often fostered to serve national political goals. **Nationalist histories** are usually not concerned with individual rights and responsibilities; rather, they tend to champion one nation over another and often elicit demands for retribution to right past injustices. This "our group has done no wrong" version of the past is a major obstacle to political compromise.

FIGURE 1.3 Irish woman during the famine begging for help from American ships.
SOURCE: Library of Congress.

For example, some Irish Catholics interpret the centuries-old British
presence in Ireland as imperial conquest rather than settlement. Many
Irish Catholics still blame the British for the loss of their land, the potato
famine, and the lingering poverty in the Northern Irish Catholic community. Oliver Cromwell, the Union Jack, and the English crown are reminders of British imperialism and frustrated national expression. In contrast,
Northern Irish Protestants driving through Belfast might take a nostalgic
look at the giant cranes of the defunct dry dock where the *Titanic*, a symbol of the modern economic progress and relative wealth of their community, was built in the early twentieth century. The presence of British
political institutions in Northern Ireland is a comforting reminder to them
of close links to the British Empire.

Diametrically opposing versions of history are used to justify Israeli or
Arab claims on Palestine. Israelis reference the Hebrew Bible to make the
"we were here first" argument. That is ancient history to Arabs, who argue
that their presence in Palestine over the last 1,200 years is a more legitimate historical claim. Arab **Muslims**, Jews, and Christians lived in the
area for centuries before European Jewish immigrants began arriving in significant numbers after World War I. Israel has won the three wars against
Arab states since partition in 1947, prompting many Israelis to shrug and
say that might makes right. Israelis celebrate the birth of the new Israeli
state in 1948, while Palestinians term it the *nakba* (catastrophe).

Most Israeli and Palestinian history books give different versions of the
Palestinian flight to the West Bank and Gaza Strip in 1947 and 1948. The
Israelis certainly terrorized some of the Palestinian community into leaving the UN-designated area of Israel, as Palestinians maintain, but many
Arabs left of their own accord. Whether or not Palestinians have a right
to return to their homes in Israel hinges on this historical debate, which
contributed to the failed peace process of the late 1990s. The tragedy of
the Arab-Israeli conflict is that both sides have legitimate historic claims
to Palestine.

Historians make semantic choices that often reveal bias. Palestinians
might refer to their suicide bombers as martyrs on a political, military, and
religious mission, while Israelis label them criminals and mass murderers.
Nationalist Serbs embrace their militias in Bosnia during the Yugoslav
Civil War in the 1990s as heroic defenders of the nation, not rapists or
mass murderers. The Nicaraguan Contra rebel group fought the leftist
Sandinista government in the 1980s. They were paramilitary remnants
of the thuggish deposed dictatorship of Anastasio Somoza, but President Ronald Reagan gave them the moniker "freedom fighters." Are the
Chechen rebels in Russia a legitimate resistance movement fighting for
independence from Russian imperialism, or a bunch of sadistic terrorists?
Some observers claim that the **janjaweed** bands operating against the indigenous populations in the Darfur region of western Sudan are government supported; the government prefers to call them "rogue bandits."

When nationalists are confronted with criticism of their people, they
react with denial and verbal attacks on other peoples. They view history
as an inexorable struggle of nation against nation and, therefore, criticism
of one's own history as treasonous. Serbian nationalists point out that

FIGURE 1.4 The Temple Mount in Jerusalem is a disputed holy site for both Jews and Muslims. SOURCE: Library of Congress.

Croatians and Bosnian Muslims committed mutual atrocities during the war. True enough, but that does nothing to exonerate Serbian criminals.

India and Pakistan use opposing versions of history to stake their claims to Kashmir. When the British granted independence to India in 1947, the state fell into communal strife between Muslims and Hindus. Two new Islamic states of West and East Pakistan (today Pakistan and Bangladesh, respectively) emerged, leaving hundreds of thousands dead and millions of people displaced. Whether Muslim-majority Kashmir should be part of these Islamic states or part of India depends on the details of the complicated processes by which rajahs turned over their states to these newly formed nations more than sixty years ago. Pakistan and India have fought three wars since then, and low-level fighting over Kashmir continues. Both states have nuclear weapons, making the area one of the most dangerous threats to regional and world peace. Historical dissonance persists over which side was the aggressor and how many people were forced to leave their communities.

Defense of the nation becomes synonymous with defense of the national myth. Several years ago, an Indian education minister mandated a
revisionist version of Indian history texts to recast former Muslim rulers
of India as uncivilized, brutal despots. In 2003, a US author published a
much-acclaimed book that some Indians believed maligned the reputation of a seventeenth-century Hindu king. Former Prime Minister Atal
Bihari Vajpayee warned foreign authors not to "play with our national
pride. We are prepared to take action against the foreign author in case
the state government fails to do so" (Dalrymple 2005, 62).

Who are the keepers of authentic Chinese history, the nationalist
Chinese in Taiwan or the Communist regime on mainland China? In the
Marxist version of Chinese history, the Taiwanese leaders are the bour-
geois capitalist lackeys of Western imperialists. The nationalists teach
their children that the Red Chinese overthrew the legitimate Chinese
government in 1949, killing hundreds of thousands of innocent people in
the process. They point out that Mao Zedong's Great Leap Forward in the
late 1950s caused a famine that killed 30 million Chinese and that Beijing
has yet to hold a free democratic election. At present, the differences in
these histories are a clear reflection of the political stalemate across the
Strait of Taiwan.

Another potential Asian flashpoint is the Chinese-Japanese relationship. Despite—or perhaps because of—a tremendous increase in economic
intercourse between the two countries in the past decade, contested nationalist histories create tensions. It strikes a raw nerve in China when the
Japanese whitewash the brutality and cruelty of their invasion and occupation of China in 1937, or when the Japanese downplay the destruction of
the incident the Chinese call the "rape of Nanjing."

Japanese leaders often pander to right-wing nationalists by paying hom-
age to fallen Japanese soldiers at the Yasukuni shrine in Tokyo, where
convicted war criminals are also buried. The Chinese leadership is always
outraged at this pilgrimage, which they view as an implicit sanction for
Japanese aggression in China. Japanese nationalists prefer to emphasize the
industrial progress that Japanese imperialists brought to continental Asia.

In 2007, the Japanese prime minister claimed that women in conquered
areas—so-called comfort women—willingly entered into prostitution to
serve Japanese soldiers. Some Japanese scholars have discovered convinc-
ing documentary evidence that the Japanese army had a program to set up
military brothels in Korea, China, and Southeast Asia.

FIGURE 1.5 Japanese soldiers in Manchuria in the 1930s. SOURCE: Library of Congress.

"History is a nightmare from which I am trying to awake," lamented Stephen Dedalus, an Irish character in James Joyce's *Ulysses*. Joyce's Haines, an Englishman, understood the plight of the Irish: "I can quite understand that an Irish man must think like that, I dare say. We feel in England that we have treated you rather unfairly. It seems history is to blame" (Joyce [1922] 1984, 38). It is a sign of a mature democratic society when scholars enjoy the freedom to criticize their own people for crimes against humanity. Germans have conducted a thorough examination of the Holocaust and other atrocities committed in their name by the Third Reich. The South African Truth and Reconciliation Commission has tried to reconstruct the crimes of the South African apartheid regime in an effort to move race relations and democracy forward. Confronted with a mountain of physical evidence of the mass murder of Bosnian Muslims by Serbs in Srebrenica in 1995, the new democratic government in Belgrade has hunted down and prosecuted the perpetrators. In contrast, authoritarian regimes imprison or kill their critics, rather than seek absolution for past crimes committed by the state.

WHAT IS GOOD HISTORY?

If all history is subjective, how can we trust any rendition of the past? The recent worldwide expansion of written and electronic media now puts thousands of different sources at one's fingertips. Much to the chagrin of history teachers, students can cull sources from websites of unknown credibility.

Obviously, some sources are more trustworthy than others. The historical field, like medicine or law, has professional historical associations and professional journals. For example, the American Historical Association publishes the *American Historical Review,* and the Society for Historians of American Foreign Relations publishes *Diplomatic History.* Articles are refereed by other historians. Reputable publishing houses and university presses put prospective books through a similar vetting process.

Some university presses will even operate at a loss to ensure that important new research is published, even if the work is not marketable to a general audience. Histories published by a reputable university press are generally more reliable than private television productions, the popular press, blogs, or other websites of doubtful reliability. Universities and research centers in the free world hire historians on the basis of their professional training and prior publishing record. These institutions afford scholars the opportunity to write without fear of political reprisal or pressure to turn a profit.

Popular histories are less accurate narratives of the past, but they have a great capacity to influence public opinion. If authors must convince an editor of the marketability of their work, they will be tempted to embellish the story. A question often posed regarding historical novels and movies is whether they are historically accurate. It is a fair question if one recognizes that the producer will add dramatic effect whether or not it has any connection to the known historical record. Movies such as *Titanic, Lincoln,* and *Saving Private Ryan,* or novels such as *The Da Vinci Code,* attract mass audiences because they combine realism with a captivating, if not entirely accurate, version of past events.

THEORIES OF HISTORY

Historians construct theories of the past to explain and understand the human condition. Theories guide the historian's method, approach, and sources. For example, Western historians have tried to explain Europe's rise to global ascendancy in the last five centuries. Some theorize that the key factor was Europe's advantageous geographical and climatic position, or the **balance of power** among European states that spawned intense scientific and technological competition, or Europeans' navigational skills and resistance to disease. Others emphasize Christianity and its peculiar rational means to understand the Bible and the world. Historians use available evidence to test these hypotheses, although theory will often determine the direction of their research.

The historical debate about the origins of humans between evolutionists and those who believe in intelligent design hinges on the testability of these respective approaches. Evolution can be verified or disproven through observation, but intelligent design is a belief that cannot be subjected to the rigors of the historical method. Intelligent design is not provable.

Some people think of history as **providential** (Benjamin 1991, 12–13). From this perspective, meaning in life derives from the belief that a higher power is operating in the world, if not always in explicable ways. God must have had some reason for unleashing the worldwide AIDS epidemic, the tsunami in Southeast Asia in 2004, or the earthquake in Haiti in 2010. Some people believe that God has given their nation a special mission to fight evil (often another nation), promote global freedom, or spread their religion and culture. This view, like other determinist theories of history, reduces the importance of individual free will and responsibility. Most professional historians leave the question of divine intervention and the meaning of life to philosophers and theologians, and concentrate on the historical events they can observe.

Another way to make sense of the past is a **progressive** view of history. In the early nineteenth century, German philosopher Georg Hegel wrote that as new ideas challenged old traditions, a new synthesis would result to develop better political, economic, and social structures. In other words, through education and rising standards of living, people can rid society of past wrongs such as slavery, war, and inequality, and learn to live in peace and harmony. This is an essential element of Western thought, and it provides the rationale for universal education and liberal democracy. Marxism is also a progressive view of history. The end of history will be a utopian classless society in which all people will "make according to their ability and take according to their needs."

A more pessimistic **theory of history** is that the past is cyclical. In other words, there are discernible patterns in the past that are likely to repeat themselves. In the history of capitalism, for example, economies have cycles of growth and recession. Some realists argue that any new rising power will challenge the power of the older, and a military clash is likely. Those who adhere to this view of history foresee an inevitable Sino-American conflict over dominance in Asia.

These theories of history bring some **rationality** and meaning to our daily lives. We are most uncomfortable with the randomness of historical events. When we read of a murder in the newspaper, we are comforted to find out that the perpetrator knew the victim. No one wants to contemplate walking down the street and being killed by a stranger. Random violence has no meaning, and there is no way to avoid it. Terrorists can create a disproportionate fear in people, although we have a greater chance of getting hit by lightning than dying in a terrorist act. Over three thousand people simply went to work on September 11, 2001, and died in the terrorists' attacks. Highway deaths worldwide vastly dwarf the terrorists' death toll, but people's fears of dying in a car crash are not great enough to create the political will to do much about it.

Casinos have capitalized on people's desire to believe in logic and patterns of the past. Roulette wheels now have a "history board" informing potential players of the numbers and colors that have hit in the last several hours. Suppose for example that "red seven" has not come up all day. By what mathematicians call the *law of independent trials*, red seven has no better odds of hitting on the next or any subsequent spin of the wheel than does any other number, including those that have already come up, perhaps several times. Nonetheless, people passing by the history board impulsively plunk their money down on red seven on the expectation that it is "due" to come up.

Historians try to identify some patterns in the past to help understand the present, but historians do not agree about which variables caused events. Causation is one of the trickiest problems in writing about the past, and historians' conclusions can have far-reaching effects on future policy. If Germany were mainly responsible for the catastrophe of World War I, then the Germans should have paid with an even harsher treaty than Versailles. If one believes that US containment policy caused the fall of Soviet communism, not Soviet Premier Mikhail Gorbachev's bold new foreign policies, then American leaders might exaggerate US power to influence world politics in any way it wants. The essential question in the war on terror is this: Did US policies cause September 11, or did the terrorists merely hate the United States because it is free? How historians answer these questions has direct impact on the way we think about the present. The dilemma for policymakers is that historians have many different answers.

Historians often elevate their particular focus on the past to create a theory of causation. Environmental historians might emphasize climate, environment, geography, and natural resources to explain human development (Diamond 2003, 2005). Political historians study power relationships and the influence of leaders' decisions on social systems and people's lives. Marxists believe that economic relationships are the main determinants of human history, while intellectual historians raise the significance of ideas to cause change. International studies not only employs an interdisciplinary approach to global issues but also recognizes that many independent or interdependent forces can influence human behavior and cause historical events.

ARE THERE LESSONS OF HISTORY?

An old history essay question asks students to compare and contrast certain events, implying that there are discernible patterns of history from which to draw lessons. People often express the belief that "history tells us" to make a particular choice, but the relationship among the past, present, and future is a conundrum, a puzzle with many missing pieces. Geographers can help us understand where we stand and where we are going, but history cannot always tell us what will happen along the way or if or when we will get there. Human agents can alter history in unforeseen ways, and events take accidental turns that are dependent on random occurrences.

Policymakers frequently invoke historical analogies to make and justify decisions, in the belief that history teaches particular lessons. Yet historians and philosophers are not so sure. Hegel said that what we learn from history is that we do not learn from history. Aphorisms such as "history repeats itself" or "those who do not remember history are condemned to repeat it" are based on the notion that history is something we can know and build predictive models from.

Historical analogies provide clarity, rationality, and logic to current affairs, and historians often contribute to the idea that history teaches great lessons by declaring that certain works are "definitive" or "the last word." Obviously, decision making requires comparison to previous policy successes and failures, but historical analogy drawn from unique events can lead policymakers down a dark alley. Erroneous presumptions about what happened in the past constrain an accurate analysis of and creative thinking about the present.

Definitive lessons of history are impossible to derive from different accounts and interpretations of the past. Many scholars have debated the causes of World War I, but what lessons do policymakers draw if there is disagreement about how and why the war started? Economists would make a killing in the stock market if economic history allowed them to predict the ups and downs of the stock exchanges.

Policymakers are often blinded by their beliefs about the past that may not have any application for the present. For example, American policymakers during the Cold War consistently used the appeasement of Hitler before World War II to argue against accommodation with the Soviet Union, which they cast as a similarly aggressive, totalitarian dictatorship. The United States acted on the erroneous assumption that if Vietnam fell to the Communists, the dominos in Asia would fall like the East European countries had to the Nazis in the late 1930s. The failure in Vietnam created another "lesson of history" that warned against armed intervention into civil conflicts, with devastating consequences in places like Yugoslavia and Rwanda in the 1990s. In the run-up to the United States' war in Iraq in 2003, the George W. Bush administration argued that if the United States could successfully occupy Germany and Japan after World War II, it could surely handle the occupation of Iraq, a much smaller country. That historical analogy turned out to be wrong as well.

Historical events, unlike scientific experiments, can never be replicated. History often yields analogies for decision makers that are more dangerous than using no history at all. Historian Barbara Tuchman cautioned, "the trouble is that in human behavior and history it is impossible to isolate or repeat a given set of circumstances" (Tuchman 1981, 249).

Although past records cannot provide blueprints for the future, a thorough grounding in contemporary world history is essential for understanding current global issues, and honest and accurate histories are indispensable for human progress and reconciliation of international conflicts.

References

Benjamin, Jules. 1991. *A Student's Guide to History*. New York: St. Martin's Press.
Bryson, Bill. 2003. *A Short History of Nearly Everything*. New York: Broadway Books.
Dalrymple, William. 2005. "India: The War over History." *New York Review of Books*, April 7.
Diamond, Jared. 2003. *Guns, Germs, and Steel*. New York: Spark Publishers.
———. 2005. *Collapse: How Societies Choose to Fail or Succeed*. New York: Viking Press.
Joyce, James. [1922] 1984. *Ulysses*. New York: Garland Publishing.
Tuchman, Barbara W. 1981. *Practicing History: Selected Essays*. New York: Knopf.
Westfall, Richard S. 1993. *The Life of Isaac Newton*. New York: Cambridge University Press.

Further Reading

Anderson, Sheldon. 2008. *Condemned to Repeat It: "Lessons of History" and the Making of US Cold War Containment Policy*. Lanham, MD: Lexington Books.
Carr, E. H. 1961. *What Is History?* New York: Vintage Books.
Collingwood, R. G. 1946. *The Idea of History*. Oxford: Oxford University Press.
Gardiner, J. 1988. *What Is History?* London: Humanities Press International.
Hoffer, Charles, and William W. Stueck. 1994. *Reading and Writing American History: An Introduction to the Historian's Craft*. Lexington, MA: D. C. Heath.
Howard, Michael. 1991. *The Lessons of History*. New Haven, CT: Yale University Press.

Journals

American Historical Review. http://www.indiana.edu/~ahrweb
Cold War History. www.tandfonline.com
Diplomacy and Statecraft. www.tandfonline.com
Diplomatic History. www.onlinelibrary.wiley.com/journal
Journal of Contemporary History. www.jch.sagepub.com/
Journal of World History. www.uhpress.hawaii.edu/t-journal-of-world-history

Films

Citizen Kane (1941). Orson Welles, director.
Judgment at Nuremberg (1961). Stanley Kramer, director.
Rashomon (1950). Akira Kurosawa, director.
The Thin Blue Line (1988). Erroll Morris, director.
Triumph of the Will (1934). Leni Riefenstahl, director.

Websites

American Historical Association. www.historians.org/teaching/links
International Interdisciplinary Organization of Scholars. www.h-net.msu.edu: history discussions and job site.
Society for Historians of American Foreign Relations. www.shafr.org
World History Association. www.thewha.org
WWW Virtual Library: International Affairs. www.etown.edu

Peoples, Places, and Patterns

Geography in International Studies

Geography is Destiny.

—*attributed to Napoleon,*
quoted by Abraham Verghese in Cutting for Stone, *2009.*

WHAT IS GEOGRAPHY?

Geography does not automatically determine the outcome of human events, as Napoleon intimates, but geography does have an impact. **Geography** is a core discipline of international studies. It is about where and why. The roots of the word *geography* (γεωγραφία) are Greek. *Geo* means "earth," while *graphy* refers to "writing." Hence geography is writing about or description of the earth. In another culture with roots in antiquity, the Chinese, the word for geography is *dili* (地理). *Di* refers to "earth," while *li* refers to "pattern or arrangement." So in Chinese *dili* means the patterns on/of the earth. Geography then, is a detailed description of both the earth and its identifiable patterns. To understand those patterns requires thorough analysis and deep understanding rather than superficial description.

"Geography is the study of the interaction of physical and human phenomena at individual places and of how interactions among places form patterns and organize space" (Dahlman et al. 2011, 2). From this definition of geography, we see that geography is a study of the activities of people as well as a study of the earth itself. The disciplines of history and anthropology study people too, but what distinguishes geography from these other disciplines is that geography considers the arrangement of these activities across the earth. Where and why do activities occur? At its core geography answers the question of where: Geographic inquiry analyzes the arrangement of people and their activities across the earth and searches for explanations of those patterns.

Geography has two main areas of study: physical and human. Physical geography examines our environment, focusing on topics such as soil, climates, plants, and animals. Subfields of physical geography include climatology, geomorphology, and resource geography. Human geography studies the activities of people; focusing on topics such as industries, cities, cultures, and transportation. Subfields of human geography include political geography, economic geography, and cultural geography. For international studies, our considerations of states, cultures, resources, and economies require an understanding of geography.

DEVELOPMENT OF GEOGRAPHY

Geography is an ancient field of study. The classical Greeks as well as the classical Chinese studied the geography of their respective known worlds. The Greek Eratosthenes (c. 275–195 BCE), who directed the library at Alexandria, Egypt, wrote a book entitled *Geography*. Greek theory posited that the lands to the south would be hotter than the temperate climes of Greece and thus uninhabitable. The oldest example of Chinese geographical work is the *Tribute of Yü* written down around 500 BCE. This tale surveys the Chinese empire, dividing the empire into nine provinces and annotating the peoples and resources. After the fall of the Roman Empire in 476 CE, geography as a discipline did not develop in Europe. Much knowledge was actually lost in the West but preserved by the Arabs. Under the patronage of the Caliph in the eighth century, the Greek and Roman geographies were translated into Arabic. During the Renaissance, Europeans relearned the geography of the Greeks through encounters with the Muslims. The age of discovery in the 1600s spurred a new awakening of European geographic thought (Dahlman et al. 2011; Martin 2005). Although the parallels of latitude were well known in navigation, the lines of longitude could not be adequately measured. The invention of the marine chronometer in 1759 by John Harrison allowed for accurate east-west measurements (Sobel 1995).

Table 2.1 Standards for Geography

1. The World in Spatial Terms
2. Place and Region
3. Physical Systems
4. Human Systems
5. Environment and Society
6. Uses

SOURCE: *GESP 2012.*

Modern geography as a science developed through the twentieth century. By the 1990s, geography educators (college and secondary) in the United States conceptualized the discipline as embodying six elements: space, place and region, physical systems, human systems, human-environment interactions, and the uses of geography (see Table 2.1). Each element has several standards, for a total of eighteen standards for geographic education (GESP 2012).

Element 1. Space is a major consideration for geographers. Geography seeks to understand the spatial relations in the world, be it spatial organization, spatial interaction, or the locational context. For example, geographers study the way people organize space in the city. The spatial element in geography examines the particular patterns of human activities across the earth. The important component here is the concept of space (see Space, under Components of Geography below) for measuring distance, form, direction, and position.

Element 2. Despite the homogenizing forces of globalization, the world is still sufficiently different from place to place that **places** are therefore quite significant in our understanding of local, regional, and global processes. For example, geographers study how city systems vary from place to place. Area studies focuses more on the particular characteristics of places and regions.

Element 3. Physical systems are useful to understand the varying processes of the natural environment. For example, geographers study the physical process of the circulation of water. Physical systems relate with the earth sciences. Study of natural processes and their relationship with people has remained a strong component of geography. The ancient Greeks and the Chinese as well as modern Europeans with their analyses of the environment form a historical foundation to our current understanding of geography.

Element 4. Human systems are central to geography; people have helped to shape the planet. For example, geographers study how trading networks utilize cities. Human systems connect with the spatial element as well as the place and region element. From Chinese and Arabs to Europeans, geographers provide a basis for our consideration of human systems of population, culture, and economy.

Element 5. The idea of **environment** and society represents the interrelationships between people and their environment. For example geographers study how cities have changed the climate of the earth. The element of environment and society portrays the links between human society and our environment.

Element 6. A final element is the uses of geography to examine the past, interpret the present, and plan for the future. All of the traditions connect to this final element. For international studies, deep knowledge of other places and regions, languages and cultures, is an instructive departure point of analysis. Modern scientific geography is based on scientific reasoning linking human and physical geography (GESP 2012).

For international studies, the utility of understanding the National Geography Standards can be illustrated through examples. For example, we can examine the structure of population patterns around the world (human systems and space). We can analyze global population trends in terms of their effects on the earth's environment. Although China has a much larger population than the United States, its ecological impact is similar (physical systems and environment and society). We can examine Chinese culture and its responses to globalization (human systems and places and regions).

A 2010 analysis of primary and secondary students in the United States shows that about 20 percent of high school seniors scored proficient or better in geography. Students in Europe and Asia do better in geography because the subject is taught more thoroughly in schools there than in the

United States. Why is this problematic? David Driscoll, chair of the National Assessment Governing Board, says that "geography is not just about maps. It is a rich and varied discipline, that now more than ever, is vital to understanding the connections between our global economy, environment and diverse cultures" (Hu 2011).

COMPONENTS OF GEOGRAPHY

The history and standards of geography point to three main components of a geographical way of thinking: (1) space, (2) region, and (3) environment. **Space** includes the locations of people. **Regions** are mental constructs with which people identify. **Environment** consists of human interaction with our natural surroundings. Geography's role in international studies is to answer the questions of spatial location, regional identity, and issues of human-environment relations (Johnston 2010). Let's examine the concepts of space, region, and environment more thoroughly.

Space

The study of space in geographic analysis is composed of location, spatial interaction, and spatial organization. **Location** is the essential element; it answers the question, where? Locations can be nominal, relative, and absolute. A *nominal location* is a name attached to a place, such as Oxford, Ohio. A *relative location* reveals a direction relative to other locations: north or south, east or west. Ohio is west of New York and east of California; Ohio is in the Midwestern United States. Finally, an *absolute location* expresses mathematical precision, such as latitude and longitude, which is an intersection of mathematical coordinates (Rubenstein 2014). Oxford, Ohio, is at 39° 30' N Lat, 84° 45' W Long. The designation of east (E) or west (W) longitude is essential because 39° 30' N Lat, 84° 45' E Long would put one in the middle of the Takla Makan Desert in northwestern China. Likewise, the designation of north (N) or south (S) latitude indicates regions north or south of the equator, respectively.

Spatial interaction involves analyzing flows, interdependence, and underlying structures. Why and how do people, resources, and ideas move? As an example, the geography of energy in an international context is the geography of localized resources of pipelines, straits, and great distances between producing and consuming areas. Oil reserves are increasingly inaccessible. The spatial pattern and arrangement of oil has impacts on cultures, economies, politics, and histories, not just geography (Dahlman et al. 2011). For example, the oil in Kazakhstan in Central Asia is located on the Caspian Sea. That oil is an important resource for Kazakhstan. To reach the global market, the route to a seaport could pass south to Iran, east to China, north to Russia, or west to Azerbaijan and Georgia. Given the current political climate, which of these routes is better for the United States? What do you think?

The study of **spatial organization** reveals how people have delineated various territories. International boundaries are one form of spatial organization. In the Pacific Ocean, small islands take on territorial significance as claims extend 200 miles out from shore. International boundaries and national jurisdiction entail an organization of space. Businesses focus on certain market areas. For example, how and why do US businesses try to get into the Asian market and vice versa (de Blij 2012)?

Hong Kong (Figure 2.1) is a good example of spatial organization and spatial interaction. Hong Kong means "fragrant harbor" in Chinese. Hong Kong was a British colony until 1997 and is now a Special Administrative Region of the People's Republic of China. Hong Kong is a major center for Asian trade. Spatial interaction is a key reason for the existence and success of Hong Kong.

For international studies, space is of critical concern. Where are the political hot spots in the world? Where are the oil reserves located? Where is the focus of international trade or migration? Of course, knowing where these phenomena are located is a first step; the next is to examine the ramifications of these locations.

Region

A region is a concept humans use to differentiate one area from another. Geographers identify two types of regions: formal and functional. Formal regions include language communities, agricultural fields, the Bible Belt, the Midwest, the South, Europe and Asia, the Middle East, and zip code and area code regions. Functional regions include hunting territories, realms of empire, grazing areas, zones of trading activities, newspaper readership regions, river basins (watersheds), commuting corridors, and airspaces (Rubenstein 2014).

FIGURE 2.1 Hong Kong. The harbor is the reason for Hong Kong. PHOTO: S. Toops.

How do geographers classify these regions? A **formal region**, also known as a **uniform region**, is an area in which selected physical or human characteristics are present throughout the region. Its identity could be a certain climate, or specific landforms, or a shared language or religion. A region's characteristics can also be technically defined: per capita income, literacy rate, televisions per capita, or hospital beds per capita. Regions can reflect organizational areas such as congressional districts, prefectures, provinces, or special economic zones. They can have everyday usage such as the South, the Midwest, or the Middle East. And usage of regional terms tells as much about the observer as the region. For example, much discussion about Iraq assumes similarity throughout the country. A regional analysis, however, points to a northern area with a mostly Sunni Kurd population, a southern area with a mostly Shia Arab population, and a central area with a mostly Sunni Arab population. Understanding the regional cultural geography of Iraq is a first step to understanding the character of the country (Allen 2012).

A **functional region** is an area in which an activity has a network, a focal point, or a node. A river system or a trading system has a network of activity that inscribes a region. The issue here is one of dynamism through connections or linkages. Commuter areas and newspaper readership areas are examples of functional regions. The bounds of these regions change daily with new connections established between the focal center and the consumers or market. The range of a television signal, a radio broadcast, a political idea, or the extent of governmental control all determine a functional region (Rubenstein 2014).

For international studies, we consider broad world regions such as North America, Europe, East Asia, South Asia, Africa, the Middle East, and Latin America (as in this book). Each of these has a territory but the boundaries may well overlap. Each is a formal region in the sense that there are established characteristics such as language, culture, history, and economy that help to define each world region. At the same time there are functional networks active in a region. The nodes of the regions are leading global cities. In East Asia global cities are Beijing, Shanghai, Singapore, and Tokyo; in South Asia, Mumbai and Delhi; in the Middle East, Dubai and Jerusalem; in Latin America, Mexico City and Sao Paulo; in North America, New York City and Los Angeles; in Africa, Johannesburg and Cairo; in Europe, London, Paris, Zurich, and Moscow (Rowntree et al. 2014).

Within these world regions, however, there are strong regional differences. In Africa, many different cultural, economic, and political identities hold sway. In South Africa, for example, Zulu, Xhosa, Khoi-San, Sotho, and Afrikaaner provide a diverse cultural mosaic. Asia, because of its size, is very differentiated. We can identify strong cultural distinctions among Uzbekistan, China, India, and Indonesia as countries respectively from Central Asia, East Asia, South Asia, and Southeast Asia. European identity also varies but it is coalescing due to the European Union. The Middle East may be mostly Arab, but Jewish, Turkish, and Persian peoples are quite significant to the area politically, economically, and culturally. In contrast North America and Latin America have less variation. The English language dominates in North America, most people speak Spanish and Portuguese (but not Latin) in Latin America.

Zurich, Switzerland (Figure 2.2), is a good example of region and place. Two million people live in the metropolitan area; of that, 400,000 are in the central city. In terms of economic geography, the city is a global center for finance because of the Swiss banking policy and low corporate tax rates.

FIGURE 2.2 Zurich. The largest city and financial center of Switzerland. PHOTO: S. Toops.

Interestingly, this financial center was the home of Lenin in exile where he wrote *Imperialism: The Highest Stage of Capitalism* in 1916. Zurich is a hub for Swiss railway, road, and air traffic. In terms of political geography, Bern, not Zurich is the capital of Switzerland. By the 1300s Zurich joined other cantons to form a Swiss confederacy. Switzerland has maintained its neutrality since the early 1800s. In terms of cultural geography, the locals here speak German at home, though most Swiss are multilingual, speaking French, Italian, and English also. Zurich was a focus for the Protestant Reformation in the 1500s, yet many people here are Catholic. Theaters, museums, and churches provide the base of the cultural life of the city. In terms of physical geography, the city grew up on the banks of the Limmat River where it flows into Lake Zurich. Mountains and hills covered with forests enclose the city. In sum, Zurich is a cultural and economic center for Switzerland and a financial center for the world.

The borders between these regions are more aptly called transition zones. The zone between North and Latin America is blurred in California, New Mexico, and Texas. As Turkey endeavors to enter the European Union, the distinction between Europe and the Middle East fades. Egypt and the Sudan have strong roots in the Middle East and Africa. South Sudan has broken off from Sudan and established a new state. Pakistan and

FIGURE 2.3 Istanbul. Asia is in the background, Europe is in the foreground, and in between is the Bosporus, the historical divide between Europe and Asia. PHOTO: S. Toops.

Indonesia are Asian but have cultural identities resonant with the Middle East. Russia straddles the divide between Asia and Europe (Rowntree et al. 2014).

Istanbul (Figure 2.3) lies at an intersection of regions. This largest city of Turkey is where Asia and Europe meet. The Bosporus, a strait connecting the Black Sea to the Mediterranean Sea, divides the city. Much of the city's population lives on the Europe side, where are found the Byzantine sites of the Hippodrome (300 CE) and Hagia Sophia (532 CE), and the Ottoman sites of Topkapi Palace (1453 CE) and the Sultan Ahmet Mosque (1606 CE). On the Asian side of the Bosporus are rail links to Ankara and the rest of the country. Today we may think of Turkey as part of the Middle East, but the cultural heritage of the Turks is in Central Asia. Region is indeed a mental construct.

Environment

International studies involves an understanding of the environment. Humans modify and react to the natural environment. Global environmental processes produce climates, soils, biotic communities (biomes), minerals, and landforms. The physical geographer studies the processes of the natural environment, while the human geographer is concerned more with the human interaction than with these physical processes.

Some countries have more resources than others, some have larger populations, and some have milder climates. All of these attributes of a country relate to the physical environmental processes at work in a country. A common observation is that people tend to congregate in flatter areas with access to freshwater, in climates not too hot or too cold, but with access to resources, such as plants, animals, or minerals. An analysis of population distribution around the earth would entail an understanding of climate, soils, biomes, minerals, and landforms. Simple spatial questions such as where is it flat and well watered usually indicate the locations of denser populations. Major concentrations of population are in (1) South Asia with India, Pakistan, and Bangladesh (1.78 billion); (2) East Asia with China, South Korea, and Japan (1.6 billion); (3) sub-Saharan Africa with Nigeria and Ethiopia (925 million); and (4) Europe with the United Kingdom, Germany, France, and Russia (750 million). Population is concentrated on the Yellow and Yangtze rivers of China, the Ganges River of India, and the Rhine of Europe, but also along the coasts of Japan, Bangladesh, and the United Kingdom. Location (space) is a part of the geographic attribute of a country, but so is the environment (Dahlman et al. 2011).

People and their environment are mutually interactive, each influencing the other. This contemporary view has replaced traditional conceptions going back to the ancient Greeks that the environment exerts a controlling influence over people: for example, people in cold climates can only act in a certain fashion while people in warm climates act in another fashion. This concept of **environmental determinism** is rejected by contemporary geography because of the inaccuracies of using the environment to predict how a group of people will behave. Plains in temperate climates with grasslands exist in Russia, Mongolia, and the United States. And yet the human geographies of cultures, economies, and polities of the plains of Russia, Mongolia, and the United States have all developed quite differently. Environmental determinist views still crop up. Robert Kaplan's *The Revenge of Geography* (2012) examines global politics from a relatively conservative view of the world, that somehow geography ordains European dominance in world politics. Rather people have agency and are not bound by what the land offers.

Another modern view is that people can control their environment. We can make dams, move the earth, control the waves, farm crops, raise animals, build factories, and construct cities all without regard to environmental concerns. This, however, is **human determinism**. This belief in human determinism has led us to build great dams in the former Soviet Union, China, and the United States to tame mighty rivers. The damming of the Amu Darya (River) in Uzbekistan has led to the desiccation of the Aral Sea. The damming of the Colorado River in the United States does provide Los Angeles with water and Las Vegas with electricity, but the Colorado River no longer reaches the ocean. The Three Gorges Dam on China's Yangtze River, the biggest dam in the world, has caused problems such as a reservoir plagued by garbage, sewage, and algae (Wines 2011). The huge weight of the water in the reservoir has also increased the risk of earthquakes and landslides. More power has been generated at what cost? Another view beginning in the nineteenth century is that of **environmental possibilism**. While there are some physical limits to human actions, people have various options to adapt to the physical environment. We can choose many possibilities. The physical environment does not determine what we can do but it can limit what we can achieve. Norwegians can grow bananas in a hothouse, but it is easier and cheaper for Norwegians to buy bananas from Africa. We can modify the environment using our technology, but we need to do so sensitively. Otherwise there will not be a habitable earth for future generations (Rubenstein 2014).

A good example of human-environmental interaction is the Hunza Valley in northern Pakistan (Figure 2.4). Glaciers lie high above the valley. The water used for irrigation comes down from the glaciers. Local residents, Hunzakuts, cut channels into the rugged mountains to bring the water to the fields. This is much more efficient than bringing water up from the river. This irrigation system has been vital to the continued productivity of the valley.

Resources are key components in the environment. When humanity became aware of self and needs, people became capable of identifying resources. A resource refers primarily to the functions that an object or substance may perform. A rock was simply an inanimate object until someone came along and used the rock to dig for roots or to hunt. Out of the material world, human needs and ingenuity have fashioned resources. Without human evaluation and appraisal, a rock remains a rock. Culture and technology play a major role in the determination of what a resource

FIGURE 2.4 Hunza. Pakistan. The Hunza Valley is irrigated from the glaciers in the surrounding mountains. PHOTO: S. Toops.

is. We use coal for heating but also as a basis for petrochemicals, dyes, and fibers. Yet coal was just another rock until the Industrial Revolution.

Resources are either **nonrenewable** or **renewable**. Nonrenewable resources are materials or energy that have finite amounts. Their continued use leads to exhaustion. Some nonrenewable resources are recyclable in that these materials (primary minerals) can be removed from the waste heaps humanity has created and used again. Your local recycling center makes use of aluminum, plastic, and paper. Other nonrenewable resources such as fossil fuels are not recyclable. They can be used only once; they are destroyed by their use (Dahlman et al. 2011).

Renewable resources are consumed, but they can be restored; there are two types: continuous flow and short-term renewable. *Continuous-flow resources* approach inexhaustibility because they are direct products of the actions of the sun, the earth, or the moon. Tidal power, solar power, hydropower, and geothermal power are all examples of continuous flow resources. The flow of rivers can power turbines to generate electricity. *Short-term renewable resources* are sustainable in that they can be continued with careful management. These include the usage of timber, soil, crops, or water. Water can be reused in heating and cooling processes (Brown 2011).

In international studies, we seek to understand the physical inventory of the earth and how we use its natural resources. Geography helps us to understand the human use of the earth and its resources. Our future depends upon the wise use of these resources.

To summarize, the basic components of geography—space, region, and environment—figure prominently in the essential geographic questions today. A key issue for geography is how we delineate space. A map of the world showing states (political territories) evokes a different perception than a map of the world showing rivers. As a matter of practical research, when we study pollution problems on rivers, do we frame our analysis in terms of states or watersheds? Geographers study how places and regions differ from one another. How can policies be implemented in a world fragmented socially and environmentally? Being able to explain the nature of this variability is a key challenge for geography. How has the earth been transformed by human action? Humans have altered the earth, its air, and its water on scales ranging from the global to the local. Globally, our industries inject carbon dioxide into the atmosphere in massive amounts. Locally, we create new urban environments in which we live, work, and play. Local pollution translates into global climate change. Space, region, and environment all provide concepts for the big questions in geography (Cutter et al. 2002).

Here is an example of a geography (Figure 2.5). I (Stanley Toops) grew up on a farm in Iowa with about 160 acres of a corn, soybean, wheat, cattle, and hog operation. The location of the farm is in southeast Iowa about 2 miles from Missouri and 55 miles from Illinois, part of the Mississippi River watershed. Rainfall is about 40 inches per year; the soil is good black loam, rich in humus. Native vegetation is tall-grass prairie. A nuclear family of parents and five children worked the land using tractors and combines. Brands of the farm machinery included John Deere, Allis-Chalmers, International, and Belarus. The Belarus tractor was made in the Soviet Union. Much of the corn and soybeans was fed to cattle and hogs. The livestock were sold at auction and then turned into steaks and chops. Some of the corn, wheat, and soybeans were exported to the Soviet Union and China.

There is a spatial and environmental geography to this Midwestern region. The scenery is replicated throughout the Midwest. Even on a farm

FIGURE 2.5 Farm in Iowa. A piece of land, a farm, a home, a place, a geography.
PHOTO: S. Toops.

in Iowa, the international connections linked that plot of land to China and the Soviet Union through the trade of corn, wheat, and tractors. The author grew up here; so this location is home—a place filled with memories and meaning, beyond a node in the food chain. This particular family farm is no more. The land was sold to a neighbor who had a cash grain operation of over 1,000 acres. Yet the scene remains in memory for a time.

MAPS: TOOLS FOR INTERNATIONAL STUDIES

Like numbers, writing, speeches, music, or pictures, maps are a form of communication that expresses ideas about the world. The map is a specialized picture of mathematical precision, a multifaceted tool that provides a concrete understanding of the relationships that locations have with other locations. Knowledge of a map's versatility can help one gain a thorough understanding of our world. Ken Jennings, the record-breaking *Jeopardy* game-show champion, traces a history (and geography) of maps from ancient times to the twenty-first-century digital formats of GIS and GPS in *Maphead* (Jennings 2011). Maps are fascinating tools for international studies.

Map Fundamentals

Maps convey spatial relationships. To use maps effectively requires some knowledge about the fundamentals of their preparation.

Scale. Scale is the relationship between the length of an object on a map to the length of that object in the real world. Most maps of the entire world can only show a portion of the myriad detail. Such maps of the world are small scale, perhaps 1:4,000,000 (which is a very small number). At this ratio one inch on the map represents a distance of 4,000,000 inches, which adds up to more than 63 miles in the real world. A map of a city can show more detail because it is covering less area. Such a map may have a scale of 1:25,000. This is a large-scale map. In this case one inch on the map represents 25,000 inches or about 0.4 miles in the real world (de Blij 2012).

Centering and orientation. Maps can be centered on any point on the earth. Maps produced in the eighteenth century were centered on Paris or London. The prime meridian, at 0° longitude, runs through Greenwich in London. Many maps of the world produced in the United States may have the American continents at the center. Maps centered on the Pacific or on the Atlantic convey a different view of the world. Maps 2.1 and 2.2 are centered on Europe and Africa rather than the Pacific (Allen 2012).

Projection. All maps involve some distortion of the earth's surface. The world is a three-dimensional object. To flatten the spherical globe to a plane means some characteristic—distance, direction, shape, or area—is sacrificed. Distortion is always present in world maps and other small-scale maps; in some cases the distortion is quite severe. Some **projections** have elongated shapes or distorted areas. Many atlases and cartographic products will use equal-area projections, in this way the distribution of items across the earth is kept accurate even though shapes may be altered. The practicalities are such that a flat map is more easily used, yet keep in mind that the world is a sphere (Veregin 2010).

Here are two types of map projections. The *Mercator projection* (Map 2.1), developed in 1569, preserves shape and orientation, and lines of latitude and longitude are at right angles. The Mercator projection was developed for navigation and is excellent for that purpose. However, as can be seen on the Mercator projection, the sizes of land masses in

high-latitude areas are severely distorted. Greenland looks similar in size
to South America. In reality South America is 8.6 times the size of Greenland. Thus the Mercator should not be used to show distribution of space.
In contrast, consider the *Robinson projection* (Map 2.2). This projection
is oval, thus achieving a more global (rounder) esthetic. The Robinson
projection preserves many spatial relationships, particularly in the middle
to low latitudes. South America is indeed much larger than Greenland
when viewed on the Robinson projection. Overall, the Robinson, while
not specifically accurate, represents the spatial distributions more clearly
(Dahlman et al. 2011).

A specialized type of geographic product is a geographic information
system, or **GIS**. The scale and projection are matched completely and dig-
itally so that layers of information, such as physical or human attributes,
are known for each and every location. With remotely sensed imagery
from satellites and computer facilities, a large amount of detail is available on a GIS. Much analysis in geography today utilizes GIS and remote
sensing (Gewin 2004). Satellite technology gives us an excellent method
to view complex information about our earth. Environmental issues such
as the impacts of floods in Bangladesh or deforestation in the Amazon can
all be analyzed using remote sensing and GIS (Sheehan 2000).

Lying with Maps

A picture may be worth a thousand words, but maps can be used to mis-
inform and as propaganda. The propagandist uses maps to manipulate political opinion (Monmonier 1996). Maps are used as icons to stake out a
national territory. India, Pakistan, and China all claim Kashmir. Maps in
each of those countries show Kashmir to be the rightful territory of that
country. In global atlases such as *Goode's World Atlas*, these territories are
marked to show the different claims (Veregin 2010).

Another issue open to manipulation and misinformation is projection.
The Mercator projection, which shows direction accurately and thus is
very useful for navigation, distorts the true size of the polar areas, making the upper-latitude areas appear very large. Propagandists such as the
right-wing John Birch society used Mercator projections to alert the West
to the significance of the Communist threat posed by the Soviet Union.

Map design is another useful tool for the propagandist. The Nazis designed their propaganda maps to show Germany surrounded by enemies

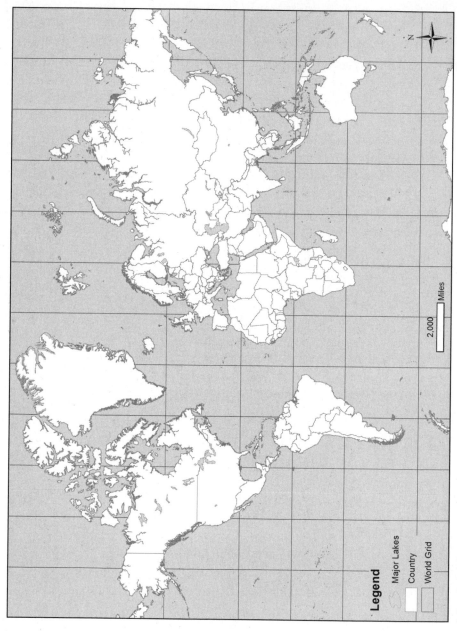

Legend

Major Lakes

Country

World Grid

2,000 ⎯ Miles

N

MAP 2.1 Mercator Projection.

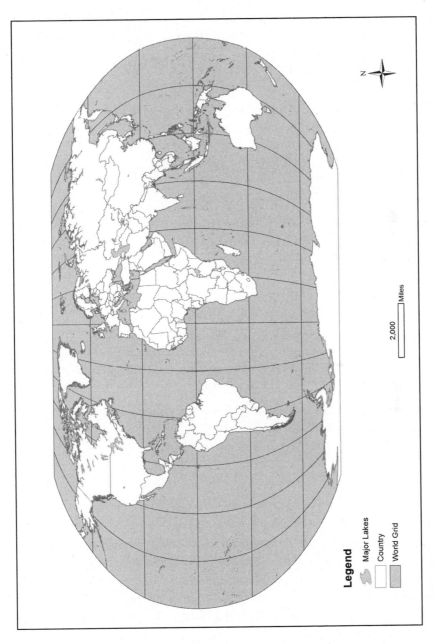

Legend

Major Lakes

Country

World Grid

2,000   Miles

N

MAP 2.2   Robinson Projection.

(the United Kingdom, France, and the Soviet Union). In one example, the outline of Germany is compared with that of the British Empire, with territories including Canada and India. With a map showing the British Empire covering over a quarter of the world's land area, Nazi Germany tried to make the case that the British Empire was the greater imperial threat. Map colors can be used to stir emotions and manipulate opinions: yellow might show warning, red might show danger, or green or blue might be used for a friendly country. Red for Russia, yellow for China, and green for the United States and Europe portrayed the Western view of the cold war. From outer space, of course, the earth is mostly blue ocean (Monmonier 1996).

The colors on a map can describe more than political views. In *Tom Sawyer Abroad*, Tom and Huck Finn set out in a hot air balloon from Missouri to Europe. Huck Finn remarks that they must still be in Illinois and not yet in Indiana. Why? asks Tom. Because Indiana is pink and Illinois is green.

> Huck: What's a map for? Ain't it to learn you facts?
> Tom: Of course.
> Huck: Well, then, how's it going to do that, if it tells lies? That's what I want to know.

A more useful knowledge of maps may aid both Huck and Tom in their excursion abroad (Twain 1894).

CONCLUSION

Space, region, and environment will be used most often in international studies. Courses in human geography—such as political geography or economic geography, which emphasize the spatial element—are important for international studies. Another group of courses is the geography of certain world regions, such as the geography of Europe, Latin America, and Asia. A third set of courses concerns the environment and physical elements such as natural resources, ecology, and climatology. There are also courses on geographic methodologies, maps, geographic information systems (GIS), and remote sensing that would prove helpful in international studies. The study of international relations must be built upon recognition of geographical concepts.

For international studies, geography is critical in a number of endeavors. International studies graduates often work in business, government, education, and nongovernmental organizations (NGOs). In the business world, retailers, banks, and firms engaged in international business rely upon location analysis to seek new markets, suppliers, labor, and raw materials. Transportation and travel sectors utilize geographic analysis as well. GIS analysis is a common career-entry path. In government, geographical skills are practical for many in international studies. In the United States, such departments and agencies as agriculture, census, commerce, NASA, state, defense, intelligence, mapping, and interior employ spatial, environmental, and regional analysis. International organizations such as the United Nations, World Health Organization, UNESCO (the United Nations Educational, Scientific, and Cultural Organization), and World Trade Organization use geographical methods to gather and analyze spatial, regional, and environmental knowledge. Education is another fertile field for international studies as jobs in high school and college are on the increase. NGOs hire international studies graduates for their skills in geography, economics, languages, politics, history, and anthropology.

As we've discussed, the main components of geography are space, region, and environment (Johnston 2010). A combined concern for these components distinguishes geography from history, political science, economics, and anthropology. Geography's role in international studies is to analyze space, regions, and environments of the earth. The map is a special tool that geography applies in its analysis of the earth. As people struggle to understand their role in a world characterized by instant global communications, shifting geopolitical relationships, and growing evidence of environmental change, we come to realize that geography needs to be rediscovered (Murphy 1998). Without geography, we are nowhere.

The events of the Indian Ocean tsunami of December 26, 2004, illustrate the utility of geography. An English schoolgirl was vacationing with her parents in Phuket, Thailand, when she noticed the ocean suddenly receding in the distance. She recalled the lesson from her geography class: "that the deep wave of a tsunami sucks the water off the beach before it returns in a massive wall that inundates the entire shoreline" (de Blij 2012). There was just enough time to alert about 100 people of the impending wave and to move to higher ground. Those who followed her advice survived. Of those who stayed behind, none survived. Geography does indeed matter.

References

Allen, J. 2012. *Student Atlas of World Geography*. 7th ed. New York: McGraw-Hill.

Brown, L. R. 2011. *World on the Edge: How to Prevent Environmental and Economic Collapse*. New York: W. W. Norton.

Cutter, S., R. Golledge, and W. Graf. 2002 "The Big Questions in Geography." *The Professional Geographer*, 54 (3), 305–317.

Dahlman, C., W. Renwick, and E. Bergman. 2011. *Introduction to Geography*. 5th ed. Upper Saddle River, NJ: Prentice Hall.

De Blij, H. 2012. *Why Geography Matters*. 2nd ed. New York: Oxford University Press.

GESP (Geography Education Standards Project), American Geographical Society of New York, Association of American Geographers, National Council for Geographic Education, and National Geographic Society. 2012. *Geography for Life: National Geography Standards*. 2nd ed.. Washington, DC: National Geographic Research and Exploration.

Gewin, V. 2004. "Mapping Opportunities." *Nature* 247: 376.

Hu, W. 2011. "Geography Report Card Finds Students Lagging." *New York Times*, July 19. http://www.nytimes.com/2011/07/20/education/20geography.html.

Jennings, K. 2011. *Maphead: Charting the Wide, Weird World of Geography Wonks*. New York: Scribner.

Johnston, R. J. 2010. "Geography and International Studies" in *The International Studies Encyclopedia*, edited by R. A. Denemark. West Sussex, UK: Blackwell.

Kaplan, Robert D. 2012. *The Revenge of Geography:* New York: Random House.

Knox, J., and S. Marston. 2013. *Human Geography; Places and Regions in Global Context*. 6th ed. Boston: Pearson.

Martin, G. 2005. *All Possible Worlds*. New York: Oxford University Press.

Monmonier, M. 1996. *How to Lie with Maps*. Chicago: University of Chicago Press.

Murphy, A. R. 1998. "Rediscovering the Importance of Geography," *The Chronicle of Higher Education* (October 30).

Rowntree, L. et al 2014. *Globalization and Diversity*. 4th ed. Upper Saddle River, NJ: Prentice Hall.

Rubenstein, J. 2014. *The Cultural Landscape*. 11th ed. Upper Saddle River, NJ : Pearson Education.

Sheehan, M. 2000. "Gaining Perspective," *World Watch* (March/April), 14–24.

Sobel, D. 1995. *Longitude*. New York: Walker.

Twain, M. 1894 (1996). *Tom Sawyer Abroad*. New York: Oxford University Press.

Veregin, H. 2010. *Goode's World Atlas*, 22nd ed. Skokie, IL: Rand McNally.

Verghese, A. 2009. *Cutting for Stone: A Novel.* New York: Knopf.

Wines, Michael. 2011. "China Admits Problems with Three Gorges Dam," *New York Times*, May 19. http://www.nytimes.com/2011/05/20/world/asia/20gorges .html.

Further Reading

Castree, N., et al., eds. 2005 *Questioning Geography: Fundamental Debates.* Malden, MA: Blackwell.

Clifford, N., et al., eds. 2009. *Key Concepts in Geography*, 2nd ed. Thousand Oaks, CA: Sage.

De Blij, H. J. 2009. *The Power of Place: Geography, Destiny, and Globalization's Rough Landscape.* New York: Oxford University Press.

Dodds, K. 2000. *Geopolitics in a Changing World.* Harlow, England: Prentice Hall.

Johnston, R. J., et al., ed. 2002. *Geographies of Global Change.* Malden, MA: Blackwell.

Rogers, A., and H .A. Viles, eds. 2003. *The Student's Companion to Geography.* 2nd ed. Malden, MA: Blackwell.

Seitz, J., and K. Hite. 2012. *Global Issues.* Malden, MA: Wiley-Blackwell.

Journals

Annals of the Association of American Geographers

Eurasian Geography and Economics

Geographical Journal

Political Geography

Professional Geographer

Films

Power of Place: World Regional Geography (1996). BBC and Annenberg/CPB Project.

Is Wal-Mart Good for America? (2004). Frontline: PBS Home Video.

Diarios de motocicleta (Motorcycle diaries) (2005). Walter Salles, director. United States: Universal.

The Story of the Weeping Camel (2003). Byambasuren Davaa, director. [München]: Hochschule für Fernsehen und Film München.

Whale Rider (2003). Tim Sanders, director. Culver City, CA: Columbia TriStar Home Entertainment.

Websites

Association of American Geographers. http://www.aag.org/
International Geographical Union. http://www.igu-net.org
Miami University, Department of Geography. http://www.units.muohio.edu
/geography/
National Geographic Society. http://www.nationalgeographic.com/
Perry Castañeda Library Map collection. http://www.lib.utexas.edu/maps/

3

Anthropology and Intercultural Relations

Understanding the web of connections that links people around the world involves more than the study of environments, historical change, economies, and power. It requires studying the ideas by which people make sense of these processes. However integrated communities become through globalization, their models of how the world works continue to be shaped by different environments, histories, economic systems, ideologies, political systems, and languages. These differences in how people understand the world lead to different ways of acting and behaving in it.

Anthropologists, the scientists who study human similarities and differences, call these differences in belief and behavior *culture*. **Culture** involves the socially mediated human capacity to differentiate, to categorize the world of experience according to what is important to pay attention to, and what is not, and to assign meanings to the categories created.

What this means, says Michael Herzfeld (2001, 1) of Harvard University, is that cultural anthropology is the comparative study of common sense. **Common sense** is that set of unstated assumptions we share with others in our community that we can most rely on in making sense of the world around us. It is what we accept to be true without questioning or analyzing it. Common sense does not need explanation because it *is* the explanation—we guarantee the truth of something by saying that it is just common sense. The problem for international social relations is that different communities have different common senses that work equally well in each one's physical and social environments. As economic, political, and environmental processes bring into contact people who operate

according to different common senses, **cultural misunderstandings** occur. A thorough understanding of the international community requires
an ability to learn and deal with **intercultural relations**: the flows of symbols across the global landscape, facilitated by transnational migration,
new information technologies, and global markets, which can lead to creativity and innovation but also to misunderstanding and conflict.

CULTURAL MISUNDERSTANDINGS
IN AN INTERNATIONAL MILIEU

In a globalizing world, both communities and the common senses constructed within them become increasingly complex, and the likelihood of
cultural misunderstanding increases. For example, Robert, an American
executive, was brought into the Egyptian office of his company to increase
efficiency.[1] One day he asked Ahmad, his top manager, when an important report would be finished. "You'll have it Monday, *insh'allah* [if God
wills]," Ahmad told him.

"I don't want to hear excuses," Robert replied. "You all need to learn
to meet deadlines. I expect to see that report on my desk Monday whether
God is willing or not." Shocked, Ahmad left the office and shared the
incident with many fellow employees, who were equally upset. A work
slowdown ensued, frustrating Robert's efforts to improve efficiency. When
corporate managers arrived from the regional headquarters to see how
things were going under Robert's management, a delegation of employees met them to complain about Robert's "sacrilegious" attitudes. It took
weeks for the whole thing to get straightened out.

At the heart of the problem was a set of misunderstandings about what
was meant by the term *insh'allah*. To Robert, Ahmad saying he would get
the report Monday "if God wills it" was tantamount to him saying that
he might not deliver the report on time. It supported a larger conviction
he had that Egyptians in general failed to take personal responsibility for
things and that this led to inefficiency and to a failure of entrepreneurial
spirit.

To Ahmad, Robert's statement was a direct attack on faith in God and
an attempt to enforce an American secularism on people who recognize the
sovereignty of God in all domains of life. The phrase is so common in everyday life among Egyptians—both Muslim and Christian—that most don't
notice when they are using it. Ahmad intended to work hard on the report,

and if he were to miss the deadline because of his own actions, he knew he would deserve criticism. But he also knew that he could be hit by a car and hospitalized and therefore fail because of things beyond his control.

Insh'allah operates in everyday Egyptian speech like clauses in business contracts that excuse companies from liability in the cases of "acts of God." It is not intended as a denial of personal responsibility but a reminder that we humans are not in control of the universe. What is more, most Egyptians feel that God chooses to let bad things happen to good people for reasons known only to him—and that one of these reasons may be as a reminder to humans that God is in charge of the universe. Saying *insh'allah* is thus a way to let God know that you recognize his preeminence so that he won't allow bad things to interfere in getting the work done. In the view of many employees, Robert's order was a blasphemy because it amounted to claiming that they had more power over the world than God.

As the discussions continued, the Egyptians were surprised to discover what Robert had really meant. Didn't he know, they asked, that Egyptians have always had a strong entrepreneurial spirit, that Arabs were writing fairy tales with merchants as heroes when Europe was still mired in a feudal economy and spinning stories about knights and princesses? Successful entrepreneurs are admired for their cleverness and skill in recognizing and taking advantage of opportunities, but most Egyptians also believe that their successes and failures are allowed or disallowed by God. Even the cleverest entrepreneur can lose cargo to a shipwreck or have an important contract lost in a plane crash.

Robert was likewise disturbed to find that most of what the Egyptians thought of him came from stereotypes of arrogant, unprincipled bosses they acquired watching American soap operas and sitcoms. He warned his employees that these stereotypes were no more accurate than the ones he held about Middle Eastern fatalism, the notion that what happens to people is a matter of destiny rather than personal initiative. As an evangelical Christian, Robert actually agreed with Ahmad's perspective about God being in charge. He told the Egyptians that the incident had been a positive one in that it had led him to think about how clearly he was carrying the principles he professed in church through to his office life. Once he understood the Egyptians, he came to respect their use of *insh'allah*. He adopted it himself, and his use of it gave him more credibility with Egyptian workers as he established clearer rules about employee responsibilities and professional conduct.

Both Robert and Ahmad had depended on their common sense to interpret what was happening. Common sense acted as a kind of cultural logic that helped them to generate behaviors, and to interpret each other's actions. But since each held to a different common sense rooted in a different way of viewing the world, they initially failed to understand one another.

Not all cultural misunderstandings occur at the interpersonal level, though. Common sense governs peoples' actions at all levels of social life, including large-scale political projects. Cultural misunderstandings in realms of policy are all too common. Anthropologist William Beeman, who served as a consultant to the Carter administration, argues that policymakers in the United States and elsewhere often rely on common-sense myths about the world even when these are out of sync with empirical realities and fail to accomplish policy goals. For example, he argues that the US State Department operates on the basis of a coherent, consistent model of the world that serves as a common-sense basis for policymaking. In this worldview, he writes, "the normal conduct of foreign policy consists of the elite leaders of nation-states meeting in seclusion discussing matters of power and economics chiefly in the context of a bipolar struggle" (previously in a cold war context, now with regard to the "war on terror") (Beeman 2003, 680). He argues that while this view of the world is consistent with US historical experience and continues to work well when dealing with European nations, many of the failures of US foreign policy elsewhere—regardless of whether the administration is Democratic or Republican—stem from policymakers having a view of the world that is sometimes out of sync with reality and not shared by policymakers in many other parts of the world, who often have quite different views of how the world works.

For example, Iranian officials tend to work with a substantively different worldview, one in which Iran is an honest, just, and moral nation surrounded by hostile enemies. These enemies seek to destroy Iran's cultural and moral purity, not only through military threat but by the seduction of false ideologies like communism or open-market capitalism. This worldview is consistent with Iranian history, pre-Islamic Persian mythology, and contemporary Shiite Islamic doctrine, but it is not always correct, and it is rarely useful in formulating policies for dealing with foreign powers, including the United States. Moreover, Iranian assumptions about how international communication should proceed are just the opposite of American assumptions. Americans tend to be egalitarian in interpersonal communications but insist on the superior position of the United States in formal international communications. Iranian culture anticipates careful attention to hierarchy in interpersonal communication but expects that nation-states will treat one another as equals in international relations.

Beeman (2003) argues that in US-Iranian relations, neither side is able to generate foreign policy that produces desired results from the other because they do not understand how the world looks from the other's viewpoint, nor do they understand one another's styles of communication. Instead, after more than thirty years in which every overture or threat by either country produces results quite different from what their politicians' common sense expects, each country accuses the other of being mad or evil.

From business to politics and in every other sphere of international relations, culture plays a crucial role. Attention to culture is therefore an essential element in understanding international situations.

What Is Culture?

The capacity to create culture is a fundamental human trait. To be human is to need to live in a world of meanings. To be able to act effectively in the universe, humans must construct models of how the world works, values that help them decide what goals are worth pursuing, and plans of action to help them achieve those goals. Yet all humans do not live in the *same* world of meanings. Groups of humans generate and elaborate different systems of meanings, and to the extent that these systems are shared, they define groups as communities. Individuals in communities create their own unique ways of acting, but they do so within the horizon of meanings defined by the community. **Culture**, then, is this learned system of meanings through which people orient themselves in the world so that they can act in it. As such, culture is symbolic, shared, learned, and adaptive.

Culture Is Symbolic

Humans live in a physical world, and they understand and manipulate that world through symbols. Everything humans produce has a symbolic aspect—from words to gestures to clothes to housing to complex technologies. A **symbol** is *something* that stands for *something else* to *someone* in *some respect*. The use of words in language is a good example. A word such

FIGURE 3.1 An example of the human world of meanings: people everywhere care for their dead with elaborate symbolism, as in this funeral in Moldavia. PHOTO: Doug Rogers.

as *horse* is a "something" (the technical word is *signifier*) that stands for something else (its *referent*)—in this case, a particular animal—to speakers of English.

When we define a symbol as a signifier standing for a referent to someone *in some respect*, we are drawing attention to special features possessed by symbolic systems. One of the most important is that signs usually have no intrinsic or essential relationship to their referent. There is nothing in the phonetic sounds of the words *horse, hassan, equus,* or *cheval* that connect them with the particular animal to which all these signs refer. Their relationship is **arbitrary**—we know the meaning of the word only if we've grown up in a community that shares the knowledge of which signifiers refer to which referents.

To say that a symbol means something only to a *someone* is to emphasize that culture is expressive. Our words, our actions, and our artifacts communicate things to others about us. Not only what we say but how we say it—intonation, volume, and pitch—communicates important information about us and what we may be thinking, feeling, or about to do. The same is true of the kinds of clothing we wear, how we cut our hair, how close we stand to people, and how we eat our food. Even the most practical of actions possesses a symbolic, communicative element. It is because we share a common set of understandings about what symbols mean that we can understand and predict one another's actions, and so cooperate as a community.

Culture Is Shared

Culture, then, involves shared understandings of symbols and their meanings that allow us to communicate, to cooperate, and to predict and understand one another's actions. Yet while culture is shared, it is not equally distributed among all the peoples of a society. Different distributions of cultural knowledge usually serve to produce and maintain differences in social positions such as gender, race, caste, or class. But in highly complex and diverse societies, differences can also distinguish people on the basis of education, occupation, or even leisure. In most societies, rights, responsibilities, and control over resources are unequally distributed to people on the basis of these social categories. The mobilization of cultural symbols to create, sustain, or resist such social inequities is called **ideology**.

Shared culture includes knowledge of history and also the whole realm of convention and belief we call tradition. Slavery is part of a shared heritage in the United States, but what it means to people differs according to their social positions and other aspects of their belief systems. These areas of similarity and differentiation intertwine in complex ways. Because of this, specific symbols may have very different meanings to different people within the same general culture; the meaning of the Confederate battle flag emblazoned on T-shirts, belt buckles, or bumper stickers, or flown in front of courthouses, differs in relation to people's understandings of the meanings of the common heritage of slavery.

Because culture is shared but unequally distributed, every society must have mechanisms to deal with two processes: the generation of similarity and the organization of difference (Wallace 1961). The **generation of similarity** involves those institutions and processes that teach and reinforce common beliefs, values, orientations, and models for action among members of a community. Family, school and peer groups, and mass media, among others, generally serve as key institutions for enculturating members of a society into the most deeply and widely held cultural symbols. But shared, uniform beliefs and values are not necessary for many cooperative activities. People from many different backgrounds can share a bus in a multiethnic neighborhood in Los Angeles; they simply need to know the rules for bus riding. Institutions concerned with the **organization of difference** include most political and social organizations with the power to regulate behavior and reward or punish behaviors from schools and police to tribal institutions.

Culture Is Learned

The fact that not all cultural knowledge is equally shared by all members of a society draws our attention to the fact that we do not simply possess culture by virtue of being born into a society, we learn our culture as we live, work, and grow. Which aspects of our society's total cultural repertoire we learn depends to a large extent on our unique experiences growing up. Yet those experiences are in turn shaped by society. Insofar as we are raised in similar ways and pass through similar institutions (like hospitals, schools, weddings, and funerals), we share common sets of cultural knowledge, values, and assumptions. Insofar as our experiences differ—because of unusual family structures, differences in wealth, and exposure to different areas of society—our cultural knowledge is different.

The processes by which members of a society pass on culture to new generations is called **enculturation**. One aspect of enculturation is **formal learning**, the acquisition of cultural knowledge that takes place within institutions specifically designed for this purpose, such as schools, apprenticeships, and on-the-job training. Each society has institutions that exist primarily to pass on to children specific knowledge and skills needed as adult members of that society.

Formal learning makes up only a small part of enculturation, however. Most enculturation takes place through processes of **informal learning**—the learning we engage in simply by watching, listening, and participating in everyday activities. Consider how you learned to speak, your taste in clothes, or your eating habits. These things are usually learned through observation, imitation, and gauging the responses of those around us.

Our deepest cultural learning often shapes our bodies and unconscious behaviors: how we speak, how we move, how we eat, how close we are

FIGURE 3.2 Most enculturation involves informal learning—the learning we engage in simply
by watching, listening, and participating in
everyday activities. PHOTO: Cameron Hay.

comfortable standing to people. This kind of enculturation is called **embodiment**. An example of embodiment is accent. As we learn the language of our community, we train our whole vocal apparatus to easily and
automatically produce a certain range of sounds. When we try later to
learn a second language, we find it difficult to produce the new sounds,
resulting in a foreign accent. Even though we are physically capable of
making the same sounds as any other human, we have trained our bodies
so as to privilege certain sounds over others. Similar embodied patterns
can be shown to exist for proximity, gesture, how we walk or sit, what we
wear (or don't), and many other elements of our everyday life. Embodied
culture is especially important because it feels completely natural to us. It
is not only difficult to change, it is difficult for us even to become aware of.

Culture Is Adaptive

And yet, culture is not only capable of changing, it is always in a process of change. Enculturation does not refer only to the process whereby children become socially adept members of a community. Cultural learning is a lifelong process, because cultural systems adapt to changing environmental, economic, political, and social conditions. All cultural systems change over time in response to shifts in context. Cultures change as they adapt to internal or external pressures. Cultures do not, however, all adapt to the same pressures in the same ways, nor do there seem to be stages that all cultures pass through. One important corollary of this is that there are no primitive or fossil cultures. Studies of foraging societies have been important in helping us understand how all humans must once have lived, but contemporary hunter-gatherers nonetheless have their own unique histories. The Ju/'hoansi !Kung people of the Kalahari desert, for example, have a centuries-long history of being pushed south by fiercer peoples. How they hunted and what they gathered changed as they were pushed into increasingly inhospitable environments and had to adapt by developing new skills and technologies (Lee 2002).

Culture adapts to changing conditions in a number of ways. Creativity is a fundamental human trait, and all societies have mechanisms for generating innovation from within. At least equally important is the capacity of communities to borrow cultural innovations from other societies and adapt them to their needs. The **diffusion** of ideas, technologies, and practices occurs through direct contact, such as migration or conquest, as well as through indirect contact, such as trade and mass media.

It is important to recognize that culture does not cease to be culture because it borrows and adapts. When the Plains Indians adopted the horse and the rifle from Spanish conquerors, traders, and settlers, they completely transformed their society. They did not, however, become Spaniards. Today it is not uncommon to see Coca-Cola franchises in Cairo or New Delhi and interpret them to be evidence of an emerging global culture, or **globalization**, a process some have even referred to as *McDonaldization*. But the McDonald's of Egypt is not the McDonald's of the United States. In the United States, McDonald's is a low-status, inexpensive, and convenient restaurant designed to serve frantically busy lifestyles, low budgets, and the desire for places children can go with their parents. In Egypt, McDonald's is a high-priced, high-status restaurant that delivers food, caters parties, and is a favorite place for young cosmopolitan Egyptians to hang out. Although the restaurants share many of the same physical characteristics, those characteristics mean very different things in their different contexts. Understanding how apparently identical things can mean very different things in different contexts is an important aspect of international studies.

LEVELS OF CULTURE

The poster for a program on multicultural education in Washington, DC, in 1989 represented culture in a way that would make any anthropologist cringe. It showed a series of identical stick figures, each wearing a different hat, such as a sombrero, a beret, and a feather headdress. The implication was that we are all basically the same, all fundamentally human, but we put on cultural differences like so many different hats.

There are many problems with such a conceptualization. The use of identical bodies to symbolize our underlying similarities belies the important role culture plays in shaping those bodies, through marriage rules, dietary practices, and routines of physical activity. The reduction of cultural difference to matters of style—something we can put on and take off—ignores the deep-seated, pervasive, and complex beliefs people hold about such things as family, faith, patriotism, and race—things that are very difficult to put on and take off.

And yet, there is something to this depiction. Cultural difference is *expressed* largely through overt behaviors such as dress and idiomatic phrases. One way to resolve this discrepancy between overt behaviors and underlying meanings is to imagine culture as existing at three levels: (1) a level of everyday practices, (2) an underlying level of reasons and logical explanations for those practices, and (3) a level of underlying assumptions about how the world works that are usually taken for granted. All of these combine to make up the common sense by which we deal with everyday life.

Cultural Practices

Cultural practices, then, refer to the everyday actions through which people in a particular community get through their day. It is the work we do, the things we say, the tools we use, the physical spaces we occupy and the ways we live and work in them, the things we buy, the ways we behave around other people, the entertainment we enjoy, the prayers we say. Cultural practices are, in brief, the surface of culture, the artifacts we produce and use, and the actions of everyday life. Because observable practices often involve material space and objects—business cards, seating arrangements, clothing, gifts, types of food—specialists in intercultural communication sometimes call this level *artifact*. Saying *insh'allah* in Egypt, presenting business cards with a bow in Japan, and having men and women eat separately in India are all cultural practices. But merely knowing about these cultural practices, and accepting or going along with them, does not reveal the deeper issues of faith, respect, or honor that generate them.

Cultural Logics

Cultural logics are the underlying mechanisms that generate meaningful human action, including routine cultural practices like those described above. Anthropologists have generally recognized two forces at work. On the one hand, people act according to ideas they have in their heads. They have goals, values that make the goals worthwhile, and strategies for achieving these goals. These do not seem to take the form of scripts and rules so much as sets of logics that generate consistent behaviors. On the other hand, people's cultural logics are always organized in part by real-world conditions. If culture is to offer us a meaningful model of reality, it must be sufficiently true to reality to work on an everyday basis. Nature, and our technological adaptations to it, enable and constrain forms of human action.

This is true even of culture logics like magic, which violate many other people's common sense. Writing of the use of magic in shipbuilding by Trobriand Islanders, Bronislaw Malinowski pointed out that magic and technology are always complementary systems of knowledge. To sail hundreds of miles across the ocean in an open boat requires sophisticated boatbuilding and navigational technology, and among the Trobrianders, excellent shipbuilders and sailors are celebrated for their skills. But even the best-built ship with the most skillful sailors can be destroyed by a sudden, severe storm. In such a case, Trobrianders believe it is the magic that sees them through. By their success in the face of the otherwise uncontrollable forces of nature, Trobrianders also recognize and respect those with particularly powerful magical skills (Malinowski 1992).

Because cultural logics are almost always self-consistent, they have ways to explain the failures of the practices they generate. Magicians have explanations as to why their magic failed, just as dentists have explanations as to why even those who brush their teeth twice a day still get cavities. Whether we believe these explanations is usually determined more by our faith in the cultural logic, and the authority of the person explaining it to us, than any objective truth of the matter.

Worldview

Although no cultural system ever forms a fully integrated whole, anthropologists have a great deal of evidence to support the notion that there are deep, systematic patterns that join logics together. The most encompassing level of cultural integration is usually called a **worldview**. *Worldview* refers to assumptions people have about the structure of the universe. A worldview is a model of reality that people use to orient themselves in the world. A worldview usually consists of fundamental principles and values that organize and generate cultural logics. These may include such propositions as the following:

- The world is made up of individuals who make choices.
- Most people's lives are shaped by circumstances not in their control.
- There are supernatural beings who may answer my prayers or petitions.
- Everything in the universe can be explained by material operations in the universe.
- All living things have souls.

These propositions are rarely stated in such bald terms by members of communities where they are held as shared assumptions, even though they often underlie many different forms of social action. In most societies, worldviews are articulated through myth, religion, drama, and art. Collectively, these comprise domains of **expressive culture**, those institutions through which we show ourselves to ourselves. Most societies include specialists in expressive culture—writers, artists, poets, theologians, performers, ritual specialists, and others—who articulate and elaborate the society's worldview in various symbolic forms.

FIGURE 3.3 Rituals are part of expressive culture, in which worldviews are articulated and elaborated in symbolic forms. PHOTO: John Cinnamon.

A worldview is often described as an encompassing picture of reality. The term *worldview* suggests that this level of cultural integration affects the ways people see the world. These visual metaphors are not accidental. Seeing is a widely used metaphor for understanding in many cultures, and worldview is often described as a set of tinted lenses that color our perceptions of reality. This metaphor helps us understand how two people can approach the same reality yet understand it and respond to it differently. A person who believes that human life is made up of a series of individual choices will generally apply this worldview in order to understand a story even if it is being told by someone who understands life to be outside human control. Someone who believes in malevolent spiritual forces will look for evidence of their presence in events that someone without this belief would shrug off as bad luck or poor choices.

Worldviews are important tools through which human beings make sense of the world around them. It is important, however, to avoid seeing worldviews as prisons that lock us into a single way of seeing the world. Many early formulations of worldview did just that. Some anthropologists and linguists argued that people learned a particular language and worldview simultaneously, and that when this enculturation process was complete, people were locked into their worldview. The argument was that, for example, people whose languages contained no word for green literally did not see the color green (they saw shades of blues and yellows), while people whose languages included words for many shades of green saw forests and grass in richer ways than those who had just one word.

Empirical studies of language and perception have clarified our understanding of worldview.[2] As we encounter the world around us, our worldview makes certain ways of seeing and dealing with reality *easier* than others. For example, one series of studies with color chips showed that people with few color words in their vocabulary had no trouble categorizing subtle differences in color (Brown and Lenneberg 1954). Although they might use the words available to them, *blue* and *yellow*, to categorize various shades of green, if pressed they could give metaphorical descriptions like "the color of a broadleaf" or "the color of grass." The general conclusion of these experiments was that humans see the same reality but they divide it up into different categories. They routinely use these categories for dealing with the world, but they remain capable of creative, outside-the-box thinking. These studies also suggest that when faced with something new we routinely try to understand the world in familiar terms. When these familiar ways of seeing the world don't work, we are capable of creatively discovering new ways of dealing with things outside our experience.

INTERCULTURAL RELATIONS

These discoveries have important implications for intercultural relations and cultural change. The easiest way to imagine culture is to imagine a people living within a geographically defined area and sharing a common language, a common worldview, and a common repertoire of cultural logics and practices. Unfortunately for social theory, this easy way of thinking about culture is not the reality for most of the world's peoples, and for many of them it never has been. People encounter one another through trade, migration, and warfare, as well as through mediated forms of communication such as the circulation of technologies, art, books, and movies. This process is called cultural **diffusion**. Cross-cultural encounters can have powerful transformative effects on both social systems and on individuals, and any theory of culture needs to be able to account for this.

One way in which cultural diffusion operates is to provide opportunities for communities to innovate and expand their cultural repertoires without particularly acknowledging the origins of their cultural innovations. For example, the Nuer people of the Sudan were originally monotheistic. As they brought wives into their tribes from neighboring Shilluk and Dinka tribes, the wives taught their own myths and rites to their children. Gradually, Nuer religion came to accept the existence of lesser gods operating under the authority of the greater God. By the time E. E. Evans-Pritchard (1940) came to study them in the 1930s, they took their polytheism for granted. Most societies develop through such processes of diffusion. Ralph Linton (1936) wrote a now-classic article in which he pointed out that almost every artifact and cultural practice an American employs in daily life is appropriated from some foreign origin. Whether something is appropriated but has no symbolic connection to its origin (for example, the fact that pajamas come to us from South Asia is irrelevant to understanding their use and meanings in contemporary North America), or whether a practice's origin is part of its meaning (like the authenticity of imported ethnic art works) is an important aspect of understanding globalization.

But intercultural relations are never only about societies. They are always also about people. As labor migrants, tourists, soldiers, and **refugees**, people move with increasing frequency across cultural boundaries, from communities where they know the rules to places where very different practices, logics, and worldviews are in play. The term **culture shock** is often used to describe the unpleasant, even traumatic, feeling people get when the rules and understandings by which they have organized their lives no longer apply.

How do people deal with culture shock? There are several ways. Some people might hold on tightly to the worldview and logics they grew up with and believe the people among whom they now live are wrong, foolish, or even immoral. Often, they surround themselves with artifacts and people from their own community. To deal with their new host culture, they focus on pragmatic knowledge of local cultural practices. Take the case of John, an American businessman who spent two to four months each year doing business in Japan. John made a conscious effort to learn customary Japanese business practices as tools to get his job done. He learned to bow and present a business card, to give and receive gifts, and other important elements of doing business in Japan without ever making the effort to understand the deeper logics underlying these practices. He never tried to learn the language beyond a few greetings, to read translated Japanese novels, or to watch dubbed movies. He kept up on news about Japan but only through newspapers and television from the United States. John was shocked when, after five years as his company's Japanese liaison, he was transferred to another part of the world and Greg, a newly hired sales representative, got his job. The chief difference between them was that Greg seemed to appreciate many aspects of Japanese society. He had studied the language in college (although he did not speak it well), he read the illustrated novels Japanese call *manga*, and he kept up with Japanese news through the English edition of the Japanese newspaper *Asahi Shinbun*. Most importantly, Greg got a feel for the logics that generate Japanese practices rather than simply trying to memorize them as rules. As a result, he was comfortable in situations where John was uncomfortable or bewildered. Japanese clients were likewise more comfortable with Greg, who usually knew when to follow formal rules and when the rules changed.

An increasing number of people around the world live for long periods of time in host communities and become at least partially enculturated. The practices of the host community become increasingly normal, and they get a glimpse of the cultural logics that generate these practices. Susan, a teacher from the United States who taught for thirteen years at an Egyptian private school, learned to dress conservatively, covering her shoulders and wearing skirts that fell below the knees. She also grew accustomed to the deference with which students treated her as a teacher. She grasped some of the underlying logics of life in Egypt, where one's behavior is a reflection of one's family, and where good people are expected to govern their lives so as to contribute to social stability. Dressing conservatively and speaking with deference to those in higher positions had nothing to do with her feelings; they were about respecting the feelings of others. When she returned to the United States and began teaching at a school in Florida, she suffered reverse culture shock. But gradually she came to recall the crucial role of individuality in the North American worldview and to understand that the Florida students' practices and modes of dress were about expressing their individuality. Susan gradually came to feel that she understood and was comfortable with both worldviews.

Not everyone is so fortunate. Oscar, a Venezuelan, and Peggy, his American wife, have lived with their three children in four different countries as they've followed Oscar's career in the oil industry. They speak Spanish at home, and their children have attended British and American schools during their postings. As his college years approached, Victor, the oldest, began to express worries about who he was and where he would go as an adult. He likes the lifestyle in the United States but feels the people are "ignorant and narrow, seeing everything in black and white." His American accent, modes of dress, and inability to understand nuances of people's behavior set him apart in Venezuela. "It's like, wherever I live I'm a foreigner," he said. Victor's plight is that although he has linguistic and educational tools for success, he is unable to comfortably orient himself in the world. A significant part of culture is its capacity to help us generate **identity,** a sense of being part of a group through shared commonalities of belief and feeling. In many cases, it is subtleties of surface practices that generate this sense of being part of a community—being around others who speak, dress, and behave more or less as you do.

STUDYING CULTURE: THE ANTHROPOLOGICAL PERSPECTIVE

As even this brief overview suggests, culture is a pervasive aspect of human life that touches on everything we do. In the United States, culture is particularly studied by cultural anthropologists as part of a larger inquiry into human nature. Broadly speaking, anthropology is the empirical study of what it means to be human. Whereas most social sciences are defined by their subject matter, anthropology is not. History studies people's records of their past. Political science examines relations of power. Geography studies the relations of people to their environments (and vice versa). Economics studies the ways people produce, distribute, and consume goods and services. Since all of these are human activities, an anthropologist may well study any or all of these.

Lacking a bounded subject matter, anthropology is defined instead by a common perspective, a particular way of looking at human activities. Employing this perspective, anthropology can be said to be comparative, holistic, empirical, evolutionary, and relativistic.

Comparative Perspective

It is normal for people to believe that the ways they behave are natural. Heterosexual American men don't usually express affection for each other through touching. The idea that men might show friendship through handholding, patting, or sleeping in one another's laps seems unnatural. Yet such displays are common in many parts of the world. For most Europeans and North Americans, the idea of a soup made of dog or guinea pig is repulsive, yet these are enjoyed thoroughly in parts of Asia and South America, respectively. Elsewhere in the world there are peoples for whom beef or pork are just as repulsive.

Because all people tend to assume their ways of life are natural, the only way one can study culture is through a **comparison** of cultural systems that shakes up this sense of normalcy, showing that what we assumed was natural and essential is actually cultural and historically contingent. Anthropology is therefore deeply concerned with understanding the similarities and differences among cultural systems.

Holistic Perspective

A second important aspect of the anthropological perspective is the capacity to understand human societies as complex systems with many interwoven elements. Taking a cue from the biological sciences, anthropologists tend to examine human social action as richly contextual. In the biological sciences, there are essentially two ways to examine organisms. One way is to examine them in laboratory settings, where their behavior can be described under controlled conditions. The other is to examine them in the ecologies in which they actually live. In the latter case, understanding an organism requires understanding adaptations to specific ecological conditions as well as its relations with other species in the same niche. This is similar to the approach anthropologists take with the study of humans. Rather than trying to reduce the complexity of social action by concentrating on one aspect of human action—like religion, social institutions, language, art, drama, or agriculture—anthropologists assume that all these aspects of human society are interconnected and that these interconnections can be discovered and described.

An example of this kind of **holism** can be found in the work of Stephen Lansing in Bali. Lansing was in Indonesia studying Balinese temple religion in 1983 when the island was going through an agricultural evolution. Indonesian and Western agronomists had introduced new breeds of rice, chemical fertilizers, pesticides, and other technologies as part of Asia's green revolution. Many of these techniques had enjoyed enormous success elsewhere in Asia. But in Bali, one of the world's leading rice producers, crop yields actually fell after these techniques were introduced.

Lansing was able to demonstrate that these problems were due in part to a failure to understand the complexity of Balinese society. At the peak of the volcanic island is a great crater lake and also the temple of Dewi Danu, the goddess the Balinese say created the island and the lake. At particular times during the year, according to detailed ceremonial calendars, priests open canal gates that flood a series of canals—but not all canals. Farming communities are organized around canal gates throughout the island, and the ceremonial calendar governs how irrigation takes place. Because farmers in different parts of the island are engaged in different stages of activity at different times, the cycle not only aids efficient rice production but also works around the life cycles of ducks, eels, and frogs, which consume insects that would otherwise eat the grain and which also form a significant protein source for the Balinese (Lansing 1991).

Lansing's work demonstrates not only that agriculture, social organization, and religion are intertwined, but that the separation of life into these distinct domains is not always relevant or useful. To the Balinese, agriculture, the farming community, and the temple rituals are all part of the same life and are not easily separable. Western agricultural experts, coming from a very different worldview, had a difficult time seeing the world from a Balinese perspective, even when the Balinese perspective yielded better harvests.

Empirical Perspective

A holistic perspective requires anthropologists to enter into the communities they study in order to gather data about everyday life. Anthropology is therefore an **empirical** science whose data are derived from direct observation and data collection by anthropologists living with the people they study. Anthropologists call what they do **fieldwork**, a term that may include a wide variety of methods, including interviewing, mapping, taking censuses, charting genealogies, and collecting stories and media produced by the people they are studying. For the most part, these methods are

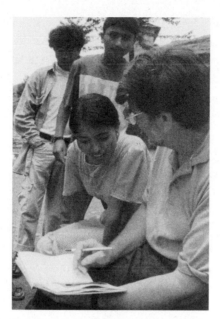

FIGURE 3.4 Fieldwork: Anthropologist James Hamill collects information from his hosts in Nepal. PHOTO: H. Sidky.

encompassed within the broader anthropological method they call *participant observation*. **Participant observation** refers to long-term engagements with a host community in which the anthropologist enters into the everyday life of the community, insofar as the hosts in that community permit.

Evolutionary Perspective

Once, anthropologists tended to assume that social systems were stable except when they were acted on by outside forces. They wrote of communities in a kind of eternal present tense as if they could capture once and for all the culture of a society. Empirical research has since demonstrated that stability is not normal for social systems. Contemporary anthropologists try to stay cognizant of the fact that all communities are in continual processes of historical change as they adapt to population pressures, environmental changes, wars, famines, new technologies, and other phenomena. This is not something new; it is inherent in social systems.

Arguing that all cultures continuously evolve by adapting to change—that they are in **evolution**—is not an argument for "survival of the fittest" thinking. Many times, a society changes to meet urgent pressures of war, famine, plague, or sudden economic change in ways that are not viable over the long term, or that lead to other urgent crises down the road. As culture change recedes into history, it becomes possible for scholars to make judgments about how communities benefited or were harmed by their particular adaptations, and why their adaptations took the form they did.

An evolutionary perspective cautions anthropologists not to take stability for granted. This might seem obvious, but how many times do you hear news stories that explain cultural practices in terms of tradition? When the Taliban regime imposed the wearing of a full body and face covering called a *burqa* on all Afghani women, it was not imposing traditional dress. In most Pashtun villages before Taliban rule, girls wore no head covering until they began menstruating, then they adopted a head scarf. They assumed the burqa only after they were married. In imposing the burqa on every human female in Afghanistan without regard to class, age, or marital status, the Taliban regime was creating an entirely new cultural institution, forcing change on villagers as much as on urban women who didn't wear the veil. The evolutionary assumption reminds anthropologists that traditions have histories. When we find a practice our hosts understand to be traditional, the anthropological question is always, why *this* tradition *now*? What does it mean to people in the contemporary community, and what functions does it serve?

Relativistic Perspective

Perhaps the most controversial—and misunderstood—aspect of the anthropological perspective is the notion of **relativism**. In order to draw meaningful conclusions about human behavior from the comparison of many different societies, as well as to gather data about these societies fairly, anthropologists assume that all human societies offer data of the same type. This means that anthropologists cannot make advance judgments about the practices of the peoples they are studying.

From any given perspective, a whole range of behaviors practiced by others will appear repugnant. To most Americans, eating dog or guinea pig, the veiling of women, female (but not male) circumcision, penis bifurcation, arranged marriages, and myriad other practices around the world are disgusting, immoral, or oppressive. Yet common American practices of premarital sex, eating pork, private ownership of land, male circumcision, making pets of dogs, talking to strangers about intimate family problems (including millions of strangers through television talk shows), and putting criminals to death are just as disgusting, immoral, or oppressive in the eyes of many other peoples. The goal of anthropology is to understand the functions of these cultural practices, the roles they play in social systems, and their meanings to those who take them for granted, rather than to privilege one system of meaning over another.

This does not mean that anthropologists do not have strong feelings about many of the practices they study. The commitment to relativism is not an abrogation of moral and ethical judgments. It is a commitment to recognizing that humans are capable of collectively generating innumerable creative solutions to the problems that beset life, and to understanding how and why they work in a particular time and place. It is a commitment to learn *from* people, not only *about* them.

One way to understand relativism in anthropology is to divide it into three types. **Methodological relativism** is the principle that, to be comparative, anthropology must treat all social practices as data of the same type, that is, as institutions that serve particular social functions in specific times and places and that are embedded in complex webs of meanings. **Theoretical relativism** is an assumption, much tested and held by most anthropologists, that all human actions make rational sense when understood in their own contexts. This is often mistaken for **philosophical relativism**, a position that claims, in essence, that whatever people do is right for them. Few, if any, anthropologists would claim to adhere wholeheartedly to this philosophy. No one believes infanticide or genocide is okay—only that they are understandable. But because anthropologists do not hurry to judgment about cultural practices that many others may condemn out of hand, they are sometimes accused of taking a position of philosophical relativism.

ANTHROPOLOGY AND INTERNATIONAL STUDIES

The anthropological perspective offers at least five key dimensions to international studies. First, anthropology emphasizes the importance of culture

FIGURE 3.5 As cultures increasingly come into contact with each other through economic globalization, there is little evidence that a shared worldview is coming into existence. Rather, we find an increasing organization of diversity. PHOTO: Mark Allen Peterson.

in explaining human actions at every level of society, from the interpersonal to the international. The concept of culture reminds us that people's symbolic worlds are just as real as the material conditions in which they live; in fact, people only apprehend the empirical world through learned models of reality. While all peoples may respond to economic pressure and military power, we cannot begin to make accurate predictions about *how* they will respond unless we have a thorough understanding of their cultural realities.

Second, anthropology urges a more sophisticated approach to cultural boundaries. Rather than writing about culture as a shifting, eminently practical set of resources for making sense of the complex worlds in which people live, many contemporary approaches to international studies tend to write about cultures when they mean communities or societies, or to imagine that culture is somehow contained by the lines on a map that demarcate the borders of states. The anthropological perspective can offer an important corrective to these tendencies to imagine nation-states as the only important locus of culture and identity or to confuse symbolic systems with social groups.

Third, anthropology urges us to remember that there are usually more than two points of view. Imagining the world in binaries is a deeply rooted part of the American and Western European shared cultural heritage. We divide the political world into left and right, the economic world into socialist and free markets, we look for two sides to every story, and so forth. When we are faced with multiple perspectives on issues, we often lump them together into two opposed views. But differences between perspectives that seem trivial to us may be matters of life and death for those who hold them.

Fourth, anthropology sometimes encourages us to think small. Dictators, presidents, ministers, ayatollahs, and military commanders are not the only political actors who matter in the world. Political policies designed to bring dictators to heel may affect hundreds of thousands of people who have no say in how their states are run. Economic plans for increasing overall national economic growth may end up benefiting only a small percentage of the population while increasing poverty among the majority. Military strategies designed to quickly overcome militant groups may so devastate bystanders as to create more people willing to join such groups. Rooted in on-the-ground empirical observation, anthropology encourages us to recognize the unintended outcomes of international actions on communities beyond their intended targets—and to consider how these will reshape the worldviews of members of these communities and so their future encounters with us.

Finally, anthropology emphasizes that international studies is always ultimately about people. It urges students to learn *from* people, not just about them. It urges us to recognize that the generation of similarities and differences is part of the human condition and to seek to understand difference, rather than fearing or dismissing it.

The contemporary world is a world of encounters across national, social, and cultural borders. Understanding culture is crucial to understanding human behavior at every level, from the individual to the nation state, in an increasingly globalized world.

Notes

1. All examples not cited are drawn from the author's fieldwork in Egypt, India, or the United States.

2. For example, Brown and Lenneberg 1954, Lenneberg and Roberts 1956, Berlin and Kay 1969, and Kay and McDaniel 1978.

References

Beeman, William O. 2003. "Iran and the United States: Postmodern Culture Conflict in Action," *Anthropological Quarterly* 76, no. 4: 671–691.

Berlin, Brent, and Paul Kay. 1969. *Basic Color Terms: Their Universality and Evolution*. Berkeley: University of California Press.

Brown, Roger W., and Eric H. Lenneberg. 1954. "A Study in Language and Cognition." *Journal of American Social Psychology* 49: 454–462.

Evans-Pritchard, E. E. 1940. *The Nuer: A Description of the Modes of Livelihood and Political Institutions of a Nilotic People*. London: Clarendon Press.

Herzfeld, Michael. 2001. *Anthropology: Theoretical Practice in Culture and Society*. London: Blackwell.

Kay, Paul, and Chad K. McDaniel. 1978. "The Linguistic Significance of Basic Color Terms." *Language* 54: 610–646.

Lansing, Stephen. 1991. *Priests and Programmers: Technologies of Power in the Engineered Landscape of Bali*. Princeton, NJ: Princeton University Press.

Lee, Richard B. 2002. *The Dobe Ju/'Hoansi*. 3rd ed. Belmont, CA: Wadsworth.

Lenneberg, Eric H., and John M. Roberts. 1956. *The Language of Experience: A Study in Methodology*. Baltimore, MD: Waverly Press.

Linton, Ralph. 1936. "One Hundred Percent American." *The American Mercury* 40: 427–429.

Malinowski, Bronislaw. 1992. *Magic, Science and Religion and Other Essays*. Westport, CT: Greenwood Press.

Wallace, Anthony. 1961. *Culture and Personality*. New York: Random House.

Further Reading

Agar, Michael. 1996. *Language Shock: Understanding the Culture of Conversation*. New York: Harper.

Besteman, Catherine, and Hugh Gusterson, eds. 2005. *Why America's Top Pundits Are Wrong: Anthropologists Talk Back*. Berkeley: University of California Press.

Farmer, Paul. 2004. *Pathologies of Power: Health, Human Rights, and the New War on the Poor*. Berkeley: University of California Press.
Gonzalez, Roberto, ed. 2004. *Anthropologists in the Public Sphere: Speaking Out on War, Peace, and American Power*. Austin: University of Texas Press.
Greenhouse, Carol J., ed. 2002. *Ethnography in Unstable Places: Everyday Lives in Contexts of Dramatic Political Change*. Durham, NC: Duke University Press.
Mainz, Beatriz. 2004. *Paradise in Ashes: A Guatemalan Journey of Courage, Terror, and Hope*. Berkeley: University of California Press.

Journals

Anthropological Quarterly
Anthropology News
Anthropology Today
City and Society
Cultural Survival

Films

First Contact (1984). Bob Connolly and Robin Anderson, directors. Filmaker's Library, www.filmakers.com.
The Goddess and the Computer (1988). J. Stephen Lansing and Andre Singer, directors. Documentary Educational Resources, www.der.org.
In and Out of Africa (1993). Ilisa Barbash and Lucien Taylor, producers. Berkeley Media, www.berkeleymedia.com.
Transnational Fiesta: 1992 (1993). Paul Gelles and Wilton Martinez, producers. Berkeley Media, www.berkeleymedia.com.
Trobriand Cricket: An Ingenious Response to Colonialism (1976). Gary Kildea and Jerry Leach, producers. Berkeley Media, www.berkeleymedia.com.

Websites

Cultural Survival. www.culturalsurvival.org.
Human Relations Area Files. www.yale.edu/hraf/index.html.
Public Anthropology. www.publicanthropology.org
Savage Minds: Notes and Queries in Anthropology. http://savageminds.org/
Zero Anthropology. http://zeroanthropology.net.

4

Economics and International Development

The global economy continues to struggle with the ongoing aftereffects of what many have come to call the **Great Economic Crisis,** a sharp downturn in the world economy that began in the United States in 2008 and had devastating worldwide ramifications. Considered by most analysts to be the worst economic slump since the Great Depression of the 1930s, the crisis began in the United States with a sharp decline in banking **liquidity**—the ability to pay debts when they come due without incurring unacceptable losses. Because the United States is a global financial hub, the crisis spread quickly, resulting in the collapse of giant investment firms, bank bailouts by national governments, and stock market slumps around the world. In many areas, the housing market also suffered, causing a sharp rise in evictions, foreclosures, and prolonged vacancies. The crisis led to steep declines in consumer wealth in the trillions of US dollars, ultimately leading to a severe global economic recession in 2008. Although most economists declared the recession over in 2009, the economic consequences have persisted well into the next decade, with no end in sight.

Why were so many American banks suddenly unable to pay their debts? The answer lies back in 2007 with the collapse of a long-term real-estate bubble in the United States. For more than a decade, US land and housing prices had risen steadily, encouraging lenders to offer home ownership loans at increasingly higher risk; the logic was that if the borrowers were foreclosed on, the banks could recoup their loss by selling the property. When the housing bubble burst, many lending institutions found themselves holding more debt than they could manage. Similar bubbles burst in several European countries, as well as in Argentina, Australia, New Zealand, Lebanon, South Africa, Ireland, Israel, South Korea, India, Russia, Ukraine, and China.

But the problem was made worse by US banking deregulation, which since the 1980s had rolled back many protections that had been put into place after the Great Depression. These reforms allowed savings banks, whose purpose is accepting savings deposits and paying interest on them, to also operate as investment banks, which underwrite or act as agents for issuing securities. The deregulation also allowed banks and investment firms to create complicated high-risk, poorly understood new financial instruments. Thus the crisis "was not a natural disaster, but the result of high risk, complex financial products; undisclosed conflicts of interest; and the failure of regulators, the credit rating agencies, and the market itself to rein in the excesses of Wall Street," according to a 2011 US Senate report (United States Senate 2011).

One of the immediate consequences was a dramatic downturn in the US stock market, which dropped from a high of 14,000 points in October 2007 to a low of 6,600 in March 2009. US market volatility was quickly reflected in stock markets in Asia and Europe. Twenty-five banks failed in 2008 and were taken over by the Federal Deposit Insurance Corporation (FDIC), including Washington Mutual Bank, the largest bank failure in US history. Another 140 failed in 2009, 158 in 2010, 92 in 2011, and 51 in 2012.

The crisis grew rapidly into a global economic shock that resulted in a number of European bank failures, falling stock indexes, and large reductions in the market value of commodity goods and equities. Beginning with the United Kingdom, governments responded with bailouts of foundering banks and large corporations to put more money in circulation, while cutting interest rates to help borrowers.

The continuing fiscal crisis in the United States affected many other countries worldwide. The US economy had been spending and borrowing at very high rates for many years, and much of the rest of the world depended on the US consumer as a source of global demand. With a decline in borrowing and drop in spending by US consumers, economic growth elsewhere was affected. Even countries that avoided the worst effects of the recession were hit by the drop in global shipping in 2009, in which, for example, exports from Taiwan dropped 42 percent, South Korea 30 percent, and Japan 27 percent.

In Europe, countries fared differently. Poland, which had imposed strict austerity measures as a result of financial problems in 2000, was the only member of the European Union to avoid a recession; the country even saw modest growth during this period. In Iceland, on the other hand, the entire international banking system collapsed. It was the greatest financial disaster to strike any country in modern history. Furious at their government's handling of the crisis, people began protesting, culminating in 2009 with the resignation of the entire ruling conservative party and its replacement by a left-leaning government.

The word **recession**, generally referring to any period of reduced economic activity, can be used in two ways. In the formal economic sense, it refers specifically to two consecutive quarters of declining economic growth. By this definition, the recession ended in the United States in the summer of 2009, and as much as six months earlier or later in most other countries. However, people often continue to use the word in a more general sense to refer to continuing high unemployment, escalating federal debt problems, inflation, rising gas and food prices, and ongoing declines in home values, leading to an increase in foreclosures and personal bankruptcies, which marked many economies well after the recession technically ended.

This was particularly dramatic in the **Eurozone**—those parts of Europe where the euro (€) is the common currency. In late 2009, alarm grew over the possibility of a **sovereign debt crisis**, an inability of a country to pay back its debt. Sovereign debt had increased dramatically throughout Europe as a result of the European bank bailouts, with Greece, Ireland, and Portugal seen as particularly vulnerable. The fear was that if countries like these defaulted on their debts, it would pull down countries that held their debt, like Italy and Spain. The collapse of these larger economies would in turn threaten the economies of European economic powerhouses, most importantly Germany.

In May 2010, the **International Monetary Fund** (IMF) and the Eurozone countries agreed to a €110 billion loan for Greece, in exchange for harsh austerity measures including tax hikes, scaling back public benefits, and cutting pensions. This was followed by similar rescue packages for Ireland six months later and Portugal six months after that. These austerity measures led to massive public protests, and it was not clear that the Greek government would not fall, as Iceland's had. Worse, it did not solve the problems, which resurfaced a year later over the refinancing of Greek public debts. Again in 2012 the Greek government managed to pass a new package of austerity measures, and **European Union** (EU) leaders passed a bailout package to sustain the country, but many economists began to question the viability of the European joint financial system. By 2013, the EU still had 27 million people out of work, and less than one-half of one percent economic growth.

Latin American states suffered during the first stage of the crisis, but came through comparatively unscathed by 2010. Initially, stock markets became extremely volatile during the crisis, and currencies fell sharply. Except for Peru, industrial growth fell. Unemployment grew, leading to marches and protests in many countries. However, as foreign investment in Latin America declined, domestic banks, especially in Brazil, stepped in to fill the gap. The loss of US and European investments also led many countries to build stronger ties with China. Latin America had suffered major economic crises in the 1980s and again in the 1990s, and the economic reforms instituted over the past decade, especially in Bolivia, Brazil, Ecuador, El Salvador, Nicaragua, and Venezuela, led to more resilient and better-managed economies.

Major Asian economies experienced the same stock-market volatility and rising unemployment as the rest of the world, but while China, India, and South Korea experienced slowed growth and accompanying social and political unrest, they avoided a technical recession. Other Asian nations fared very poorly. Cambodia fell from 10 percent economic growth to nearly zero, and Bangladesh faced a sharp rise in the number of families living below the poverty line. Many Asian countries implemented strict austerity measures to try to avoid further economic problems. Cutting of benefits and pensions, rising unemployment, layoffs of public-sector workers, and wage cuts provoked strikes, protests, and riots across Asia from Cambodia, South Korea, and Taiwan to Japan and Hong Kong.

Although oil-producing countries in the Middle East lost enormous sums in international investments, they were generally less severely affected by the crisis than many other parts of the world because of continuing high world oil prices. Iran, largely cut off from global financial markets due to US sanctions, apparently did not even sink into recession.

Countries with less petroleum fared worse. It is no coincidence that countries with fewer petroleum reserves (such as Egypt, Syria, and Tunisia), and those in which the public enjoys a smaller share of revenues from oil sales (like Libya and Yemen) were the countries in which the so-called

Arab Spring emerged. Already facing high unemployment and rampant government corruption, protests in these Arab countries did not decline as they did in most other parts of the world, but grew dramatically, toppling apparently strong governments like that of Ben Ali in Tunisia and Hosni Mubarak in Egypt. In Libya, it turned into a full-fledged armed revolution that ousted Muammar Qaddafi, while in Syria protests escalated into civil war.

In Africa, the global economic crisis swept "away firms, mines, jobs, revenues, and livelihoods," plunging the continent into "a full blown development crisis" (AfDB 2009). For more than a decade, African states and international development agencies had sought relatively strong economic growth by integrating Africa into the international financing market, but these efforts, while producing economic growth, made most African countries more vulnerable to the global economic downturn. The decline in global trade led to a drop in demand for many African commodities, such as diamonds, coffee, and rubber, which in turn led to rising unemployment. For example, in the once-prosperous Katanga province of the Democratic Republic of Congo, 60 percent of enterprises closed and more than 300,000 people were laid off in 2009. Income from remittances by Africans living in developing countries has also declined as workers faced the consequences of the global crisis in those countries. In Kenya, for example, remittances declined by 13.3 percent in late 2008 compared with the same period in 2007. Domestic investment also declined precipitously. For example, the Nigerian stock exchange lost 66 percent of its value in 2009.

Poor African countries that depend heavily on overseas development assistance, such as Benin, Comoros, Ethiopia, Liberia, and Niger, saw reductions in aid. This means states have less to spend on social programs like education and health, and they see further increases in the number of people living under the poverty line. The number of people living in poverty in Ghana, for instance, rose by 230,000 by the end of the year 2009. Since then, the economy has remained stagnant in most African countries.

How do social scientists describe and understand what happened to world trade and finance in the years leading up to the global downturn? How do governments decide what policies to enact to lessen the effects of the crisis, to shorten its duration, or to reverse its effects? How do we measure whether or not those policies are effective? **Economics** is the social science that studies, describes, models, and makes projections about the production, distribution, and consumption of goods and services. It does so by focusing on the choices made by individuals about alternative uses of scarce resources to satisfy needs and wants.

In most contemporary definitions of economics, the meaningful unit of analysis is some individual actor seeking utility or pleasure by gratifying needs and wants, although the unit might also be a corporation, institution, or state. While wants are presumed to be unlimited, human beings have only limited resources to satisfy them. In the dominant contemporary economic theories, "rational" individuals seek to maximize utility by expending the fewest resources (or costs) to obtain a need.

There is an implied definition of human nature in this way of looking at human activity. It assumes first, that all humans have unlimited desires; second, that all humans have limited resources; third, that humans are rational in the narrow sense that they evaluate the costs and benefits of their actions; and finally, that humans are inherently self-interested. These assumptions have been contested by other social sciences, as well as within economics, but proponents argue that even if human nature does not operate strictly by these principles, models based on these principles still work at a statistical level.

This point of view is widely accepted by economists in the United States, but remains a point of debate among economists in many other parts of the world. The assumptions economists make about human behavior, operations of institutions, the creation of wealth, and other aspects of economics can be roughly grouped into three economic **paradigms** that guide economists and policymakers throughout the world. These are liberal economics, nationalist economics, and Marxist economics. Understanding the basics of all of the major different theories of political economy is important in international studies because they all remain influential, and aspects of them can be found in most economic systems.

LIBERAL ECONOMICS

Liberal economic theory is a theory of political economics first clearly articulated during the Enlightenment in Adam Smith's *Inquiry into the Nature and Causes of the Wealth of Nations* (1776). Smith conceived of wealth as produced by a nation through the efficient division of labor and use of resources. From these roots, the science of economics took on its double role as both an academic enterprise and a practical project aimed at developing the practical foundations for the efficient production, distribution, and consumption of resources on a global level. Many theoretical variations of liberal economics have emerged with differences revolving around the relative importance of labor, the value of specific scarce resources, or the effect of changes in demand on the creation of wealth.

Liberal economic schools of thought all hold a consistent commitment to **markets** with minimal government intervention. In an absolute form, liberal economic theory assumes a perspective on human beings as "economic man," *Homo economicus*, who act to gain the highest possible well-being, or **utility**. Such individuals are rational in the sense that they seek to achieve their goals at the least possible cost. This does not mean that individuals' goals are rational or that individuals necessarily know fully what their long-term best interests are, only that they try to fulfill needs and desires at minimal cost to themselves. This concept of **rationality** is fundamental to *rational choice theory*, which, in its basic form, assumes that social systems arise as the result of the actions and interactions of individual actors motivated by self-interest.

Liberal economics assumes that humans have unlimited wants and desires, thus creating **demand**, but have limited resources to fulfill them, creating **scarcity**. Trade-offs are therefore an inherent aspect of economic decision making, and part of the decision to meet one set of desires requires not meeting another set of desires. Imagine a young woman choosing between a party dress and a new softball bat. She can afford only one. Her choice involves both objective costs (the price of the party dress or the bat) and the subjective value of being well dressed and of improved athletic performance. Once she chooses to buy one rather than the other, there is also the cost of the desire that is not met; buying the dress comes at the cost of forgoing the bat, and vice versa. The value of demands not met is called **opportunity cost**. According to liberal economic theory, such dynamics of consumer choice are best played out where a single individual can assess these costs and benefits in a free market with free flows of information. Critics of the theory argue that the social, historical, cultural, and individual complexities of even this simple-minded example are far more complicated. The young woman is not making this decision in isolation from a number of other complexities, including her social relationships to her parents, her coach, her dance date, peers, and many others.

According to liberal economic theory the best decisions about the use and transmission of wealth and resources occur without coercion. Without coercion, individuals will automatically make rational decisions about how much pleasure is obtained by each additional unit of cost for a good or service. Individuals will purchase goods/services so that the satisfaction gained equals the labor or costs invested in obtaining that satisfaction. The goal of business is to increase the point where consumer satisfaction is gained. This is called the theory of **marginal utility**, and the models derived from the theory allow for sophisticated model building on which market strategies are based.

Buyers and sellers are all trying to maximize utility. The buyers' demand can be represented by a **demand schedule** that lists the goods that buyers are willing to buy at certain prices. As the price of a good or service increases, the quantity demanded of those goods and services decreases. The **law of demand** asserts that there is an *inverse* relationship between the price of a good and the quantity demanded of that good. Price, of course, is relative not only to demand but also to the availability of money. As the income of buyers increases, so too will the demand for goods and services. These relations between price and demand can be represented graphically in a **demand curve**.

But buyers' demands for goods are not the only factor determining price in the market place. The seller's **supply** of goods also plays a role in the market price. (Like the buyer's demand, supply economists can depict supply models as a supply schedule and graphically in a **supply curve**.) As the price of a good increases, sellers are motivated to increase the supply of that good. According to the **law of supply**, a direct relationship exists between the price of a good and the quantity of supply of the good. In the market, the decisions of buyers interact simultaneously with those of sellers and there is a tendency for the demand to equal the supply of a good or service. When the demand for a good equals the supply of that good, the market for that good is said to be in **equilibrium**.

The place where optimal decisions about supply, demand, scarcity, utility, and the evaluation of opportunity costs can be made is in the free market. Successes in the free market abound in an increasingly globalized economy. In Europe, Australia, and Asia, movies such as *Monsoon Wedding* and *Bend It Like Beckham*, produced in partnership with India's movie industry, have been hits in part because they depict Indian or Asian families' adaptations to Western values. In a free market, unrestricted by high tariffs or import quotas, Japanese car manufacturer Toyota has managed to outsell US auto manufacturing giants General Motors and Ford. The loosening of impediments to optimal decision making in the international market has, from the perspective of free marketers, enhanced effective economic decisions and benefited both sellers and buyers.

From the perspective of liberal economics, then, the global recession actually serves as evidence that the free-market system works. The decade-long housing bubble, the overextension of debt, the creation of ridiculously complex financial instruments all created a "distorted" market that was not responsive to true financial conditions. The global recession and continuing crisis were a case of the market "correcting" itself. The enormous human suffering caused by this process was an unfortunate but natural and necessary effect of the operation of the global market economy. Interventions to minimize that suffering—bank bailouts, artificially low interest rates, government investment in new businesses—are a mistake, in this view, because they slow the market's return to balance and normalcy.

ECONOMIC NATIONALISM

The notion that state interventions are inherently bad sets liberal economics apart from those approaches that can be covered by the term **economic nationalism.** *Economic nationalism* refers to policies that are guided by the protection of national labor, production, and wealth accumulation. The fundamental principle of economic nationalism is that the economy is not independent of a country's social and political system, but is an integral part of the nation state, and must be guided to perform in the nation's best interests, both domestic and international. Establishing minimum wages and setting limits on the work week, regulating manufacturing standards, policing which chemicals are allowed in foods, setting aside resources as public lands, limiting monopolies, setting terms on investments by foreign countries, and enacting tariffs and other barriers to foreign trade are examples of ways economic nationalists seek to subordinate economic activity to national interest, as opposed to liberal economics, which views economic interests as best served by unregulated markets.

Economic nationalism has its roots in an earlier set of theories popular during the colonial era, known as mercantilism. **Mercantilism** is a theory of political economy that holds that the economic well-being of a nation is directly related to its control over the global volume of capital. In early forms of mercantilism, the volume of global trade was seen as constant and unchanging, and it was calculated in known values of precious metals held by the state. The power of the state was believed to be best improved by an economic system that appropriated as much of this constant capital as possible. This required having high quantities of exports and smaller quantities of imports. The role of government, therefore, was to enhance a positive balance of trade by enforcing **protectionist** policies such as **tariffs** on imported goods, creating **subsidies** to protect businesses from risks, and imposing **import quotas** to prevent other nations from dumping cheap products on national markets. Protectionist policies were imposed to limit other nations' competitive advantages because it was believed that one nation's advantage required another nation's loss. This **zero-sum approach** to economics was the dominant political-economic paradigm during the emergence of the **nation-state** in Europe between the sixteenth and eighteenth centuries. Historically, protectionist policies gave industry time to develop their production systems and accumulate capital until they could compete in the international marketplace.

Economic nationalism and its predecessor, mercantilism, have experienced changes since their inception in the period of European expansion. Moreover, manifestations of mercantilism were differently expressed in different countries, often on an ad hoc basis, and were not characterized by any unifying theories or models such as is found in liberal economic or Marxist paradigms. Nevertheless, there is a central idea in economic nationalism that the interests of the state are inherently tied to economic activity and that economic activity itself is subordinate to national interests. Today, this idea remains influential, and all states continue to enact forms of protectionism as means of enhancing their own economic strengths. These forms can range from tax breaks or subsidies for local businesses to outright **nationalization** of industries. For example, Venezuela and Bolivia recently took steps to nationalize their petroleum and natural gas industries and appropriate larger **royalties** from multinational petrochemical corporations.

Economic nationalism is inevitably tied to ideologies of national belonging and citizenship. Nationalistic ideology focuses on the nation-state as the exclusive and essential institution, and individuals are defined according to their membership in it and their subservience to it. The nation is usually represented as a fixed homeland, a homogeneous identity and language, a high degree of autonomy, complete sovereignty, and a unity of identity. Political elites will therefore often attempt to protect the nation from outside influences. For example, in 2005, the Chinese National Off-shore Oil Corporation's (CNOOC) failed in an attempt to take over the US-based multinational petroleum corporation, Unocal. The CNOOC bid met with intense lobbying efforts from the US-based petrochemical giant Chevron. The Republican-dominated US Congress eventually fore-stalled the deal. Chevron's lower bid on Unocal gained economic credibil-ity, although this whole episode ran counter to the Bush administration's free-trade agenda.

China is keenly interested in acquiring oil companies because China's economic growth and its lack of petroleum reserves are contributing to increased global demands for oil, an indispensable, strategic, and finite resource. Easing China's access to petroleum to further its productive ca-pacity may be consistent with efforts to liberalize international trade, but it is not consistent with US foreign-policy interests that see China as a potential political threat and economic rival. In this context, the policies formulated by the US Congress were meant to encourage US investments in Unocal and discourage foreign investments. These efforts were clearly motivated by American nationalist concerns.

Economic nationalism assumes a complementary relationship between national power and the nation's domestic welfare. This is at odds with liberal economic theory that would see fundamental contradictions in seeking national welfare through militarization or any form of state inter-vention. Liberals would also argue that all nations would best benefit not from protectionist or any nationalist policies but rather by instituting ex-actly the opposite, by opening trade between nations without restrictions or nationalist intervention. Economic nationalists see sovereign states in competition with one another and not well served by the formation of economic interdependencies.

Protection of national economic interest can become a national-security interest very quickly. When this happens, nationalism as a polit-ical philosophy gains increasing importance and is supported by judicial, police, and military power. The important issue for nationalism is therefore not mutual economic gain among the community of nations, but the rel-ative gain between nations. Global liberal economic institutions, from the World Bank to the McDonnell Douglas Corporation, however, could not have developed as they have without the support of the most powerful and self-interested liberal nation-state, the United States, whose interests are at once consistent with and at odds with nationalism. Efforts by all states to protect their economic interests are normal and recurring themes in international studies as conflicts between national industries, particularly over scarce and finite resources, become apparent in the international community.

Adherents to economic nationalist approaches, then, applaud interventions into national economic institutions and processes designed to alleviate economic hardship and minimize the collapse of banks and businesses, and strengthen employment. Economic nationalists take comparative note of the countries that suffered most and least from the global recession, and express concerns about the relative power between rival countries recovering at different rates. These concerns can, in turn, spur further efforts at market regulation and state investment.

MARXISM

Marxism refers to a range of systems of economic analysis based on the notion that the value of goods and services stems not from supply and demand in a market but from the human labor, both physical and mental, required to produce it. This has profound implications for economic analysis, because it means that markets, rather than establishing values through supply and demand mechanisms, can be means of exploiting people by setting the prices of goods lower than the cost of the labor required to produce them. Based on various interpretations of the works of Karl Marx and Friedrich Engels, Marxist theories have evolved in significant ways since their basic formulations in the mid-nineteenth century. Marx's analytical approach, **historical materialism**, analyzes the causes of change in human societies by focusing on how societies organize the production and distribution of goods and services. This approach pays attention to the relationships between economics, politics, social structure, and ideology.

Marx argued that the driving force of historical change was the relationship between people who worked to transform natural resources into goods, and those who profited from this labor without contributing to it. From the rise of river-valley agricultural civilizations to feudal systems to global capitalism, there have existed fundamental economic contradictions between laborers and the elites who enjoyed, and profited from, the goods produced by those laborers. Every era thus resulted in **class struggle**, which eventually led to a series of social transformations resulting in the emergence of a new economic system. Marx believed that the contradictions inherent in global capitalism would eventually lead to its collapse, and the emergence of a utopian, classless society called **communism**.

These theories were based on Marx's observations in Germany and England in the mid-nineteenth century, where he saw extreme forms of labor exploitation, distinct class divisions, and a **political economy** that, in his view, both created and required these inequalities. Marx said that what made the system structurally unequal was that some people owned the **means of production**. They owned the means of doing business, the resources it required, the labor it needed, the capital derived from it, and even the ideas required for it (which can be copyrighted or trademarked). They devised a political, legal, and military system to legitimize their ownership. The owners were able to accumulate **capital** without themselves contributing significantly to the actual productive process. While capital could be put to use in a variety of ways, Marx argued that the owners of the means of production, the capitalist class, controlled the uses to which capital was put and, in that context, capital accumulated in the hands of a small segment of society, the capitalist class itself. Labor, in his view, owned little or no capital but was responsible for actually creating the capital appropriated by the capitalist class. The working class never receives the true **value of its labor**.

Marx referred to the relations between social classes as the **relations of production**. These are the social relations that are *necessarily* formed by the way societies produce and reproduce their material lives. The relations of production determine how incomes, products, and assets are socially distributed, and they constitute the social structure of the society. In capitalism, according to Marx, these relations of production are necessarily those of exploitation of labor and denial of basic human rights to most of the population. In many modern instances, the philosophical perspectives of Marxism gained support through the aspirations of peasant and labor groups seeking economic and political liberty from authoritarian and oligarchic capitalist regimes in Latin America, Asia, and Africa.

Modern forms of Marxism can be divided into two separate movements: Marxism-Leninism and social democracy (Gilpin 1987, 30). **Marxism-Leninism** was characterized in the political economy of the Soviet Union. As a form of totalitarian state-run or command economy, it no longer holds any legitimacy. **Social democracy** refers to a variety of egalitarian political economies that are not too different from forms of egalitarian liberalism. That is, these social democratic systems generally embrace industrial production and market systems, but include governmental and social controls intended to mitigate the tendencies of market systems to exacerbate social inequalities, including partial or full state ownership of businesses or industries. Most European countries have some form of a social democracy. Countries that have instituted these social reforms have largely market-based economies that include sole proprietorships as well as multinational corporations (Saab and Ikea, in the case of Sweden, for example). In modern forms, these countries encourage private entrepreneurial activities and foster forms of capitalist industry but also offer a wide range of social safety nets, universal healthcare, and well-financed public education. As a consequence, these countries also enjoy high life expectancies, low unemployment, low crime rates, and small national debts. The trade-off is usually higher taxes and lower overall economic growth than in countries structured by economic liberalism.

In most modern applications of Marxist theory, the goal is not to overthrow capitalism, but to reform it and remove the apparent economic inequality and social injustices that, according to Marxism, are inherent in capitalism. In the *Communist Manifesto*, Marx claimed that, in capitalism, workers become a commodity. He also argued that as the drudgery of the work increases, wages decrease. This was clearly true in the nineteenth century, but over time in Europe and the United States wages generally improved and the drudgery of work decreased with technological innovation. In the less-developed world, however, and with the freeing of international trade in globalization, labor again has become increasingly commoditized. Corporations seeking increased profits have relocated their production to the Third World, where labor costs are far lower than in the developed world. Consequently, there has been a rise in "sweatshop labor" despite economic research suggesting that profits would not be significantly lowered if better wages and working conditions were offered (Pollin et al. 2002). US garment manufacturers like Abercrombie and Fitch and J. Crew are seen as particularly guilty of subcontracting to sweatshop operators in Asia while reaping huge profits. A global backlash against these manufacturers and Nike Corporation has resulted in some changes in hiring practices, but generally these conditions persist, leading to a continued interest in Marxist-inspired economic reform in many developing countries.

Political movements advocating socialist reforms have been popular in many less-developed countries and have drawn their inspiration more from local organizers than from Marxist theory. These movements vary considerably in their concerns, organization, and goals, and they may not identify themselves as socialist, but their basic struggle can be couched in terms of opposition to the political and economic inequalities of a capitalist economic system. These movements seek a more equitable distribution of economic resources, increases in wages, social justice, and liberty.

For example, these sorts of Marxist-informed political ideologies have reemerged in Bolivia, Venezuela, and other Latin American countries. They have made political economic reforms such as nationalizing domestic petroleum resources and major industries to improve social services and ease persistent and egregious levels of poverty. The Mexican rebel, Subcomandante Marcos, represented some of the impoverished peasant groups in southern Mexico, the Zapatistas, and the major ethnic groups of Chiapas. He denied any affiliation with socialist governments, but demanded peasant rights to farm their own land, reasonable healthcare, public education, and justice. As such, these peasants represented what is recognized as the underlying interests of social democracy, universal rights, and freedom from exploitation. As Blackman (2005) points out, "very few of the Mexican peasants who joined the Zapatistas had read Marx or Engels."

For Marxist economists, the global financial crisis was the result of fundamental contradictions in the system of global capitalism, specifically the way wealth aggregates in the hands of a small percentage of the global population, but from whom it is inefficiently redistributed to the rest of the world's population. Bank and corporate bailouts add to the problem by shifting debt from failing institutions to nation-states. All efforts to solve the crisis by regulation will ultimately fail, Marxist economics argues, because of another contradiction: because the markets are now global, only a global system of financial regulations can fix it. But the key players are nation-states, none of whom are willing to give up their sovereignty and national interests to an international regulatory agency (Beams 2008).

MICROECONOMICS AND MACROECONOMICS

Contemporary economic analysis proceeds primarily not through elaborate essays and monographs like those of Smith and Marx but through the construction of models of economic behavior. The field of economics is divided into two large branches: micro- and macroeconomics.

Microeconomics is concerned with studying specific market systems on a small scale, such as the economic behavior of individuals, firms, and industries, to understand the relative prices of goods and services and the alternative uses to which resources can be put in a particular market system. Microeconomics assumes that there is a host of buyers and sellers in the market, none of whom can effectively control the price structure in the market. Real-market transactions, of course, do include individuals or groups who can influence prices, and this complicates microeconomic analysis. For example, the Organization of the Petroleum Exporting Countries (OPEC) and the chaotic political climate in many oil-producing countries such as Nigeria and Iraq clearly influences the supply and cost of petroleum products. The environmental costs of using these products are increasing as well. Sophisticated models in microeconomic analysis are used to formulate business policies for a firm or industry in the context of these politically, environmentally, and economically complex marketing environments.

Macroeconomics is concerned with the study of the combined performance of all markets in a defined market system. Macroeconomics may have nation-states or global regions as its unit of analysis, and aggregate information about a nation's economy is gathered. A particularly important indicator of economic performance in this arena is **gross domestic product** (GDP), defined as the total value of all goods and services produced in a country in a year. The goal of macroeconomic analysis may include data analysis and modeling to inform government or institutional policies. The Federal Reserve Board in the United States, for example, was established in 1913 to regulate the amount of capital and credit available in the American economy. Macroeconomic analyses crucially inform the board in regulating the nation's money supply. The Federal Reserve influences the amount of Federal Reserve funds available to banks, thus controlling interest rates. "The Fed" can do this by purchasing US government securities, by increasing or decreasing the discount rate (the interest the federal government charges to banks to borrow money from the government), and by regulating the proportion of monetary reserves banks are required to keep on hand before making loans. The higher the reserve requirement, the fewer funds are available to distribute as loans, and the availability of capital is thus adjusted.

DEVELOPMENT ECONOMICS

Development economics studies growth strategies in less-developed countries. Defining *developing countries* is difficult but the label refers to countries

where standards of living are consistently low compared to the so-called
First World economies in Europe, the United States, Canada, and Japan.
Most of these countries are located in sub-Saharan Africa, South Asia, and
Latin America, but poor countries are also found in East Asia (e.g., Vietnam), Central Asia (e.g., Kazakhstan), Eastern Europe (e.g., Romania), as
well as the Middle East. The goal of economic development is to create
an economic environment where people enjoy long, healthy, and creative
lives. Obviously, there is more to economic development than growth in
incomes but the concept begins with developing economic structures to
facilitate higher standards of living. Since World War II there have been
several policy-informing models seeking to enhance the economic development of the Third World. (The Second World consisted of the Communist
bloc countries before they collapsed at the end of the 1980s.) The first such
model was offered in the 1950s by W. W. Rostow who presented an evolutionary paradigm in his *The Stages of Economic Growth: A Non-Communist
Manifesto*. Rostow posited that nations pass through five consecutive stages
before reaching the "stage of high mass consumption" characteristic of
the United States. This simplistic theory was criticized for not recognizing
that, although capital accumulation was *necessary* for development, it was
not *sufficient* to guarantee it. Structural-change theory suggested a series
of sequential economic policies that would foster economic development,
particularly in industry and trade. This theory failed to consider forms of
rural economic development, and the policies therefore failed to improve
the standards of living of most of the developing countries' populations. A
central problem with early developmental theories was that they looked at
how American and Western European countries became wealthy (often in
idealistic ways that excluded the contributions of slavery, colonialism, and
appropriation of land from Native people) and constructed idealistic "one
size fits all" models that paid little or no attention to the actual ecological, social, and historical conditions of the countries they were supposed to
help. International dependence theories originated in developing countries
and came as a reaction to the failed policies of structural change policies.

Immanuel Wallerstein and Andre Gunder Frank were among those
who offered critiques of liberal economics, especially of Rostow's structural-
change theory. They argued that both capitalist and Marxist economic theories were inappropriate for modeling economic development in the Third
World because they were derived from Western European historical experiences. A similar perspective informed the pan-Arab movement in the

1960s and 1970s. More recently, Arturo Escobar (1995) has laid the failures of development of many nations in the Third World at the feet of Western economic powers, arguing that development projects and economic policies based on growth-oriented, capitalist economic models often fail when applied to societies that operate according to different cultural logics.

Underlying these criticisms is the empirical fact that very few development projects work as planned. Many have unexpected local consequences, such as draining ecosystems or disrupting traditional forms of social and political organization. Many fail to achieve the predicted economic outcomes, with the result that recipients cannot pay off loans and thus sink even further into debt. Still other programs increase overall wealth as measured by national GDP, but the new wealth is concentrated in the hands of a few, increasing the gap between rich and poor.

Contemporary economic-development theory is associated with efforts to open trade and restrict government interference in economic activity. These theories, which gained popularity under Margaret Thatcher and Ronald Reagan in the 1980s, were a radical reaction to dependency theories and similar critiques. There are several variations of such neoliberal theory but all advocate a free-market approach and less government intervention. The dominant model associated with the World Bank advocates opening free markets but recognizes that the unsophisticated financial institutions of many developing nations require some government intervention to ensure the proper evolution of industry and export markets.

GLOBALIZATION

In *The Wealth of Nations*, Adam Smith considered the magnitude of the discovery of America and the links established even then between Europe, the Americas, and the East Indies. He foresaw that "uniting, in some measure, the most distant parts of the world, by enabling them to relieve one another's wants, to increase one another's enjoyments, and to encourage one another's industry, their general tendency would seem to be beneficial" (2005, 508). Although prescient in his reasoning, Smith was aware of the depredations of imperialisms, driven by nationalistic ideologies, in this process. Now, however, with the governing principles of global economics superseding nationalist interests, many economists believe that a seamless system of global trade in goods and services will yield benefits to all nations and decrease the likelihood of international conflicts (Sachs, 1998).

Globalization generally refers to the expansion of global communication and market connections, growing social and political interdependencies on a global scale, and the development of a planetary rather than national awareness among many of the world's people. In some perspectives, globalization involves consolidation and homogenization of global social relations. Certainly, globalization involves many processes, financial transactions, market expansion, electronic communication, and growing interconnections, but which of these factors is most important in understanding globalization is a matter of some contention. It is, in any case, a socially and historically complex process not easily defined or explained.

Neoliberalism is the economic theory and ideology that has served as the primary backdrop to what is commonly referred to as *globalization*. It is an adaptation of liberal economic theory applied to a world economy, and suspicious of many of the notions of "common good" (reserves, public lands, public schools, and hospitals) accepted by earlier schools of liberalism, on the theory that markets will always be more efficient than states or local communities in managing such resources.

The goal of neoliberalism is generally to ease restrictions on trade between different countries, to free the movement of goods and services, and to maximize economic efficiency and profits. This is to be accomplished by removing controls such as tariffs, regulatory measures, and restrictions on investment, as well as relegating government services to private firms whose market orientation increases the efficiency of service delivery. During the last half of the twentieth century, deregulation of industry and privatization of government services has opened economies to imports of goods as corporations seek new markets and new sources of less expensive labor than they had found in the developed world. Technological advances in communication and transportation of commodities has reduced costs and encouraged expansion of trade and foreign investments. Moreover, the advances in communication have resulted in a much more integrated system of international finance, allowing for rapid exchange of currencies. The overall effect of these changes has been an increase in businesses participating in trade beyond the borders of their own nations.

One of globalization's greatest champions, Thomas Friedman, described globalization in *The Lexus and the Olive Tree* as "the inexorable integration of markets, nation-states, and technologies to a degree never witnessed before in a way that is enabling individuals, corporations and nation-states to reach around the world farther, faster, deeper and cheaper than ever before" (1999, 7). For Friedman, globalization is not merely a trend but represents the transformation of global political economy after the Cold War, with its own logic and incentives. In fact, he defines globalization in contrast to the Cold War. The Cold War was characterized by division while globalization is, he says, characterized by integration. Friedman suggests that 80 percent of globalization is driven by technological advancement, which deliberately eliminates barriers to transactions of every kind. The barrier most directly influenced by these technological advancements is that of national prohibitions or restrictions.

Economist Jeffery Sachs (1998, 110) notes that the world is now joined in a single global marketplace and that the focus of **international economics** must be on how national economies respond to this international system. Sachs defines international economics as "concerned with the trade and financial relations of national economies, and the effects of international trade and finance on the distribution of production, income and wealth around the world and within nations." As a form of political-economic transformation, globalization has happened so quickly that its consequences and implications for economic growth, patterns of trade, global and national transfers of currencies, and the resulting distribution of wealth in the world economy are still poorly understood. What does seem to be the case is that national economies are becoming more integrated and interdependent in several ways: through increased trade, foreign direct investment, international production, and through international treaties and legal institutions to regulate the system. However, although it is true that global trade has increased steadily since World War II, much of this is through large multinational corporations. This means that a great deal of trade and investment between countries are transactions within the same multinational company (Sachs 1998). As much as one-third of investment and its resulting trade of goods are actually shipments of component products to various production plants of the same business firm whose production processes are conducted in several different countries.

The **World Trade Organization** (WTO) has been both praised and criticized as the consummate representative of globalization. The WTO was created in 1995 as part of the **General Agreement on Tariffs and Trade** (GATT), which was part of a postwar process to lower tariffs. The WTO is an international organization for negotiating, monitoring, and regulating international trade agreements. The goal of the WTO is to help producers of goods and services conduct business without fear of trade restrictions and government intervention. Consumers and producers benefit by having secure supplies of goods at low prices and having greater choices of products, raw materials, and services. Producers and exporters can predict that foreign markets will remain open to them, resulting in a more "prosperous, peaceful and accountable economic world," as the WTO's website states (WTO 2011).

Critics of globalization, neoliberalism, and the WTO argue that these agreements are part of a corporate-inspired agenda targeting any protectionist policy that might negatively influence free trade and benefit citizens over companies. Arguments have been made that the WTO can essentially override any law meant to protect workers or the environment if the law can be seen as restricting the capability of corporations to trade freely. Economist Joseph Stiglitz in *Globalization and Its Discontents* (2002) has claimed that globalization has not brought economic benefits to the world's poorest countries. He points out that in the 1990s, while global income rose by 2.5 percent, the number of people living in poverty increased by 100 million and that 43 percent of the world's population live on less than $2.00 per day. Stiglitz criticizes the policies of global financial institutions, particularly the **World Bank** and the **International Monetary Fund (IMF)**, for these growing economic inequalities. One of his major arguments is that rich nations, like the United States, became wealthy in part by protecting their own industries when they were too immature to compete on a larger global level. Yet the current policies of the IMF and the World Bank do not take these developmental issues into account when they authorize loans that require the borrowing nations to liberalize their markets and increase external trade rather than protect their industries. For Stiglitz, the theories that guide the IMF and the World Bank are empirically flawed and the conditions where perfect liberal markets are successful are historically rare. According to Stiglitz, recent advances in economic theory demonstrate that markets only function optimally in places where people have lots of information with which to make reasonable choices, which is almost never true in developing countries. Stiglitz claims that in most situations there are desirable government interventions that can improve the efficiency of market mechanisms to benefit poorer nations.

These criticisms of neoliberal policies are not only of theoretical importance; they influence political activity at many levels. This has been readily apparent in Latin America. In 2005, the Summit of the Americas failed to establish an agreement on the Free Trade Area of the Americas

(FTAA). The **Summit of the Americas** is a set of meetings held every two years between leaders of countries in North America, South America, Central America, and the Caribbean to discuss economic issues. It was established in the early 1990s to allow the leaders of the **Organization of American States** (OAS) to discuss the implementation of the principles of the **Washington Consensus**, a set of neoliberal policies aimed at instituting free markets for the entire Western Hemisphere. These principles included fiscal discipline, anti-inflation policies, privatization of state enterprises, elimination of state interference in the economy, deregulation of the private sector, and liberalization of investment policies. At the first Summit of the Americas in 1994, Latin American leaders had endorsed the economic principles outlined by the Washington Consensus and began reforming their economies to conform to their policies. These reforms, however, failed to produce expected economic growth or to raise the living standards of the 50 percent of Latin Americans living in poverty. Across Latin America, people began electing governments that promised to alter or to abandon these neoliberal policies and to reinstitute social programs to mitigate growing poverty.

The election of Hugo Chavez in Venezuela in 1998, despite strong US opposition to his candidacy, became a symbol of the threat to the policies of the Washington Consensus. Chavez began his Bolivarian Revolution to replace it with a Latin American economic community based not on competition but on cooperation to further regional goals of increased economic and social equality. By 2005, the strains between Latin America and the United States became clear when FTAA policies were rejected. More ardent voices in this debate argued that neoliberal policies were inherently imperialist, and, with Chavez, called for a new "socialism for the 21st century."

NON-WESTERN ECONOMICS

A very different critique of classical economics has arisen in anthropology, sociology, social psychology, geography, and other humanistic sciences concerning economy's claim that there is a universal form of economic rationality. These social scientists have studied the economic behaviors of non-Western actors and economics in small, often remote villages. An alternative vision of economic rationality was derived from these studies; foremost among these was Marshall Sahlins's argument in *Stone Age Economics* that economy is a category of culture and, as such, is not about the "need-serving activities of individuals, but the material life process of society" (1972, xii). In one famous paper, Sahlins suggested that the foraging society of the !Kung of the Kalahari people in southern Africa generally desired little, and so were able to easily meet their desires and be content, even in one of the harshest environments on earth. There was evidence among these people that "happiness" was not gained by hard work and the accumulation of wealth but rather through their having limited wants, limited demands on labor, much leisure time, and strong community and family ties.

Sahlins did not deny that economic rationality operates in non-Western societies, but he insisted that it was only one form of cultural logic, and that multiple forms of rationality exist, some of which contradicted Western ideals of individualized, wealth-maximizing behavior.

In this perspective, there is no universal form of economic rationality but rather an infinitely diverse set of rationalities contingent upon a very complex interaction of cultural, social, environmental, individual, and historical contexts; people make different but equally "rational" decisions in different times, places, and social contexts. For example, in a classic ethnographic work by Richard B. Lee, *The !Kung San: Men, Women, and Work in a Foraging Society* (1979), Lee argued that a primary "rational" characteristic of the !Kung, was a form of anti-individualism that prohibited individuals from "maximizing their individual gain." Mike Evans (2001), working in the Kingdom of Tonga in the South Pacific, eloquently demonstrated the persistence of non-Western forms of kin-based exchange systems and gift giving in Tonga that do not easily conform to liberal economic models of maximizing individual utility.

Subsequent studies turned these arguments on their head, arguing for the continued existence of nonrational market activities in large-scale modern civilizations. For example, Gretchen Hermann showed that people holding garage sales were likely to price goods differently, based on personal relationships rather than market competition (Hermann 1997). Julia Elyachar (2005) showed that cooperative commercial activities by craftsmen in Egypt, reinforced by social pressures and fear of the **"evil eye"** (a supernatural punishment produced by envy and brought on by greed) actually made these craftsmen more able to survive market pressures than the Westernized college students setting up export businesses with government loans. These and other studies led to the conclusion that non-Western agriculturists and peasants do not calculate their costs and benefits at the margins, and that "in its most extreme form, methodological individualism is highly ethnocentric" (Halperin 1994, 14).

Sustainability

This empirical critique of economic assumptions gained some attention as global concerns arose about the sustainability of economic development. **Sustainability** refers to the capacity of a political economic system to meet the needs of present communities without reducing the ability of future generations to meet their own needs. As agencies monitoring global development looked at how economic projects had operated over the decades, they realized that in many cases "successful" projects had damaged ecologies, sold off limited resources, or otherwise traded short-term gains for long-term costs. The economics of sustainability insists on including resource depletion as a cost in economic models.

The debates on the universal applicability of formal rational theory led to a host of studies on economic and agricultural activities at the household and community level that seem to preserve the natural resource base. For example, Robert Netting found that relatively self-sufficient farmers in areas as diverse as Nigeria and Swiss Alpine valleys manage resources in such a way as to preserve the environment on which their economic activity depends. These resource-management activities not only constitute a form of rational utility, but also provide a model for possible future forms of sustainable production. These studies provide important information on the complexity of human/environment interaction and describe forms of sustainable economics activities that are useful for creating more sustainable food production and distribution systems in an increasingly crowded and resource-scarce world. The underlying argument is that perpetual growth and pure economic efficiency is not sustainable. It cannot long continue in a world of limited resources.

This work fit well with serious criticism of the environmental consequences of unregulated liberal-economic decision making. The most famous of these early critical voices came from *The Limits to Growth* models (Meadows et al. 1972) where scientists developed computer models predicting that economic growth could not continue indefinitely due to the limited availability of natural resources, particularly oil, and of the inability of the earth's systems to replenish themselves as rapidly as they were being depleted. Using then-new concepts such as **carrying capacity**, they outlined the consequences of human systems of economic growth in the context of limited and finite global resources. They argued that continuing growth-oriented economic development would lead to the exhaustion of the earth's resources and the subsequent collapse of global economic and environmental systems. These debates initiated a drive by economists to reformulate economic models to better understand ideas of valuation of natural resources.

The well-documented environmental problems often created by industrial capitalism sparked strong arguments from within the capitalist camp as well. Economists Robert Costanza, Kenneth Boulding, Herman E. Daley, and others developed the field of **ecological economics** in the early 1990s (Costanza 1991). Convinced that existing forms of economic organization were incapable of guaranteeing sustainable production or healthy ecological systems, these economists sought to include a reasonable method of explicating the value of such things as clean water, vibrant environmental systems, and future resource needs.

The future costs of such things as controlling resource depletion, global warming, and maintaining biodiversity, have little economic relevance or value today. There is a desire in conventional economics to maximize resource flows and gain the greatest financial return in the short term. This approach to accounting discounts the well-being of future generations. Ecological economists have begun to reconsider this narrow form of accounting and have presented accounting methods to translate the future values of environmental impacts into equivalent values in today's monetary units in order to better formulate environmental constraints in economic modeling. In 1987, a report by the Brundtland Commission made sustainable development the official principle endorsed by the United Nations.

CONCLUSION

The global economic crisis led to dramatic social and political upheavals as people in many countries lost faith in their governments. In addition to those already mentioned, several waves of protests swept the world. In April 2009, protests in London over global economic policy, banking executives' salaries and bonuses following bailouts, climate change, and the war on terror were timed to coincide with the **Group of Twenty (G20)** summit. Although the majority of the protests were peaceful, many protesters were forcibly detained and there were widespread accusations of police brutality, including the death of one protester at the hands of police. A month later saw a series of international protests in conjunction with the May First, International Labor Day. Traditional marches turned violent in Germany and Venezuela, and banks and shops were attacked in Turkey. May Day protests also occurred in Cuba, Hong Kong, Italy, Japan, the Philippines, Russia, and Spain. In 2011, a wave of protests swept across the United States. These included protests in Ohio and Wisconsin in the spring over state efforts to overturn union protections for public workers. Later that year, thousands turned out in New York for weeks of "Occupy Wall Street" protests, followed by sympathetic protests in Boston, Chicago, Albuquerque, New Mexico, Spokane, Washington, and Los Angeles. In the wake of this unrest, new political parties and projects have emerged, such as the "Abenomics" program of new Japanese Prime Minister Shinzo Abe. New social movements have emerged around the globe as groups seek to deal with deeply unpopular austerity measures, including cuts in public wages, tax hikes, and reductions in social spending. Politically volatile countries—such as Somalia, Iraq, Libya, Afghanistan—face greater risks of increased social and political unrest as economic challenges affect the political will of international bodies to police, aid, or intervene. Such turbulence seems likely to grow in the near future until a new economic stability is established internationally.

References

AfDB (African Development Bank Group). 2009. "Impact of the Global Financial and Economic Crisis On Africa." www.http://www.afdb.org.

Beams, Nick. 2008. "The World Economic Crisis: A Marxist Analysis." The World Socialist Web Site. www.wsws.org/en/media/documents/legacy/nb-lecture-1208.pdf

Blackman, Andrew. 2005. "What Is the Soul of Socialism?" *Monthly Review* 57(3): 104-113.

Costanza, Robert, ed. 1991. *Ecological Economics: The Science and Management of Sustainability.* New York: Columbia University Press.

Elyachar, Julia. 2005. *Markets of Dispossession: NGOs, Economic Development and the State in Cairo.* Durham, NC: Duke University Press.

Escobar, Arturo. 1995. *Encountering Development: The Making and Unmaking of the Third World.* Princeton, NJ: Princeton University Press.

Evans, Mike. 2001. *Persistence of the Gift: Tongan Tradition in Transnational Context*. Waterloo, ON: Wilfred Laurier University Press.

Friedman, Thomas L. 1999. *The Lexus and the Olive Tree*. New York: Farrar, Straus and Giroux.

Gilpin, Robert. 1987. *Political Economy of International Relations*. New Haven, CT: Princeton University Press.

Halperin, Rhoda H. 1994. *Cultural Economies: Past and Present*. Austin: University of Texas Press.

Hermann, Gretchen M. 1997. "Gift or Commodity: What Changes Hands in the US Garage Sale?" *American Ethnologist* 24 (4): 910–930.

Lee, Richard B. 1979. *The !Kung San: Men, Women, and Work in a Foraging Society*. Cambridge and New York: Cambridge University Press

Meadows, Donella, Denise Meadows, Jergin Randers, and William H. Behrens III. 1972. *The Limits to Growth*. New York: Universe Books.

Pollin, Robert, Justine Burns, and James Heintz. 2002. "Global Apparel Production and Sweatshop Labor: Can Raising Retail Prices Finance Living Wages?" Political Economy Research Institute. Working Papers Series. Number 19.

Sachs, Jeffery. 1998. "Brookings Papers on Economic Activity." (no. 1). Washington, DC: Brookings Institution Press.

Sahlins, Marshall. 1972. *Stone Age Economics*. Chicago: Aldine-Atherton.

Smith, Adam. 2005. An Inquiry Into the Nature and Causes of the Wealth of Nations. Pennsylvania State University Electronic Classics Series. http://www2.hn.psu.edu/faculty/jmanis/adam-smith/wealth-nations.pdf

Stiglitz, Joseph. 2002. *Globalization and Its Discontents*. New York: W. W. Norton.

United States Senate. 2011. "Wall Street and the Financial Crisis: Anatomy of a Financial Collapse." http://hsgac.senate.gov/public/_files/Financial_Crisis/FinancialCrisisReport.pdf

WTO (World Trade Organization). 2011. http://www.wto.org

Further Reading

Frieden, Jeffrey. 2007. *Global Capitalism: Its Fall and Rise in the Twentieth Century*. New York: W. W. Norton.

Gilpin, Robert. 2001. *Global Political Economy: Understanding the International Economic Order*. Princeton, NJ: Princeton University Press.

Marx, Karl, and Friedrich Engels. 1967. *The Communist Manifesto*. New York: Harmondsworth: Penguin Books.

Tett, Gillian. 2009. *Fool's Gold: How Unrestrained Greed Corrupted a Dream, Shattered Global Markets and Unleashed a Catastrophe.* New York: Free Press.
Varoufakis, Yanis. 1998. *Foundations of Economics: A Beginner's Companion.* London: Routledge.

Journals

Economic Affairs
The Economist
The Financial Times
International Economics and Economic Policy
Wall Street Journal

Films

B.A.T.A.M. (2005). Liam Dalzell, Per Erik Eriksson, Johan Lindquist, directors.
Life & Debt (2001). Stephanie Black, director.
The Golf War (2000). Jen Schradie and Matt DeVries, directors.
King for a Day (2001). Alex Gabbay, director.
The Perfect Famine (2002). Steve Bradshaw and Chris Walker, directors.

Websites

Economic Policy Institute. http://www.epinet.org/
Economic Scenarios. http://www.economicscenarios.com/
History of Economic Thought. http://cepa.newschool.edu/het/
Marxist's Internet Archives. http://www.marxists.org/
Political Economy Research Institute. http://www.peri.umass.edu/
The world's first and only stand up economist. http://www.standupeconomist.com/

5

Power, Conflict, and Policy

The Role of Political Science in International Studies

What do political scientists study? The answer ranges from subjects as disparate as international legal treaties to the backroom maneuverings of legislative aides on Capitol Hill, from textual analyses of Plato's *Republic* to statistical scrutiny of voter turnout in Argentina. The single thread that links all political scientists' inquiry is politics. No matter the country or the subject matter we research, our questions are political in nature.

How does one define *politics*? A typical dictionary definition points to issues of government and governance. And although governmental topics are certainly a dominant theme in political science, they nonetheless remain only a subset of what is considered political. Everything that a government does may be political, but all political actions do not involve government actors. The types of political behavior that occur in a government (e.g., negotiations, power plays, financial allocations, alliance building) also occur in business offices, community organizations, and even families. A fuller definition, therefore, addresses not a particular type of institution (e.g., government) but instead a set of behaviors or conditions. A fitting definition, then, is that **politics** concerns human interactions that involve both *power* and *conflict*. Power is an essential element of politics because political issues are conflicts about who wins and who loses. An issue over which no one disagrees is not political, but rather consensual. The power-and-conflict definition encompasses all governmental decisions and actions and also decisions and actions that occur outside of the government purview but that are nonetheless intensely political. Therefore political science makes a fundamental contribution to international studies.

Where does international studies lie in relation to political science? Many international studies programs in the United States are housed in departments of political science. The terms *international studies* and *international relations* are so similar that most people consider them synonymous, but they are quite distinct in important ways. International studies refers to an interdisciplinary approach to exploring the world. As such, international studies scholars rely on many fields, including political science, to inform their discourse and conclusions. In contrast, international relations is a specific subfield of political science, rather than an interdisciplinary one.

MAJOR FIELDS

As it is practiced in the United States, the political science discipline is divided into a number of major fields. One's field determines research areas, courses taught, professional association membership, and peer group. Two subfields of political science pertain most to international studies: **comparative politics** and **international relations**. Both study political phenomena largely outside of US borders. The remaining key subfields are **American politics, political theory**, and **public administration**. The subject matter of each of these fields frequently touches on topics in international studies, but these subfields do not seek to examine the global arena per se.

Comparative Politics

Comparative politics is the domain of scholars who study domestic politics mostly outside of the United States. The term *comparative* refers to the fact that scholars in this field often analyze their subjects by using the comparative method. They glean findings from research that compares, for example, judicial behavior in two different countries, or in the same country but across different time periods. They use carefully chosen case studies to generate reliable conclusions about political behavior in settings as diverse as a Russian parliament and a Peruvian bureaucracy.

Comparative politics researchers tend to be regional specialists. They frequently self-define as Latin Americanists, Africanists, or Eastern Europeanists, for example. Thus, while particular scholars likely focus their research on one or a few countries, they would teach a course in politics of the region. Seek out a course in European or Asian politics and you are

FIGURE 5.1 The political spectrum: communism on the far Left and fascism on the far Right.

likely to have a comparative politics specialist as your instructor. Whereas most comparativists are regional specialists, others concentrate on thematic areas. Democratization, gender politics, post-Communist transitions, and civil war are among the specialties that a comparativist scholar might assume.

Comparativists are also the specialists in government systems and policy behaviors that stem from their differences. Understanding the modern world's various political systems is important for international studies. Political systems range from **communism** on the far Left to **fascism** on the far Right (see Figure 5.1). Some of these political systems are in fact political economies, defined not necessarily by a political structure but by the role of government in the economy.

The father of communist thought, Karl Marx, called for the violent overthrow of the capitalist system, a dictatorship of the proletariat (working classes), and the eventual formation of a classless society with the motto, "from each according to his ability, to each according to his needs." Marx foresaw communist revolutions coming in industrialized societies with a large working class, but communism has never succeeded there. Vladimir Lenin and the small Bolshevik Party created the first communist government in the largely underdeveloped, rural Russia, and all subsequent communist systems have taken hold in rural societies. Communism, as it was practiced in the Soviet Union, is in theory the most totalitarian political system, in that the government monopolizes all aspects of society: the armed forces, the press, cultural activities, and the economy, in addition to the government itself. Communist governments keep their citizens under control with a ubiquitous secret police.

After the fall of the Soviet satellites in 1989 and the collapse of the Soviet Union in 1991, only China, Cuba, North Korea, and Vietnam still call themselves communist, although all but North Korea have loosened state control of their economies and have allowed some independent cultural institutions. Communist regimes committed horrible atrocities in the twentieth century, but communism still has adherents who argue that

Lenin, Stalin, Mao, and others warped Marx's utopian idea. They decry the inequities of capitalism today. In Marx's theory **socialism** was a stage on the road to full communism, but today the term is used to identify less-dogmatic Marxists and states that combine a one-party regime with vestiges of capitalism. Even the Italian Communist Party, which operates within the Italian liberal democratic system, has no illusions about effecting a Marxist revolution, at least in the short term.

In the late nineteenth century the communist movement split between radicals who believed in the violent overthrow of the capitalist system and moderates who believed that they could achieve evolutionary change in the system through the ballot box. The division in the working class between communists and social democrats enabled the fascists in Italy and Nazis in Germany to come to power in the interwar period. After World War II social democrats disavowed destruction of the capitalist system and democracy in favor of a modified free market that protected workers' rights, provided a broad social welfare net, and permitted state control of key industries. Most European countries have some form of **social democracy**. The United States government plays a more limited role in the economy.

To the right of the political spectrum are **constitutional monarchies**, in which the monarch serves as the head of state and a parliament runs the affairs of government. In most constitutional monarchies today, such as Great Britain, Norway, and Japan, the monarch plays little or no political role, but is rather a symbol of national unity. In some Middle Eastern and Asian countries, however, the powers of the **monarchy** are not circumscribed by constitutional law but are in fact royal dictatorships.

Monarchies' legitimacy rests on blood lines and tradition. They usually claim to represent an imagined, unified religious and/or ethnic community. Domestic support usually comes from the privileged classes or ethnic groups, the armed forces, and religious leaders. **Authoritarian** regimes such as Syria and Iran have similar bases of support, but its leaders do not come from royal families. Authoritarian military dictatorships typified Latin American and African countries in the last quarter of the twentieth century.

In the **Arab Spring** of 2011, a grassroots, anti-authoritarian movement rose up against Egyptian president Hosni Mubarak, who had ruled Egypt for nearly thirty years. Although the protests and anti-Mubarak sentiment were widespread in the Egyptian populace, they were loosely organized and not rooted in any political movement that could readily assume control of the government. Once Mubarak resigned under enormous public and international pressure, the military stepped in to run the government and oversee a transition to civilian and democratic rule. At the time, Egyptians supported the military as the most qualified and able Egyptian institution to assume governing duties. A government dominated by the Islamist Muslim Brotherhood was elected in 2012, and mass protests against the Brotherhood's illiberal rule prompted the military to depose President Mohammed Morsi in the summer of 2013, leaving the future of Egyptian democracy in doubt, and other liberal democracies in a quandary about how to conduct relations with an illegitimate military regime.

Turkey is another important Muslim country that has a long tradition of military intervention into political affairs. A large segment of Turkish society has viewed the military as insurance against an Islamist government that might try to reverse nearly a century of secular civil society. The military has conducted three coups d'état in the second half of the twentieth century, coups that were highly antidemocratic but not particularly unpopular. In each case, the military ceded authority back to civilian institutions, albeit after the "offending" government officers were removed from public life. In 2013 Prime Minister Recep Tayyip Erdogan, leader of the Islamist Justice and Development Party, faced large public demonstrations against his increasing authoritarianism, prompting new speculation about the military's intentions. Turkey's desire to join the European Union is likely to put a brake on military intervention.

Fascism is on the far right of the political continuum. Fascism is a dictatorship of one party and a single, charismatic leader. Populist authoritarian leaders often maintain the trappings of democracy, but fascist leaders do away with it. Fascist parties promote extreme nationalism, and in the Nazi case, a racist ideology. After the Benito Mussolini's fascist debacle in Italy (1922–1943) and the military aggression and genocide committed by Adolf Hitler's Nazi regime in Germany (1933–1945), no dictators today call themselves fascist, although they might have similar ideas and policies.

As the Cold War between the United States and the Soviet Union emerged after World War II, Western political scientists and politicians, hoping to spread fear of communist expansionism, used the term **totalitarian** to describe both the far Left (communism) and the far Right (fascism). After the terrible atrocities of the Nazis were revealed to the world, this strategy of equating the two systems as inherently inhumane and aggressive

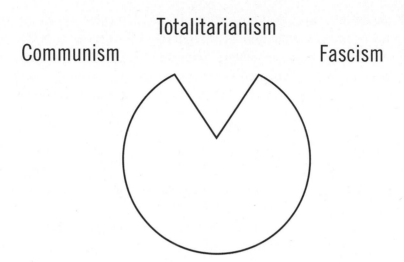

FIGURE 5.2 Communism—totalitarianism—fascism.

was an effective propaganda strategy. These anti-communists argued that communist and fascist regimes shared much in common: a single ideology, a secret police to spread terror, total control over the military, suppression of the press, and control of the economy. This theory of totalitarianism blurred the great differences in two ideologies: the Nazi regime theoretically acted in the interests of the German nation only, whereas communism preached the liberation of the worker all over the world. Brutal and immoral though Hitler's regime was, government control over the cultural scene and the economy was not total. Although some businesses linked to the German war machine were forced to produce what the state wanted, most of the economy was still privately owned. And churches and private schools, for example, were among the many cultural institutions that were allowed to function under the Nazi regime. In contrast, Stalinist communism called for total state control over the economic and the cultural spheres in the Soviet Union.

Democracies sit in the middle of the political spectrum. **Democracy** is a governing structure rather a system to promote a right or left agenda. An open society enjoys freedom of expression and a system for choosing leaders in a multiparty polity. A **liberal democracy** is defined as one in which there is a balance of power between the legislative, executive, and judicial branches of government, smooth succession processes, and a respect for civil rights, such as those found in the US Bill of Rights. Most European and North American governments are liberal democracies, as are most of the Pacific Rim countries, among others. Latin American countries are now liberal democracies for the most part, while some African and Asian countries have struggled to develop liberal political systems.

Although liberal democratic countries have parties on the left and the right, none of them advocate radical change of the democratic system itself. On the political spectrum one could term them center left and center right. Put simply, **the right** believes in limited government whereas **the left** believes in expanded government. In policy terms, this means that the right wants less government involvement in education, healthcare, consumer protection, welfare, promotion of science and industry, regulation of business practices, and the environment. The right also is less inclined to tax citizens to pay for these types of programs. In contrast, the left believes that government has an important role in the public welfare, which includes greater government intervention in the areas mentioned above. The left promotes taxation as a way of spreading the wealth and assuring national prosperity and health. In US *politics*, the term *conservative* is often used to describe the right and *liberal* to describe the left, although in classical *economic* terms a liberal believes in less government involvement in the free market.

Democracies share the idea that political leaders are elected by the people, although, once chosen, leaders can act in undemocratic ways by rigging elections, suppressing dissent, and changing constitutional law. There are numerous single-party, authoritarian systems that hold regular elections, such as China, Cuba, and Vietnam. Some authoritarian leaders are **populists**, such as the late Hugo Chavez in Venezuela, who legitimize their rule by wooing the masses with government largesse. Some observers worry that in recent years Russia, with ostensibly democratically elected leaders, has backtracked toward authoritarianism.

There are two main types of democratic systems, although some are combinations of both. The United States and most Latin American countries have presidential systems with a separation of powers between the executive and legislative branches. The president is usually elected by popular vote and is not only the chief executive but the head of state. In a parliamentary system the executive, or prime minister, is elected by the majority vote of a popularly elected parliament, such as the House of Commons in Great Britain. Most European countries and Japan, for example, have parliamentary systems. France is among those countries with a hybrid government in which the president shares powers with the prime minister and a Chamber of Deputies.

Political gridlock can occur in both systems if the president represents a different party than the majorities in the legislative houses, or if no party in parliament has a majority and parties cannot agree on a **coalition** government and a prime minister. Maintaining a coalition across party lines requires compromise. Furthermore, parliaments can demand a new election by passing a vote of no confidence in the executive's leadership. Both systems frequently require the type of compromise a robust democracy anticipates and requires.

The type of political system a country adopts has an impact not only on its domestic constituency but also on its neighbors and the rest of the world. According to democratic peace theory, liberal democracies do not war against each other. True liberal democracies have only existed in the last century or so, and not one has initiated a war against another. Although liberal democracies such as Great Britain and the United States have gone to war with undemocratic states, war is most likely between two undemocratic states. If democratic peace theory holds true, it follows that a world full of democracies would be more peaceful than its alternative. Hence, the existence of democracy would be a boon not only for a domestic population enjoying the benefits of choosing its leaders, but also for the greater global environment as well.

International Politics

Also known as *international relations* (the terms are interchangeable), **international politics** is the domain of scholarship that examines political behavior *outside of or across domestic political borders*. Its subfields include peace and conflict, international security, foreign-policy analysis, international political economy, global organization, and international law, among others. The common theme among all these areas is that they involve international exchange and do not operate at the domestic level alone. Domestic politics is invariably one of the strongest inputs into foreign-policy behavior, however, but because foreign policy involves a country's interaction with actors beyond its own borders, foreign-policy analysis remains within the field of international politics.

Students of international studies must understand the fundamental ways in which political scientists approach the study of international politics, that is, how they explain the world's political events. This section introduces merely two of the most important theories of international politics: **realism** and **idealism**. First, a brief discussion of the meaning and uses of theory merits attention.

A theory of international politics performs two crucial yet distinct functions. First, a theory *provides the concepts* necessary to understand the phenomena in question. That is, a theory gives us the tools we need to examine, explain, and critically evaluate global events. Second, a theory *explains* global political outcomes. As social scientists, scholars of international politics seek out variables—such as events, behaviors, trends—that can account for outcomes—such as war, peace, levels of defense spending, and foreign-policy actions. In social science language, we call "the explainers" *independent variables* and "the explained" *dependent variables*. For example, a theory might posit that income inequity (independent variable) explains the outbreak of civil war (dependent variable). In the recent civil war in Syria, the political power of an Alawite religious minority and a poorly performing economy could be the independent variables. Another way to think of independent and dependent variables is as causes and effects. Some theorists might argue that the huge US federal debt in the 2010s will constrain the country from intervention into foreign conflicts. A theory of international politics, then, creates a framework of independent variables to explain a series of outcomes, or dependent variables, that we call world politics.

Some theories take on a third function: prescription, or policy advocacy. Whereas all political scientists agree that a theory must perform the analytical role described above (concepts and explanation), they disagree on the role of prescription. A prescriptive theory goes beyond explanation and offers solutions to world problems. Some political scientists believe that engaging in policy prescription clouds researchers' judgment in their fundamental task of explaining global events. Others argue that in a world of violence, injustice, and poverty, analysis without advocacy makes no sense. Why, they argue, would scholars spend years researching the causes of war, only to remove themselves from the debate over how to implement foreign policy?

A final important feature of theory is **parsimony**. Parsimony refers to theoretical brevity and elegance. In other words, a parsimonious theory explains a large dependent variable (war and peace) with few independent variables. Clearly, the political world is hugely complex, engaging nations, individuals, non-governmental organizations, ethnic groups, supranational entities, and many other actors every day. Any theory that could account for all these actors' behaviors in every setting would be unwieldy. A parsimonious theory therefore reduces global complexity to its most important elements. The goal is to account for large variation in the dependent variable with as few independent variables as possible. In creating a parsimonious theory, then, political scientists necessarily depict global complexity in simplified terms. But if they can account for that complexity, or a large portion of it, they have performed their theoretical task.

Idealism/Liberalism

The body of theory known typically today as **liberalism** went by the term *idealism* for most of the twentieth century. Idealist theory is rooted in the more general liberal tradition, which holds that humans are moral beings, that they have free agency, and that public institutions moderate their behavior. The crucial tenets of liberalism in international politics (adapted from Kegley and Wittkopf 2004, 70–71) include:

- Humans have a capacity for good.
- Selfish and violent behaviors come not from human nature but from institutions that promote such behavior.
- The primary public institution leading to war is the state, because it promotes nationalism and selfishness over global welfare.
- Multilateral action and institutions help to prevent war.

Idealists embraced the idea that the pursuit of global peace and the appeal to humanity's better nature could generate a less violent world. After World War I demonstrated the horror that humans could wreak on each other, idealists sought to create institutions that would mitigate violence and greed. The so-called war to end all wars was so heinous that idealists believed it could catalyze global changes to ensure that such carnage would not happen again. The fundamental idealist goal in this period was international organization, the development of a global governance structure that could negotiate grievances through hearings and diplomacy rather than through force. Idealists advocate **collective security** over national defenses. Under collective security, states organize and agree to rules of international engagement. Deterrence comes in the form of the collective will and force of the group, which agrees to take action against transgressions against any member of the group—in other words, an attack on one is an attack on all.

This optimistic worldview motivated idealists such as President Woodrow Wilson to create the League of Nations between World War I and World War II. President Wilson maintained that war was largely a product of nondemocratic countries and that US participation in World War I was necessary to "make the world safe for democracy." As such, Wilson reflected the same faith in democratic peace as philosopher Immanuel Kant. Additionally, President Wilson argued that war could be prevented with the creation of international organizations to settle disputes between countries and further promote the values of peace and democracy. Few idealists believed that the elimination of the state as the principal unit of international politics was ever possible. But Wilson and other thinkers of his day were visionary in imagining an alternative to the every-state-for-itself system that dominated in the eighteenth and nineteenth centuries.

Although idealism suffered a serious blow with the collapse of the League of Nations and the outbreak of World War II, liberalism as a theoretical approach remains strong. Liberalism in international politics (not to be confused with liberalism in US politics) retains its focus on individual rights, the ethical behavior of political actors, and the ability of states and other global actors to create just and peaceful institutions such as the United Nations. Witness the growth in regional and global trade organizations. Liberals hold that organizations such as the **North American Free Trade Agreement** (NAFTA) and the **World Trade Organization** not only bind countries into peaceful trading relationships but also promote political cooperation and peaceful relations. Once countries' economic prosperity is reliant on one another, it is less likely they will go to war.

This theory's best example is the **European Union** (EU). Today it is not only an enormous free-trade area but also a full political entity for which war among its constituent members is unthinkable. It is wise to recall that the EU behemoth began in 1951 as a modest coal and steel community among a few European states, including France and Germany, which had battled each other in two vicious world wars. Proponents of liberal theory point to the type of functional cooperation that the European Union represents as the basis for peaceful coexistence, if not full political cooperation. At the end of World War II, few could have imagined that France and Germany would today have set aside their hostilities in favor of cooperating in a united Europe.

The EU example points to another liberal/idealist tradition within international politics, **complex interdependence**. The coiners of this phrase, Robert O. Keohane and Joseph S. Nye (1977), argue that peoples, institutions, corporations, states, and other entities are fundamentally and globally connected in ways that dampen the attraction of interstate warfare. In contrast to realism, which views states as inherent competitors, complex interdependence conceives of a world in which multiple types of actors engage in much more cooperative behavior than in conflict. They develop institutions, rules, and practices aimed at enhancing that cooperation because they all benefit from it. If this theory is valid, there is no reason to heed the warning of some realists of a coming conflict between the United States and China, because the two powers are connected in so many economic, political, and cultural ways. Liberals are less threatened by the rise of China.

Serious challenges to the European Union's success as an economic institution and its members' adherence to the union emerged in the 2010s. Greece's de facto default on its debt, combined with severe debt- and currency-related crises in Ireland, Spain, Italy, and Portugal, call into question whether the euro currency, and even the European Union itself, can be sustained. Healthy economies with well-functioning democracies, namely Germany, are understandably resentful of having to financially rescue their underperforming neighbors. How the European Union will weather the global financial crisis, and how it will manage its defaulting members, remain to be seen. Yet liberal theorists would point to the fact that EU members continue to address these problems in diplomatic fashion. No talk of violent conflict, or even intra-European alliances, has emerged. In other words, liberal theorists would argue, the European Union's existence ensures that its own serious challenges are managed in a peaceful way.

Liberals point to advances in democracy, respect for human rights, international law, and increasing levels of supranational organization as evidence that international politics can work to advance humanitarian ideals. Furthermore, liberalism is a prescriptive theory. Liberal theorists

advocate for institution building, transnational cooperation, demilitariza-
tion, and multilateralism as means to overcome global conflict.

Realism

Realism as an international theory is quite distinct from *realism* in everyday English parlance. People who say they are "realists" usually mean that
they are cynical, or at least pragmatic, about their expectations of human
behavior. Do not confuse this definition of realism with its use as a theory
of international politics. Although the two uses share some very general
meanings, realism as a theory connotes very specific concepts, assumptions, and expected global political outcomes.

Realism is also referred to as **realpolitik.** The foundations of a realist
theory of international politics date to Thucydides's fifth-century BCE account of the Peloponnesian War, in which the well-armed Athenian army
explained to the neutral and unarmed peoples of Melos: "The strong do
what they can and the weak suffer what they must" (1982, 351). In the
sixteenth-century city-state political world in Italy, Niccolo Machiavelli
famously advised his patron, the prince, that "whoever becomes the ruler
of a free city and does not destroy it, can expect to be destroyed by it"
(cited in Porter 1989, 169). About a century later, Thomas Hobbes famously wrote that in the absence of a dictator to maintain civil society,
humans would resort to killing each other and "the life of man" would
be "solitary, poor, nasty, brutish, and short" (cited in Porter 1989, 254).
These and other authors laid the literary foundations for modern political
realism, which is in its simplest form a theory of *power politics.*

In the late nineteenth century Prussian Chancellor Otto von Bismarck,
in reference to the possible unification of the German states, came up with
probably the most famous declaration of *realpolitik:* "The great questions of
the day will not be settled by means of speeches and majority decisions but
by iron and blood." In the twentieth century, World War II and especially
the Holocaust, as well as the collapse of the League of Nations, effectively
undermined idealist theory. Diplomats, political scientists, historians, and
ordinary citizens viewed World War II as evidence that a global organization such as the League of Nations and the appeal to humans' sense of
decency were insufficient to prevent war and atrocities.

Hans Morgenthau, a refugee from Hitler's Germany, codified realism
into a theory of world politics for the modern age. Morgenthau's *classical*

realism combines with more recent iterations of the theory to generate a series of assumptions and propositions about international politics (adapted
from Kegley and Wittkopf 2004, 74–75):

- Human nature is self-interested and power hungry.
- The primary entity in world politics is the **state**. States act as an
  extension of humans and therefore are also self-interested and
  power hungry.
- States behave as rational actors. They pursue their interests
  within the limits of their own resources and abilities.
- States' goals are national interests defined as power.
- Power is expressed in political, economic, and military might.
  Of these, military power is the most important in world politics.
  Economic development is a means to create military might.
- States operate in a world of **anarchy**, defined as *the absence of a
  global government.*
- In an anarchical world system, states operate in a self-help sys-
  tem, looking out for their own interests alone.
- States pursue alliances to the extent that they provide defense
  and power enhancement.

Realists do not assume that the realist worldview is one of constant
war, assassination, and discord, however. Not unlike the market's invisible
hand in liberal economic theory, anarchy generates balances of power that
ensure stability. Because military and economic power are so unevenly
distributed, most states will seek to ally with major powers, such as the
United States today or France and the United Kingdom a century ago.
These major powers are known as **hegemons**. Hegemons can be organized
in multipolar, bipolar, or unipolar systems. Although hegemony is contested and won through war, realists argue that hegemonic systems bring
about decades of coexistence without outright war between the major
powers. Perhaps their best example is the twentieth century's Cold War.
This supposedly bipolar system dominated by the United States and the
Soviet Union saw enormous spending on armaments, including nuclear
weapons; wars in places such as Korea, Vietnam, and Afghanistan; proxy
wars and interventions throughout the Third World; and recurrent political tension. Although an estimated twenty-five million died in conflicts

during the Cold War, realists still contend that this global system based on power politics and military might was generally peaceful.

Theoretical Diversity

Idealism/liberalism and realism are but the two most prominent theoretical traditions in international politics. They also predominate because their fundamental assumptions so strongly oppose each other. There is nonetheless much greater theoretical diversity in international politics than a cursory review of these two theories would suggest. Neoliberalism and neorealism are modern variants of the classical traditions.

Neorealists maintain that a result of the lack of a higher authority in the structure of the world systems is that countries have to go to war to settle their disputes. A neorealist notes that if human nature was the cause of war in 1914, then human nature was also the cause of peace in 1918. According to Kenneth Waltz, countries that struggle for power are driven instead by the anarchy of the international system. As states attempt to survive in the absence of a higher authority to adjudicate their disputes, they must rely solely on themselves and their own power. As a result of this anarchical system, war becomes inevitable. (Waltz 1959: 28, Waltz 1979: 87).

Neoliberalism developed in the 1970s and 1980s partly as a response to the events surrounding the 1973 oil crisis that revealed how actors (such as OPEC) other than states could have a profound effect on the course of international events. In other words, although states remained the primary actors on the world stage, they were no longer the only actors. Complex interdependence (Keohane and Nye 1977) described this transformation in the international system. Countries were tied together through trade and other economic interactions and exchanges, and these ties increased interdependence and thereby lessened the likelihood of conflict. Whereas realists of all stripes maintained that power (hard power) was primarily military in nature, neoliberals saw economics as another important form of power (soft power) equally capable of furthering a state's interests.

Consider the different views that neorealists and neoliberals hold with regard to the rise of China in the international system. A realist argues that the rise of China can only be viewed as a threat to US interests. When President Obama made a pivot toward Asia aimed at bolstering US defense ties with countries throughout the region and expanding the US naval presence, that pivot was a realist move. Secretary of Defense Leon Panetta reassured US allies, many of whom harbored concerns about China's rise, that "the United States is going to remain a presence in the Pacific for a long time." Neoliberals, on the other hand, are less threatened by China's rise. They point out that the close economic ties and interdependence of the two countries will make conflict less likely over time.

Other important theoretical perspectives in international relations are feminism, Marxism, globalization, and interdependence, as well as constructivism. *Constructivism* is a theory of knowledge or tool of analysis positing that reality is socially constructed based on an actor's identity, ideas, interests, and understanding of social norms. It is fair to say that all draw on the two classical traditions, liberalism and realism, in one form or another. They all must answer the primary question posed by these two theories: What drives international politics—unchangeable human nature or variable human decisions? One's answer to this question places a theorist in the realist camp or the liberal camp.

As opposed to domestic politics, the left-right distinction in foreign policy is somewhat less well defined. On economic policy, the right generally promotes free markets and opposes protectionist trade barriers. The left is more likely to favor tariffs, quotas, or specialized preferences in the global marketplace, arguing that these are necessary to protect its workers and nurture domestic industries. On global political issues, namely so-called national security policy, the right tends to act like *hawks*, whereas the left represents the *doves*. Hawks generally believe in strong militaries, heavy defense spending, and using lethal force and military intervention to address global problems. In contrast, doves prefer smaller armies and defense budgets, as well as diplomatic and noninterventionist responses to global challenges. These archetypes oversimplify the thinking of most policymakers but they represent general approaches to foreign policy. It is important to note that a right-winger on domestic policy could very well be a dove in the international arena, and vice versa. Indeed, although in the US political context the Democratic Party has the reputation of being leftist, Democratic presidents such as Bill Clinton and Barack Obama have engaged heavily in overseas military action.

With their keen attention to the dynamics of power, conflict, and ideology, political scientists contribute a necessary element to any understanding of global dynamics. That said, politics alone cannot explain today's global issues, such as war, trade, debt negotiations, and environmental agreements. In order to provide the most comprehensive and intelligent analysis of these problems, knowledge of the political landscape, along with a study of the relevant history, culture, economics, and geography, is essential.

References

Kegley, Charles W., Jr., and Eugene R. Wittkopf. 2004. *World Politics: Trend and Transformation*, 9th ed. Belmont, CA: Thomson/Wadsworth.

Keohane, Robert O., and Joseph S. Nye. 1977. *Power and Interdependence*. Boston: Little, Brown.

Porter, Jene M. 1989. *Classics in Political Philosophy*. Scarborough, ON: Prentice Hall Canada.

Thucydides. 1982. *The Peloponnesian War*. Translated by Richard Crawley and revised by T. E. Wick. New York: Modern Library.

Waltz, K. (1959) *Man, the State, and War: A Theoretical Analysis*. New York: Columbia University Press.

Waltz, K. (1979) *Theory of International Politics*. Boston: McGraw-Hill.

Further Reading

Rosenbloom, David H., and Robert S. Kravchuk. 2002. *Public Administration: Understanding Management, Politics, and Law in the Public Sector*. Boston: McGraw-Hill.

Roskin, Michael G., et al. 2005. *Political Science: An Introduction*, 9th ed. Upper Saddle River, NJ: Pearson Prentice Hall.

Snarr, Michael T., and Neil Snarr. 2002. *Introducing Global Issues*, 2nd edition. Boulder, CO: Lynne Rienner.

Films

Dr. Strangelove (1964).

The Candidate (1972).

Indochine (1992).

The Fog of War: Eleven Lessons from the Life of Robert S. McNamara (2003).

Rules of Engagement (2012). PBS Frontline.

Journals and Websites

American Political Science Association, www.apsanet.org
Foreign Policy, www.foreignpolicy.com
International Affairs, http://www.chathamhouse.org/publications/ia
International Studies Association, www.isanet.org
Perspectives on Politics: A Journal of Political Questions and Issues of Our Day.
University of Colorado at Denver's School of Education website on political theory and critical thinking, http://www.cudenver.edu/~mryder/itc_data /postmodern.html

PART TWO

INTERDISCIPLINARY APPROACHES TO REGIONAL AND INTERNATIONAL TOPICS

6

North America and International Studies

A Brief History of the United States in the World

This chapter focuses on the United States and Canada (Mexico is covered in the Latin America chapter). Obviously the United States plays a major role in international affairs, and a brief discussion of its position in the world provides illuminating comparisons between this familiar part of the world and foreign lands. The character of the people, power relationships, place, production, and the past—that is anthropology, politics, geography, economy, and history—define North America.

In his farewell address of 1796, US President George Washington warned the fledging nation against involvement in the political affairs of Europe:

> Our detached and distant situation invites and enables us to pursue a different course. . . . Why, by interweaving our destiny with that of any part of Europe, entangle our peace and prosperity in the toils of European ambition, rivalship, interest, humor or caprice? . . . It is our true policy to steer clear of permanent alliances with any portion of the foreign world.

At the end of the eighteenth century the United States was in no position to project its power anyway. After a costly war with Great Britain from 1812 to 1815, the United States concentrated on westward expansion, where it met little resistance from the indigenous peoples. Until the

FIGURE 6.1 Mt. Rushmore. The sculpture in South Dakota memorializes George Washington, Thomas Jefferson, Theodore Roosevelt, and Abraham Lincoln. PHOTO: S. Toops.

late nineteenth century the United States was preoccupied with North American matters, expanding to the Pacific by mid-century and then fighting a civil war from 1861 to 1865.

By the turn of the century the United States was the greatest industrial power and had the resources to play a greater role in world affairs. In 1911, the country was producing over 24 million tons of steel, outstripping Germany's 14 million tons and Britain's 6.5 million tons (Hause and Maltby 1999, 757).

The United States began to wield its newfound power abroad, fighting a war with Spain in 1898 and taking Puerto Rico and the Philippines. In 1907–1908, President Teddy Roosevelt sent the "Great White Fleet"— warships painted garishly white—around the world to show that the United States was now a power to be reckoned with. The United States built and operated the Panama Canal (1904–1914) to allow passage for a two-ocean navy and to facilitate US trade in the Western Hemisphere and Asia.

From its inception the United States has considered itself an exceptional country, a "city upon a hill," a free, democratic republic, a beacon of righteousness far removed from the Europe of perpetual war, monarchy, aristocracy, and mercantilism. President Woodrow Wilson furthered this notion when he said that the United States had entered World War I to make the world safe for democracy. The United States helped defeat the Central Powers in that war and the Axis powers in World War II, confirming in American minds that the United States was indeed an indispensible agent for freedom, peace, and prosperity. The United States emerged from the war as the world's greatest power, although the Soviet Union became a formidable military and ideological rival in the Cold War.

The United States sought to establish a liberal economic, democratic postwar order. Washington birthed free-market institutions such as the **World Bank** to reconstruct the war-torn world, the **International Monetary Fund** (IMF) to regulate currency exchanges and bail out bankrupt economies, and the **General Agreement on Tariffs and Trade** (GATT), a periodic round of talks among capitalist economies to gradually lower tariffs and encourage trade. GATT evolved into the **World Trade Organization** (WTO) in 1995.

The demise of the Soviet Union in 1991 seemed to confirm that there would be no more significant challenges to this liberal economic paradigm and the political power of the United States. The United States has the world's largest economy, although in aggregate the EU GDP surpasses the US GDP by about $2.6 trillion. China is the world's biggest trader, with exports totaling $1.9 trillion in 2011, and imports of $1.7 trillion. The United States is second with exports in 2011 valued at $1.5 trillion, and imports at $2.27 trillion (WTO 2013). The size of the US economy, as well as its dependence on trade, mandate that the United States will be engaged throughout the world to maintain the stability of this free-trade system.

US NATIONAL INTERESTS

Although the United States does not face any serious existential threats as it did in the Cold War, the increasingly globalized world has created new challenges. Washington feels responsible—as the reputed "indispensible" power—to meet them, whether head on or "leading from behind."

As the wealthiest country in the world, the United States also feels obligated to come to the aid of the needy in times of natural disasters and other humanitarian crises. The United States spends more on its military than the next fifteen countries combined, providing the means necessary to intervene in any part of the world on a moment's notice. The United States maintains military bases in more than 60 countries to protect its interests (Global Research).

Today the United States has significant security and economic interests in all of the regions below:

Asia

US President Barack Obama declared a "pivot" to Asia, in other words a redirection of US diplomatic and economic interests in the most populous region in the world. Japan remains Washington's main ally in the region. China's rapid economic growth has created new opportunities for US trade and investment although China's military spending is seen by some as a threat. China is a vital partner in US efforts to denuclearize the Korean peninsula. Washington also sees opportunities for cooperation with the rapidly growing India.

The Middle East

Turmoil in the Middle East has the potential to draw the United States into a major war. Despite Obama's desire to focus more attention on Asia, the wars in Iraq and Afghanistan started by his predecessor forced him to devote more resources to this region. US troops left Iraq in 2011, but the war and occupation cost nearly 4,500 Americans and tens of thousands of Iraqi dead. The withdrawal left Iraq in a precarious security situation. Communal violence between Sunnis and Shiites reached a new high in September 2013 with almost 1,000 deaths. About 60,000 American troops remained in Afghanistan in the fall of 2013, although most were scheduled to leave in 2014.

Obama has drawn two red lines in the Middle East that, if crossed, could ignite renewed US military action in the region. The president has said that Iran will not be allowed to build a nuclear weapon. In the fall of 2013, the new Iranian president, Hassan Rouhani, made new overtures to begin negotiations to regulate Iran's nuclear program, but it remains to be seen if Iran is sincere.

Obama also warned the Syrian regime of Bashar al-Assad not to use chemical weapons against rebel opposition fighters in the civil war that began there in 2011. When Assad did use them in 2013, Obama threatened air strikes, but Russia, Assad's partner, stepped in to broker a deal to put Assad's chemical arsenal under UN control.

In 2013, Obama's Secretary of State, John Kerry, launched a new diplomatic effort to forge a final peace deal between Israel and the Palestinians. Most pundits consider that prospect a long shot.

Africa

The United States has renewed interest in Africa, and not only for economic development or humanitarian concerns. Countries such as Somalia, Mali, and Nigeria have seen the rise of extremist Islamic terrorist groups that threaten not only the people in these countries, but neighboring countries, Europe, and the United States. In 2009, a Nigerian national linked to al Qaeda tried to blow up a US airliner, and in 2013, the Somali terrorist group al-Shabab attacked a shopping mall in Nairobi, Kenya, killing at least 70 people.

Latin America

When President George W. Bush came into office in 2001, he promised renewed efforts to increase US ties to Latin America. After the terror attack on the United States on September 11, 2001, Latin America was moved to the back burner. Bush did try to push the Free Trade Agreement of the Americas (FTAA), but rejection of neoliberalism in the region brought few results. Obama has not pushed this agenda either.

Europe

With the notable exception of Russia, Europe continues to be America's most trusted and important political, military, and economic partner. Russian President Vladimir Putin challenged the notion that the United States is an "exceptional" country, and has supported the Assad regime in

Syria and wrenched Crimea from Ukraine in 2014, much to the outrage of the EU and the United States.

THE UNITED STATES IN THE WORLD ECONOMY: TOO BIG TO FAIL

The US economy is the largest in the world by any measure. It comprises nearly 25 percent of the global GDP (the total values of all goods and services produced in the world in a year). It is the world's largest manufacturer, manufacturing a fifth of global goods, and it is the second-largest trading nation in the world (after China). It possesses the world's largest and most influential financial market, with foreign investments more than double that of any other country. Nearly 60 percent of global currency reserves are invested in US dollars (as compared to 24 percent for the euro). The New York Stock Exchange leads the world in number of shares traded, and more than one-quarter of the world's 500 largest companies are headquartered in the United States, twice that of any other country (CIA *World Factbook* 2013).

America's wealth derives from abundant natural resources, a well-developed infrastructure, high productivity, and a broadly mixed economy. The United States has the world's largest coal reserves, and is the world's third-largest producer of oil and second-largest producer of natural gas. It also has significant holdings of copper, lead, molybdenum, phosphates, uranium, bauxite, gold, iron, mercury, nickel, potash, silver, tungsten, zinc, and timber. Heavy investment in infrastructure both by the government and the private sector, particularly after World War II, created sophisticated water, rail, and highway transportation systems; a highly effective power grid; and a water-distribution system that enable business growth and high quality of life. The United States is a world leader in petroleum, steel, motor vehicles, aerospace, telecommunications, chemicals, electronics, food processing, consumer goods, lumber, and mining, among other products. This highly diversified economy means that global downturns in any one major market have only minor effects on the US economy, as opposed to many countries that have only a handful of industries.

The American economy is a market-oriented system in which private businesses and individuals operate largely independent of the government. Corporations in the United States have greater flexibility to expand or close their businesses, dismiss workers, and develop new products than do business firms in most other nations, even strongly market-oriented economies like Germany and Japan. Overseas firms also face fewer barriers entering US markets than American firms usually do when entering foreign markets. Only three places in the world—Hong Kong, Singapore, and New Zealand—make it easier to do business (World Bank 2014).

With a few exceptions, such as the Post Office, the Veterans Health Administration, the Corporation for Public Broadcasting, and the Federal Deposit Insurance Company, federal and state governments own and operate few businesses, contracting with private corporations for needed goods and services. An example of this is the recent national healthcare reform. Instead of creating a government healthcare system to compete with private healthcare, as most nations do, the Affordable Care Act required citizens to acquire insurance from private insurers, while mandating certain basic requirements for all insurance plans.

The United States is not only the wealthiest but the most militarily powerful country in the world. The US Department of Defense maintains more than 900 bases and other military installations overseas, and is the world's largest employer, with more than 3 million employees. Combined spending on military agencies—the departments of Defense, Veterans Affairs, and Homeland Security—exceeds spending on all other government agencies combined (OMB 2013). Military spending, along with Medicare and Social Security costs, make up more than three-quarters of spending of the United States, with the result that the country, in spite of its great wealth, is rarely able to balance its budget and must year after year borrow money, mostly from foreign countries like China, Japan, and Brazil, to pay its bills.

As the United States excelled in technological innovation, becoming a world leader in computers, medical equipment, aerospace products, and military armaments, it developed a "two-tier labor market" between professional and skilled labor, and other workers (Saint-Paul 1996). Since the mid-1970s, practically all gains in household income went to those in the top 20 percent, while those without professional skills have failed to get comparable pay raises, health-insurance coverage, and other benefits. This has led to what many call "the erosion of the middle class" (Gunderson 2013, Reich 2010). Nearly 15 percent of Americans now live below the poverty level. By the twenty-first century the gulf between rich and poor in the United States exceeded that of many developing countries (*CIA World Factbook* 2013).

Rising debt and the weakening of the working and middle classes made the global recession of 2008 hit particularly hard. Foreclosures doubled during 2006–2008 as rising oil prices forced many families to purchase gasoline at the expense of falling behind in their mortgage payments. Soaring oil prices also caused a decline in the value of the dollar and increased the US trade deficit. Wars in Afghanistan and Iraq—totaling $900 billion in direct costs and more than a trillion in indirect costs such as veterans benefits, military pensions, homeland security, and international aid—further strained national resources, added to the budget deficit, and increased public debt (Crawford 2013). Because US revenues from taxes are lower, as a percentage of GDP, than those of most other countries, much of this war spending had to be borrowed. As a result of these pressures, in 2008 America fell into the longest and most severe economic downturn since the Great Depression of the 1930s.

The US government acted quickly to help reduce the duration and impact of the recession. In October 2008, the US Congress allocated $700 billion for the Troubled Asset Relief Program (TARP), through which the government invested in local development projects and bought interests in US banks and corporations deemed "**too big to fail**" (meaning that their failure would have greater fiscal consequences than the economy could absorb). In January 2009, the US Congress authorized an additional $787-billion fiscal stimulus to be used for investment and tax cuts to create jobs and to help the economy recover. And in July 2010, the president signed the Dodd-Frank Wall Street Reform and Consumer Protection Act, a law designed to ensure that many of the complex and predatory banking practices that led to the recession could not be repeated.

Following these measures, unemployment declined, spending by the government slowed, and the deficit shrank from 9 percent to 7.6 percent of GDP. Whether these signs of economic recovery were a result of the government's efforts remains hotly contested. And many long-term problems remain, including stagnation of wages for lower-income families, deteriorating infrastructure, rising medical and pension costs of an aging population, energy shortages, and huge deficits in both state and national budgets.

The slogan "too big to fail" was also sometimes applied to the United States as a whole to explain why foreign countries like Japan and China that held huge US currency reserves did not change their borrowing habits in the face of the US economic downturn. The argument was that these nations held so much US debt that they could not take any actions that might further devalue US currency for fear of the impacts it would have on their own fragile economies.

THE AMERICAN DREAM

Much of what is unique about American culture can be located in a North American ethos that promises everyone an opportunity to build a better life than the one they were born into through hard work. Although the term "**the American Dream**" was not coined until 1931 (Truslow 1931), the roots of this cultural system are expressed in the US constitution:

> We hold these truths to be self-evident: that all men are created equal, that they are endowed by their Creator with certain unalienable Rights, that among these are Life, Liberty and the pursuit of Happiness.

Articulated as a **meritocracy**, a system in which people succeed according to their own skills without regard for such social distinctions as caste, class, religion, race, ethnicity, sex, age, or kinship networks, this ethos is heavily coded into America's expressive culture, from films to games to novels to political speeches. Anthropologists who have studied contemporary North American culture have noted that the American dream entails an entire worldview that sees human life as comprising free-willed individuals whose lives are a product of the choices they make when confronted with opportunities and obstacles.

This individualistic, meritocratic view shapes America's actions in the world in three important ways. First, it shapes the division between political camps that control power in the United States. Second, it plays significantly into political, legal, and social debates about migration to the United States from elsewhere in the world, and management of the cultural differences they bring with them. Third, it shapes America's wider dealings with the world as it exerts power through economic aid and military force.

Many of the internal problems of US society—racism, immigration, gender imbalances, costs of education—are tied to cultural contradictions in the American dream. The quintessentially American board game *Monopoly* expresses the values of the American Dream: starting from a level playing field, through luck, strategy, and skill at seizing opportunities, players acquire wealth. In real life everyone does not start out with the same opportunities: some start out already owning Park Place and Boardwalk, while others have only a fistful of dollars; people get very different amounts of cash when they pass Go; and the same rules often do not apply equally to everyone.

US politics are importantly shaped by this contradiction between a worldview that emphasizes the importance of a meritocracy of individuals, on the one hand, and the inequities of everyday life for many people in the United States, on the other. American political culture has become polarized around two competing ideologies that differ largely on how the American dream is to be achieved. American political culture can be roughly divided into two strands, liberalism and civil republicanism (Sarat and Berkowitz 1998). *Liberalism* proposes that all individuals should be free to express themselves as they wish and go their own way, with civic order maintained by the state through laws (Fitzpatrick 1992). *Civil republicanism* is suspicious of the state, preferring to emphasize America as a nation, a body of people sharing a core set of common values that cross-cuts differences (Michelman 1988).

A key cultural issue that emphasizes these differences involves who is to be considered "American." Although America's origin myths emphasize its significance as a "land of immigrants," nativist discourses have also always existed. US citizenship is derived either from birth to citizens or birth within national boundaries, so that one can find US citizens who have lived their entire lives elsewhere in the world and non-citizens who have grown up in the United States and know nothing of the countries from which their parents emigrated. Who is truly American? The person who is born in the country, or the person who chooses to live there? These debates turn around a key cultural problem: does being "American" mean sharing a common cultural identity, or is it about citizenship and loyalty to the United States?

This problem is closely tied to issues of racial, linguistic, and cultural difference, in which a normative standard—hard-working, English-speaking (and traditionally white) persons who struggle to make a better life for themselves and their families—becomes a model against which other Americans are measured. These issues are often expressed in civil republican terms through powerful cultural metaphors such as "the melting pot" through which differences are assimilated into a common, normative national character. In the early twentieth century, many liberal

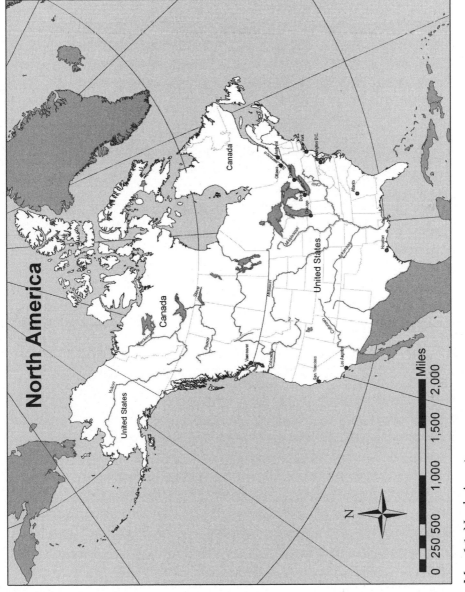

MAP 6.1 North America

religious, political, and intellectual leaders began to propose an alternative to assimilationist models called the *cultural pluralism model* (subsequently renamed *multiculturalism*), which proposed that differences within society are valuable and should be preserved. Cultural pluralists have offered alternative metaphors for America's heterogeneity such as the "mosaic" (Gibbon 1938), "kaleidoscope" (Fuchs 1990), or "salad" (Chua 2007) to capture alternative ways of understanding difference in the United States. Many of these ideas spread to the United States from Canada.

The United States' exertion of power in the world has also been shaped by its desire to spread the American Dream as part of a vision for global social progress through economic aid, diplomacy, and military might (Rosenberg 1982). The idea that every country could become like the United States through democratic and liberal economic reform has long shaped US development programs (Escobar 1995). Even when expediency and national interest create partnerships that might seem to be at odds with American values—close ties with monarchs and dictators, for example—the United States generally requires them to make at least a show of implementing social and political reforms in line with American values.

Belief in the power of most people to achieve the American dream has significantly wavered in the United States in recent years, especially following the 2008 recession, but the values implied in it—the importance of the individual, the notion that all people should have equal opportunities, and the idea that merit should be rewarded with material prosperity—remain important in contemporary American life, and seem likely to do so well into the future.

CANADA AND THE WORLD

In 1961, US President John F. Kennedy told the Canadian parliament: "Geography has made us neighbors. History has made us friends. Economics has made us partners. And necessity has made us allies."

Canada is often overshadowed by its bigger neighbor to the south, but it is among the most developed countries in the world, and its vast size puts it in an advantageous position for continued growth in the twenty-first century and a greater role in global affairs. Canada has the world's second-largest land mass (behind Russia), although because of its proximity to the Arctic Circle, under 5 percent of the land is arable. Ninety percent of the population of 34.5 million lives within 100 miles of the US border. Access to fresh water will be a serious issue in the twenty-first century as many arid regions in the world drain off their rivers, lakes, and aquifers. Canada has the most fresh water in the world (CIA *World Factbook* 2013).

If one does not mind the long, cold winters, Canada is a good place to live. Canada ranks nineteenth in the world in per capita GDP. Unlike its neighbor to the south, Canada has a publicly funded healthcare system. Although there is also debate in Canada about the inefficiencies and quality of health delivery, Canadians are as a whole healthier than Americans. Life expectancy is 81.6 years, ranking thirteenth in the world, and the infant-mortality rate is among the lowest (CIA *World Factbook* 2013).

Canada has the eleventh-largest economy in the world and is a partner in the G8. Like most of the developed world, Canada's economy stagnated after the financial crisis of 2008. Canadian banks had followed relatively conservative financial policies, however, and the economy rebounded to average between 2 and 2.5 percent growth rates from 2010 to 2012. Canada has the third-largest proven oil reserves in the world; over three-fourths of Canadian exports go to the United States, much of it in gas and oil shipments. Canada is on pace to balance its federal budget by 2015, in part because its military spending is relatively low, ranking one hundred twentieth in the world (CIA *World Factbook* 2013).

As democracies go, Canada's political parties have reached a modicum of consensus about federal fiscal policy, environmental regulation, healthcare, military spending, and social policies—issues that have caused a wide divide between the Republican and Democratic Parties in the United States. In many ways Canada has more in common with European social democracies than with the United States. Canada has no death penalty but does have stricter gun laws, higher student test scores, a healthier population, and a higher per capita GDP than the United States.

Canada's vast size, abundant resources, and developed economy ensure that the country will play a significant role in international affairs in the twenty-first century.

GEOGRAPHY, TRADE, AND THE GLOBALIZATION OF NORTH AMERICA

Globalization is readily apparent in the daily lives of North Americans. On the streets of Toronto, Montreal, New York, Los Angeles, or a small town in Ohio or Ontario, one can taste, see, and hear the global connections of market and production, culture, and politics. North Americans consume food from Latin America (orange juice made of oranges from Brazil), Africa (chocolate made of cacao from Ghana), Asia (apple juice made of apples from China), and Europe (pasta made of wheat from Italy). North American versions of tacos and burritos, pizza, and spaghetti are found in most towns. Larger cities have their forms of General Tso's chicken and aloo gobi. Musical influences such as salsa from Latin America and African-inspired jazz beats fill the airwaves and Internet. Movies from all over the world challenge the cultural power of Hollywood.

The United States and Canada have some 350 million residents. Yet because of buying power and trade, North America has a role in global economics far beyond the size of its population. Consumer goods, food, and popular culture from North America are diffusing across the world. The affluence of the United States and Canada derives from their **post-industrial economy**. Technology and culture combine to produce high levels of resource consumption in the United States and Canada. Globalization is a two-way street; perhaps a good metaphor is a fiber-optic cable net as flows occur in many directions simultaneously.

North American agricultural products, manufactures, and technologies link the region to the world. Canada exports wheat from Saskatchewan to China. Nissan exports the Altima from Tennessee to the Middle East (Olsen 2012). Apple iPhones, while designed in California, are manufactured in China. Global exports include licenses for software, patents, movies, and TV shows. Travel to the United States and Canada counts as US and Canadian exports when the travelers from other countries spend money to buy goods and services.

North America is connected by NAFTA, a trade bloc from the Yukon to the Yucatan, but also to the rest of the world. In 2010, the main US export partners included (in rank order) Canada, Mexico, China, Japan, the United Kingdom, and Germany (US Census Bureau 2013a). US exports included car parts to Canada, petroleum products to Mexico, soybeans to China, aircraft to Japan, gold to the United Kingdom, and vehicles to Germany. Canada's top export destinations are the United States, China, the United Kingdom, Japan, and Germany. Canada exports oil to the United States, ore to China, gems and precious metals to the United Kingdom, oil to Japan, and vegetable oil seeds to Mexico. US imports include electronics from China, oil from Canada, electronics from Mexico, vehicles from Japan, machinery from the United Kingdom, and vehicles from Germany.

FIGURE 6.2 Los Angeles, viewed from Griffith Park. On the horizon is the central city. PHOTO: S. Toops.

TRANSFORMING THE ENVIRONMENT

Five hundred years ago most of the eastern areas of the United States and Canada were forested, but today much of it is cropland. European settlers transformed the environment by cutting down forests and planting new crops. They plowed under native grasses in the Midwest and Great Plains, making way for large fields of corn, soybeans, or wheat today, none of which are native to the region or the prairie. Urbanization meant the concentration of people in metropolises such as New York, Los Angeles, and Toronto. In suburbs people created a new landscape of shopping malls and green lawns, even in areas like southern California and Arizona where there was hardly enough water or land to do so.

Water

India and China surpass the United States' total consumption of water, but the US per capita consumption is far greater. The water footprint of the average consumer in the United States is 2,842 cubic meters per year, whereas the average consumer in China has a water footprint of 1,071

Figure 6.3 Niagara Falls. Water from Lake Erie passes to Lake Ontario. Niagara Falls has highest flow rate of any waterfall on earth. PHOTO: S. Toops.

cubic meters per year. The global average is 1,385 cubic meters per capita (Hoekstra and Mekonnen 2012).

The Colorado River, which supports water users in Los Angeles, barely reaches the Gulf of California in Mexico. All of the states in the river basin (Colorado, Utah, Wyoming, New Mexico, Arizona, Nevada, and California) use the water for irrigation, residential, and industrial purposes. Population growth as well as per capita consumption in the southwestern United States depletes the river's flow. The United States has a desalinization plant to clean the Colorado River before it reaches Mexico (Berg and Hager 2009, Rogers 2008).

The Colorado River basin is in a dry climate, but water issues also affect humid areas. Water pollution in the Great Lakes is a serious issue for Canada and the United States. Together the five Great Lakes (Superior, Michigan, Huron, Erie, and Ontario) account for one-fifth of the world's fresh surface water. Almost 40 million people live around the Great Lakes and use the water. By the 1960s many pollutants, including sewage, fertilizer runoff, and industrial wastes, contaminated the Great Lakes. In the

1970s Canada and the United States began working together to clean up the Great Lakes. The lakes are much cleaner today, but constant development of the shoreline around the cities has resulted in a continued loss of habitat (Berg and Hager 2009).

Climate Change

Most scientists agree that human activity is having a dramatic impact on the climate. Burning carbon-based fuels such as coal and oil puts more carbon dioxide into the atmosphere. The carbon dioxide acts as a blanket, keeping in the heat from the solar radiation reflected off the earth's surface, just like the translucent roof of a greenhouse traps the sun's heat inside the building.

Overall global temperatures are rising. What are some possible impacts in North America? Some models forecast that the Great Lakes area will become wetter by 2100, and southwestern United States will become drier, further straining the Colorado River basin. Climate change may portend longer growing seasons along the US-Canadian border. Greater heat may also mean a drier climate in the interior. Northern Canada and Alaska will see ice melting and transformation of the tundra, with unknown ecological impacts (Fouberg et al. 2012).

The melting of the Antarctic and Greenland ice sheets and glaciers will result in a rise in the sea level, jeopardizing the densely populated North American coastline (Rowntree et al. 2014). Low-lying areas in Florida, such as Miami and Tampa, would be inundated. By 2070, over $3.5 trillion of Miami's assets would be at risk. The sea rise also means salt water would enter and affect Florida's water system. Similarly, over $2.1 trillion of New York City's assets would be jeopardized. New York could become the Venice of the West (Folger 2013).

NORTH AMERICA'S CHANGING POPULATION

In general, North America has a very mobile and affluent population, much of which lives in huge urban areas. The megalopolis from Boston to New York and Washington DC forms an urban corridor known as BosNyWash. Chicago to Pittsburgh, and San Francisco to Los Angeles are also great metropolitan areas. The Canadian "Main Street" runs from

FIGURE 6.4 Toronto, Canada. Toronto is the most populous city in Canada. The CN Tower is the tallest freestanding structure in the Western Hemisphere. PHOTO: S Toops.

Montreal to Ottawa and Toronto. Canada has 34.5 million people, of which 81 percent live in urban areas. The United States has 316.7 million people with 82 percent in cities (*CIA World Factbook* 2013).

Until the Civil War, most immigrants to the United State came from Northern Europe, and from Africa through the slave trade. Immigrants came from Southern and Eastern Europe between the Civil War and World War II. Since World War II most of the immigrant population has come from Latin America and Asia (Rowntree et al. 2014).

The United States measures resident population by race. In the 2010 census, whites accounted for 79.5 percent of the population, Hispanics 16 percent, blacks 12.9 percent, Asian and Pacific Islanders 4.9 percent, multiracial 1.8 percent, and American Indians one percent. Hispanics can be of any race. The United States has the fifth-largest Spanish-speaking population in the world. Almost 13 percent of the population today is foreign born. Population projections show that by 2070 the United States will be 47 percent non-Hispanic white, 29 percent Hispanic, 13 percent black, 11 percent Asian and Pacific Islander, and one percent American Indian (multiracial may account for 5% of the population). Because of globalization and the continued attraction of the United States to immigrants, and the higher birth rates of the non-white population, the United States will be much more diverse in 2070 (U.S. Census Bureau 2013b).

Canada has fairly open migration laws. The 2011 census shows that 20.6 percent of the population is foreign born. The largest share of recent migrants comes from Asia (including the Middle East). Canada keeps records of the ethnic origin of people's ancestors. Forty-two percent report more than one ethnic origin. The most common are Canadian, English, French, Scottish, Irish, German, Italian, Chinese, First Nation (American Indian), Ukrainian, East Indian, Dutch, and Polish. Canada also has records by visible minority (19 percent), including South Asian 4.8 percent, Chinese 4.0 percent, black 2.9 percent, and smaller percentages of Filipinos, Latin Americans, Arabs, Southeast Asians, and West Asians (Statistics Canada 2013). Canada and the United States are globally connected not only in terms of trade, but also in terms of population.

Although the US and Canadian cultural, economic, political, and historical ties are greater to Europe, North America's connections to China are becoming more and more important. For example, in 1982, one of the authors (Toops) traveled from Seattle to Vermont to continue his study of the Chinese language at Middlebury College. Air travel was cheaper in Canada in those days, so he took a flight from Vancouver, British Columbia, to Montreal, Quebec. He took an airport bus to downtown Montreal and was searching in vain for the bus station to find a bus to Middlebury, Vermont. Without French-language skills, he was fortunate to stumble upon on a Chinese restaurant where he asked in Chinese for directions. North America is indeed fully globalized.

TIMELINE OF CONTEMPORARY
NORTH AMERICAN HISTORY

1821	Mexican independence from Spain
1867	Canadian independence from Great Britain
1898	Spanish-American War. United States acquires Puerto Rico, controls Cuba
1903	United States takes Panama Canal Zone
1914	Panama Canal opens
1914, 1916	United States intervention in Mexican Revolution
1917	United States enters the First World War
1941	Japan bombs Pearl Harbor, Hawaii; United States enters Second World War
1945	United States employs nuclear weapons against Japan
1959	Cuban revolution. Castro seizes power
1961	United States failed Bay of Pigs invasion of Cuba
1961	United States cuts ties to Cuba
1962	Cuban Missile Crisis
1978	United States hosts the Camp David Accords
1983	Reagan mines Nicaraguan harbors in support of Contras against Sandinista government; United States invades Grenada
1986	United States amnesty for illegal immigrants
1989	United States invades Panama
1990–1991	First Gulf War
1994	North American Free Trade Agreement
1994	Mexican peso crisis
1996	United States Helms-Burton Act codifies Cuban embargo into law
1999	United States cedes Panama Canal to Panama
1999–2013	Anti–United States Hugo Chavez president of Venezuela
2000	Election of Vincente Fox of Mexico's Alliance of Change, ending decades of PRI rule
2001	Al-Qaeda terrorists attack New York City and Washington, DC; United States and allies invade Afghanistan
2003	United States invades Iraq, initiating the Second Gulf War

Table 6.1

Population and Rate of Growth

Country	Population	RNI%
Canada	34,568,211	0.77
U.S.A.	316,668,567	0.9
Mexico	116,220,947	1.07

This chart shows the population and rate of population growth among the countries of North America
SOURCE: *CIA World Factbook 2013*

Gross Domestic Product and GDP Real Growth

Country	GDPpc	GDP real growth
Canada	$43,400	1.80%
U.S.A.	$50,700	2.20%
Mexico	$15,600	3.90%

This chart shows the GDP per capita and rate of GDPpc real growth among the countries of North America.
SOURCE: *CIA World Factbook 2013*

Literacy Rates and Life Expectancy

Country	Lit	LE-yrs
Canada	99.00%	81.57
U.S.A.	99.00%	78.62
Mexico	93.50%	76.86

This chart shows the Literacy Rates and Life Expectancy (in years) among the countries of North America.
SOURCE: *CIA World Factbook 2013*

Major Religions

Country	Religion
Canada	Roman Catholic 42.6%, Protestant 23.3%
U.S.A.	Protestant 51.3%, Roman Catholic 23.9%
Mexico	Roman Catholic 82.7%

This chart shows the percentage of major religions among the countries of North America.
SOURCE: *CIA World Factbook 2013*

Type of Government

Country	Government
Canada	Const. Monarchy, Par. Democ., and Fed.
U.S.A.	Constitution-based Federal Republic
Mexico	Federal Republic

This chart shows the form of government among the countries of North America.
SOURCE: *CIA World Factbook 2013*

References

Berg, L. R., and M. V. Hager. 2009. "Freshwater Resources and Water Pollution." *Visualizing Environmental Science*. Hoboken, NJ: Wiley. 242–268.

Chua, Amy. 2007. *Day of Empire: How Hyperpowers Rise to Global Dominance and Why They Fall*. New York: Anchor Books.

CIA World Factbook. 2013. https://www.cia.gov/library/publications/the-world -factbook/

Crawford, Neta. 2013. "U.S. Costs of Wars through 2013: $3.1 Trillion and Counting. Summary of Costs for the U.S. Wars in Iraq, Afghanistan and Pakistan." Brown University and Boston University: Costs of War Project. http://www .costsofwar.org/sites/default/files/UScostsofwarsum_March2013.pdf [accessed 7 Nov. 2013].

Escobar, Arturo. 1995. *Encountering Development: The Making and the Unmaking of the Third World*. Princeton, NJ: Princeton University Press.

Fitzpatrick, Peter. 1992. *The Mythology of Modern Law*. London: Routledge.

Folger, Tim. 2013. "Rising Seas." *National Geographic*. September. http://ngm .nationalgeographic.com/2013/09/rising-seas/folger-text

Fouberg E.H., A. B. Murphy, and H. J. de Blij. 2012. "The Humanized Environment." *Human Geography*. Hoboken, NJ: Wiley. 434–463.

Fuchs, Lawrence H. 1990. *The American Kaleidoscope: Race, Ethnicity, and the Civic Culture*. Middleton, CT: Wesleyan University Press.

Gibbon, John Murray. 1938. *Canadian Mosaic: The Making of a Northern Nation*. Toronto: McClelland & Stewart.

Global Research. Centre for Research on Globalization. www.globalresearch.ca.

Gunderson, Steven. 2013. *The New Middle Class: Creating Wages, Wealth, and Opportunity in the 21st Century*. Austin, TX: Greenleaf Books.

Hause, Steven, and William Maltby. 1999. *Western Civilization: A History of European Society*. Belmont, CA: West/Wadsworth.

Hoekstra, A., and M. Mekonnen. 2012. "The Water Footprint of Humanity." *Proceedings of the National Academy of Science* 109 (9) 3232–3237.

Michelman, Frank. 1988. "Law's Republic." *Yale Law Journal* 97: 493–537.

Office of Management and Budget. 2013. "Outlays by Function and Subfunction: 1962–2018." http://www.whitehouse.gov/sites/default/files/omb/budget/fy 2014/assets/hist03z2.xls [accessed 9 Nov. 2013]

Olsen, Patrick. 2012. "Auto Exports from the US on the Upswing." *USA Today*, April 2. http://usatoday30.usatoday.com/money/autos/story/2012-04-02 /honda-usa-plant-anniversary-marysville/53957210/1

Reich, Robert. 2010. *Aftershock: The Next Economy and America's Future*. New York Vintage Books.

Rogers, P. 2008. "Facing the Freshwater Crisis." *Scientific American*, August, 46–53.

Rosenberg, Emily S. 1982. *Spreading the American Dream: American Economic and Cultural Expansion 1890–1945*. New York: Hill and Wang.

Rowntree, L., et al. 2014. *Globalization and Diversity*. 4th ed. Upper Saddle River, NJ: Pearson Prentice Hall.

Saint-Paul, Gilles. 1996. *Dual Labor Markets: A Macroeconomic Perspective*. Cambridge, MA: MIT Books.

Sarat, Austin, and Roger Berkowitz. 1998. "Disorderly Differences: Recognition, Accommodation, and American Law." In *Democracy and Ethnography: Constructing Identities in Multicultural Liberal States*. Carol Greenhouse, ed. Albany: State University of New York Press. 81–102.

Statistics Canada. 2013. "2011 National Household Survey." http://www.statcan .gc.ca/daily-quotidien/130508/dq130508b-eng.htm

Truslow, James. 1931. *The Epic of America*. Boston: Little, Brown and Co.

United States Census Bureau. 2013a. "U.S. Exports, imports and merchandise trade balance by country." http://www.census.gov/compendia/statab/2012 /tables/12s1307.pdf

United States Census Bureau. 2013b. "Resident population projections by Race, Hispanic Origin Status, and Age 2010." http://www.census.gov/compendia /statab/2010/tables/10s0011.pdf

World Bank. 2014. *Doing Business 2014: Understanding Regulations for Small and Medium-Size Enterprises*. World Bank and International Finance Corporation Global Indicators and Analysis Unit. http://www.doingbusiness.org/reports /global-reports/doing-business-2014

World Trade Organization. www.wto.org

Further Reading

Agnew, John, and Jonathan Smith, Eds. 2002. *American Space/American Place*. New York: Routledge.

Hofstadler, Richard. 1948. *The American Political Tradition*. New York: Knopf.

Morton, Dennis. 2001. *A Short History of Canada*. Toronto: McClelland and Stewart.

Steinbeck, John. 1939. *The Grapes of Wrath*. New York: Viking.

Williams, William Appleman. 1961. *The Contours of American History*. Cleveland, OH: World.

Journals

American Studies. https://journals.ku.edu/index.php/amerstud/
American Review of Canadian Studies. www.acsus.org/display.cfm?id=297
The Atlantic. www.theatlantic.com/
Canadian Review of American Studies. www.utpjournals.com/Canadian-Review-of
    -American-Studies.html
New York Review of Books. www.nybooks.com/

Films

America: the Story of US (2010). US miniseries.
American Exceptionalism: Monopoly on Democracy (2013). Anissa Naouai, producer.
Black Robe (1991). Bruce Beresford, director.
The Canary Effect (2006). Fobin Davey, director.
Monsieur Lazhar (2011.) Philippe Falardeau, director.

Websites

American Studies Association. www.theasa.net
The Globe and Mail. www.theglobeandmail.com
Government of Canada. www.canada.ca
International Council for Canadian Studies. www.iccs-ciec.ca
The New York Times. www.nytimes.com
United States Government. web portal. www.usa.gov

7

Europe and the Modern World

In 1900, Europeans and their cultural offspring (including, for example, Americans, Canadians, and Australians) controlled nearly 85 percent of the earth's land mass. European dominance in the modern world was by no means determined five hundred years ago, but a potent mix of geographical, historical, political, cultural, and economic advantages has enabled Europe to put its stamp on global development to this day. Europeans defined the meaning of the term *modern*, which includes a rapid rise in agricultural production, currency-based trade, exchanges of goods and services over long distances, rapid improvements in industry and technology, an increase in life expectancies, lower birth rates, universal elementary education, and urbanization. **Globalization** in the late-nineteenth century was mainly a Western phenomenon.

European thinkers developed the important ideas that frame global debates today. Are democracy and human rights universally applicable to all people, regardless of ethnicity, culture, gender, or tradition? Is the capitalist, free-market economic system a model for economic development and human happiness everywhere? Does free trade best serve the interests of impoverished countries and poor people worldwide? Does the European idea of the **nation-state** have any relevance to nation-building efforts in other parts of the world?

An understanding of European political and economic development is essential to the study of international affairs today. European colonialists disseminated their political, economic, and social culture into the Western Hemisphere, Africa, and Asia. Westerners created most of the international

159

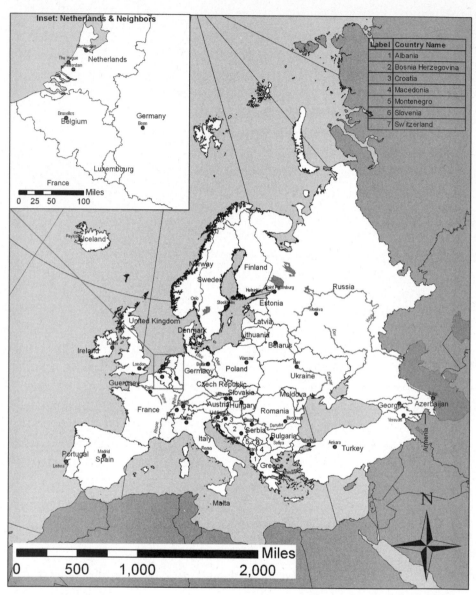

MAP 7.1 Europe.

institutions of global governance. After World War I, the Western allies formed the first global political organization to prevent war. The League of Nations failed, but following World War II the United States and Great Britain spearheaded efforts to resurrect a new United Nations, which codified the Universal Declaration on Human Rights in 1947. As the world's greatest economic power, the United States created financial and trade institutions such as the **International Monetary Fund** (IMF) and the **World Trade Organization** (WTO) to promote a stable global capitalist system. The twenty-eight members of the **European Union** (EU) form the largest free-trade area in the world.

WHAT IS EUROPE?

Europe has different and often conflicting geographic, historic, political, ethnic, and cultural definitions. The traditional **geographic definition** of the continent of Europe describes it as extending from the tip of Norway in the north to Gibraltar in the southwest and the Bosporus in the southeast, and from Iceland in the Atlantic to the Ural Mountains in central Russia. That leaves over half of Russia in Asia and puts a part of Istanbul, the largest Turkish city, in Europe.

Europe has been blessed by nature with a temperate climate, abundant rainfall, a long growing season, navigable waterways, and accessible oceans and seas. European industrialization and modernization had many causes, but its geographical advantages were significant. Europe's ample timber and coal resources provided the energy necessary for early industrialization, although Europe is now largely dependent on petroleum products from outside the region.

Europe has a distinct **historical definition** as well. The Roman Empire brought the Judeo-Christian tradition to the heart of Europe in the early centuries of the first millennium CE. The Renaissance in Italy and the Reformation in Germany in the fifteenth and sixteenth centuries began an enlightened age that propelled the continent's political and economic development past the Ottoman and Chinese empires. In 1492, the powerful Spanish monarchy sent Christopher Columbus to the so-called New World, destroyed Europe's largest Jewish community, and defeated Granada, the last Muslim state in Western Europe.

European modernization was characterized by a flourishing of diverse religious, political, scientific, and technological thought. The European balance of power ensured competition among the states for the best inventors, scientists, businessmen, tradesmen, and intellects. For example, in 1697, seeing that Russia was far behind technologically, Tsar Peter the Great toured Western Europe incognito to glean innovations in sailing and weaponry.

Europe gradually acquired the military power, maritime technology, and scientific knowledge to begin its unprecedented domination of the world. It was a toxic brew that gave Europeans the power to do great harm to themselves and others. In the seventeenth and eighteenth centuries, Europeans surpassed the rest of the world in terms of modern development: relatively stable political and legal structures, standing armies, intellectual exchange, progressive social policies, industrialization, technology, urbanization, and capitalization.

The political definition of Europe has changed since World War II. The continent was divided into two camps after the war. Most West European states had democratic governments, capitalist economies, and a military alliance with the United States and Canada, forming the **North Atlantic Treaty Organization** (NATO). Six West European countries created the European **Common Market** in 1957, which has evolved into the EU. The Soviet Union's satellite states in Eastern Europe formed the **Warsaw Pact** in 1955, completing the division of Europe. Southeast European states such as Greece fell into the Western sphere, while Yugoslavia, despite its communist system, remained nonaligned. Most of Finland, Sweden, and Austria lay east of the Warsaw Pact boundary, but their neutral status and democratic systems defined them as more Western than Eastern.

After the **Iron Curtain** fell in 1989, the economic definition of Europe became nearly synonymous with membership in the EU. In 2004, the fifteen members of the EU expanded to twenty-five. With the accession of Finland, the three Baltic states (Estonia, Latvia, and Lithuania), Poland, the Czech Republic, Slovakia, Hungary, Slovenia, Cyprus, and Malta, some observers have suggested that there is a new East-West political and economic division of Europe. Bulgaria and Romania joined the EU in 2007, and Croatia in 2013, leaving Russia, Belarus, and Ukraine on the outside looking in. Are the Caucasian states and Turkey eligible to join the EU? Israel plays in the European soccer championships, and there is some discussion that it might join the EU as well (see Chapter 14).

FIGURE 7.1 Hitler and Mussolini in Munich, Germany, circa June 1940. SOURCE: National Archives.

The cultural definition of Europe is perhaps the most controversial. Europe traces many of its cultural influences to the Mediterranean area, from the ancient civilizations of Egypt, Palestine, Greece, and Rome. Europe is predominantly Christian, and before the Holocaust had a substantial Jewish population. The Balkan Slavs are mainly Orthodox, and their Slavic and Hungarian neighbors to the north are mostly Roman Catholic. During the Reformation, Protestantism took hold in Prussia and Saxony (northern and eastern Germany today), England, and Scandinavia. The major Western Catholic countries are Italy, Spain, France, and Ireland.

But organized religion no longer plays an important role in the lives of most Western Europeans. Despite the Catholic Church's conservative attitude toward birth control, Italy and Spain have among the lowest birth rates in Europe. Poles (Catholic) and the Balkan peoples (Catholic and Orthodox) tend to be more devout, and their religion remains a central element in their national identity. For example, Serbs distinguish themselves from other Yugoslavs (South Slavs) in part by their Orthodox faith.

Language is a deeper national fault line in Europe. The major Indo-European languages fall into three major groups: Germanic (English, German, and the Scandinavian languages); Romance (Spanish, French, Italian, and Romanian); and Slavic (Russian, Ukrainian, Polish, Czech, Slovak, Serbian, Slovene, Croat, Bulgarian, and Macedonian). Finnish and Hungarian belong to a distinct Finno-Ugric language group unrelated to any other European language. English is becoming the European lingua franca, but it will not replace national languages as the mother tongue in the foreseeable future.

EUROPE AND THE WORLD'S PROGRESS TOWARD LIBERAL DEMOCRACY

The philosophical discourse about the most just and fair political systems today is informed by Europe's long evolution toward **democracy**, from the ancient Greek city-states and the laws and practices of the Roman Empire to the American and French revolutions in the late-eighteenth century. The world's first modern democracies were formed in Europe and North America.

Liberal democracy is a system of government that institutionalizes majority rule and equality under the law. Democratic institutions are characterized by free elections, an independent judiciary, a constitution or body of law, civilian control of the military, and basic civil rights such as freedom of speech, religion, assembly, and the right to trial. In theory, liberal democracies apply the law equally to all groups and guarantee the rights of the electoral minorities.

Democracies are liberal to varying degrees. Elections in and of themselves do not define liberal democracy. Many countries such as Iran and Belarus hold elections, but the outcomes are controlled by screening the candidates allowed to run for office, monopolizing the press, rigging elections, or harassing and even jailing the opposition. Constitutions can limit the rights of women and ethnic minorities and restrict civil rights. Theocracies engrave religious law into civil law. Endemic corruption is also the bane of liberal democratic rule.

In his now famous book *The End of History and the Last Man* (1992), Francis Fukuyama theorized that the fall of communism in 1989–1991 in Eastern Europe and the Soviet Union signaled the end of history. He argued that with the fall of communism and the ideological bankruptcy of Marxism, there were no other political philosophies to rival Western liberal democracy and its enlightened ideas of free political and economic thought, tolerance, and equality under the law. The inability of centrally planned Communist economies to compete with liberal-economic systems supposedly meant the end of economic history as well. **Liberal economics** is in ascendancy today, despite a growing disparity between the rich and poor classes and rich and poor countries.

Although most European countries are liberal democracies now, a short walk through modern European history should give pause to Westerners who muse about the superiority of their culture and progressive political and economic development. Europeans and their cultural offspring have made great contributions to liberal democratic thought, but their unrivaled economic and technological power of the last three centuries has enabled them to bring greater good and wreak greater havoc on the world than any other people. On the one hand, they have given the world the railroad, the automobile, the airplane, computers, constitutional law, and the protection of human rights. On the other, they have produced weapons of unparalleled lethality and have used them in war after war after war. Five million people died in the Napoleonic Wars, six hundred thousand in the American Civil War, and another 50 million in the two world wars. Western science produced the nuclear bomb, which the United States used to obliterate two Japanese cities to end World War II. Europeans and Americans killed and enslaved millions of Africans, and Western imperialists destroyed peoples and mangled foreign cultures. Nearly 25 million Third World peoples perished in Cold War conflicts.

Enlightened political philosophers such as John Locke, Montesquieu, Jean-Jacques Rousseau, Voltaire, and Thomas Jefferson developed many of the liberal democratic ideas manifested in the American and French revolutions at the end of the eighteenth century. Both revolutions borrowed heavily from the Glorious Revolution of 1688 in England, when parliament asked the executive (King William III) to share power. The old regime of divine-right monarchy, aristocratic privilege, and inequality under the law came under siege in the nineteenth century when the middle and working classes, as well as oppressed nationalities, challenged the status quo.

In the late-eighteenth century, the great Prussian philosopher Immanuel Kant (1788/1997) wrote that "the universal and lasting establishment

FIGURE 7.2 Nagasaki after the atomic bomb. SOURCE: National Archives.

of peace constitutes not merely a part, but the whole final purpose and end of the science of right as viewed within the limits of reason." Current threats from terrorism, weapons of mass destruction, global warming, and genocide seem to mock Kant's optimistic vision of the ultimate reason and rationality of human beings, and his progressive view of history. But the march toward democracy in the world in the last two centuries has been inexorable, albeit with many hurdles and setbacks along the way. Liberal democratic revolutions rocked most of the illiberal empires of Europe in 1848, but the forces of reaction prevailed. The major European states could not extinguish the fire of democratic freedom for long. Britain and France gradually broadened the franchise, the German and Austrian empires had national assemblies (Reichstag), and even the ultraconservative Russian tsar acceded to a parliament (Duma) in 1906.

There were no liberal democracies in 1900, and only about twenty after World War II. At the end of the twentieth century, **decolonization** and the fall of communism enabled the formation of many new democratic states, although at the start of the twenty-first century only one-third of the 192 states in the United Nations are true liberal democracies (Diamond 2000, 413–418). With the exception of Belarus, all of the European states have democratic systems of some sort, although Russia and Ukraine have yet to prove their liberal democratic credentials.

Europe's exhaustion after World War II enabled the colonized peoples of Africa and Asia to demand the same right to national self-determination that was a theoretical hallmark of Western liberal political thought. Ho Chi Minh in Vietnam, Mohandas Gandhi in India, and Nelson Mandela in South Africa were among the many independence leaders who invoked Western political ideas to demand their countries' independence from European rulers.

In the mid-nineteenth century, Karl Marx introduced the most threatening revolutionary idea to liberal democracy. Marx theorized that workers in the capitalist system would never receive the value of their labor from the owners of the machines. Marx argued that the political system that protected and promoted the capitalist system had to be violently overthrown. The horrendous conditions of working-class life in early industrial Europe provided a fertile recruiting ground for the Communist parties.

Marx said that religion, racism, and nationalism were the ideological weapons of the upper classes to keep the working classes passive and obsequious. Christianity's promise of an afterlife, Marx argued, was so much hokum to keep workers from fighting the natural order of things on earth.

Although the Soviet Marxist experience died in 1991, many of the world's poor ask themselves today whether a capitalist system that was built on colonialism and exploitation of non-European peoples is just. The world's one billion poor have not benefited from the growth in world trade, and their traditional livelihoods have in fact been threatened by the globalization of the world's economy. They have many allies in marginalized workers and leftists in the developed world. Every meeting of the **World Bank**, the IMF, or the G8 (the **Group of Eight**: Canada, France, Germany, Italy, Japan, Russia, the United Kingdom, and the United States) is met by anti-globalization and anti–free trade demonstrations that have often turned violent. In the last decade, Latin America's impoverished masses have elected a host of left-leaning leaders.

Europeans also incubated one of the most dangerous mass ideologies of the modern age: nationalism. National unity is based on a common history, language, religion, and territory. Often nations have defined themselves in relation to an enemy, such as Serbia's battles against the Ottoman Turks and Poland's struggles against Germans and Russians.

National pride has proven to be the most powerful group identifier, trumping the Marxist appeal to workers' solidarity with fellow laborers on the factory floor. **Imperialism** in Africa and Asia fueled the national competition between European countries and rallied the upper, middle, and working classes behind national goals. "If you wish to avoid civil war [at home]," British empire builder Cecil Rhodes declared, "then you must become an imperialist" (cited in Lenin 1974, 256–257). When World War I erupted in 1914, the working classes and their parties again backed the national cause. Few German, British, or French workers refused to serve in the trenches or go over the top in futile offensives.

The power of national identity was an important factor in the ultimate collapse of communism in Eastern Europe in 1989, and the failure of Marxist ideology as a whole, but nationalism is not a political system or economic program; it is an authoritarian ideology of exclusion. European governments were moving in the direction of greater liberalism in the early-twentieth century, but the power of nationalism helped bring on and prolong the carnage of World War I (1914–1918).

World War I was the catalyst for rapid and radical political change in Europe. At the end of the war, the four great Eastern empires—Germany, Austria, Russia, and Turkey—collapsed. Germany, Austria, and Turkey created republics with varying degrees of liberal democratic government. The new independent states of Finland, Estonia, Latvia, Lithuania, Hungary, Poland, Czechoslovakia, and Yugoslavia were carved out of the ruins of the old empires. All of them established democratic governments.

But liberal democracy could not survive the economic, social, and psychological damage done by World War I. Threats came from the far left and the far right. The **Bolshevik Revolution** in Russia in 1917 created the first communist state, and **fascism** in Italy and **Nazism** in Germany emerged to meet the communist challenge to religion, nationalism, and capitalism. In contrast to liberal democracy's dilatory reaction to the economic crises and communist agitation, fascists on the far right promised action to protect national interests.

Italy created the first fascist state in 1922. Italy had allied with Britain and France in World War I but was humiliated when the Paris peacemakers denied it any significant territorial spoils of the war. Fascist leader Benito Mussolini capitalized on wounded Italian national pride to overthrow the

Italian democracy. Mussolini's fascist ideology was a dynamic and spirited answer to Italian economic ills and political infighting. He promised to bring law and order to a land in profound political, economic, social, and psychological turmoil. Fascism promised to move Italy forward even if it came at the expense of Italian democracy and civil rights. The fascists glorified Italy's past, censored the press, and undermined the appeal of Marxism to workers by employing them in state works' programs and by implementing controls over management-labor relations. Mussolini promised to put millions of men under arms to project Italian power abroad.

Italians were willing to go along with one-man rule as long as Mussolini stabilized the economy and ended domestic strife. This popular attraction to the promises of authoritarian rule—to bring order out of political, economic, and social chaos—remains a constant threat to liberal democracy today. Citizens in democracies have shown a dangerous tendency to sacrifice many of their civil rights for greater security and political and economic stability. Despite revelations in 2013 of a far-reaching personal-data-collection program run by US national-security agencies, there was little outcry from Americans.

Adolf Hitler modeled his mass movement in Germany after Italian fascism. Nazism was the antithesis of liberal democracy. The Nazis papered over Germany's deep social and economic divisions with appeals to **anti-Semitism**, nationalism, racism, and militarism. Songs, mass rallies, symbols, creeds, marches, and messianic promises of returning Germany to first place among nations lent a fanatic religious and spiritual tone to the Nazi movement. The demonization of other groups is staple propaganda of dictatorships today, such as Iran, Syria, and North Korea, and demagoguery is always a threat to undermine democratic rule. Hitler's rise to power is a case in point. The Nazi party garnered less than three percent of the German vote before the most serious depression in the history of modern capitalism hit in 1929. With millions out of work, the stress became too much for the democratic middle to save the fledgling Weimar Republic. By 1932, the Nazi Party was polling one-third of the vote, becoming the largest party in Germany. Hitler took over the chancellorship in January 1933 and quickly snuffed out any opposition to Nazi rule.

Hitler's early economic and diplomatic successes caused many skeptical Germans and Europeans to ignore his undemocratic methods and virulent anti-Semitism. Nazism was no accident, as some scholars have argued, but a logical if not predictable product of German and European modern

Figure 7.3 NATO meeting in Estonia, 2010. SOURCE: State Department Photos.

political culture. Nineteenth-century German Marxist August Bebel called anti-Semitism "the socialism of fools." At that time the political and economic power brokers knew that they could deflect working-class hostility from themselves onto Jews; theories proliferated about Jewish conspiracies to exploit the Christian working classes. Hitler borrowed from theories of racial superiority to argue that Jews were a threat to the purity of German blood. The mass slaughter of five and a half million Jews during World War II was the terrible result of this fanatical nationalism and racism. Although no leader since then has wanted to be labeled a fascist or a Nazi, many have established fascist dictatorships and have committed genocide, such as Pol Pot in Cambodia in the 1970s and the Hutu leaders in Rwanda in the 1990s.

Liberal democracy in Eastern Europe and Spain fared no better between the wars. **Authoritarian** nationalist dictatorships relied on support from the upper classes, large landowners, churches, and conservative elements in the armed forces. By the early thirties, every Eastern European state save Czechoslovakia had an authoritarian regime. The Spanish rebel *caudillo*, Francisco Franco, defeated the Spanish Republic in the bloody Spanish civil war (1936–1939). By the start of World War II in 1939, France,

Belgium, the Netherlands, Luxembourg, Finland, Norway, Denmark, Sweden, and Switzerland were the only remaining democratic governments on the continent, and the Germans defeated all but the latter two neutral countries in the first year of the war. By the middle of 1940, the United States, Great Britain, Canada, and Australia were the only major liberal-democratic states left.

The United States emerged from World War II as the world's unparalleled economic and military power. The dynamic of the superpower confrontation and the division of Europe by the Iron Curtain from 1949 to 1989 compelled the countries of Western Europe to cooperate with the United States on the liberal-democratic paradigm. The success of the American democratic and economic system along with the Soviet threat spurred transatlantic cooperation. Fascism was obviously discredited, and the crimes of Soviet leader Joseph Stalin's odious regime had been exposed. **Stalinism** held no appeal for West Europeans. All of Western Europe save Spain and Portugal developed liberal democratic political systems.

Europe has experienced a truly dramatic turnaround since those dark days of fascism, Nazi-dominated Europe, and the Cold War. Virtually all of Europe's governments today are democracies, albeit with varying degrees of liberalism. Europe's story challenges those who argue that the world is becoming progressively more dangerous, more unstable, and more violent. Europe has been all of that in the twentieth century, but it has also emerged as one of the most peaceful and prosperous regions of the world.

The Western contribution to liberal democratic development is undeniable. Every member of the United Nations has signed on to the UN Declaration on Human Rights. Even in times of national crisis, few leaders openly promote principles of government contrary to the declaration, such as government of and for the minority; divine or hereditary right to rule; arbitrary rather than electoral bases of power; consolidation of executive, legislative, and judicial power; government restriction of civil rights; government control over religion; restrictions on freedom of speech, the press, and the right to assemble; restrictions on economic choices; unequal treatment of women and minorities; and arbitrary imprisonment. Even authoritarian states that operate under these undemocratic principles, such as China, Saudi Arabia, and Zimbabwe, do not trumpet their illiberal policies openly. Beijing has implicitly acknowledged the legitimacy of democratic government by holding elections on the local level, even if the leadership has no intention of giving up its monopoly on power. More liberal democracies exist than ever before. It appears that Kant might be vindicated after all.

From the Scourge of Nationalism to the European Union

The European Union is a liberal answer to Europe's long tradition of national conflict. Europe's modernization in the last two centuries laid the groundwork for the formation of national identities. The advent of universal education, increased literacy, transportation links, urbanization, and mass media allowed political elites to inculcate the masses with a pride in nation. But **nationalism** was the bane of European peace and prosperity in the twentieth century. At the beginning of World War I many Europeans were excited about the prospects of a war that could prove their country's national superiority. Over nine million Europeans died in that war. Nazi nationalist and racist propaganda effectively convinced Germans to attack and subdue most of Europe in World War II and to continue fighting even when it was obvious that Germany would be defeated. Thirty-five million more Europeans died as the result of Germany's nationalist mania.

Japan was the one non-Western state that borrowed Western technology to become the most modern and powerful country in Asia. A chauvinist national identity developed in Japan that was used to justify Japanese domination of East Asia during World War II. The power of Japanese nationalism was evident at the end of the war in the kamikaze attacks on US ships and the martial ethic of fighting to the death. Nationalism is the ideology of scoundrels, but it is a product of modern Western society, and its power over people's imaginations continues to cause interstate and civil war.

Americans often use the terms *nation* and *state* interchangeably. A **state** is a governing political structure, while a **nation** is a distinct group of people. *Nation* is a loaded term, because it implies that a nation should have its own state. The definition of *ethnic group* is nearly the same as *nation*, but the international community usually accepts the minority status of ethnic groups within a state dominated by another national group. The Kurds in Turkey, the Tibetans in China, and the **Basques** in Spain are examples of this phenomenon.

National groups are distinguished by some of these common characteristics: language, religion, culture, an agreed-upon history, and a link to a particular piece of land. Most nations develop a historical mission, such as the defense of the nation against an alien people or the spread of the nation's way of life.

No one is born with a national identity. Nationalism is learned from the family, community, schools, and the media. Toward the end of the nineteenth century, the newly formed German Empire was one of the first states to mandate universal elementary education. Berlin sought to overcome local and regional identities with a pan-German patriotism. After World War I, the United States developed social studies courses to inculcate a distinct American national identity among its various immigrant groups. National histories often distort the truth to glorify founding fathers and heroic defenders of the nation, and raise the nation's cultural and technological achievements above others.

During the French Revolution, at the end of the eighteenth century, nationalism became a potent means of mobilizing the masses toward a common goal. Revolutionaries toppled the French monarchy and reduced the power of the nobility and the church, and French armies carried the people's revolution to the rest of Europe. Napoleon proclaimed himself emperor in 1804 and became a despot and conqueror rather than a liberator. German and Russian national feelings were awakened as the result of French imperialism and chauvinism, and Napoleon's crusade into central Europe and Russia in 1812 foundered in the Russian winter.

National myths appeal to emotions rather than reason. English poet Lord Byron captured the essence of romantic nationalism in his panegyric to the martyred Greeks fighting for independence from the Turks in the early nineteenth century:

> *They never fail who die*
> *In a great cause: the block may soak their gore;*
> *Their heads may sodden in the sun; their limbs*
> *Be strung to city gates and castle walls—*
> *But still their spirit walks abroad.* (Byron 1821)

Lord Tennyson immortalized the futile British "Charge of the Light Brigade" during the Crimean War (1854–1856) against Russia in similar romantic style. When the order was given, the soldier was to do his duty and accept a noble and heroic death on the battlefield:

FIGURE 7.4 Charge of the Light Brigade. SOURCE: Library of Congress.

Theirs not to make reply
Theirs not to reason why
Theirs but to do and die
Into the Valley of Dead
Rode the Six Hundred. (Tennyson [1854] 1964)

In the nineteenth century, European nationalism developed in tandem with industrialization, urbanization, class divisions, and increased literacy. Europeans forged further ahead in science and technology, sometimes misrepresenting science to make seemingly rational explanations for racism, anti-Semitism, and imperialism. Pseudosciences such as phrenology and examinations of brain sizes and facial characteristics were used to justify the superiority of one race over another.

Nationalists in the divided German and Italian states wanted to pull together their peoples into single countries, respectively, based on a common language, culture, and history. This was not necessarily a natural development for either nation. Germans were Protestant, Catholic, and Jewish, they spoke different dialects, and they were divided into thirty-nine states with very different histories. Protestant Prussia in the north and Catholic

FIGURE 7.5 Eleanor Roosevelt and the United Nations Universal Declaration of Human Rights in a Spanish text, November 1949. SOURCE: National Archive, ARC.

Bavaria and Austria in the south were the largest German states, although Vienna controlled an empire with a majority of non-Germans.

A German national myth had to be developed on the basis of ostensibly superior literary, artistic, scientific, philosophical, and industrial achievements. German nationalism had a negative orientation as well, as a reaction against French political and cultural imperialism, and German superiority over the less-developed Slavs to the east, primarily Poles and Russians. Many German nationalists considered Jews to be outside of the community of German peoples (*das Volk*).

There were deep cultural, economic, and historical fissures on the Italian peninsula as well, some of which persist to this day. Italian nationalists whipped up national passions by harkening back to the halcyon days of the Roman Empire, the progressive Italian city-states, and the beauty and grace of Renaissance culture. Italian unification would have to come at the expense of the Austrian Empire, which controlled two key northern Italian states, Lombardy and Venice.

The multinational Austrian Empire had the most to lose from the rise of nationalism. The empire was home to eleven different nationalities: Austrian Germans, Italians, Czechs, Ukrainians, Hungarians, Slovenes, Croats, Serbs, Romanians, Macedonians, and Poles. Russia and Prussia also possessed substantial portions of old Poland, which had been partitioned by the three eastern empires (Austria, Russia, Prussia) in the late eighteenth century. Russia supported fellow Orthodox Slavs in the Balkans—Bulgarians and Serbs—who sought liberation from the Turkish Ottoman Empire.

The relatively peaceful attempt by professors, lawyers, and other middle-class leaders to usher in constitutional government in Europe in 1848 failed for lack of arms. Vienna was temporarily paralyzed by the revolutionaries but vanquished them within a year. As one historian observed, "the Austrian emperor has a standing army of soldiers, a sitting army of officials, a kneeling army of priests, and a creeping army of informers," and they were up to the task of crushing the rebellion, albeit with the help of archconservative Tsar Nicholas I, who sent Russian troops in 1849 to crush a Hungarian national revolt (Sheehan 1989, 723).

Conservatives in the Italian state of Piedmont-Sardinia and the German state of Prussia co-opted the nationalist appeal to the masses by promoting a **conservative nationalism** of their own, characterized by imperial conquest and loyalty to the monarchy. Piedmont-Sardinia and France defeated Austria in 1859 to begin a unification process that was completed in 1870. Prussia fought wars against Denmark (1864), Austria (1866), and France (1870) to unite the German states into the Second German Reich. The success of these unifications by war created national myths for both Italy and Germany based on what one historian termed "the armed deed" (Wandycz 1988). Unfortunately, Prussian Chancellor Otto von Bismarck put a militaristic, conservative, nationalist, and illiberal stamp on the new German state.

Bismarck was disinterested in expanding the German Empire into Asia and Africa, but he, like other conservative leaders in Europe, realized that imperial conquest was an effective palliative against working-class discontent and demands for greater democratic rights. The so-called yellow press fanned the flames of national pride by reporting the exploits of their imperial armies.

National pride metastasized into a martial theology of racial superiority, which would eventually become an essential element of fascist ideology. Charles Darwin's theory of the survival of the fittest in nature was transposed onto societies. Superior European culture, racial character, and technological achievement justified wars on other races. British imperialist Cecil Rhodes, whose name is borne by a prestigious scholarship, proclaimed that "we are the finest race in the world and the more of it we inhabit the better it is for the human race" (cited in Flint 1976, 27–28). In 1895, Teddy Roosevelt revealed his firm Darwinian belief in the invigorating benefits of war for a nation: "Let the fight [with Great Britain] come if it must. I rather hope that the fight will come soon. The clamor of the peace faction has convinced me that this country needs a war" (cited in Miller 1992, 235). When the Spanish-American War broke out in 1898, the *Washington Post* gushed with glee at the chance for the United States to prove its mettle: "Ambition, interest, land hunger, pride, the mere joy of fighting, whatever it may be, we are animated by a new sensation. . . . The taste of Empire is, in the mouth of the people even as the taste of blood in the jungle" (*Washington Post* 1898).

Most Europeans fought loyally for their respective states in World War I, but the German soldier was the best of the lot. Germans, more than their major continental rivals in both wars—the French and the Russians—were imbued with a sense of obedience to higher command, a fervent belief in the superiority of German blood, and a national myth that called for ultimate and unquestioning sacrifice for the German nation. Nineteenth-century German philosopher Friedrich Nietzsche, whose ideas were later warped to suit the Nazis' racial ideology, said that "the Germans are responsible for . . . the sickliness and stupidity that oppose culture, the neurosis, called nationalism, from which Europe suffers; they have robbed Europe itself of reasoning and intelligence. They have led it into a blind alley" (Stromberg 1994, 165). Pride in positive national achievements contributes to national unity, but denial of any wrongdoing by members of the national community and the dehumanization and demonization of the enemy is a recipe for international conflict.

The bankruptcy of national idealism was laid bare in the futile trench warfare of World War I and the total war of World War II. In the course of the world wars, the word *German* became synonymous with militarism, extreme nationalism, blind obedience, and brutality. French national pride was at a nadir after the nation's defeat at the hands of the Nazis in 1940. The leader of the free French, Charles de Gaulle, rallied French resistance forces against the Nazi occupiers and developed a new French national myth. American and British troops pushed the Nazis out of France in 1944, but a French division marched into Paris first and de Gaulle bravely walked down the Champs-Elysées as if the French had played the dominant role in liberating France.

Even the communists in the Soviet Union had to admit that Russian nationalism spoke to people's hearts more than class solidarity. Desperate to save the Soviet Union after Hitler's invasion in 1941, Stalin subordinated Marxist propaganda and dubbed the defense of Mother Russia "the Great Patriotic War." Stalin's compromise with nationalism foreshadowed the demise of the Soviet Union in 1991. The head of the Russian Republic, Boris Yeltsin, appealed to Russian nationalism to rescue Soviet leader Mikhail Gorbachev from a hard-liners' coup attempt in 1991. In this case, however, the strength of Russian nationalism and the bankruptcy of Soviet ideology meant the end of the communist state.

At the end of World War I, President Woodrow Wilson outlined American interests in free and unfettered international trade, but the depression put a brake on global trade when capitalist countries raised tariffs to protect their industries. It was the wrong prescription for bringing the world out of the economic crisis. And just as economists and policymakers were beginning to recognize the folly of protectionist policies, World War II broke out.

After World War II, the United States was determined not to repeat the failed economic policies of the interwar period and embarked on a **classical liberal** economic program. In the United States, the term *liberal*, related to the word *liberty*, often means tolerance, less government intervention into religious and personal moral affairs, and progressive government on behalf of the middle- and lower-class majority. American liberalism differs from European classical liberalism by promoting progressive tax policies and social programs to ensure equal economic opportunity. American liberalism is more akin to European social democracy.

Classical liberalism stems in part from Adam Smith's 1776 work *Inquiry into the Nature and Causes of the Wealth of Nations*. Smith argued that economies functioned most efficiently when the invisible hand of supply and demand is free to operate without burdensome government regulation. Classical liberalism calls for limited government ownership of economic enterprises. With the notable exception of billions of dollars in farm subsidies and defense contracts, the United States has one of the most liberal economies in the world. For example, the United States is the only major industrial country without a government-run universal health insurance program. President Barack Obama passed through Congress a broadened public healthcare program in 2010, but many Americans still opposed it. The troubled rollout of the Affordable Care Act in the fall of 2013 provided more fodder for critics who argue that the federal government should not force Americans to buy health insurance.

Memory of the catastrophic world wars, the Great Depression (which many scholars blame for the rise of Hitler), and the postwar communist threat were the compelling motives for European integration after World War II. The theory of **comparative advantage** also pushed the Europeans toward greater economic liberalism. The United States tried to prevent a postwar recession by creating institutions to promote free markets and international economic cooperation. The **World Bank** made loans to spur economic development, the **IMF** tried to keep currencies stable, and the **General Agreement on Tariffs and Trade** (GATT) provided a framework for gradually reducing barriers to freer trade between states. In 1995, GATT evolved into the WTO, which is dedicated to arbitrating international trade disputes and further lowering trade barriers. Today, the world is closer to the liberal economic model for international commerce than ever before.

In contrast to Stalin's exploitation of the East German and East European economies, the United States financed a $13-billion aid program called the **Marshall Plan** (1948–1952) to jump-start the Western European economies. The rapid West European economic recovery in the 1950s ended any real threat from a united Communist movement. Liberal democracy in Western Europe thrived in the context of the Cold War.

The Marshall Plan was the first step toward Western European economic integration. The United States viewed economic cooperation with Western Europe as a way to bolster a community of free-market economies and liberal democracies as a counterweight to the Soviet bloc. Western Europe's economic and political stability became a strategic imperative.

Formal European economic integration began with the **European Coal and Steel Community** of 1951, which lowered tariffs and controlled production among France, Germany, Italy, and the Benelux countries (Belgium, the Netherlands, and Luxembourg). The ECSC was an agreement for managed trade rather than free trade, and it worked. The "Six" expanded the scope of their economic cooperation by forming the **European Economic Community** (EEC), or Common Market, in 1957, which lowered tariffs on trade as a whole and created a common external tariff. Great Britain stayed out, preferring to preserve economic ties to the empire and cultivate its special relationship with the United States. The rapid economic growth of the Common Market countries and the disintegration of the British Empire prompted a change of heart in London. Great Britain, Ireland, and Denmark joined the EEC in 1973.

In 1790, President George Washington predicted that one day there would be a "United States of Europe." In 1992, the European Economic Community took a major step toward achieving that goal when member states decided to drop border controls, issue a common currency, and create a common foreign policy and defense policy. The **euro** was launched in 1999, joining the dollar and the yen as one of the world's major currencies. Not since the heyday of the Roman Empire has Europe been so united. But unlike an empire, the EU is a voluntary union based on liberal democratic principles.

The European Common Market gradually expanded its scope into political and military cooperation, culminating in the creation of the European Union in 1992 and the adoption of the euro by eleven EU members in 1999. The Eurozone has expanded to seventeen of the twenty-eight countries in the EU. Great Britain, which has always held the EU at arms' length, is a notable Eurozone outlier. The euro makes transactions easier between the Eurozone members and for travelers; one currency provides a welcome relief from exchanging bills and coins at each European border, and having to pay an.exchange fee each time. The EU's open borders have also eliminated time-consuming passport checks.

The Greek debt crisis of the 2010s revealed that the Eurozone, and to a certain extent the EU as a whole, had pushed ahead with economic union without the requisite political legitimacy. While the Eurozone looked good on paper, not all members have played by the financial rules, and there was no real means of punishing the profligate governments. When the Greek government faced default, Germany, which is the strongest economy in the EU, was forced to bail them out or risk the collapse of the Eurozone. German voters asked themselves why they should pay taxes to save Greece, a country that had, unlike Germany, spent money that it did not have. Furthermore, the Greeks' penchant for not paying their taxes also grates on the rest of those in the Eurozone who do.

The EU has fostered a common economic culture. Most European countries have systems that fall somewhere between a liberal and a command economy. European **social democracy** combines a free-market economy with extensive social benefits and substantial government regulation. All governments in the EU provide universal healthcare, generous unemployment and pension benefits, nearly free higher education, and subsidized election campaigns. Some national governments own airlines, railways, and other major industries.

Some major continental economies such as France and Italy have struggled to maintain these generous social benefits, and suffer from chronic high unemployment. An aging population is putting strains on pension and health insurance programs in most of the EU states. When employees in a private company lose their jobs, they have little recourse. But politicians jeopardize their own positions when they try to cut government workers, and attempts to trim social welfare spending in some European countries have been met with public protests, as have changes in work rules for private firms. Greece's financial crisis has forced Athens to make draconian cuts in state spending, which has sparked repeated public demonstrations. European states face difficult choices about the role of immigrant workers in alleviating labor shortages and about revamping welfare states to promote economic growth.

In the late twentieth century, the United Kingdom and Ireland moved closer to American **laissez-faire** policies, and the two economies showed strong economic growth, suggesting to other EU countries that their social welfare systems were too generous. But Ireland's financial system crashed in 2009, and its unemployment nearly doubled from 2008 to 2009 (Eurostat 2011). The UK's economy has also seen sluggish growth.

The EU has not yet realized George Washington's prediction. The EU member states have been reluctant to give up national sovereignty on defense and foreign-policy issues. The EU has decided to create a sixty-thousand-strong Rapid Reaction Force but has been slow to find the necessary funding. The EU's failure to act decisively to end the Yugoslav civil war in the 1990s and divisions within the community over going to war in Iraq in 2003 exposed the weakness of the common EU foreign and defense policy. American policymakers have been increasingly critical of the EU's lack of defense spending, as evidenced by NATO's dependence on US weaponry in the campaign to oust Libyan dictator Muammar Qaddafi in 2011. No European country took the lead in responding to the Syrian government's use of chemical weapons against its citizens in 2013.

The EU, as some have suggested, is still a "United Europe of States." Most Europeans identify themselves as nationals first and EU citizens second. The European idea is under siege. Some Europeans describe the capital of the EU, Brussels, as representing a cold, technocratic, bureaucratic despotism—a "government of strangers." In 2005, French and Dutch voters rejected a European constitution. One anti-EU slogan in the Netherlands read, "We want to stay Dutch" (Pfaff 2005, 26). The United Kingdom has not adopted the euro, and given the problems the Eurozone has faced in the 2010s, that decision seems vindicated. The United Kingdom has also complained about its monetary contributions to the EU and the billions of euros in Common Agricultural Policy funds subsidizing French and other EU farmers.

Open EU borders have resulted in questions about the dilution of national cultures. In the fall of 2005, widespread rioting broke out in French cities among immigrant communities, which have not been integrated into French political, economic, and cultural life. In early 2006, many European Muslims protested a Danish newspaper's publication of cartoons depicting the Prophet Muhammad in a derogatory way. Protesters in the Middle East boycotted Danish companies and attacked European embassies. And if the EU cannot achieve higher rates of economic growth and lower an unemployment rate that hovers around ten percent, more and more people will ask EU leaders if integration is really benefiting them.

As a result, more anti-immigrant, nationalist right-wing parties have sprung up in Europe, and they have been gaining in strength. France's Front National Party has polled over ten percent in national elections, and has elected several mayors and deputies to the National Assembly. The party is particularly strong in the Mediterranean southeast, as a reaction against immigration there from north Africa. Germany's mainstream parties have debated banning the far-right, xenophobic National Democratic Party. In 2013, a leader from Italy's Northern League stooped to a new low when he said that a black government minister reminded him of an orangutan. In the fall of 2013, the Greek government arrested the leadership of the Golden Dawn Party, which was behind the murder of a popular anti-fascist singer, Pavlos Fyssas. This neo-fascist demagoguery feeds on the high unemployment in some regions of the EU, where it is easy to blame foreigners and the EU for undermining national power.

The EU is bent on combating these nationalist tendencies and mitigating tensions between nation-states. The migration of ethnic groups from one European state has been a source of some right-wing reaction, but the EU is dedicated to the idea of equal rights for all of its citizens, no matter where they live.

The EU is a solution to the most intractable international question of our time; which nation deserves to have its own state. Woodrow Wilson popularized the idea of **national self-determination** at the end of World War I. He saw the origins of that war in the repression of national groups in the illiberal Eastern empires and felt that European imperialism in Africa and Asia denied peoples their inalienable human rights. One way to prevent further wars and to ensure justice for deserving nations, Wilson believed, was to give them a state of their own. It was an ironic solution coming from a country in which national heritage was supposed to play no legal role. Wilson envisioned that the international community, through his proposed League of Nations, would adjudicate the legitimacy of a nation's right to a state.

Wilson was fully aware that a pure nation-state was impossible. The victorious powers forced the new or expanded states of Eastern Europe to sign treaties ensuring the rights of minorities. Nonetheless, minorities in Poland, Romania, and Yugoslavia suffered from discrimination.

The nation-state idea was impossible to realize in Europe without terrible wars of unification and two world wars. The international community and the United Nations still struggle with the dilemma of ethnic groups' desire for a political entity of their own when no pure ethnic boundaries exist. Africa has been particularly hard-pressed to establish legitimate boundaries that allow for self-determination. Europe has been no model of development on this front, as the Yugoslav civil war in the 1990s attests. When the Yugoslav civil war broke out in 1991, it became evident that nationalism was still a potent political force in Europe, although it was no prescription for governing multinational states.

With few viable options after World War I, Slovenes and Croats from the Austrian Empire and Serbs in the independent state of Serbia reluctantly formed a new Yugoslav state. In an effort to bring Rome to their side in 1915, Britain and France had promised Italy parts of the Austrian Empire. Not wanting to remain in a reconstituted Austro-Hungarian Empire or to lose territory to victorious Italy, the Slovenes and Croats chose the least objectionable of three evils, agreeing to join the Serbs in the so-called Kingdom of Serbs, Croats, and Slovenes in 1918.

The Yugoslav (south Slav) national idea, however, was a weak bond. South Slavs had some linguistic similarity but very different histories, religions, and levels of economic development. The northernmost south Slav people, the Catholic Slovenes, resided in the Austrian half of the empire. They tended to be wealthier than their fellow south Slavs. The Croatians are also Catholic and held a privileged position in the Hungarian half of the empire. Spoken Serbo-Croatian is nearly the same among these groups, but the Slovenes and Croatians use the Latin alphabet, the Serbs the Cyrillic. Neither the Slovenes nor the Croatians have had modern political entities or "armed deeds" on which to build a national history.

Serbs had the strongest sense of national identity of the constituent nationalities in the new Yugoslav state. Serb nationalism is virtually indistinguishable from Orthodox Christianity. For centuries, the Serbs prided themselves on defending the frontier of Christian Europe against the Muslim Ottoman Turks. Martyrdom is an essential element of Serbian identity; the Serb national holiday commemorates the national defeat at the hands of the Turks in Kosovo in 1389. Serbia gained its independence from the Ottoman Empire in 1878 and finally helped chase Turkey out of Europe in the First Balkan War (1912). Serbia more than doubled its territory in that war, and the Bosnian Serb who shot the Austrian archduke in 1914 wanted a greater Serbia to include Bosnia.

Serbia fought on the side of the eventual victors of war, but it was handed yet another defeat at the hands of the Central Powers in 1915. The ultimate defeat of Austria and Bulgaria in 1918 enabled the Serbs to join the Slovenes and Croats in what the Serbs viewed as greater Serbia. Serbs held the positions of power in the new kingdom; the monarchy was Serb, and Serbs dominated the armed forces and bureaucracy. In 1929, King Alexander established a royal dictatorship and changed the state's name to Yugoslavia in a vain attempt to foster a south Slav national identity.

When Hitler attacked Yugoslavia in 1941, the state fell apart in a week; Serbia was occupied, Slovenia was annexed by the Third Reich, and Croatia was established as a puppet fascist state under Italian tutelage. Modern Croatian state history has this fascist burden to bear. The Croatian fascists were called the Ustase, and with the help of some Bosnian Muslims (Bosniaks), the Ustase murdered hundreds of thousands of Serbs.

A civil war ensued between Serb nationalists, the Croatian fascists, and Josip Broz Tito's partisan communist movement. Tito emerged victorious at the end of World War II. His postwar communist state (1945–1991) papered over the atrocities committed during the war, and when Yugoslavia fell apart in 1991, Serbian collective memory of suffering at the hand of the Croats in the war rekindled fears for the fate of the Serbs living in Croatia and Bosnia. The Serb perpetrators of the ethnic murders and ethnic cleansing during the Yugoslav civil war in the 1990s reminded their compatriots of the centuries-long history of Serb persecution at the hands of the Turks, as well as the Ustase atrocities in World War II. In Serb minds, Yugoslavia was synonymous with the greater Serbia for which Serbs had fought three twentieth-century wars. In 1991, when the new Croatian independent state began to use the flag, songs, and other trappings of the wartime Ustase state, Serb fears seemed to be confirmed.

Belgrade-supported Serbian militias and the Serb-dominated Yugoslav army launched attacks in Croatia in 1991 and Bosnia in 1992. Croatian militias followed suit in Bosnia, and a tragic three-way ethnic civil war lasted until 1995, when NATO forces bombed Bosnian Serb positions. Europe was demoralized by its most devastating war since World War II. Over 250,000 people died, and many more were wounded, raped, tortured, and driven from their homes. Western Europeans, who had buried their extreme nationalist ideologies in favor of international cooperation in the EU, could barely comprehend the barbarity of this bloody conflict.

Europe and the United States were reluctant to intervene in a conflict between peoples with supposedly ancient animosities. In effect the West adopted the same view of history as the minority of Yugoslavs who perpetrated this civil war. Except for the fascist period, Serbs, Croats, and Bosniaks had lived together in peace in Bosnia for centuries. Its capital, Sarajevo, was a beautiful cosmopolitan city of ethnic tolerance before the extreme nationalist forces tore it asunder.

The final chapter of the war began in 1999, when Belgrade began to force hundreds of thousands of Albanians out of the Serb province of Kosovo, killing about ten thousand. After seventy-eight days of NATO bombing of Serbia, the Serbs again capitulated. NATO, EU, and UN forces now keep an uneasy peace in Bosnia and Kosovo. Serbian strongman Slobodan Milosevic was ousted in 2000 and put on trial at the International Court of Justice in The Hague. In hopes of bettering its chances to join the

EU, in 2011 Serbia arrested General Radko Mladic, who had orchestrated the torture and massacre of thousands of Bosnian Muslims during the war.

The EU is a hopeful remedy to the national hatreds that have plagued Europe in the past, and perhaps an inspiration for other national conflicts. Slovenia joined the EU in 2004, Croatia in 2013, Serbia has applied for membership, and Bosnia-Herzegovina, Montenegro, and the former Yugoslav Republic of Macedonia are in accession talks.

The European Union and Basque, Irish Republican, and Islamic Extremism

Ethnic minorities who have grievances against their national governments now have recourse in the European Union. The EU has standardized civil rights among its members, and can put enormous diplomatic pressure to ensure its members' respect of those rights. It was not always so.

Terrorism today is mainly associated with the Middle East, but Europe has a long history of terrorist activities to demand political rights. Russian revolutionaries in the nineteenth century used terrorist tactics to oppose tsarist rule, culminating in the assassination of Alexander II in 1881. Serbian Gavrilo Princip's assassination of the Archduke of Austria in 1914, which led to World War I, fell into a nineteenth-century tradition of national groups using terrorist methods to attack the symbols and institutions of an oppressive state. When conventional war against a stronger military and police force is impossible, nationalists often turn to so-called asymmetrical guerrilla war, or terrorist attacks on vulnerable state institutions.

Extremist Islamists conducted terrorist bombings on the transportation systems in Madrid in 2004 and in London in 2005, killing more than one hundred people. But Spain and the United Kingdom have experienced terror attacks from sources even closer to home. For decades the Basque terror group **Euskadi Ta Askatasuna** (ETA) has sought independence of the northern Basque region from Spain. For nearly a century the **Irish Republican Army** (IRA) fought for the end of British rule in Northern Ireland and unification with the Republic of Ireland.

The Basques of northwestern Spain have a unique linguistic and cultural heritage. Their language is unrelated to any other Indo-European language. Only about half of the people in the Basque provinces claim Basque heritage, and fewer than that speak Basque (Euskera). Economic nationalism plays a role in Basque separatism, but unlike most nationalities struggling for independence, the Basques have the highest standard of living per capita in Spain. The Basque provinces have ample reserves of iron ore and lumber as well as deep, sheltered harbors in the Bay of Biscay. Bilbao is a major industrial center and San Sebastian a key northern Spanish port. Poorer Spaniards have been attracted to the region's economic opportunities, changing the demography of the Basque region.

The Basque region enjoyed considerable autonomy from Madrid before the Spanish Civil War (1936–1939). The regime of Francisco Franco executed Basque nationalists, threw thousands of Basques into prison, repressed Basque cultural expression, and restricted the use of Euskera. Franco's policies created a breeding ground for Basque terrorism. ETA's most notorious act was the 1973 assassination of the authoritarian-minded Prime Minister Luis Carrero Blanco. After the end of Franco's dictatorship in 1975, the new constitutional monarchy of King Juan Carlos granted the Basques a measure of autonomy in 1979 that they had not enjoyed since the end of the republic in 1939. The move eventually shoved ETA onto the margins of Basque political life. There have been few attacks in the past few years, and there is little support among Basques for ETA's terrorists.

Ireland has been struggling for independence from the United Kingdom for more than a century. In 1914, the British government passed an Irish home rule measure but suspended it until the end of World War I. On Easter Sunday 1916, Irish nationalists began a rebellion in Dublin and declared an Irish Republic. British forces quelled the poorly organized Easter Rebellion and executed fifteen of the ringleaders. Irish Catholics were shocked into siding with the revolutionaries, and the Irish Republic was proclaimed in 1918. London did not recognize its legitimacy or its claim of sovereignty over the whole island of Ireland, including the northern provinces of Ulster.

The Irish Republic created the IRA as a defense force for the breakaway Irish government, and it began to conduct guerrilla attacks on British forces. London responded by sending army veterans to serve in the Royal Irish Constabulary, which raided and terrorized Irish communities. Both sides committed terrorist acts. Finally, in 1921 the British Parliament agreed to recognize the Irish Free State. Six predominantly Protestant Northern Irish provinces remained in the United Kingdom, however, and Irish nationalists have sought to unite the island of Eire ever since.

Those provinces have been the source of the so-called **Troubles** that began in the 1960s, with the IRA and the Irish Catholic Nationalist community on one side and the Protestant Loyalists and the Royal Ulster Constabulary, the British army, and several Ulster paramilitary groups on the other. Spurred on by the civil-rights movement in the United States and the French student riots in 1968, Irish Catholics in Northern Ireland demanded their own equal civil and economic rights. Rioting and communal fighting prompted London to send in the British army, which openly sided with the forces of the status quo. The Irish Catholic community viewed them as imperial forces dedicated to repression of their human rights. Continued violence prompted London to institute direct rule over Northern Ireland in 1972.

The seminal event of the Troubles was the massacre of thirteen Irish Catholic marchers by British paratroopers in Londonderry (Derry to Nationalists) in 1972 on a day now known as Bloody Sunday. British soldiers inflamed Catholic passions by scrawling "Paras 13, Catholics 0" on a lookout tower overlooking the site of the shootings.

In the next three decades, IRA and Loyalist paramilitaries killed over 3,600 people and injured another 40,000. By the end of the 1970s, Belfast and Londonderry looked like war zones. The bombings and paramilitary intimidation led to even greater segregation in Belfast and Londonderry neighborhoods and schools.

British Prime Minister Margaret Thatcher (1979–1987) took a no-compromise position toward IRA demands. She refused to treat convicted IRA members as political prisoners, categorizing them as common criminals. Bobby Sands and nine other prisoners went on a hunger strike in protest. Sands was elected to parliament in March 1981, but Thatcher would not bend. He died in prison in early May and became a cause célèbre for the Irish Nationalist community.

By the 1990s, realism had overcome nationalism in Irish and British policy toward the Northern Ireland problem. Ireland's membership in the European Economic Community and its rapid economic growth in the late 1980s and 1990s, coupled with Northern Ireland's economic stagnation and civil strife, made the province a burden to both the Irish and British governments. Dublin had nothing to gain from inheriting the Troubles, and London wanted to rid itself of the terrorist threat and Northern Ireland's drain on the British Exchequer (treasury).

In 1997, Labour Prime Minister Tony Blair, Irish Prime Minister Bertie Ahern, and US President Bill Clinton went to work on the Northern Ireland issue. All parties sought a political solution to the violence. Reversing Thatcher's hard-line stance, they negotiated with the IRA and its political wing, **Sinn Fein,** and a ceasefire was reached in 1994. The IRA's promise to keep weapons caches buried in place prompted one wit to quip, "may they rust in peace." An IRA bomb killed two in London in 1996, but instead of ending the peace process Blair pressed ahead. Two years later, former US Senator George Mitchell brokered the so-called Good Friday Agreement, which called for a Northern Irish parliament (Stormont), disarmament of the paramilitaries, a reformed police force, outreach programs between the communities, and an economic development fund. Stormont disbanded in 2002 because Unionist parties claimed that the IRA had not kept its promise to disarm. Nonetheless, progress continued on other tracks of the peace process and an uneasy peace held. In July 2005, the IRA finally agreed to decommission, and hopes were again raised for a permanent end to the violence. In May 2007, Sinn Fein and the Northern Irish Loyalists agreed again to political reconciliation and self-rule.

Both ETA and the IRA have been affected by the rise of radical Islamic terrorism in the early twenty-first century. In the 1960s and 1970s, ETA and the IRA sympathized with other national liberation groups in Palestine, Latin America, and Africa. Terror groups often attack what they consider to be legitimate targets, such as the army, police, or government officials and institutions. For example, on September 11, 2001, al Qaeda attacked the World Trade Center towers and the Pentagon as symbols of American economic and military power. The IRA often called in warnings of imminent bombings to prevent collateral damage. Of course, innocent victims died anyway. The advent of suicide bombing and the wanton and deliberate killing of innocent civilians has discredited any group using terror to affect political change. After a cell of British Muslims killed over fifty people on subways and buses in the summer of 2005, the IRA renounced the use of violence to achieve its goals.

Al Qaeda is an international terrorist network formed by members of the *mujahideen* (guerrilla resistance fighters) resistance against the Soviet occupation of Afghanistan in the 1980s. The group was initially financed by its late leader, Osama bin Laden, who was a member of a wealthy Saudi family. Bin Laden's goals were to rid Arab lands of foreign armies, free the Muslim world from pervasive Western influence, and erect Islamic fundamentalist regimes. Al Qaeda used cells in Germany to plan the September 11 terrorist attacks in the United States, and a Muslim terrorist shot Dutch filmmaker Theo van Gogh in 2004 for allegedly blaspheming Islam. His killer, a Moroccan Dutch, said, "I acted purely in the name of my religion." The train and bus bombings in Spain and the United Kingdom in 2004 and 2005 heightened fears of Islamic fundamentalism. Nationalist parties in France, the Netherlands, and Germany have grown in popularity as a direct result of immigration from Islamic countries. There are approximately 25 million Muslims living in Europe, including at least 5 million in France, 3 million in Germany, 2 million in the United Kingdom, and over a million in Italy.

The challenge posed by Islamic and other non-European cultures, as well as high unemployment rates following the financial crisis of 2009, has fostered a serious debate in the EU about immigration, freedom of speech, security measures, sedition laws, and deportation of foreigners. The French Republic has been adamantly secular, and the French worry that their culture is being undermined by a devoutly religious and insular Islamic community. France passed a law in March 2004 prohibiting all religious expression in public schools. The measure was directly aimed at Islamic girls who wear the traditional North African head scarf, called a *hijab*. More recently, France banned the wearing of the face-covering *niqab* in public (see Global Issue on veiling). Perhaps even more surprising is the backlash against immigrants in Sweden, which has been unusually tolerant in the past. In 2010 an anti-immigrant party won 6 percent of the vote, enough to gain representation in the Swedish parliament. The wife of a truck driver from the southern city of Malmo captured the essence of this new anti-immigrant attitude: "They do not respect Swedish people. As long as they learn the language and behave like Swedes, they are welcome. But they do not. Immigration as it is now needs to stop" (Daley 2011).

Nonetheless, Europe's experience with terrorism on the continent and in its colonies has prompted a measured response to the new threat from extremist Islamic terrorists. The EU has been critical of the United States' military approach to fighting terrorism and the idea of preventive strikes. Europe tends to view terrorism as a criminal activity to be dealt with by intelligence agencies and police forces. It is also engaged in serious debates about eliminating the causes of terrorism, which can lead to criticism of Western policies in the Middle East.

EUROPE'S IMPORTANCE IN THE WORLD TODAY

The world wars diminished Europe's power in the world. Europeans were demoralized, and their countries' economies were in shambles. During the Cold War, the Soviet Union dominated one half of the European continent, and the other half was dependent on US military and economic might. It was also at this time that the Europeans' control of their empires abroad crumbled.

However, Europe still plays a dominant role in world affairs. The United States and the EU have some of the world's largest economies and the biggest and most sophisticated militaries. Western ideas still dominate the global debates on modern political and economic development.

European unity has allowed the region to regain its international importance. It is one of the most healthy, well educated, and wealthy areas of the world. Life expectancy in the EU is fourth highest in the world, following Japan, Australia, and South Korea. The EU's gross national product per capita ranks fifth behind the United States, Canada, Australia, and Japan, only because in the last two decades the EU has absorbed less-developed countries in eastern and southeastern Europe (Eurostat 2013).

The EU is the largest free-trade area in the world, with over 500 million people. The EU comprises 7.3 percent of the world's population (China has nearly 20%), but the EU accounts for 25.8 percent of the world's **GDP** (gross domestic product) and nearly 20 percent of global trade. The EU has a common internal tariff, which means that imports unloaded in Naples or Hamburg will be assessed the same duty (Eurostat 2013).

In 2007, the EU formed the Transatlantic Economic Council with the United States and Latin America to reduce trade and investment barriers. The United States and the EU are each other's largest trading partner. The United States takes 17.3 percent of the EU's total exports, followed by exports to China and Russia. The United States supplies 11.5 percent of EU imports, which is third on the list behind China and Russia (Eurostat 2013).

The EU has made significant efforts to increase trade with countries that have less-developed economies. In 2001, the EU instituted a program called the General System of Preference, which eliminated all tariffs on imports from the poorest forty-nine economies, most of which are in Africa. The EU has also launched trade and development strategies with many countries in the Caribbean, Africa, Asia, the Middle East, and Latin America. Excluding fuel imports, the EU imports more from developing countries than China, the United States, Japan, and Canada combined (Eurostat 2013).

The EU has struggled to recover from the financial crisis in the late 2000s. Unemployment has hovered near 10 percent for several years, and in some countries like Greece and Spain it is over 25 percent. With an aging population (only Japan has an older median age), there are worries that the welfare state that Europeans have come to expect is not sustainable in the long run.

Europe is dependent on foreign energy sources. Russia supplies over two-thirds of Europe's oil and gas supplies, and the EU has been reluctant to criticize the hemorrhaging of Russia's democracy, President Vladimir Putin's support of Syrian leader Bashar al-Assad, and Putin's annexation of Crimea in 2014. Europe receives about 45.7 percent of Russia's exports and supplies 35.5 percent of Russia's imports, and the EU supported Russia's entry into the WTO in 2012 (Eurostat 2013). Putin soured relations with the United States by providing asylum for Edward Snowden, a fugitive from American justice for leaking top-secret documents from US intelligence agencies, and by calling into question America's claim to be an exceptional country and an indispensable force for good in the world. Putin has played the nationalist card, even to the point of whitewashing the crimes of Josef Stalin. The intense media coverage of the Winter Olympic Games in Sochi in 2014 brought these issues into the full light of day. Putin's meddling in Ukraine also tempered the generally positive international reaction to the Games.

The United States and the EU countries share basic beliefs in democracy and capitalism, but after the collapse of the communist states some of their cultural differences have come to the fore. The United States has always pushed the EU for lower tariffs and freer trade in general. EU tariffs on industrial imports average four percent, while US tariffs average three percent (ABC Doha 2011). In 2007, the US trade representative asked Europe to eliminate all tariffs of five percent or less. The EU has balked (USTR 2011). Nonetheless, tariffs on the goods exchanged between the

United States and the EU average under three percent, and trade disputes amount to less than two percent of their trade volume (EU 2011).

The EU and the United States have also tangled over subsidies for major industries and agriculture. For years, the United States has accused the EU of giving Airbus, the joint European aircraft manufacturer, illegal debt relief and research-and-development monies. The EU has countered that US-based Boeing receives indirect government subsidies through US military contracts (Klapper 2007). The EU has also brought suit against US tariffs on some European information technology imports. The WTO is adjudicating these disputes. The environmentally conscious EU states have banned meat products from hormone-injected livestock and refuse to accept US genetically modified foods (WTO 2011).

European and American values have diverged on social issues as well. The EU has banned the death penalty, considering it a barbaric act for the state to put a prisoner to death. Europeans are highly critical of the role of money in US politics and the electoral power of right-wing Christian fundamentalists. Organized religion plays little role in mainstream Western European politics. Fewer than 20 percent of Western Europeans go to church twice a month. That number is even lower in Britain. About 34 percent of Irish Catholics attend mass weekly, but that number was 90 percent in the 1980s. About 43 percent of Americans go to a religious service every week (Shorto 2007, 63).

Europeans wonder about the lack of a universal healthcare system in the United States and the exorbitant cost of higher education, which seems to favor wealthier Americans. Some Europeans also decry the global influence of what they consider to be American lowbrow culture, from the Big Mac to Hollywood action films.

Europeans as a whole are much more environmentally conscious than Americans. Green parties play an important role in several EU countries. Europeans willingly support subsidies for environmentally friendly mass-transportation systems, and they are critical of Americans' gas-guzzling autos. Europe is responsible for approximately 15 percent of the world's carbon dioxide emissions. The United States has a smaller population but emits about 25 percent of global carbon dioxide emissions. In March 2007, the EU agreed to cut its greenhouse gas emissions by 20 percent (compared with 1990 levels) by 2020. If non-EU states agreed to reduce emissions significantly, the EU promised to make cuts of up to 30 percent ("Europe to Cut" 2007). Chinese and United States indifference to climate change makes that target unlikely. Nonetheless, Europe is on the front line of the effort to stop global warming.

European political and economic development is an inspirational story for other regions of the world that have experienced ethnic strife, brutal tyranny, and devastating war. Out of the horror in the trenches of northern France and Flanders in World War I, and the bombed-out European cities and Holocaust of World War II, Europe has reconciled its ideological and national differences to enjoy unprecedented peace and prosperity. Some ethnic issues and terror threats persist, but war among the twenty-eight members of the EU is nearly unthinkable today. The EU is, as one scholar put it, "the most progressive political development of our time" (Cohen-Tanugi 2005, 67).

TIMELINE OF TWENTIETH-CENTURY EUROPEAN HISTORY

1914–1918	World War I. Central Powers: Germany, Austria-Hungary, Turkey, Bulgaria. Entente: Britain, France, Russia, Italy (entered in 1915).
1917	Bolshevik Revolution in Russia.
1918	German, Austrian, Turkish empires collapse. Germany creates Weimar Republic (1918–1933).
1918	New independent states formed: Finland, Estonia, Latvia, Lithuania, Poland, Czechoslovakia, Hungary, and Yugoslavia.
1919	Paris Peace Settlement. Versailles Treaty with Germany is part of this settlement.
1921	Irish Home Rule.
1922	Mussolini's fascist coup in Italy.
1929	Worldwide economic depression.
1933	Adolf Hitler's Nazis take power, end the Weimar Republic, and establish the Third Reich.
1939–1945	World War II. Axis powers: Germany, Italy, Japan. Allies: France, Britain, Soviet Union (entered in 1941), United States (entered in 1941).
1945	Victory in Europe (May).

1945	United States drops two atomic bombs on Japan; end of war in Asia (August).
1945	World Bank and International Monetary Fund created.
1945–1949	Soviet Union annexes the Baltic states and imposes communist regimes in Poland, Bulgaria, Romania, Hungary, Czechoslovakia, and East Germany.
1948–1952	European Recovery Program (Marshall Plan).
1949	North Atlantic Treaty Organization created.
1949	West Germany (liberal democracy) and East Germany (communist) created, completing the division of Europe after World War II.
1955	West Germany joins NATO.
1955	Soviet-led Warsaw Pact formed.
1957	European Economic Community (EEC or Common Market) established.
1972	Bloody Sunday massacre in Londonderry.
1973	Great Britain, Ireland, and Denmark join the EEC.
1981	Irish Republican Army prisoner Bobby Sands starves to death in prison.
1985	Mikhail Gorbachev becomes General Secretary of the Soviet Communist Party.
1989	Gorbachev allows the collapse of the communist regimes in Eastern Europe.
1990	German reunification: East Germany incorporated into West German Federal Republic.
1991	Soviet Union disintegrates after hard-liners' failed attempt to depose Gorbachev.
1991–1995	Yugoslav civil war.
1992	European Union.
1993	Czech Republic and Slovakia declare independence.
1998	Northern Ireland Good Friday Agreement.
2002	European Monetary Union; euro adopted as new currency.
2004	Terrorist attack on Madrid trains.
2005	Terrorist attack on London transport system.
2007	Bulgaria and Romania admitted to the EU.
2007	Terrorist attack on Glasgow airport.
2011	Greek debt crisis threatens unity of Eurozone.

Table 7.1 Population and Rate of Growth

Country	Population	RNI%	Country	Population	RNI%
Albania	3,011,405	0.29	Latvia	2,178,443	−0.61
Armenia	2,974,184	0.14	Lithuania	3,515,858	−0.28
Austria	8,221,646	0.02	Luxembourg	514,862	1.13
Belarus	9,625,888	−0.18	Macedonia	2,087,171	0.22
Belgium	10,444,268	0.05	Malta	411,277	0.34
Bosnia and Herzegovina	3,875,723	−0.10	Moldova	3,619,925	−1.02
Bulgaria	6,981,642	−0.81	Montenegro	653,474	−0.56
Croatia	4,475,611	−0.11	Netherlands	16,805,037	0.44
Cyprus	1,155,403	1.52	Norway	4,722,701	0.33
Czech Republic	10,162,921	−0.15	Poland	38,383,809	−0.09
Denmark	5,556,452	0.23	Portugal	10,799,270	0.15
Estonia	1,266,375	−0.66	Romania	21,790,479	−0.27
Finland	5,266,114	0.06	Russia	142,500,482	−0.02
France	65,951,611	0.47	Serbia (Yugoslavia)	7,243,007	−0.46
Germany	81,147,265	−0.19	Slovakia	5,488,339	0.09
Georgia	4,555,911	−0.33	Slovenia	1,992,690	−0.21
Greece	10,772,967	0.04	Spain	47,370,542	0.73
Hungary	9,939,470	−0.20	Sweden	9,119,423	0.18
Iceland	315,281	0.66	Switzerland	7,996,026	0.85
Ireland	4,775,982	1.16	Turkey	80,694,485	1.16
Italy	61,016,804	0.42	Ukraine	44,573,205	−0.63
Kosovo	1,847,708	NA	United Kingdom	63,395,574	0.55

This chart shows the population and rate of population growth (natural increase) among the countries of Europe.

SOURCE: *CIA World Factbook 2013*

Table 7.2 Gross Domestic Product and GDP Real Growth

Country	GDPpc	GDP real growth	Country	GDPpc	GDP real growth
Albania	$8,200	1.3%	Latvia	$18,600	5.6%
Armenia	$5,900	7.2%	Lithuania	$22,000	4.0%
Austria	$43,100	0.8%	Luxembourg	$81,100	0.1%
Belarus	$15,900	1.5%	Macedonia	$10,800	−0.3%
Belgium	$38,500	−0.2%	Malta	$27,500	0.8%
Bosnia and Herz.	$8,400	−0.7%	Moldova	$3,500	−0.8%
Bulgaria	$14,500	0.8%	Montenegro	$11,900	1.5%
Croatia	$18,100	−2.0%	Netherlands	$42,900	−0.9%
Cyprus	$27,500	−2.4%	Norway	$55,900	3.0%
Czech Republic	$27,600	−1.2%	Poland	$20,900	2.0%
Denmark	$38,300	−0.6%	Portugal	$23,800	−3.2%
Estonia	$22,100	3.2%	Romania	$13,000	0.3%
Finland	$37,000	−0.2%	Russia	$18,000	3.4%
France	$36,100	0.0%	Serbia	$10,600	−1.8%
Germany	$39,700	0.7%	Slovakia	$24,600	2.0%
Georgia	$6,000	6.5%	Slovenia	$28,700	−2.3%
Greece	$24,900	−6.4%	Spain	$31,100	−1.4%
Hungary	$20,000	−1.7%	Sweden	$41,900	1.2%
Iceland	$39,900	1.6%	Switzerland	$46,200	1.0%
Ireland	$42,600	0.9%	Turkey	$15,200	2.6%
Italy	$30,600	−2.4%	Ukraine	$7,500	0.2%
Kosovo	$7,600	2.6%	United Kingdom	$37,500	0.2%

This chart shows the GDP per capita and rate of GDPpc real growth among the countries of Europe.

SOURCE: *CIA World Factbook 2013*

Table 7.3 Literacy Rates and Life Expectancy

Country	Literacy	LE-years	Country	Literacy	LE-years
Albania	97%	78	Latvia	100%	73
Armenia	100%	74	Lithuania	100%	76
Austria	98%	80	Luxembourg	100%	80
Belarus	100%	71	Macedonia	97%	76
Belgium	99%	80	Malta	92%	80
Bosnia and Herz.	98%	76	Moldova	99%	70
Bulgaria	98%	74	Montenegro	98%	NA
Croatia	99%	76	Netherlands	99%	81
Cyprus	99%	78	Norway	100%	80
Czech Republic	99%	78	Poland	100%	75
Denmark	99%	79	Portugal	95%	79
Estonia	100%	74	Romania	98%	74
Finland	100%	80	Russia	100%	70
France	99%	82	Serbia	98%	75
Germany	99%	80	Slovakia	100%	76
Georgia	100%	78	Slovenia	100%	78
Greece	97%	80	Spain	98%	81
Hungary	99%	75	Sweden	99%	81
Iceland	99%	81	Switzerland	99%	82
Ireland	99%	80	Turkey	94%	73
Italy	99%	82	Ukraine	100%	70
Kosovo	92%	NA	United Kingdom	99%	80

This chart shows the Literacy Rates and Life Expectancy (In Years) among the countries of Europe.

SOURCE: *CIA World Factbook 2013*

Table 7.4 Major Religions

Country	Religion
Albania	Muslim 70%, Albanian Orthodox 20%, Roman Catholic 10%
Armenia	Armenian Apostolic 95%, Christian 4%, Yezidi 1%
Austria	Roman Catholic 74%, Protestant 5%, Muslim 4%, unspecified 2%, none 12%
Belarus	Eastern Orthodox 80%, other 20%
Belgium	Roman Catholic 75%, Protestant or other 25%
Bosnia and Herz.	Muslim 40%, Orthodox 31%, Roman Catholic 15%, other 14%
Bulgaria	Eastern Orthodox 59%, Muslim 8%
Croatia	Roman Catholic 88%, Orthodox 4%, Muslim 1%, none 5%
Cyprus	Greek Orthodox 78%, Muslim 18%
Czech Republic	Roman Catholic 10%, Protestant 1%, other and unspecified 55%, none 34%
Denmark	Evangelical Lutheran 95%, other Christain 3%, Muslim 2%
Estonia	Evangelical Lutheran 14%, Orthodox 13%, other Christian 1%, other 66%, none 6%
Finland	Lutheran 82%, None 15%
France	Roman Catholic 83%, Muslim 5%, Portestant 2%, Jewish 1%, unaffiliated 4%
Germany	Protestant 34%, Roman Catholic 34%, Muslim 3.7%
Georgia	Orthodox Christian 84%, Muslim 10%, Armenian-Gregorian 3.9%
Greece	Greek Orthodox 98%, Muslim 1.3%
Hungary	Roman Catholic 52%, Protestant 19%, Greek Catholic 3%, other Christian 1%
Iceland	Lutheran 81%, Roman Catholic, 2%
Ireland	Roman Catholic 87%
Italy	Roman Catholic 80%, atheists and agnostics 20%
Kosovo	Muslim 90%, Orthodox Christian 10%
Latvia	Lutheran 20%, Orthodox 15%, unspecified 64%
Lithuania	Roman Catholic 79%, Russian Orthodox 4%, Protestant 2%, unspecified 6%, none 9%
Luxembourg	Roman Catholic 87%, others 13%
Macedonia	Macedonian Orthodox 65%, Muslim 33%
Malta	Roman Catholic 98%
Moldova	Eastern Orthodox 98% Jewish 1%, Baptist, and other 1%
Montenegro	Orthodox 74%, Muslim 18%, Catholic 4%, unspecified 3%, atheist 1%
Netherlands	Roman Catholic 30%, Protestant 20%, Muslim 5.8%, none 42%
Norway	Church of Norway 86%, Pentecostal 1%, Roman Catholic 1%, other Christian 2%, Muslim 2%, other 8%
Poland	Roman Catholic 90%, Eastern Orthodox 1%, other 9%

continues

Table 7.4 Major Religions *continued*

Country	Religion
Portugal	Roman Catholic 85%, other Christian 2%, unknown 9%, none 4%
Romania	Eastern Orthodox 87%, Protestant 7%, Roman Catholic 5%
Russia	Russian Orthodox 15-20%, Muslim 10–15%, other Christian 2%
Serbia (Yugoslavia)	Serbian Orthodox 85%, Catholic 5%, Protestant 1%, Muslim 3%, unspecified 3%
Slovakia	Roman Catholic 69%, Protestant 11%, Greek Catholic 4%, none 13%
Slovenia	Catholic 58%, Muslim 2%, Orthodox 2%, other or unspecified 23%, none 10%
Spain	Roman Catholic 94%, other 6%
Sweden	Lutheran 87%, other 13%
Switzerland	Roman Catholic 42%, Protestant 36%, Muslim 4.3%, Orthodox 1.8%, other 5.3%, none 11.1%
Turkey	Muslim 99.8%
Ukraine	Ukrainian Orthodox 84%, Ukrainian Catholic 8%, Roman Catholic 2%, Protestant 2%, Jewish 0.6%, other 3%
United Kingdom	Christian 72%, Muslim 3%, Hindu 1%, other 2%, unspecified or none 23%

This chart shows the percentage of major religions among the countries of Europe.

SOURCE: *CIA World Factbook 2013*

Table 7.5 Type of Government

Country	Government	Country	Government
Albania	Parliamentary democracy	Latvia	Parliamentary democracy
Armenia	Republic	Lithuania	Parliamentary democracy
Austria	Federal republic	Luxembourg	Constitutional monarchy
Belarus	Republic in name, although dictatorship	Macedonia	Parliamentary democracy
		Malta	Republic
Belgium	Federal parliamentary democracy under constitutional monarchy	Moldova	Republic
		Montenegro	Republic
Bosnia and Herz.	Emerging federal democratic republic	Netherlands	Constitutional monarchy
		Norway	Constitutional monarchy
Bulgaria	Parliamentary democracy	Poland	Republic
Croatia	Parliamentary democracy	Portugal	Republic, parliamentary democracy
Cyprus	Republic		
Czech Republic	Parliamentary democracy	Romania	Republic
Denmark	Constitutional monarchy	Russia	Federation
Estonia	Parliamentary republic	Serbia	Republic
Finland	Republic	Slovakia	Parliamentary democracy
France	Republic	Slovenia	Parliamentary republic
Germany	Federal republic	Spain	Parliamentary monarchy
Georgia	Republic	Sweden	Constitutional monarchy
Greece	Parliamentary republic	Switzerland	Confederation
Hungary	Parliamentary democracy	Turkey	Republican parliamentary democracy
Iceland	Constitutional republic		
Ireland	Republic, parliamentary democracy	Ukraine	Republic
		United Kingdom	Constitutional monarchy

This chart shows the form of government among the countries of Europe.

SOURCE: *CIA World Factbook 2013*

References

ABC Doha. 2011. American Business Coalition for Doha (Round of Trade Talks). http://www.polity.org.za/topic/american-business-coalition-for-doha

Byron, George Lord. 1821. *Marino Faliero, Doge of Venice*. London: John Murray.

Cohen-Tanugi, Laurent. 2005. "The End of Europe?" *Foreign Affairs* (November–December): 55–67.

Daley, Suzanne. 2011. "Swedes Begin to Question Liberal Migration Tenets." *New York Times*. February 26. http://www.nytimes.com/2011/02/27/world/europe /27sweden.html?_r=1&ref=sweden

Diamond, Larry. 2000. "The Global State of Democracy." *Current History* (December): 413–418.

"Europe to Cut Greenhouse Gases 20 Percent by 2020." 2007. *Environmental News Service*. March 8. www.ens-newswire.com

Eurostat. 2011. http://epp.eurostat.ec.europa.eu/statistics

Eurostat. 2013. http://epp.eurostat.ec.europa.eu/statistics

Flint, John. 1976. *Cecil Rhodes*. London: Hutchinson.

Fukuyama, Francis. 1992. *The End of History and the Last Man*. New York: Penguin Books.

Kant, Immanuel. (1788) 1997. *Critique of Practical Reason*. Cambridge, UK: Cambridge University Press.

Klapper, Bradley S. 2007. "WTO to Give Glimpse into Boeing-Airbus Subsidy Dispute." *Seattle Post-Intelligencer*, March 19. seattlepi.nwsource.org

Lenin, Vladimir Ilyich. 1974. "Imperialism, the Highest Stage of Capitalism." In *Collected Works*, vol. 2. Moscow: Progress Publishers.

Miller, Nathan. 1992. *Theodore Roosevelt: A Life*. New York: Morrow.

Pfaff, William. 2005. "What's Left of the Union?" *New York Review of Books*. July 14, 26–29.

Reuters. 2007. "EU's Mandelson Tells Russia: No Politics in Energy." June 10. www.reuters.com

Rich, Norman. 1992. *Great Power Diplomacy*. New York: McGraw-Hill.

Sheehan, James J. 1989. *German History, 1770–1866*. New York: Oxford University Press.

Shorto, Russell. 2007. "Keeping the Faith." *New York Times Magazine* (April 8): 39–63.

Stromberg, Roland N. 1994. *European Intellectual History since 1789*. Englewood Cliffs, NJ: Prentice Hall.

Tennyson, Alfred Lord. (1854) 1964. *The Charge of the Light Brigade*. New York: Golden Press.

USTR (Office of the US Trade Representative). 2011. www.ustr.gov

Wandycz, Piotr S. 1988. "East Central Europe 1918: War and Peace, Czechoslovakia and Poland." In *Revolution and Intervention in Hungary and Its Neighboring States*, edited by Peter Pastor. Boulder, CO: Social Sciences Monograph: 397–408.

Washington Post. 1898. Editorial. April 25.

WTO (World Trade Organization). 2011. www.wto.org

Further Reading

Bomberg, Elizabeth, et al. 2008. *The European Union: How Does it Work?* New York: Oxford.

Coogan, Tim Pat. 2000. *The IRA*. New York: Palgrave.

Gellner, Ernest. 1983. *Nations and Nationalism*. Ithaca, NY: Cornell University Press.

Gilbert, Felix, and David Clay Large. 2009. *The End of the European Era*, 6th ed. New York: Norton.

Hobsbawm, Eric. 1990. *Nations and Nationalism since 1870: Programme, Myths, Reality*. Cambridge, UK: Cambridge University Press.

Hunter, Shireen T. 2002. *Islam, Europe's Second Religion*. Westport, CT: Praeger.

Jolly, Mette. 2007. *The European Union and the People*. New York: Oxford.

Judt, Tony. 2005. *Postwar: A History of Europe since 1945*. New York: Penguin.

Kurlansky, Mark. 2001. *The Basques in History*. New York: Penguin.

Mazower, Mark. 2000. *Dark Continent: Europe's Twentieth Century*. New York: Vintage.

Milward, Alan. 2005. *Politics and Economics in the History of the EU*. New York: Routledge.

Unwin, Tim. 1998. *A European Geography*. New York: Prentice Hall.

Wilkinson, James, and H. Stuart Hughes. 2004. *Contemporary Europe: A History*. Upper Saddle River, NJ: Pearson Prentice Hall.

Journals

Central European History. journals.cambridge.org/action/displayJournal

Contemporary European History. journals.cambridge.org/action/displayJournal

European History Quarterly. ehq.sagepub.com
Journal of European Studies. jes.sagepub.com
Journal of Modern History. www.press.uchicago.edu/ucp/journals/journal/jmh

Films

Ashes and Diamonds (1958). Andrej Wajda, director.
Battle of Algiers (1965). Gillo Pontecorvo, director.
Bloody Sunday (2002). Paul Greengrass, director.
The Lives of Others [*Das Leben der Anderen*] (2006). Florian Henckel von Donners-
    marck, director.
No Man's Land (2001). Danis Tanovic, director.

Websites

British Broadcasting Company (BBC). www.bbc.co.uk
EU. www.europa.eu
The Financial Times. www.ft.com/home/europe
NATO. www.nato.int
The Times. www.timesonline.co.uk

8

East Asia, the Pacific, and International Studies

Demography and Development

A revolution is not a dinner party, or writing an essay, or painting a picture, or doing embroidery; it cannot be so refined, so leisurely and gentle, so temperate, kind, courteous, restrained and magnanimous. A revolution is an insurrection, an act of violence by which one class overthrows another.

—*Mao Zedong, 1927*

If a cat catches mice, what does it matter if it's black or white?

—*Deng Xiaoping, 1961*

INTRODUCTION: WHY STUDY EAST ASIA AND THE PACIFIC?

Several items point to the significance of **East Asia** and the Pacific. First is the huge geographic scale. East Asia comprises two regions: **Northeast** and **Southeast Asia**. East Asia is the most populated region of the world's most populated continent. Thirty percent of the world's population lives in East Asia. Of the ten most populous countries, three are in East Asia. China has 1.35 billion people, while Indonesia has 251 million and Japan has 127 million. Environmentally, East Asia is quite diverse, ranging from the Tibetan plateau to broad river valleys to tropical rain forests.

FIGURE 8.1 The Great Wall of China, while not visible from space, is an important symbol of China. PHOTO: S. Toops.

The **monsoon** affects much of the climate of East Asia. The Pacific covers a wide expanse of territory, yet only 36 million people live in the region.

Second is the long history associated with Asian civilizations. Four to five thousand years ago, the Chinese civilization flourished along the Yellow River valley. The Great Wall is a symbol of China's history, the power of the empire (Figure 8.1). The civilizations along the Mekong, Chao Praya, and Irrawaddy are the base of Thailand, Burma, Cambodia, and Vietnam today. The island countries of Japan, the Philippines, and Indonesia all took particular arcs of historical development. The continuity of these civilizations to the present day is remarkable. European colonialism broke the power of the Asian states, but the twenty-first century points toward a world where Asia will have a significant presence. While Australia was settled very early 50,000 years ago, the islands of Polynesia were the last place on earth to be settled, 400–800 CE.

Third is the cultural variety of East Asia. Belief systems of Buddhism and Confucian philosophies originated in Asia; Islam and Christianity came to the area by the Middle Ages. The linguistic variety is even more complex. For example, Indonesian and Chinese are both quite distinct in scripts, grammars, and vocabularies; these are just a few of the many and diverse Asian languages. The Pacific Islands have a multicultural mosaic from aboriginal inhabitants and European settlers in Australia to

Polynesian culture in Hawaii. Modern forces of **globalization** challenge the variety of East Asian and Pacific culture.

Fourth is the rising economic power of Asia. China surpassed Japan as the world's second-largest economy and will surpass the United States by 2040. Japan is an economically developed power, while China is a rising economic star. The **newly industrialized countries (NICs)** of South Korea, Taiwan, and Singapore play a strong role in the Asian economy. At a per capita level China's income is low, while Japan's per capita income is quite high. Many goods and services are produced in Asia. Japanese companies play a major role in the global economy; Chinese businesses are growing strong. Economies range from the more-developed world in Australia and New Zealand and the less-developed economies of Papua New Guinea and the Solomon Islands.

Fifth and finally, the political power and strength of Asia is of significance to the world. Asia was a major theater of World War II, and Korea and Vietnam were war zones in the Cold War. A variety of political systems uneasily coexist in Asia. Democracies such as Japan, South Korea, Indonesia, and the Philippines contrast with the authoritarian regimes of China and North Korea. Burma is in transition from an authoritarian to a democratic regime. Although China is the only Asian permanent member in the UN Security Council, Japan is trying to secure a permanent seat. In terms of economic and political power, East Asia is already a major player on the world stage. Political circumstances in the Pacific point to many states with strong ties to other regions. France still has colonies in the Pacific (New Caledonia and French Polynesia). Many former British colonies of the Pacific (Australia, Fiji, New Zealand, Papua New Guinea, etc.) are in the Commonwealth. And the United States has one state (Hawaii) and several territories (Guam, American Samoa, and Northern Marianas) in the Pacific.

This chapter begins with discussions of the regional character of East Asia and the Pacific, and then focuses on demographic and development issues in East Asia, highlighting China, a rising powerhouse. The chapter closes with a discussion of East Asia's role in the twenty-first-century world.

GEOGRAPHY

Regions are mental constructs that we use to help organize the world geographically (see Chapter 1). The word *Asia* is derived from the language of the Phoenicians (ancient seagoing traders on the Mediterranean), who spoke of a region associated with the sunrise, the east. Europe was associated with the sunset in the west. This east-west distinction is still a common way to think of the world, but the historical complexities make it more reasonable to consider Asia as a variety of regions. The vast continent of Asia is usually divided into four regions: Northeast Asia, Southeast Asia, South Asia, and Central Asia. The following chapter considers South and Central Asia. The map of Asia (Map 8.1) shows the relative locations of the countries. The Pacific countries include the larger island countries of Australia and New Zealand as well as the smaller island countries stretching from Papua New Guinea to French Polynesia.

Northeast Asia encompasses China, Japan, Taiwan, and North and South Korea. There are some cultural similarities here, including Mahayana Buddhism and Confucian philosophy. The languages are less interrelated and the ethnic groups are distinct in terms of history and political identities. China and Japan are both powerful economic and political forces in the world, but with quite distinct economic and political systems. Geographically, the Koreas have acted as a bridge between China and Japan. The identities of these countries are tied up with their relative location; China has a continental influence, the Koreas are peninsular, while Japan has an island influence (Fairbank et al. 1989; Reischauer 1995).

Southeast Asia includes the mainland countries of Burma (Myanmar), Thailand, Vietnam, Cambodia, Laos, the peninsular countries of Malaysia and Singapore, and the island countries of Indonesia, the Philippines, Brunei, and East Timor. This region is a crossroad of influences from China and India. Islam came from South Asia to Malaysia and Indonesia in particular. Buddhism came from South Asia to Thailand, Burma, Cambodia, and Vietnam. Many Chinese settled in Malaysia and Singapore, as well as Indonesia, Thailand, Vietnam, and the Philippines. The Chinese diaspora is an important part of the region's economy, comprising much of the commercial class. Singapore has the most developed economy. Malaysia, Thailand, and the Philippines have lagged behind, but have experienced healthy growth rates in the past few years. Thailand and the Philippines have liberal democratic political structures. Malaysia, Singapore, and Indonesia have democratic governments with fewer liberal credentials. Myanmar is moving from a rigid authoritarian regime to more democratic structures, while Vietnam and Laos have communist dictatorships (Friend 2003; Dixon 1991).

The **Pacific** countries include several components. Australia and New Zealand have some characteristics in common given that the majority of

209

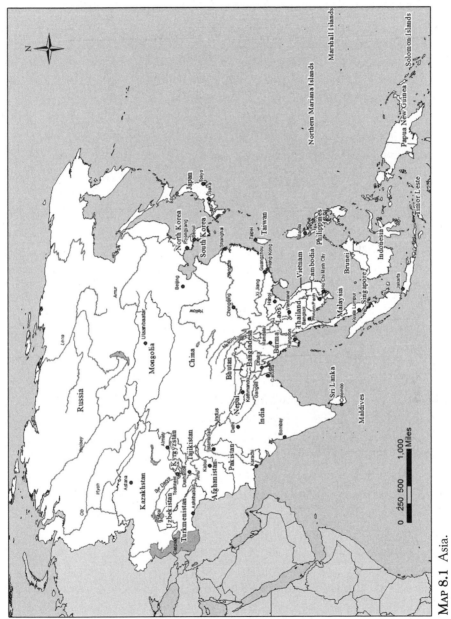

MAP 8.1 Asia.

the populations have European ancestry. **Melanesia** includes the countries of Papua New Guinea, Solomons, Vanuatu, Fiji, and the French territory of New Caledonia. **Micronesia** includes the countries of Nauru, Marshalls, Kiribati, Federated States of Micronesia and the US territories of Guam and the Northern Marianas. **Polynesia** includes the countries of Tonga and Samoa, French Polynesia and the US territory of American Samoa, and the state of Hawaii (McKnight 1995). One significant environmental issue affecting the region is global climate change. Many of the low-lying islands, particularly Tuvalu, Kiribati, and the Marshalls in the Pacific, are vulnerable to sea-level rise.

Hazards of the natural environment include earthquakes, floods, hurricanes, and tsunamis. The Indian Ocean tsunami of 2004 affected Thailand and Indonesia. A major earthquake damaged China in 2008. A major earthquake and tsunami hit Japan in 2011, resulting in a nuclear disaster in Fukushima. Hurricane Haiyan devastated the Philippines in 2013. Asia Pacific countries have to deal with these damaging natural hazards.

History

Indigenous kingdoms and empires have dominated East Asia through its long history. The ideals that guided the Chinese empires were established in the Yellow River valley in 2000 BCE. Chinese political formation remained essentially the same from 200 BCE to 1911 CE, that is, an empire with the basic governing precepts of Confucianism formulated 2,000 years ago. The Japanese empire dates back to 50 BCE; the present-day emperor traces his line back to Japan's antiquity. Khmer, Thai, Viet, and Sri-vijaya kingdoms all controlled Southeast Asia. These very early civilizations developed by being able to produce agricultural food surpluses. These early empires were quite sophisticated culturally and possessed well-developed technologies (Fairbank et al. 1989; Mackerras 1995).

European colonialism was very strong in Southeast Asia but less so in Northeast Asia. The Dutch secured Indonesia, the French colonized Indochina, the British colonized Malaya, and the Spanish captured the Philippines. All of the European powers gained some territorial control in China. Japan and Thailand alone escaped colonial control. At first the United States did not have a specific territory but rather sought influence and trade in many areas, but by 1898 the United States took over the Philippines from Spain (Borthwick 2014).

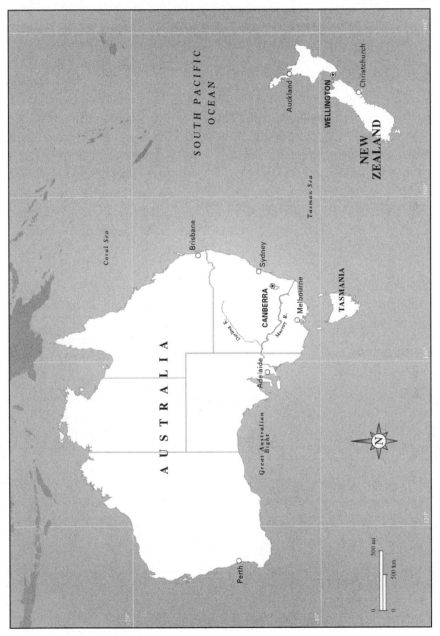

MAP 8.2 Australia and New Zealand.

Resistance to European colonialism took the form of nationalism in the 1900s. Ho Chi Minh in Vietnam, Sukarno in Indonesia, and **Mao Zedong** in China were all national leaders regardless of their political philosophies. By 1949 India and Indonesia were free from **colonial rule**, and after a brutal civil war, China became a communist state. France began to withdraw from Vietnam in 1954. Fearing communist takeover of the whole country, the United States defended South Vietnam from the early sixties to 1973. Two years later the country fell to Ho Chi Minh's communist regime.

Japan made a turn from traditionalist to a modern state in the 1880s. Emulating the Western imperialist powers, Japan became a colonial power, taking Taiwan and Manchuria from China and colonizing Korea. With the Japanese surrender in 1945 at the close of World War II, Japan's imperial era came to a close (Brower 2005).

After World War II, the new nationalisms in East Asia meant the creation of new states in China, Korea, Vietnam, Indonesia, Malaysia, and the Philippines. The Cold War meant the divisions of China, Korea, and Vietnam into competing states. Whereas Vietnam reunited in the 1970s, China is still divided between Taiwan and mainland China, and the demilitarized zone (DMZ) still separates North and South Korea.

Settlement in the Pacific begins with the aboriginal inhabitants 50,000 years ago. Papua New Guinea was settled prior to 2500 BCE. Micronesia and the rest of Melanesia were settled by 1200 BCE. Polynesia was settled by 400–800 CE. French, British, Germans, and Americans all had colonies in the Pacific. Australia became independent in 1901. By the 1970s, many Pacific islands became independent states. The United States and France still have dependent territories in the Pacific.

CULTURE

Asia has a significant degree of diversity. Every country has its own language system for the most part. Current belief systems include Buddhism, Islam, Christianity, Daoism, and philosophies such as Confucianism. Southeast Asia has Buddhism, Islam, and Christianity, and Northeast Asia has Buddhism, Confucianism, Daoism, Shinto, and Christianity (see Table 8.4 on religions).

The first waves of technological innovation originated in the Yellow River valley. In terms of religion, the oldest beliefs are Daoism in China.

Daoism merged with other philosophical perspectives in China. Daosim is rooted in nature worship and stresses spiritual harmony.

The next religious wave of innovation occurred in 500 BCE. **Buddhism** diffused throughout Southeast Asia. Today, in Sri Lanka, Burma, Thailand, Cambodia, and Laos, adherents practice Theravada Buddhism. One structural characteristic of Theravada Buddhism is a large number of monks and nuns, who focus their lives on religious devotion.

At roughly the same time as the Buddha in India (approximately 500 BCE), Confucius was teaching in China. Confucian philosophies permeate China, Korea, and Japan today. Confucius articulated philosophies rather than a set of religious beliefs. Confucius's philosophy pointed toward social stability based on human relationships. By 600–700 CE, Buddhism expanded into northeast Asia. In China, Japan, and Korea, the Buddhism practice is Mahayana. Mahayana is distinct from Theravada today in that there is less of a focus on monks or nuns to fulfill religious obligations. In China, most individuals practiced Buddhism, Daoism, and **Confucianism**, more as a syncretic compilation of beliefs and practices than as an organized religion. In Japan the syncretism combines Buddhism, Confucianism, and Shinto, the traditional belief system of the Japanese.

The next wave of a religious innovation occurs by 1000 CE. Islam, a monotheistic religion, progressed through Central Asia and then to South and Southeast Asia. Traders brought Islam to Malaysia and Indonesia by 1200 CE. Unlike the syncretism of Buddhism, Daoism, and Confucianism in East Asia, people in Southeast Asia practiced Islam or Buddhism exclusively.

The West brought the next wave of religious innovation by 1600 CE. With the power of colonial administration behind them, European missionaries made converts throughout Asia. Christian missions were particularly successful in the Philippines and also parts of Indonesia. South Korea and Taiwan have many Christian adherents.

The final wave was secularism. By 1950 Marxist atheism prevailed over traditional religions in China and North Korea (and to a lesser extent in Vietnam). Leaders in China today, particularly Communist Party members, are still required to be atheist. While technically there is freedom of religion in China, there is still a state control over religious practices, particularly for Islam, Tibetan Buddhism, and Christianity.

Religious innovation and diffusion shaped the complex diversity of East Asian peoples. The challenge today is how to retain the myriad cultural identities in Asia in the midst of globalized cultural forces. Japan, South Korea, Hong Kong, and Taiwan all have capitalist cultures that respond to global culture by making the global into the local. McDonald's restaurants are everywhere, but they take on a local flavor, offering soup and tea. As China has liberalized its economy, an urban popular culture with fast food, karaoke, and theme parks has blossomed. These Chinese versions are more similar to Korean or Japanese versions than to American. South Korea and Japan are heavy innovators of cell phone, Internet, and computer technology. Access to the Internet has developed in China as well, but Internet access is monitored by the state.

East Asian culture has also spread to other parts of the world. Even in small towns in Ohio one can find Chinese restaurants and karaoke. Chinese and Japanese movies are also available for video rentals, either dubbed or subtitled. Hong Kong has become one of the world's leading producers and distributors of films in the United States. Americans have begun to appreciate Chinese or Japanese culture through movies and food (Kristof and WuDunn 2000).

In the Pacific, cultural complexities vary from the aboriginal peoples of Australia to Maori culture in New Zealand. In Papua New Guinea a great variety of local languages are spoken as well as Pijin (Pidgin English), which utilizes English vocabularies with a Melanesian grammar. Traditional Polynesian culture developed class-based relationships between elites and other inhabitants. One note of distinction, almost half of Fiji's population is South Asian in origin so Hinduism is common there.

How does local culture interact with global culture? There are strong cultural variations from country to country. One model may be that of North Korea or Burma, both of which have resisted outside culture. Another model is that of Japan which has accommodated itself to global culture but on its own terms. Another example is the case of China, where there are distinct global influences, but at the same time there are marked Chinese influences in the rest of the world. Global cultural influences go from the US to China and back again (Borthwick 2014).

Economics

The impacts of Asian economies are felt worldwide. Japan is the economic leader in terms of **gross domestic product** per capita (GDP pc). The general metaphor for Asian development has been that of a goose flock

FIGURE 8.2 Agricultural activity in Southeast Asia focuses on rice production as shown here in Thailand. PHOTO: S. Andrus.

migrating. One goose is in the lead and the others follow the leader. Japan has been that economic leader. Close behind are Singapore, Taiwan, Hong Kong, and South Korea, often referred to as the **newly industrialized countries** (NICs). The third group is composed of countries like Thailand, Malaysia, and soon China. Indonesia is in the fourth group. Among poorer countries like Cambodia, various factors such as conflict have severely limited the possibilities for economic growth (Frank 1998). (See Table 8.2.)

While Asia is a center of business, many in Asia still work in the agricultural sector (see Figure 8.2). A traditional sector in Asia has been services. A strong segment in Asia has been industrial production including Japanese, Korean, and Chinese businesses. A newer sector that developed after World War II includes finance and high technology.

The countries have tried various methods for economic growth. Asian governments such as Japan, South Korea, and China have been actively involved in promoting export-led industrialization as a development strategy. Asia has an important role to play in the global economy, providing numerous exports as well as imports. Of the top twenty countries in exports, six are in Asia: China, Japan, South Korea, Singapore, Taiwan, and India. Hong Kong, a part of China, has exports equal to that of Singapore. The overall difficulty will be for all Asians to achieve economic satisfaction; at a local level in China, for example, there are still districts of poverty alongside high-tech districts. Global economic successes such as Japan and more recently China are set in the context against the economic difficulties of Cambodia.

In the Pacific, Australia and New Zealand have a developed economy based on the processing of primary products. In many of the other countries of the Pacific, a subsistence economy including shifting cultivation or fishing is maintained. Exports from other locations include nickel from New Caledonia, phosphates from Nauru, coconuts and fish from the Solomons. In Hawaii and French Polynesia, tourism is a significant portion of the economy (Patterson and Macintyre 2011).

POLITICS

East Asia has had two models of state formation since the 1950s. Japan in the aftermath of World War II became a democratic country, though more conservative than liberal. China in the aftermath of World War II and a civil war became a communist country under Chairman Mao (Figure 8.3). Through the twenty-first century, the rise of China's global power may mirror Japan's rise in the twentieth century. At a local level, political freedoms and human rights remain issues for countries such as China with its authoritarian regime. Recall that Taiwan, South Korea, and Japan also had strong authoritarian regimes before developing their democratic systems (Gamer 2012).

In Southeast Asia, current political tensions are strongly related to the colonial past. Singapore is a democracy but with a strong streak of paternalistic rule. Vietnam has a communist regime, while Burma is moving from a military dictatorship to a democracy. Thailand is a constitutional monarchy but the military had a bloodless coup in 2006–2007. Global dimensions of politics include the development of **ASEAN**, the Association of Southeast Asian Nations, a supranational organization that facilitates political cooperation in the region (Mackerras 1995).

The Pacific has a number of political facets. Many Pacific Island states became independent in the 1960s and 1970s. While many islands are

FIGURE 8.3 Tiananmen Square in Beijing. Chairman Mao's portrait is at the center. On the left, the banner says 10,000 years to the People's Republic of China. On the right, the banner reads 10,000 years to the great unity of the peoples of the world. PHOTO: S. Toops.

self-governing and independent, the United States and France as well as New Zealand control substantial territory. Indigenous land rights in Australia, New Zealand, and Hawaii are still problematic. The style of governance is democracy, with the exception of Tonga, which maintains a constitutional monarchy. According to the UN Convention of the Law of the Sea, territorial control extends 200 miles in an Exclusive Economic Zone. All of the islands then have economic rights including fishing and minerals over a large territory of ocean beyond their surface land. Many of the countries are members of the Pacific Islands Forum Secretariat that seeks to enhance political governance and security for the region.

The political tensions in Asia show twin tendencies. One is the authoritarian method. The other method takes into concern the aspirations of the people. In the modern world this tension is one of dictatorship or democracy. Asia has both, but the rising tide is toward democratic systems (Brower 2005).

SOCIAL ISSUES: DEMOGRAPHY

Two issues illustrate the challenges facing Asia in the twenty-first century. This section focuses on Asia's demographic dilemma. The next section uses the example of China to demonstrate Asian economic development.

One factor of the demographic dilemma is the level of population growth. The population of Northeast Asia is about 1.5–1.6 billion; however, growth rates are relatively low. Southeast Asia has a little over 630 million. In contrast, the Pacific Islands total about 36 million people.

Asia has sixty percent of the world population (see Table 8.1). China has over 1.3 billion people. In Asia both rural and urban densities are high especially on the Yangtze River in China. Strict family planning in China has led to a lower rate of population increase. Governments have made various choices to deal with population growth. China decided to limit the level of population growth by fiat: one child per family. Japan and South Korea have low rates of population increase as the result of modern economic development and urbanization.

In Southeast Asia, Thailand has low rates of population increase due to a heavily promoted government program of family planning. Indonesia has moderate levels of population increase; the issue here is one of transmigration as people move out of the center islands to the periphery. Singapore has a low level of population growth, so the government has embarked on a pro-natalist policy, encouraging people to have more children (Population Reference Bureau 2013). (See Figure 8.1.)

In the Pacific, there are two demographic clusters. Australia and New Zealand have larger populations characterized by low population growth rates, high urbanization rates, and a higher percentage of population over the age of 65. In contrast most of the other states of the Pacific have smaller populations, with high population growth rates, varying levels of urbanization, and lower percentages of the population over the age of 65.

Another demographic issue is the level of urbanization. Many people in Asia are moving from the countryside to the city. Cities are becoming quite large, including Beijing, Shanghai, Chongqing, Tokyo, Jakarta, and Manila. Overall the level of urbanization is lower in Southeast Asia than Northeast Asia. At the same time huge cities with populations over 1 million are common. A city of 200,000 is a small town. In contrast, Northeast Asia has a higher level of urbanization. Japan and South Korea are highly

FIGURE 8.4 Most people in Singapore live in huge housing complexes supported by the government. PHOTO: S. Toops.

urbanized (over 70 percent). Few people are engaged in farming in Japan and South Korea. In Southeast Asia most countries have primate cities, single large urban settlements that overshadow all others. Countries such as Thailand, the Philippines, and Indonesia are encouraging the growth of secondary cities. Singapore is essentially a city-state. Overall, planning for housing is a major issue in Asian cities (Karan 2004).

China's demographic predicament dwarfs that of the rest of East Asia. One way to solve a population problem is to produce more food. This was the method preferred by Mao. According to Mao, each stomach has two hands attached. The more people the better. Government policy was to keep subsistence ahead of population growth. Population growth rates approached 2.5 percent in 1957. The greatest demographic disaster in China was the famine resulting from the Great Leap Forward of 1958–1960, when 20–30 million people died due to poor harvests and poor planning. After the famine, birth rates soared and a baby boom in the mid-1960s increased population (Gamer 2012).

Between 1949 and 1976, China's population had nearly doubled. The country embarked on a policy of late marriages and fewer births. In Reform China, under **Deng Xiaoping**, pragmatism took hold. The government's policy of population control limited couples to one child. This policy was most effective in the cities, but in the countryside it had limited effect. In 2000 China's population growth rate was only 1 percent, an impressive feat for a developing country. Only through the centralized authoritarian government could such a policy work. By the 2000 census, most areas of China really had a two-child policy, except for the most overcrowded cities. A new policy in 2013 indicates that if one person in a couple is a single child, then the couple may have two children (Veeck et al. 2011).

Population control has been an important element of China's economic reform; without the limits on population, gains in the economy would not have registered. The impacts of population controls on society are strong. Within the space of a generation China has shrunk its family size. Families that now have one child in the city or two children in the country are the norm. This has raised two social issues. First, how does the Chinese family adapt to having only one or two children? All the aunts and uncles, grandmothers and grandfathers dote on that little girl or boy. Some have become quite spoiled; they are called "little emperors." Second, who will support the elderly? In traditional China, children and grandchildren supported the old (see Figure 8.5). In Maoist China, the state was responsible for retirees. In reform China, while the state looks after public-sector retirees, private-sector retirees are on their own.

Demographic issues pose major challenges for Asia. There is a strong need for economic improvement. Generally speaking, changes in the economic structure, from agricultural to industrial and services, lead to a greater urbanization. A demographic transition occurs with more people being urban than rural. However, a country with a large population faces greater stress in the system when moving from a rural agrarian system to an urban industrial system. One such country experiencing these challenges today is China.

FIGURE 8.5   This family in Shanghai has their future hope pinned on the success of their granddaughter. PHOTO: S. Toops.

ASIAN ECONOMIC SITUATION

Historical change within human communities has occurred as the people of a territory involve themselves in and interact with the world at large. After World War II the study of such change was generally restricted to economic growth; development was considered primarily a question of economic growth. Through the 1950s, this type of development meant the ability of a national economy to sustain an annual increase in GDP at 5 percent or more (Todaro and Smith 2009).

By the 1960s, some states in the Third World were meeting this over-all requirement, yet the standard of living for many people remained unchanged. To get at the real meaning of development meant to get beyond a single statistic, GDP, and include other variables. The definition of development continued to evolve. The development of a country was viewed by scholars as including not just economic growth but also as involving a decline of inequality, unemployment, and poverty (Seers 1969).

By the 1980s the term *development* expanded to include the achievement of political and cultural as well as social and economic goals, in short, the enrichment of the quality of human life. The good life is composed of three transcultural core values, or goals, held in common by all people. The first value is life sustenance, the provision of food, shelter, medicine, and protection to all people. The second value is self-esteem, a society's retention of dignity, worth, and respect in the midst of contact with a materially more prosperous society. The third value is freedom from servitude, an expanded range of choice, a reduction of dependence on nature, ignorance, misery, dogma, and other societies (Goulet 1985).

Without a consideration of the cultural and ethnic diversity in human community, without putting people in their development, our understanding of development is not complete. On a practical level, development projects may not achieve their expected fruition without including the human factor. Development "from below" approaches, with a further consideration of the cultural dimension, have added to the wholeness of development. "Culture, not economics, technology, or politics, is the primordial dimension in development" (Goulet 1985, 272). The twenty-first-century definition points toward an organic complexity of development that goes beyond a strictly economic measure. The United Nations Human Development Index utilizes **life expectancy,** income, and literacy in calculating development. **Sustainable development** seeks to balance economic growth, social equity, and environmental protection for the long term (Potter et al. 1999; Sen 2000; Todaro and Smith 2009; Rowntree et al. 2014).

The most common method for Asian economic growth has been export-led growth. Most Asian economies are capitalist-market-focused economies. Japan is a good example of an economy that conforms to market pressures and is the most developed country in Asia. The focus of Japan and South Korea has been big business; large corporations and most people have benefited from that development. Just as Japan and Indonesia have varieties of democracy, they also have varieties of capitalism. A contrasting example is that of China which has a mixed-market economy; there are still elements of a state-run sector.

In East Asia, the general model for economic growth has been one in which the state is heavily involved in setting goals and aims for the economy (very different from the US version of capitalism). In Japan, the government bureaucracy works in tandem with integrated corporations (*keiretsu*) to build the economy. South Korea has modeled itself on the Japanese system with large industrial conglomerates (*chaebol*). In both cases the countries have moved from exporting consumer products to heavy industry and then to high-tech goods and services. Both Japan and South Korea have built industrialized, urbanized economies (Borthwick 2014).

China has a different economic situation in that (1) the economy was totally controlled by the state until the 1980s and (2) the bulk of the population was in agriculture with industrial activity focused on heavy industry. With the economic reforms since the 1980s, the state has encouraged a new-style economy with extensive planning, combined with a market economy. This mixed-market economy has maintained high economic growth focusing on light industry. Labor is still relatively inexpensive, so China has been able to produce many consumer goods for export. Overall, the transition from agriculture to industry to services resembles the pattern established in Japan and South Korea, although state planning is still well entrenched in China.

Southeast Asia has a mix of economies. The legacy of British, Dutch, Spanish, and French colonial control held back economic development in Southeast Asia. Economically successful countries such as Singapore, Thailand, and Malaysia have followed programs of export led development, exporting consumer goods, similar to East Asia. Singapore is the financial hub of Southeast Asia. Indonesia with its focus on raw materials, oil, and timber has been less successful. Primary products such as oil and timber are exported to other countries such as Japan that derive the benefit from the raw materials. Vietnam, recovered economically from its civil wars, has recently been using a Chinese model of mixed-market economy. Economic difficulties are common in Cambodia and Laos as well as Burma, due to political conflicts and a lack of infrastructure. Globalized industrial production based in Southeast Asia—for example, the manufacture of DVD players or sports shoes—has meant a labor-intensive production with low wages. The countries outside of this globalization are not doing as well in terms of economic growth. However, the concern is that the low-wage character of these industrial jobs does not contribute to local development (Dixon 1991; Dayley and Neher 2013).

Leaders in terms of GDP per capita are Japan and then the NICs such as Singapore, Taiwan, and South Korea. All of these have had strong government intervention in the business sector: government bureaucracy plans economic development. Japan, Singapore, South Korea, and Taiwan are also leaders in terms of life expectancy and literacy. At the next level are the rising economies of Thailand and Malaysia. Thailand and Malaysia have production centers that feed into the global market for consumer goods. The next set of countries are the most populous, China and Indonesia. The large population is a major factor: how to provide for all. Another issue is that of regional development; these large countries have regions of economic growth as well as regions of economic stagnation. Real poverty is entrenched in North Korea and Burma, but that has more to do with past and current political regimes and conflicts rather than the availability of resources (Potter et al. 1999).

In addition to GDP per capita, other measures of development include more social variables. The ability to read and the overall health of the population are two indicators of social development. Japan is a leader in life expectancy and literacy. Levels of literacy above 90 percent are common in Northeast Asia and some Southeast countries (see Table 8.3). The current socialist countries have placed an emphasis on literacy. High life expectancies in Northeast Asia and some Southeast Asian countries such as Singapore and Thailand are good indicators of a better life. Countries such as Laos and Cambodia have low levels of life expectancy.

Regionally, a number of Pacific Rim counties in Asia and the Americas formed the Asia-Pacific Economic Cooperation (APEC) forum in 1989. Since then APEC seeks to promote free trade in the region. Asian members include China, Hong Kong, Japan, Taiwan, South Korea, Brunei, Indonesia, Malaysia, Philippines, Singapore, Thailand, and Vietnam. Pacific members include Australia, New Zealand, and Papua New Guinea. American members include Canada, Chile, Mexico, Peru, and the United States. Russia is also a member. India and other Asian countries as well as Costa Rica and Colombia have expressed interest in admission but the organization has limited its admissions since 1995.

In sum, whether measuring economic or social development, the Asian countries such as Japan, Singapore, the Republic of China (Taiwan), and South Korea rank high. Thailand and Malaysia are next followed by People's Republic of China. Oil states such as Brunei also rank well. Lower levels of development indicators in Laos, Cambodia, and Burma point to major difficulties.

Development and China

Why profile China to illustrate one type of economic development in Asia? The scale of China is one reason. China has 1.3 billion people in a territory the size of the United States; over 90 percent of the population is concentrated in the eastern half. China is a multicultural society, but only 8 percent of the population is not ethnic Chinese (Han). China's territory is the third largest in the world. One-fifth of humanity speaks Chinese.

The second reason to consider China is its recent rapid economic growth. New China embarked upon a period of reform in December 1978. The government calls this "socialism with Chinese characteristics" (Gamer 2012). The Chinese economy has had growth rates of 8 to 10 percent per annum since the 1980s, yet the per capita income is still low. China has the tenth-largest economy (measured in gross national product) and that economy is growing fast (Veeck et al. 2011).

The third reason is China's political and cultural role in the world. China is a major voice in world affairs, a permanent member of the UN Security Council; yet the state is an authoritarian regime controlled by the Chinese Communist Party. Chinese culture has responded to the forces of globalization. Chinese culture, food, and movies are readily available outside the country, while foreign cultures are readily visible in the urban centers of China (Gamer 2012).

In the Chinese zodiac, the dragon is also the symbol of a beginning. A dragon is part of the ceremony at the opening of a business. When the eyes of the dragon are dotted, the dragon awakes. And the new enterprise begins. Outsiders have also linked the imagery of China and the dragon. Napoleon (probably apocryphally) said "The dragon is asleep. Let it sleep. When it awakes the world will shake" (Croll 2006, 9). China is at the dawn of a new era, an era that some suggest will be a Pacific Century. Political events as well as economic realities draw the world's attention to China as a key link in Pacific Asia (Borthwick 2014).

The People's Republic of China came into being based on the peasantry. Agriculture remains a key part of the economy, especially since so many people are peasants. Under Mao, China's agricultural system rapidly changed. First, in the early 1950s through land reform, land confiscated from the landlords was given to the peasants. Then, in the mid-1950s land was worked collectively. In 1958, Mao Zedong set up the commune system as part of the Great Leap Forward. The scale of the commune, 8,000 to 80,000 people, covering large segments of farmland, structured this Maoist landscape. The focus of production was rice and wheat to the exclusion of all else. A common slogan was "take grain as the key link." The government used the surplus produced by the peasants to stimulate industrial activity. However, when crops began to fail in the late 1950s, the commune system was disorganized and many people died during the great famine (Spence 1999).

In the countryside, the change from Mao's policies came early in 1979 and took effect quickly. A return to family farming is a key feature of Deng Xiaoping's policies in Reform China. Families do not own the land, but they keep the right to work the land. The scale is different now—one family instead of 20,000, an acre instead of thousands. Production of most crops increased dramatically with the reforms. Grain is no longer the key link; vegetables, fruits, and other cash crops are preferred as farmers diversify. More machinery is in use. Surplus agricultural labor turns toward rural industry, construction, and transport. Farmers on the east coast have benefited most from the reforms.

China under Mao emphasized heavy industry. The industry program followed the Soviet Union, since the Communists under Mao had more experience with the countryside than the city. To strengthen industrial expansion the government targeted increases in coal, steel, and oil production. Steel was the key link. In the 1950s, China planned to build up its industrial structure. The Great Leap Forward was a crash course in industrialization. The government promoted industry and agriculture at all scales of development. Workers had an "iron rice bowl" that could not be broken; the state guaranteed the jobs. At the end of the Maoist era, China focused on heavy and large-scale industry controlled by the state. Theoretically, all regions were to develop equally. The north and northeast had the most developed industrial system (Borthwick 2014).

The reforms at the end of the 1970s meant much change in industry. The previous emphasis on heavy industry meant a shortage of consumer goods like bicycles or radios. Now light industry is more favored. Cities now have a variety of factories producing many goods for local, domestic, and foreign markets. The state still runs many of the heavy-industry factories, but light industry is often run by private entrepreneurs or with foreign interests. Light industry has a large domestic market and a strong export market; clothing and textiles are important products very visible in the stores in the United States. Retail trade has also picked up considerably with the reforms. The coastal region has performed well.

An important part of the reforms has been the boom in trade and services. China initially relied on the Soviet Union for trade, but by 1960 the country was following a policy of self-reliance. With the reforms under Deng, China embarked on an open-door policy. Now China seeks foreign investment and trade. Exports and imports are both important to the Chinese economy. Coastal cities have fared very well with the "open-door" policy. While trade and investments declined in 1989, the 1990s saw a strong resurgence. New elements of the Chinese economic landscape include the recent boom in telecommunications and tourism. Before the economic rise and the reforms, most Chinese did not have a telephone. In the coastal cities in particular, access to telephones, fax, microwave and satellite links, or fiber-optic cables has now tied China into the global economy in a brand new way. In the late 1970s China also opened its doors to international tourists. China's tourism suffered a decrease in 1989 as a result of publicity surrounding the Tiananmen Square protests but recovered through the 2000s (Gamer 2012).

The economy is at the heart of the reform in China. New railroads, new technology, new businesses, and new farming systems complete a picture of economic reform in China. The coastal region has reaped the benefits of reform. Hong Kong returned to China in 1997, bringing its vibrant market economy to China. The next step is for economic growth in the interior.

For China, the reform period's efforts at development are noteworthy. In China millions have been brought out of poverty. From a basic definition of development, in China there is economic growth and less poverty (Seers 1977). With the continuation of China's changing economic reforms, many have been left unemployed, as the state sector has restructured. Inequalities are arising as well (all were equal under Communism, although some were more equal than others). The basic needs of people in China have been met. Life sustenance in China is still a major issue for the poor, who, like those in the United States (Black Hills, Appalachia, Deep South) are primarily agricultural, tilling poor soil, and far from markets. Of course the United States, and now China, has urban poor as well. In China, as in the United States, minority ethnic groups are relatively poorer compared to the more populous and powerful elements of society. Beyond life sustenance, two elements of a broader conception of development—self-esteem and freedom—are rather more difficult to achieve (Goulet 1985; Sen 2000). Self-esteem and freedom are goals all over the world, not just in China or Asia.

Perhaps China's biggest challenge in the twenty-first century is to reconcile its rapid economic development with an authoritarian regime whose ideology is bankrupt and its legitimacy questioned. In contemporary Reform China, the "expert" of technology and management has replaced the "red" of politics. Deng, a key member of the Party since the 1920s, had long been an advocate of the expert in guiding China. For Reform China the new goal is the transformation of China into a socialist market economy, combining good elements of both communism and capitalism. According to Deng, "If a cat catches mice, what does it matter if it's black or white?" This pragmatism of Deng has been a hallmark of China's reform. The leaders after Deng Xiaoping have followed in his footsteps. In early 1989 students, intellectuals, and workers joined a pro-democracy movement to redress political problems of China, calling for universal freedom. The pro-democracy movement occupied Tiananmen Square in April 1989. The government responded with a violent repression under martial law on the night of June 3, 1989. The dawn of June Fourth showed thousands killed by tanks and troops. Tiananmen Square was the site of a massacre; the army under the leadership of the Party had killed Chinese people. Twenty-five years have passed, but the memory lingers (Gamer 2012).

The new leader of China, Xi Jinping, assumed Communist Party leadership in 2012 and rose to president of the People's Republic of China (PRC) in 2013. He has called for renewed efforts to boost the economy, rein in corruption, and consolidate political control of China. The new slogan in China is "achieve the Chinese dream," which alludes both to individual self-improvement and the revitalization of the nation. In 2013 and 2014, the government of the PRC reinvigorated its sea power and air power over the South China Sea and the East China Sea. The PRC has territorial disputes over islands with Japan and the Republic of China (on Taiwan) in the East China Sea. The South China Sea dispute with Vietnam, the Philippines, Malaysia, Brunei, and Indonesia is over the Spratly and Paracel Islands. These geopolitical disputes with surrounding countries point to a rising China in Asia. Finally, the PRC landed a rover on the moon in 2013. The rover, named Jade Rabbit (Yutu), after a Chinese mythological figure, paves the way for a future manned mission to the moon (Long 2013; Elleman et al. 2013; Huang and Patman 2013; "Reaching for the Moon" 2013).

The Great Wall of China is a symbol of Chinese power. But the Wall also represents the spirit and labor of the Chinese people. The fact that the Great Wall is now on a credit card in China is emblematic of the serious challenge facing the present Chinese government to maintain its position as the economic and political power of the people grows (Gamer 2012). China is an important player in the twenty-first century.

THE ROLE OF EAST ASIA IN THE WORLD

Asia is poised to play a significant role in the global order in the twenty-first century. Asia was the center of the world economically until the 1500s and the rise of Europe. After World War II, the United States and the USSR contended for global domination. While the United States is currently the most powerful state, Europe and Asia are also formidable entities, precisely because they are not continents led by just one state. China is the strongest power in East Asia. With its long history, rising economy, large population, diverse cultures, and compelling politics, China is a model for the developing world and is on the cusp of entering the developed world. The political weight of Northeast Asia and the economic growth of Southeast Asia are both a part of Asia's future.

Historical ties of Asia with the Americas, Africa, Europe, and the Middle East foreshadow developments in the twentieth century. In ancient times, Asia was connected to Europe and to the Middle East through trade and migration. (One can argue that Europe and the Middle East are historical offshoots of Asia.) The overland trading routes of the Silk Road connected China and India to the Mediterranean. The Silk Road was a crossroads for cultural and economic communication between East and West. Trade from China reached Africa in the Middle Ages. With European colonialism the direction of the flows began to change. Control of the flows also shifted from Asian to European hands. Spanish trading ships in the 1500s linked Asia with the Americas. Labor flows brought Asians to the Americas as well (Chinese and Japanese). During the twentieth century as colonialism was lifted, Asia shifted from European imperial control to new nation-states.

Asia's global connections have become stronger in this early segment of the twenty-first century. Descendants of Asian migrants were already vital components of communities around the world. Chinese in Australia, the United States, and Canada; Filipinos in the United States; Vietnamese in France; and Indonesians in the Netherlands are all examples of the migration of Asians around the world. Part of the process includes colonialism, but it also includes globalization as skilled engineers and scientists seek employment in the world high-tech centers. California and New York have both become melting pots with the advent of Asian immigrants.

Cultural transfusion comes with the Asian immigrants. Beyond the immigrants themselves, cultural components of life such as religion, film, and food enter the global medium. Films from China, Japan, South Korea, and Hong Kong bring enjoyment throughout the world. Ang Lee's *Crouching Tiger, Hidden Dragon* (2000) began the twenty-first century by filming in China with a starring cast from Hong Kong, Malaysia, China, and Taiwan, a director from Taiwan, writers from Taiwan, China, and the United States, and a global market. The 2006 US blockbuster, *The Departed*, was modeled on a 2002 Hong Kong action picture, *Infernal Affairs*. Clint Eastwood's 2006 *Letters from Iwo Jima* was in Japanese with Japanese actors. With these two films, Hollywood is making Asian movies. Chinese tai chi, and Korean taekwondo are all popular in the West. Most towns in the United States have Chinese restaurants and many have Japanese or Thai restaurants as well. Elements of East Asian culture are known and recognized worldwide.

Economic networks link countries and businesses. Japanese firms such as Toyota, Sanyo, and Nissan, and Korean firms such as Hyundai, Samsung, LG, and Kia, are recognizable to Western ears. Large Chinese firms such as Lenovo, Haier, and Alibaba, and Taiwanese firms such as Acer, Giant, and Tingyi are also moving on the market. Products range from electronic goods, software, IT, automobiles, and bicycles to noodles. Asian firms have markets globally, including China's push to Africa as well as Latin America. Global transnational corporations are also heavily invested in Asia. Asia offers a large skilled workforce as well as large market. So both production and consumption in Asia attract the global economy.

Political power and security issues also point toward the Asian connection. China is a permanent member of the UN Security Council and as such has veto power as do Russia, the United Kingdom, France, and the United States. Considerations of expanding the UN Security Council include discussion of India and Japan as possible members. The current UN secretary general is Ban Ki-moon from South Korea, so Asia has an important presence at the United Nations. China has nuclear weapons, and North Korea has tested nuclear weapons. In political and security terms, Asia is a significant component of the global system.

East Asia is globally connected. Global transnational corporations have their production centers in Asia. Asian markets are also key constituents of global consumption. Asian companies have markets in the United States, Europe, Latin America, and the Middle East. Middle East oil is a valuable commodity to Asia. Asian trade is critical to Europe, Africa, and the Americas. Asians are knowledgeable not only in the global language of business, but also of diplomacy. Asian political connections link the countries to the Americas in particular through the Asia Pacific Economic Cooperation forum, which includes all countries of the Pacific Rim. Asian countries were linked with Africa during the 1955 Bandung conference of nonaligned states. The Group of 77 now includes some 130 Asian, African, Latin American, and Middle Eastern countries who work jointly to promote their interests in the United Nations. South-South communication and cooperation for development is a key part of the Group of 77's mission.

International studies, as a discipline, examines East Asia's global connections around the world. For example, East Asia's trading connections are, of course, part of the global economic transaction. From an international studies perspective, East Asian trade has political, historical, geographic, sociological, and anthropological components. For a company, how to best market its wares in Asia depends on what country and culture it is connecting to. US political relations affect US trade with Japan and China. The spatial and temporal rhythms of trade bring in the geographical and historical components.

Beijing hosted the 2008 Olympics and has made its mark on the world just as Seoul and Tokyo did with their 1988 and 1964 Olympics, respectively. South Korea will host the winter Olympics in 2018. Market economic reforms, law-based governments, open access to technology, environmentally friendly societies, and cultural pluralism are components to a positive Asian-Pacific future. Flexibility, discipline, and drive are keys to that future.

TIMELINE OF TWENTIETH-CENTURY EAST ASIAN–PACIFIC HISTORY

1900	Boxer Rebellion in China.
1901	Australia independence.
1905	Japan annexation of Korea.
1911	Fall of Chinese Empire.
1912	Chinese Nationalist Party formed.
1921	Chinese Communist Party formed.
1931	Japanese invasion of Manchuria.
1932	Japan withdraws from League of Nations.
1934	"Long March" of Chinese Communists.

1937–1945	Sino-Japanese War (WWII in Asia).
1940	Japanese conquest of Indochina.
1941	Japan attacks US (Hawaii, Philippines) and British territories (Malaya, Singapore).
1942–1945	Pacific theater of World War II.
1945	Atomic bombs dropped on Hiroshima and Nagasaki; Japan surrenders.
1945	Partition of Korea.
1946	Philippine independence.
1947	New Zealand independence.
1945–1949	Civil war in China.
1946–1954	French colonial war in Indochina.
1946–1949	Dutch colonial war in East Indies.
1949	People's Republic of China on mainland, Republic of China on Taiwan.
1950	Formation of Vietnam, Cambodia, and Laos.
1950	Sukarno president of Indonesia.
1950–1953	Korean War.
1950	Chinese conquest of Tibet.
1954	French withdraw from Indochina.
1955	Creation of North and South Vietnam.
1955	Bandung Conference of non-aligned states.
1956	Japanese economic boom.
1959–1971	Tibetan revolt.
1959	Dalai Lama flees to India.
1958–1960	China's Great Leap Forward.
1962	Samoa independence.
1963	US military aid to South Vietnam.
1964	Tokyo Olympics.
1965	US military intervention in Vietnam.
1965	Singapore forms independent state.
1966	Suharto rules Indonesia.
1966–1975	China's Cultural Revolution.
1970	Fiji independence.
1973	US troops withdraw from Vietnam.
1975	Papua New Guinea independence.
1975	Chairman Mao dies.

1975	Communist conquest of South Vietnam and Cambodia.
1978	End of collective farms in China.
1980	Deng Xiaoping leads China's economic boom.
1981	One-child policy in China.
1988	Seoul Olympics.
1989	Tiananmen Square incident in China, suppression of democracy movement.
1989	Formation of Asia-Pacific Economic Cooperation (APEC).
1997	Deng Xiaoping dies.
1997	Asian financial crisis.
1997	Britain returns Hong Kong to China's control.
2004	Indian Ocean Tsunami.
2008	Sichuan earthquake in China.
2008	Beijing Olympics.
2011	New Zealand earthquake.
2011	Japan earthquake and tsunami.
2011	Burma forms new, nominally civilian government.
2013	Hurricane Haiyan devastates Philippines.
2013	Xi Jinping new president of People's Republic of China.
2013	Reform of China's one-child policy.

Table 8.1 Population and Rate of Growth

Country	Population	RNI%	Country	Population	RNI%
Southeast Asia:			**Northeast Asia:**		
Brunei	415,717	1.67	Japan	127,253,075	−0.10
Cambodia	15,205,539	1.67	North Korea	24,720,407	0.53
East Timor	1,172,390	2.47	South Korea	48,955,203	0.18
Indonesia	251,160,124	0.99	Republic of China	23,299,716	0.27
Laos	6,695,166	1.63	People's Republic of China	1,349,585,838	0.46
Malaysia	29,628,392	1.51			
Myanmar (Burma)	55,167,330	1.05			
Papua New Guinea	6,431,902	1.89			
Philippines	105,720,644	1.84			
Singapore	5,460,302	1.96			
Thailand	67,448,120	0.52			
Vietnam	92,477,857	1.03			

This chart shows the population and rate of population growth among the countries of Southeast and Northeast Asia.

SOURCE: *CIA World Factbook 2013*

Table 8.2 Gross Domestic Product and GDP Real Growth

Country	GDPpc	GDP real growth	Country	GDPpc	GDP real growth
Southeast Asia:			Northeast Asia:		
Brunei	$55,300	1.3%	Japan	$36,900	2.0%
Cambodia	$2,400	6.50%	North Korea	$1,800	0.8%
East Timor	$10,000	10.0%	South Korea	$32,800	2.0%
Indonesia	$5,100	6.2%	Republic of China	$39,400	1.3%
Laos	$3,100	8.3%	People's Republic of China	$9,300	7.8%
Malaysia	$17,200	5.6%			
Myanmar (Burma)	$1,400	6.3%			
Papua New Guinea	$2,800	9.1%			
Philippines	$4,500	6.6%			
Singapore	$61,400	1.3%			
Thailand	$10,300	6.4%			
Vietnam	$3,600	5.0%			

This chart shows the GDP per capita and rate of GDPpc real growth among the countries of Southeast and Northeast Asia.

SOURCE: *CIA World Factbook 2013*

Table 8.3 Literacy Rates and Life Expectancy

Country	Literacy	LE-years	Country	Literacy	LE-years
Southeast Asia:			**Northeast Asia:**		
Brunei	95%	77	Japan	99%	84
Cambodia	74%	63	North Korea	100%	70
East Timor	58%	68	South Korea	98%	80
Indonesia	93%	72	Republic of China	96%	80
Laos	73%	63	People's Republic of China	95%	75
Malaysia	93%	74			
Myanmar (Burma)	93%	66			
Papua New Guinea	62%	67			
Philippines	95%	72			
Singapore	96%	84			
Thailand	94%	74			
Vietnam	93%	73			

This chart shows the Literacy Rates and Life Expectancy (In Years) among the countries of Southeast and Northeast Asia.

SOURCE: *CIA World Factbook 2013*

Table 8.4 Major Religions

Country	Religion
Southeast Asia:	
Brunei	Muslim 67%, Buddhist 13%, Christian 10%, other 10%
Cambodia	Buddhist 96%, Muslim 2%, other 2%
East Timor	Roman Catholic 98%, Muslim 1%, Protestant 1%
Indonesia	Muslim 86%, Protestant 6%, Roman Catholic 3%, Hindu 2%, other 3%
Laos	Buddhist 67%, other and unspecified 33%
Malaysia	Muslim 60%, Buddhist 19%, Christian 9%, Hindu 6%, traditional Chinese 3%, other 2%
Myanmar (Burma)	Buddhist 89%, Christian 4%, Muslim 4%, Animist 1%, other 2%
Papua New Guinea	Roman Catholic 27%, Protestant 69%, indigenous beliefs 3%
Philippines	Roman Catholic 83%, Muslim 5%, other Christian 10%, other 2%
Singapore	Buddhist 43%, Muslim 15%, Taoist 9%, Hindu 4%, Catholic 5%, other Christian 10%, other 15%
Thailand	Buddhist 95%, Muslim 5%
Vietnam	Buddhist 9%, Catholic 7%, Hoa Hao 1%, Cao Dai 1%, none 81%
Northeast Asia:	
Japan	Shintoism 84%, Buddhism 7%, Christianity 2%, other 8%
North Korea (DPRK)	traditionally Buddhist and Confucianist, mostly atheist
South Korea (ROK)	Christian 32%, Buddhist 24%, other or unknown 1%, none 43%
Republic of China (ROC)	mixture of Buddhist and Taoist 93%, Christian 4%, other 3%
People's Republic of China (PRC)	Atheist (officially), Daoist (Taoist) 1%, Buddhist 18%, Christian 5%, Muslim 2%

This chart shows the types of religions among the countries of Northeast and Southeast Asia.

SOURCE: *CIA World Factbook 2013*

238

Table 8.5 Type of Government

Country	Government
Southeast Asia:	
Brunei	Constitutional sultanate
Cambodia	Multiparty democracy under a constitutional monarchy
East Timor	Republic
Indonesia	Republic
Laos	Communist state
Malaysia	Constitutional monarchy
Myanmar (Burma)	Parliamentary government
Papua New Guinea	Constitutional parliamentary democracy
Philippines	Republic
Singapore	Parliamentary republic
Thailand	Constitutional monarchy
Vietnam	Communist state
Northeast Asia:	
Japan	Constitutional monarchy with parliamentary government
North Korea (DPRK)	Communist state, dictatorship
South Korea (ROK)	Republic
Republic of China (ROC)	Multiparty democracy
People's Republic of China (PRC)	Communist state

This chart shows the form of government among the countries of Northeast and Southeast Asia.

SOURCE: *CIA World Factbook 2013*

Table 8.6 Population and Rate of Growth

Country	Population	RNI%	Country	Population	RNI%
Australia	22,262,501	1.11	**Micronesia Region:**		
New Zealand	4,365,113	0.85	Federated States of Micronesia	106,104	−0.38
			Guam (US)	160,378	1.34
Melanesia Region:			Kiribati	103,248	1.21
Fiji	896,758	0.73	Marshalls	69,747	1.79
New Caledonia (France)	264,022	1.45	Nauru	9,434	0.58
Papua New Guinea	6,431,902	1.89	Northern Marianas (US)	51,170	0.09
Solomons	597,248	2.12			
Vanuatu	261,565	2.06	**Polynesia Region:**		
			American Samoa (US)	54,719	−0.40
			Cook Islands	10,447	−3.07
			French Polynesia (France)	277,293	1.00
			Samoa	195,476	0.59
			Tonga	106,322	0.14

This chart shows the population and rate of population growth among the Pacific countries.

SOURCE: *CIA World Factbook 2013*

240

Table 8.7 Gross Domestic Product and GDP Real Growth

Country	GDPpc	GDP real growth	Country	GDPpc	GDP real growth
Australia	$43,300	3.6%	**Micronesia Region:**		
New Zealand	$30,200	2.5%	Federated States of Micronesia	$7,500	1.4%
			Kiribati	$6,100	2.5%
Melanesia Region:			Marshalls	$8,800	1.9%
Fiji	$4,900	2.1%	Nauru	$5,000	NA
New Caledonia (France)	$37,700	0.6%	Northern Marianas (US)	$13,600	NA
Papua New Guinea	$2,800	9.1%			
Solomons	$3,400	5.5%	**Polynesia Region:**		
Vanuatu	$5,000	2.7%	American Samoa (US)	$8,000	3.0%
			Cook Islands	$9,100	0.1%
			French Polynesia (France)	$22,000	−0.4%
			Samoa	$6,300	1.2%
			Tonga	$7,700	1.4%

This chart shows the GDP per capita and rate of GDPpc real growth among the Pacific countries

SOURCE: *CIA World Factbook 2013*

Table 8.8 Literacy Rates and Life Expectancy

Country	Literacy	LE-years	Country	Literacy	LE-years
Australia	99%	82	**Micronesia Region:**		
New Zealand	99%	81	Federated States of Micronesia	89%	72
			Guam (US)	99%	79
Melanesia Region:			Kiribati	NA	65
Fiji	94%	72	Marshalls	94%	72
New Caledonia (France)	96%	77	Nauru	NA	66
Papua New Guinea	62%	67	Northern Marianas (US)	97%	77
Solomons	84%	75			
Vanuatu	83%	72	**Polynesia Region:**		
			American Samoa (US)	97%	75
			Cook Islands	95%	75
			French Polynesia (France)	98%	77
			Samoa	99%	73
			Tonga	99%	76

This chart shows the Literarcy Rates and Life Expectancy (in years) among the Pacific countries.

SOURCE: *CIA World Factbook 2013*

242

Table 8.9 Major Religions

Country	Religion
Australia	Protestant 27%, Catholic 26%, other Christian 10%, other 36%
New Zealand	Protestant 39%, Roman Catholic 13%, other 16%, none 32%, unidentified 10%

Melanesia Region:

Country	Religion
Fiji	Protestant 55%, Hindu 28%, Roman Catholic 9%, Muslim 6%, other 1%
New Caledonia (France)	Roman Catholic 60%, Protestant 30%, other 10%
Papua New Guinea	Roman Catholic 27%, Protestant 69%, other 4%
Solomons	Protestant 74%, Roman Catholic 19%, other Christian 4%, other 3%
Vanuatu	Protestant 56%, Roman Catholic 13%, other Christian 14%, other 18%

Micronesia Region:

Country	Religion
Federated States of Micronesia	Roman Catholic 53%, Protestant 42%, other 5%
Guam (US)	Roman Catholic 85%, other 15%
Kiribati	Roman Catholic 55%, Protestant 36%, Mormon 3%, other 6%
Marshalls	Protestant 55%, Roman Catholic 8%, other Christian 34%, other 2%
Nauru	Protestant 46%, Roman Catholic 33%, other 21%
Northern Marianas (US)	Christian

Polynesia Region:

Country	Religion
American Samoa (US)	Protestant 80%, Roman Catholic 20%
Cook Islands	Protestant 70%, Roman Catholic 17%, Mormon 4%, other 10%
French Polynesia	Protestant 54%, Roman Catholic 30%, other 10%, no religion 6%
Samoa	Protestant 60%, Roman Catholic 20%, other Christian 18%, other 2%
Tonga	Christian

This chart shows the types of major religions among the Pacific countries.

SOURCE: *CIA World Factbook 2013*

Table 8.10 Type of Government

Country	Government
Australia	Federal parliamentary democracy
New Zealand	Parliamentary democracy

Melanesia Region:

Fiji	Republic
New Caledonia (France)	French territory
Papua New Guinea	Constitutional parliamentary democracy
Solomons	Parliamentary democracy
Vanuatu	Parliamentary republic

Micronesia Region:

Federated States of Micronesia	Constitutional government
Guam (US)	US territory
Kiribati	Republic
Marshalls	Constitutional government
Nauru	Republic
Northern Marianas (US)	Commonwealth; self-government

Polynesia Region:

American Samoa (US)	US territory
Cook Islands	Self-government, parliamentary democracy
French Polynesia (France)	French territory
Samoa	Parliamentary democracy
Tonga	Constitutional monarchy

This chart shows the form of government among Pacific countries.

SOURCE: *CIA World Factbook 2013*

References

Borthwick, M. 2014. *Pacific Century*. Boulder, CO: Westview Press.

Brower, D. 2005. *The World in the Twentieth-Century*. 6th ed. Upper Saddle River, NJ: Prentice Hall.

Clayre, A. 1986. *The Heart of the Dragon*. New York: Houghton-Mifflin.

Croll, E. 2006. *China's New Consumers: Social Development and Domestic Demand*. London: Routledge.

Dayley, Robert, and Clark D. Neher. 2013. *Southeast Asia in the New International Era*. Boulder, CO: Westview Press.

Dixon, C. 1991. *Southeast Asia in the World Economy*. Cambridge: Cambridge University Press.

Elleman, Bruce A., Stephen Kotkin, and Clive H. Schofield. 2013. *Beijing's Power and China's Borders: Twenty Neighbors in Asia*. Armonk, NY: M. E. Sharpe.

Fairbank, J., E. Reishchauer, and A.Craig. 1989. *East Asia: Tradition and Transformation*. Boston: Houghon-Mifflin.

Frank, A. G. 1998. *Reorient: Global Economy in the Asian Age*. Berkeley: University of California Press.

Friend, T. 2003. *Indonesian Destinies*. Cambridge, MA: Harvard.

Gamer, R., ed. 2012. *Understanding Contemporary China*. Boulder, CO: Lynne Rienner.

Goulet, Denis. 1985. *The Cruel Choice: A New Concept in the Theory of Development*. Lanham, MD: University Press of America.

Huang, Xiaoming, and Robert Patman, eds. 2013. *China and the International System*. New York: Routledge.

Karan, P. P. 2004. *The Non-Western World*. New York: Routledge.

Kristof, N., and S. WuDunn. 2000. *Thunder from the East: Portrait of a Rising Asia*. New York: Knopf.

Long, Simon. 2013. "A Long Winter." *The Economist: The World in 2014*, 59.

Mackerras, Colin, ed. 1995. *East and Southeast Asia*. Boulder, CO: Lynne Reinner.

McKnight, T. 1995. *Oceania: The Geography of Australia, New Zealand, and the Pacific Islands*. Upper Saddle River, NJ: Prentice Hall.

Meier, G. M., and J. E. Stiglitz, eds. 2001. *Frontiers of Development Economics: The Future in Perspective*. Washington, DC: World Bank/Oxford University Press.

Patterson, Mary, and Martha Macintyre. 2011. *Managing Modernity in the Western Pacific*. St Lucia, Australia: University of Queensland Press.

Population Reference Bureau. 2013. *World Population Data Sheet 2013*. Washington DC.

Potter, R., et al. 1999. *Geographies of Development*. Harlow, UK: Pearson Education.

Reischauer, E. 1995. *The Japanese Today*. Cambridge, MA: Harvard.

"Reaching for the Moon," 2013. *The Economist* (December 21): 68–69.

Rowntree, L., et al. 2014. *Globalization and Diversity*. Upper Saddle River, NJ: Prentice Hall.

Sen, Amartya Kumar. 2000. *Development as Freedom*. New York: Anchor Books.

Seers, Dudley. 1969. "The Meaning of Development." *International Development Review*, 9 (4) 2–6.

_____. 1977. "The Meaning of Development." *International Development Review*, 17 (3) 2–7.

Spence, J. 1999. *The Search for Modern China*. New York: Norton.

Todaro, M. P., and S. C. Smith. 2009. *Economic Development*. 10th ed. Boston: Addison Wesley.

Veeck, Gregory, Clifton W. Pannell, Christopher J. Smith, and Youqin Huang. 2011. *China's Geography: Globalization and the Dynamics of Political, Economic, and Social Change*. 2nd ed. Lanham, MD: Rowan and Littlefield.

Further Reading

Chang, Jung, 1991. *Wild Swans: Three Daughters of China*. New York: Simon & Schuster.

Diamond, Jared M. 2005. *Collapse: How Societies Choose to Fail or Succeed*. New York: Viking.

Gifford, Rob. 2007. *China Road: A Journey into the Future of a Rising Power*. New York: Random House.

Schell, Orville, and John Delury. 2013. *Wealth and Power: China's Long March to the Twenty-First Century*. New York: Random House.

Wasserstrom, Jeffrey N. 2010. *China in the 21st Century: What Everyone Needs to Know*. New York: Oxford University Press.

Weightman, Barbara. 2011. *Dragons and Tigers: A Geography of South, East, and Southeast Asia*. Hoboken NJ: John Wiley.

Zha, Jianying. 2011. *Tide Players: The Movers and Shakers of a Rising China*. New York: New Press.

Journals

Asian Affairs
China Quarterly
East Asia: An International Quarterly
Journal of Southeast Asian Studies
The Pacific Review

Films

Crouching Tiger, Hidden Dragon (2000). Ang Lee, Director. Sony Pictures Classics and Columbia Pictures Film Production Asia (China).

Infernal Affairs (2002). Andrew Lau, producer. Andrew Lau & Alan Max, directors. Miramax Films, Media Asia Films presents a Basic Pictures production (Hong Kong).

Letters from Iwo Jima (2006). Clint Eastwood, director. Warner Home Video.

Pacific Century (1992). Written and produced by Alex Gibney, directed by Christopher Ralling. A co-production of PBI/Jigsaw Productions in association with NHK-Japan, KCTS/Seattle, and Antelope Films, Ltd. S. Burlington, VT: Annenberg/CPB Project,

Sunset at Chaopraya (1996). Euthana Mukdasanit, director (Thailand).

Websites

Asia Society. http://www.asiasociety.org/
Asia-Pacific Economic Cooperation. http://www.apec.org/
Association of Southeast Asian Nations http://www.asean.org/
UN Economic and Social Commission for Asia and the Pacfic http://www.unescap .org/
Virtual Library Asian Studies. http://vlib.org/AsianStudies

9

South and Central Asia and International Studies

Environment and Population

Long ago we made a tryst with destiny, and now the time comes
when we shall redeem our pledge, not wholly or in full measure,
but very substantially . . . a moment comes, which comes but rarely
in history, when we step out from the old to the new, when an age
ends, and when the soul of nation, long suppressed, finds utterance.
—*Jawaharlal Nehru, 1947*

Victory attained by violence is tantamount to a defeat, for it is
momentary.
—*Mohandas Gandhi, 1919*

INTRODUCTION:
WHY STUDY SOUTH AND CENTRAL ASIA?

The significance of **South** and **Central Asia** lies in their historical challenges, geographical realities, political risks, cultural complexities, and economic possibilities. First is the long history associated with South and Central Asia. Five thousand years ago, the Harappan civilization flourished along the Indus valley. Along with China, Mesopotamia, and Egypt, these are generally considered the beginnings of civilization. The roots of today's societies in South Asia lie in this Indus Valley Civilization. South and Central Asia will occupy a significant presence in our twenty-first-century world.

Second is the major geographic scale of South and Central Asia. The region accounts for 25 percent of the world's population. Three very large countries populate the region: India has over 1.2 billion people, Pakistan has 193 million, and Bangladesh 164 million. By 2050 India will surpass China as the world's most populous country. In terms of the environment, the region varies from the world's highest mountain range of the Himalayas, the tropics of Sri Lanka, to the landlocked deserts of Uzbekistan. The summer monsoon brings life-giving rain to much of South Asia.

Third is the cultural complexity of South and Central Asia. **Hinduism** and **Buddhism** originated in South Asia and **Islam** came to the region by the Middle Ages. Today Islam predominates in Central Asia, Pakistan, and Bangladesh, while Hinduism is most common in India, and Buddhism in Sri Lanka and Mongolia. In terms of language, Hindi and other north Indian languages vary considerably from the Dravidian languages of South India. Turkic languages include Kazakh, Uzbek, and Kyrgyz. Tajik is related to Persian. Urdu in Pakistan is like Hindi but is written in a modified Persian script. Global forces have changed the cultures in South and Central Asia since ancient times, and they continue to do so through the Internet or satellite television.

Fourth is the growing economic power of South Asia. India is a rising economic star, and yet overall per capita income is not so high. Many goods and services are produced, consumed, and transferred in South Asia. Indian companies play a major role in the global economy. India is one of the "Big Four" (Brazil, Russia, India, and China, or BRIC) countries that have jump-started their economies. With the exception of Kazakhstan and its oil economy, Central Asia is relatively poor.

Fifth, the political significance of South and Central Asia is seen in the world's largest democracy of India, the nuclear power of India and Pakistan, the independence of Central Asian countries from the Soviet Union in 1991, and the ongoing presence of al Qaeda and the Taliban in Afghanistan and Pakistan. India is trying to gain a permanent seat in the UN Security Council. In terms of political power, South Asia does not yet reach the levels of East Asia, but the region includes the nuclear powers of India and Pakistan. Many countries in the region have ambitions for regional and even global leadership.

This chapter begins with a discussion of the regional character of South and Central Asia, considering geographic, political, historical, cultural, and economic relations. An interlude on the Silk Road links historical and contemporary realties. The next section examines population and environment in the region focusing on India, a rising power in South Asia. The chapter closes with a discussion of global connections of South and Central Asia in the twenty-first century.

How Is South Asia Connected to the West?

From culture to history, polity to economics, multiple connections link South Asia to the West. The languages of North India such as Hindi are Indo-European languages. The scripts are very different from the Roman-derived scripts of most European languages, but many basic words are historically related. For example "mother" is *matr* and "father" is *pitr* in Hindi. Relations between the West and India date back to Alexander the Great, who extended his conquest to the Indus and the Ganges in 326 BCE. Of course the colonial connections of the British make this part of Asia especially familiar to the English-speaking world. There are many words in English of Indian origin including *pajama, cot, bungalow, loot, khaki, shampoo, guru, curry,* and *cummerbund.* Leaders of nonviolence movements such as Dr. Martin Luther King Jr. studied the tactics of Indian independence leader Gandhi. Gandhi's philosophy was *satyaghra,* "grasping truth." India is the world's largest democracy. And technology links India and the West through call centers such as that featured in the hit film *Slumdog Millionaire.*

GEOGRAPHICAL REALITIES

Regions of Asia include Northeast Asia and Southeast Asia (profiled in the previous chapter) and South and Central Asia (profiled in this chapter). These regions can overlap; for example, Central Asia is often categorized with the Middle East. Straddling the two regions is Afghanistan, sometimes considered part of Central Asia and sometimes as part of South Asia. Because Pakistan is a Muslim-majority state playing a significant role in the US-sponsored "war on terror," the country is sometimes included in definitions of Central Asia (Karan 2004; Weightman 2011).

FIGURE 9.1 Pakistan. The Gilgit River (left) flows into the Indus River. The author is in the foreground. PHOTO: S. Toops.

South Asia includes India, Pakistan, Bangladesh, Nepal, Sri Lanka, and two small states, Bhutan and Maldives. India is the largest and strongest of the countries in this region. Both Pakistan and Bangladesh were once part of the Indian empire. The dominant religions are Hinduism in India and Nepal, Islam in Pakistan and Bangladesh, and Buddhism in Sri Lanka. India is the strongest political power in the region. Its rival Pakistan is also a regional political power, and both have nuclear weapons. The historical center is the Indus River; today's center of activity is the Ganges River (Figure 9.1). Most South Asian countries have two-tiered economies. Well-developed, technologically sophisticated economies exist alongside subsistence agriculture (French 1997; Wolpert 2004).

Central Asia is a landlocked region that emerged from Soviet control after the breakup of the Soviet Union in 1991. Uzbekistan, Turkmenistan, Kazakhstan, Kyrgyzstan, and Tajikistan were former Soviet Republics. There was also strong Soviet influence in Mongolia and a Soviet presence in Afghanistan. Western China (Tibet and Xinjiang) is also a part of this region. All of the countries in this region except Mongolia (Buddhist) are Muslim and have been so since the 900s. In ethnic terms, most of their peoples are Turkic, relatives of the Turks in today's Turkey. The Mongols, Tajiks, Tibetans, and some Afghan peoples are distinct ethnic groups. Geographically, dry climates dominate, and the region is very rural (Brunn and Toops 2012; Hanks 2013).

Two world empires, the Mongol and Timurid, controlled Central Asia in the Middle Ages. In the twentieth century, Soviet influence dominated the region. Economic **development** in Central Asia has been saddled with a difficult transition from Soviet-style command economies to market-oriented systems. The region has been troubled with a declining importance of cotton in agriculture, the rising role of the oil industry in places such as Kazakhstan, and the demise of pastoral nomadism. Politically the region is coming out of communist dictatorship. Many of the local governments, with the exception of Mongolia, are authoritarian. Afghanistan, in particular, with a Soviet invasion, civil war, Taliban conflict, and US invasion has suffered enormous political hardships (Meyer 2003; Shaw 1995; Lewis 1992; Megoran and Sharapova 2013).

South Asia is poised to join East Asia as one of the most powerful regions in the world. How the region handles its historical challenges, cultural complexities, political risks, and economic opportunities will determine the speed of its development.

HISTORICAL CHALLENGES

Indigenous kingdoms and empires dominated Asia through its long history. The Indus Valley civilization goes back to 3000 BCE. A succession of empires from the Mauryan to the Mughals ruled the subcontinent till the 1700s. Parthia and Kushan ruled the Central Asian lands, then the Persians, and then the Arabs controlled the area. By 1200 the Mongols ruled over all of Central Asia. These very early civilizations developed by being able to produce food surpluses (mostly agricultural, with the exception of Central Asia). These early empires were quite sophisticated culturally and possessed well-developed technologies.

By the 1500s, the advent of Western empires into South Asia, then Southeast and Northeast Asia, reversed the tide of Asian power. Internal conflicts in India and China set the stage for European expansion. The economic expansion of Europe and the political conquest of colonial lands proceeded with a cultural colonialism as well. After decades of competition with Dutch, Portuguese, and French rivals, the British dominated

FIGURE 9.2 The Gandhi monument shows the spinning wheel, symbol of his movement. PHOTO: S. Andrus.

India, while the Russians conquered Central Asia (Borthwick 2013). For a century the two Western empires employed diplomacy, espionage, and military support for local political actors in and around Afghanistan. Called the "Great Game" by British authors and the "Tournament of Shadows" by Russians, this Cold War between the two empires three times exploded into proxy wars (Meyer and Brysac 1999).

Western imperialism engendered Asian national movements. Dozens of resistance movements dedicated to freeing Asian lands from Western domination emerged in the late nineteenth and early twentieth centuries. The most successful was the nonviolent Quit India movement led by Mohandas Gandhi. While Gandhi's leadership was cut short by an assassin in 1948, his legacy is crucial for India (Figure 9.2). By 1949 India was free from colonial rule (Brower 2005). Disputes over how India's large Muslim population should be represented in the new nation led to a violent division of the country. Partition in 1949 meant the creation of two new states: India and Pakistan. Pakistan was further subdivided in 1971 with the creation of Bangladesh.

Before western colonialism, Asia was, in the words of Jawaharlal Nehru, master of its destiny. The advent of the West subjugated Asian peoples. The rising nationalism after WW II meant that Asia could once again be free. With the ascendancy of Asia, especially India in the world today, Asia is increasing in power and playing a stronger role after years of European dominance.

CULTURAL COMPLEXITIES

The level of diversity in Central and South Asia is quite high. In contrast to the Middle East or Latin America, or even Europe, there is nothing that really unites the region culturally. Current belief systems include Hinduism, Islam, Christianity, Buddhism, Sikkhism, Jainism, and Zoroastrianism in South Asia, while Central Asia has Islam, Christianity, and Lama Buddhism (see Table 9.4). Both regions also harbor pockets of local shamanistic traditions.

Language diversity is also high. In Central Asia, Turkic languages are dominant, including Uzbek, Kyrgyz, Kazakh, Turkmen, and Azeri. After years of Russian colonization, Russian is a common language. Tajik like Dari (in Afghanistan) is a Persian-related language. In the northern parts of South Asia Indo-European languages prevail. Hindi in India and Urdu in Pakistan are mutually intelligible but are written in Devanagari and modified Persian scripts, respectively. Bengali in Bangladesh and Sinhalese in Sri Lanka are also members of the Indo-European language family. In southern India, languages such as Tamil and Telugu belong to the Dravidian language family. Due to British colonization, English is a common tongue in many parts of South Asia.

The first waves of technological innovation originated in the Indus River Valley. In terms of religion, the oldest beliefs are Hinduism in India. Traders spread Hinduism to coastal locations of Indonesia. Today this tradition is still found in Bali. Hinduism remains the dominant religion in India.

The next religious wave of innovation was centuries later. By 500 BCE, the Buddha began teaching in India, and 250 years later Buddhists ruled most of the subcontinent. **Buddhism** diffused through South Asia, but ironically, declined in the land of its origin. By 1000 CE, there were few Buddhists in India. By 600–700 CE, Buddhism expanded into Central Asia. In Central Asia today, Tibetans and Mongols still practice the

FIGURE 9.3 A wedding ceremony in Khiva, Uzbekistan, complete with a trip to the local mosque and wishing well. PHOTO: S. Toops.

Tibetan variant of Buddhism. In Sri Lanka, Theravada Buddhists form the majority of the population.

By 1000 CE the next wave of a religious innovation occurred with the arrival of Islam, a monotheistic religion (see Figure 9.3). The Turkic peoples of Central Asia brought Islam to South Asia. Muslim rulers of India such as the Mughal (1500s–1800s), who originated in Central Asia, dominated the region (much as Buddhist rulers had dominated the region previously). In the northwest and northeast many South Asians converted to Islam. Today these areas form Pakistan and Bangladesh. Muslims and Hindus lived side by side amiably for a thousand years. People in South Asia practiced Islam or Hinduism exclusively.

Although Syrian Christians had reached India by 200 CE, the religion had not taken hold outside small enclaves in South Asia. European colonialism brought Christianity into the region. European missionaries made additional converts in India. With the advent of Russian colonialism in the 1800s, many Russians who followed Eastern Orthodox Christianity settled in Central Asia.

The last wave was secularism. By 1930 Marxist atheism prevailed over traditional religions in Mongolia. In Soviet Central Asia many mosques were closed. Some reopened as museums for atheism. Secular Marxism also attracted many intellectuals and political leaders in India, although it never took hold in the general populace. Islam and Christianity are both practiced in Central Asia today, as is Buddhism in Mongolia.

The waves of religious innovation and diffusion created the complex cultural landscape of South and Central Asia. Elements of the various traditions influenced one another over time, and various political and cultural theories of tolerance and coexistence emerged. In the South Asian context, the challenge of **globalization** is that it increases the likelihood of people mobilizing religious differences as part of political and economic struggles over resources. Conflicts between Islam, Hinduism, Sikhism, and Christianity began to take place during colonial rule and have continued, sometimes on a large scale, under the pressures of globalization. In Central Asia, the challenge today though is whether to combine, maintain, or create new cultural identities deriving from Muslim, Turkic, or Russian cultures in the midst of globalization.

Cultural waves of innovation and diffusion have sculpted the complex layers of identity. Mobile phones, computers, and satellite television bring new worlds into South and Central Asia. During the colonial era, the British government encouraged the emigration of educated Indians to its colonies elsewhere in Asia, in Africa, and in South America and the Caribbean. After independence, India also became a source of educated labor for the Middle East, Europe, and North America. This South Asian diaspora has marked the world with the outflow of South Asian movies from Bollywood, Indian restaurants to the UK and United States, and Indian technology entrepreneurs to Silicon Valley. Central Asia has made less of mark on the world. Uzbek or Afghan restaurants are much less common than Indian restaurants, for one example.

Local culture in India has been able to incorporate much of western culture on its own terms. There are distinct global influences in India, from the use of English as a national language to India's early adoption of communication technologies like the press, film, and computers, but there is also a definite South Asian influence in the wider world because of the diaspora. In the case of Central Asia the cultural variety is seen in the use of Russian because of the colonialism dating back to the 1800s. Central Asian communities are well adapted to Europe because of the long experience with Russia. Globalization is present in Tashkent with Korean and Turkish as well as Russian and Uzbek varieties of restaurants.

ECONOMIC OPPORTUNITIES

The impacts of Asian economies are felt worldwide. The countries have tried various methods for economic growth. Some Asian governments have been actively involved in promoting export-led industrialization as a development strategy. Within Central Asia, Kazakhstan has a good per capita **GDP** because of its oil economy, but it lacks the infrastructural development of the **newly industrialized countries (NICs)**. India and Sri Lanka are at a lower level. Poverty is big problem in South and Central Asia compared with East Asia. Among poorer countries like Afghanistan and Tajikistan, various factors such as conflict have severely limited the possibilities for economic growth (Frank 1998; Seivers 2003; Engelmann and Pavlakovic 2001). (See Table 9.2.)

India has seen explosive economic development since it began deregulating its industries in the 1990s. India, like China, is one of the countries in the BRIC group (Brazil, Russia, India, and China), indicating that the Indian economy is moving up the development scale. A strong segment in Asia has been industrial production including Indian businesses, such as automobiles geared to the Indian market or medicines for worldwide consumption. The educational system of India has produced many scientists and engineers. A newer sector, developed in the 1990s, includes high technology in places like Bangalore (the Indian equivalent of a Silicon Valley). International communication technologies have led to the development of call centers in India from which technical advice or customer service is dispensed to people in the United States or Britain. Science and technology are factors in this innovation but so is India's strong national education system, with its emphasis on English competence.

Economic development is defined as the process of improving the quality of human life. Underdevelopment, in contrast moves in the opposite direction, leading people to become worse off than before. The future of development economics needs to go beyond the examination of economic growth. A newer view is to consider development as freedom that involves human rights. So in that sense India can be said to be more developed than China, even though India has a lower GDP per capita than China (Todaro and Smith 2012; Sen 2000). Global economic successes in India contrast with the economic difficulties of Afghanistan and Bangladesh and compare well with China and Russia (Nadkarni and Noonan 2013).

POLITICAL RISKS

The political systems at work in Asia interlink with historical, geographic, cultural, and economic issues. Historically, the state in Asia, be it the Mauryan or Mughal empires of India, saw itself as responsible to its people. Issues of control and leadership historically are translated in the modern context with the need to develop the economy. In terms of geography, given the population of India, how does one state govern a billion people? Asian politics is often expressed in terms of "Asian values," which usually referred to the strong paternalism of the state. Asian nationalisms, whether in the form expressed by Nehru in India or by Nazarbayev in Kazakhstan, have produced a variety of regimes on the continent. The variety of governmental systems is shown in the table on government (Table 9.5).

In South Asia, the partition of India and Pakistan after the British colonial pullout was responsible for political tension in the area. Even after the horrors of partition, democratic rule has been the norm in India, Pakistan, and Bangladesh. India is the world's largest democracy; the country has a federal system with local governments having jurisdiction while the national government deals with foreign affairs and economic issues. Overall, India is the strongest state militarily and politically in the region. The tensions between India and Pakistan over Kashmir have led to complex and shifting relationships with China, the United States, and Russia. India and Pakistan have both developed nuclear capability. Finally, in a post-9/11 world, Pakistan has allied itself with the United States against the Taliban of Afghanistan and al Qaeda. The killing of Osama bin Laden in Pakistan by US forces without Pakistani knowledge in 2011 shows the complexity of the US-Pakistan relationship (Ganguly and DeVotta 2003; Ganguly 2006).

In Central Asia, the end of the political domination of the Soviet Union has left newly established states contending with diverse political issues. State formation and identity is one issue, as newly independent states suffer from internal cultural conflicts similar to the partition that created Pakistan in the 1940s. Tajikistan and Afghanistan have suffered under civil wars.

FIGURE 9.4 The Khyber Pass is on the border of Pakistan and Afghanistan.
PHOTO: S. Toops.

After September 11, 2001, the United States and the UK launched a major offensive against the Taliban in Afghanistan. While there are still remnants of the Taliban and al Qaeda, Afghanistan successfully held a presidential election in 2004. Forces are still looking for Taliban and al Qaeda in the borderlands of Afghanistan and Pakistan in the midst of a US drawdown in Afghanistan (see Figure 9.4). The political transitions in the other states of Central Asia may not be as complex but the issues still are. Uzbekistan, Turkmenistan, and Kazakhstan have authoritarian regimes. Kyrgyzstan is moving toward democracy. In contrast, Mongolia has a democratic system. The political vacuum left by the collapse of the Soviet Union has meant that China, Iran, Turkey, and Pakistan as well as the United States have all been trying to exercise influence in the area. And although the Soviet empire no longer exists, the Russians have not yet given up aspirations in Central Asia (Meyer 2003; Davis and Azizian 2007).

Most of the political systems in South and Central Asia are republics (see Table 9.5). A few governments are authoritarian. Uzbekistan and Kazakhstan are examples of authoritarian republics. In contrast, India is the world's largest democracy; every time there is an election held in India, it sets a record for the world's biggest election. Democracy is certainly stronger in South Asia compared to Central Asia (Adeney and Wyatt 2010).

THE SILK ROAD

The famous **Silk Road** illustrates contemporary linkages following on an historic trade artery. Westerners' search for the exotic began on the ancient Silk Road more than seven hundred years ago, when the chronicles of traveler Marco Polo fascinated the West with stories of faraway lands with strange customs and goods. The fall of Communism in the Soviet Union in 1991 and China's opening to the West in the 1980s reopened the Silk Road to global linkages. The Silk Road has a rich mix of cultural traditions, with Afghans, Turks, Uyghurs, Chinese, Kyrgyz, Uzbeks, and Russians living along the road. The landscape encompasses mountains and steppes, deserts and oases (Millward 2013).

The Silk Road was a crossroads nexus of religious, cultural, and economic communication between East and West. Trod by Rabban Bar Sauma, Ibn Battuta, Clavijo, Babur, Timur, Marco Polo, Fa Xian, and Xuan Zang, the Silk Road linked China to India, Persia, and Europe. The numerous ruins, monuments, ancient cities, Buddhist caves, temples, tombs, and garrisons of long-forgotten Uzbek, Kyrgyz, Uyghur, Iranian, Turkic, Mongol, Chinese, and Russian kingdoms, empires, and dynasties are evident in the landscape. They are an important part of the heritage of the area's people, who portray that history in a very different way. In ancient times Buddhism spread along the Silk Road from South Asia to Central Asia. In later times Islam followed the Silk Road from the Middle East, to Central Asia and South Asia (Boulnois 2004).

Uzbekistan illustrates the legacy of the Silk Road. Uzbeks are agriculturalists and traders along the Amu Darya and Syr Darya (rivers). The Russians came to the region in the nineteenth century and conquered the khanates (kingdoms) of the Uzbek and Kyrgyz peoples. The Russian czars cultivated Orthodox Christianity in the area. After the Bolshevik Revolution in 1917, Communism brought a new political ideology to the region. After gaining their independence following the collapse of the Soviet Union, officials in Uzbekistan have tried to create new national identities, some linked to the Silk Road. The new national hero in Uzbekistan is Timur, who ruled in Samarkand from 1370 to 1405 CE. From 1370 to 1507, the Timurid dynasty conquered the areas of Central Asia including what is now Uzbekistan, Iran,

FIGURE 9.5 Samarkand. The Registan complex of Samarkand, Uzbekistan, was the center of the Timurid Empire. PHOTO: S. Toops.

and Iraq, and conducted military campaigns to Delhi, Izmir, Ankara, and Moscow. The current Uzbek government has put up new statues of Timur and refurbished Samarkand's monumental architecture from the Timurid period (Millward 2013). (See Figure 9.5.)

The Silk Road is now used as a metaphor for globalization and trade linkages in Central and South Asia. Another element developed with The Silk Road Project by Yo-Yo Ma in 1998, bringing together musicians from East Asia, Central Asia, South Asia, the Middle East, and Europe. The Project promotes contemporary arts inspired by the Silk Road (Ma 2013).

One final note on the Silk Road, as the United States and NATO begin to wind down their military activity in Afghanistan in 2014, US troops and material will leave the country either through Pakistan, and thence to the Indian Ocean, or via the Northern Route, through Uzbekistan, Kyrgyzstan, and Kazakhstan, and thence to Russia. The US military airbase in Kyrgyzstan, which opened in 2001, will close in 2014. However, the removal of offensive troops in Afghanistan and the closure of the airbase in Kyrgyzstan do not mean the end of the US presence in the region. In 2011, Secretary of State Hillary Clinton spoke of a New Silk Road as a way of expanding a modern day trade network across South and Central

Asia. The US State Department articulates a "New Silk Road Vision" through economic connections linking Afghanistan to Central and South Asia. Military ventures could be followed by economic ventures along this New Silk Road. (Millward 2013; US Department of State 2014).

DEMOGRAPHIC ISSUES

Two issues illustrate the challenges facing Asia in the twenty-first century. This section focuses on Asia's demographic and environmental concerns. The next section profiles India as an example of demographic and environmental problems that face South and Central Asia.

One factor of the demographic dilemma is the level of population growth. South Asia has over 1.6 billion people. South Asian population growth rates are high, so there is definite population pressure on South Asia. The population growth in South Asia does have regional and global effects. Central Asia has smaller population sizes with growth rates of 1 to 1.8 percent. Afghanistan at 2.25 percent has the highest population-growth rate. **Life expectancy** ranges from 50 years in Afghanistan to 76 years in Sri Lanka (see Table 9.3).

Asia has 60 percent of the world population. India has over 1.2 billion people and, with its population growth rate of 1.28 percent, by 2050 will be the most populous country in the world, surpassing China. In Asia both rural and urban densities are high, especially on the Ganges River in India (see Table 9.1).

South Asia's population is growing faster than that of East Asia. India and Bangladesh have had some success with family planning, while others, like Pakistan, have not. Long years of settlement have created very dense and very large population in the Ganges-Brahmaputra lowland of India and Bangladesh, most land area is densely inhabited. In contrast, Central Asia has densely settled oases amid vacant steppes, mountains, and deserts. In the Soviet era, birth control was quite common so people in Central Asia have had smaller families. Population growth rates are lower with the exception of Afghanistan (Population Reference Bureau 2013).

India has had only moderate levels of success in family planning, in part because India, as a democracy, could not pass a draconian family law such as China's. Difficult policies for intensive family planning may be Asia's only way out of this dilemma. Low cost, culturally acceptable methods (pill, condom, perhaps IUD, not sterilization) are the key to a higher usage

FIGURE 9.6 Calcutta is one of India's largest cities. PHOTO: S. Andrus.

of contraception (Bradnock and Williams 2002). Advertising campaigns selling birth control as life choice have been more successful than state campaigns emphasizing social good (Mazzarella 2003).

Another demographic issue is the level of urbanization. Many people in Asia are moving from countryside to the city. Urban agglomerations are becoming quite large, including Delhi–New Delhi at 25 million, Mumbai (Bombay) at 21 million, Dhaka at 17 million, Kolkata (Calcutta) at 15 million, and Karachi at 15 million (de Blij et al. 2014) (see Figure 9.6). Overall, the level of urbanization is lower in South Asia than East Asia. In the cities of South Asia difficulties with housing and squatter settlements are evident. In Central Asia, urbanization is high with the exception of Tajikistan and Afghanistan (probably due to civil conflict). Overall, planning for housing is a major issue in Asian cities (Karan 2004).

ENVIRONMENTAL DIVERSITY AND CHALLENGES OF INDIA

As the largest country in South and Central Asia, both in land area and population, India provides an example of the problems and possibilities facing the region. India is divided into three environments: the rice-producing central and southern uplands, the alluvial lowland of the fertile Ganges and Brahmaputra valleys, and the Himalayan mountains of the North.

Southern India has a tropical savanna climate at the heart of the Deccan plateau. The rugged Western Ghats separate the narrow coast from the plateau. On both east and west coastal plains, fertile soils and abundant water support high population densities. Soil in the Deccan plateau is not so good, but the main problem is water. The Western Ghats block off rain from the west, giving the area a semi-arid climate. People rely on small reservoirs or tanks of water from the wet **monsoon** for irrigation of rice, sorghum, and cotton.

The Ganges-Brahmaputra-Indus lowlands have been created by mighty river systems with fertile alluvial soil, supporting a dense population. The Ganges, the mother river, has become a sacred river to Hindus and empties into the Bay of Bengal. The Brahmaputra comes down from Tibet and merges with the Ganges. The western areas bordering Pakistan is drier and rivers here flow into the Indus. People rely on these rivers as well as the rains from the wet monsoon for irrigation. Crops include wheat and pulses in the west and rice in the east.

The northern areas of the Himalayan range are formed by the subduction of the Indian Plate under the Eurasian Plate. This northern segment is tectonically active and earthquakes are common. A severe earthquake on the Pakistan side of Kashmir resulted in the deaths of 100,000 in 2005. The mountains are too rugged for much settlement, although fertile valleys host communities and some forest regions are home to India's *Adivasi*, or "indigenous" peoples. Nestled in these mountains, the Valley of Kashmir has a denser population (Rowntree et al. 2014).

The monsoon dominates climate patterns in India. *Monsoon* comes from the word for "season" in Arabic. In winter, a high-pressure system forms over Asia and brings dry air to India. In summer, a low-pressure system forms as heat builds up over South Asia and the lands westwards. By June, the summer monsoon brings moisture from the Bay of Bengal and the Indian Ocean, with as much as 70 inches of rain in June, July, and August. However the pattern is not regular and, if the rain from the summer monsoons is delayed, crop failure can result. The south is mostly tropical savanna with a wet summer and dry winter. The alluvial lowlands of the Ganges are subtropical, much like Florida with hot summer. The western area near Pakistan is desert and steppe. The far north has colder climate due to elevation (Karan 2004; de Blij 2014).

Environmental issues are common in India. Flooding in the Ganges River valleys, deforestation in the Western and Eastern Ghats, and water and air pollution in cities such as Mumbai (Bombay) and Kolkata (Calcutta) are a few of the problems. Over–irrigation coupled with Green Revolution intensification has led to a salinization of the soil in northwestern India (Rowntree et al. 2014).

The combination of climate and landforms makes South Asia susceptible to global climate change. India has many people living in low-lying areas on the coast of the Bay of Bengal. As the world begins to warm up, the polar sea ice will melt, five to ten million people could be displaced in coastal India, Bangladesh, and Sri Lanka with a one-meter rise in sea level. The whole of the Maldives could disappear under the ocean. Global climate change will also result in the retreating of Himalayan glaciers. These glaciers are the source of the Indus, Ganges, and Brahmaputra, so water supplies could be disrupted. An increase in winter temperatures will be disastrous for the wheat crops in India and Pakistan. The summer monsoon will have increased rainfall and this would result in flooding (Rowntree et al. 2014).

The economic transformation of India based on industry, in particular chemicals, has also led to an increase in pollution. A prime example of industrial pollution is the explosion of a fertilizer plant in Bhopal in 1984, killing over 2,500 people. Industrial development near Hyderabad in the Deccan plateau has created industrial waste which pollutes the local water supply. Delhi has seen an increase in industry with the attending pollution of sulphur dioxide and nitrous oxides into the atmosphere. Automobile exhaust is another source of air contamination. South of Delhi, air pollution threatens the Taj Mahal, with acid rain discoloring the white marble monument of Emperor Shah Jahan and his wife. The 400 million people who live in the Ganges River Valley are also a source of solid waste, much of which flows untreated into the river. Industrial waste as well as human waste, and non-biodegradable plastics add to pollution in the Ganges, this holy river sacred to the Hindus. The Ganga Action Plan in 1985–2000 was directed at cleaning up the river but the costs of the cleanup are very high; however, the costs of not cleaning up will be much higher. The World Bank already plans to lend India US$1 billion to work on the clean-up (Karan 2004).

What India has spent on environmental protection is not sufficient. The state has a high priority of economic development, which includes business, education, and scientific expansion. Environmental needs are, as in many countries, ranked behind economic growth and national-security interests. In recent years, more people in India have taken nonviolent action to protect the environment. These movements emulate Gandhi and his work against British colonialism. These environmental movements are moving away from a Western-inspired resource-intensive development model to one that includes sustainability. Some examples of these environmental movements are Save the Narmada and the Chipko Movement. The campaign to Save the Narmada River in central India serves to counteract a plan to develop the river with many large dams. The Chipko movement in northern India began in the 1970s to combat deforestation. In this movement to protect the livelihood of villagers, many women surrounded the trees to prevent them from being felled by loggers. This Gandhian 'tree-hugging' movement wrested control of the forest from a bureaucracy focused on products for the urban market (Rangan 2000).

POLITICAL ECOLOGY IN SOUTH AND CENTRAL ASIA

How does the environment relate to development? **Political ecology** combines aspects of geography, anthropology, sociology, and political science to examine environmental issues (Robbins 2012; Rocheleau et al. 1996). Political ecology considers the human adaptation to risk and uncertainty. In the case of the monsoon in South Asia, the risk is the uncertainty of the onset of the summer monsoon. People in villages know the natural cycle of the monsoon; they know their local ecology. They prepare by spreading risk out over the dry years, they practice water harvesting with small catchment basins and tanks, and work collectively in water conservation efforts. So the villagers are not just at the mercy of nature, but are integrated into natural patterns to reduce risk (Robbins and Moritz 1999).

Central Asia experiences great conflict over water issues. The physical environment is composed of plateaus and mountains in Kyrgyzstan, Tajikistan, Mongolia, and western China, steppe in Kazakhstan, and desert basins in Uzbekistan and Turkmenistan. The Caspian and Aral Sea basins in Turkmenistan and Uzbekistan and Southern Kazakhstan are vast arid landscapes, with hot summers and cold winters (Rowntree et al. 2014).

Up till modern times, the Aral Sea was fed by the Syr Darya and the Amu Darya (*darya* means "river") coming from the Tian Shan (Heavenly Mountains) in Kyrgyzstan, but today the Aral is shrinking. The lands in Uzbekistan were irrigated to produce cotton during Tsarist and Soviet times. Cotton was Tsar in Uzbekistan; the newly independent state of Uzbekistan continues to rely on cotton production for exports. Besides irrigation, cotton production uses significant amounts of fertilizer and pesticides. More water was required for cotton and rice irrigation as well in these arid landscapes. This meant more canals and correspondingly more evaporation of water. The canals leaked and the underlying soil is very sandy, so much water was wasted. More irrigation has meant greater salinization of the soil. Soviet planners had encouraged the production of cotton in Uzbekistan; cotton uses a great deal of water. Once most of the river water was diverted to the irrigated fields there was no water left for the Aral Sea, which is now threatened by desertification (Bissell 2003; Sievers 2003; Brunn and Toops 2012).

Other environmental challenges abound in South and Central Asia, including access to clean water in Bangladesh and desertification across Central Asia. Human activity, intentional or unintentional, is a major cause of these environmental issues. Bangladesh is built on the low-lying Ganges delta. Flooding in Bangladesh is a problem exacerbated by the deforestation of the Ganges headwaters. Economic growth and population pressures in Bangladesh led to settlement in the delta area. Metals including arsenic contaminate many of the aquifers used for drinking water (Rowntree et al. 2014).

In many of these cases and others, the countries were focusing on economic growth without taking into account the ecological consequences. The drive for economic growth to the exclusion of all else has created severe environmental problems, air and water quality in particular. Yet how can a government ignore the economic needs of its people? Economic needs have to be balanced with ecological realities. The cost of fixing such environmental disasters is more than the economic benefit from production and consumption. Environmental stresses in highly populated areas like Asia have global ramifications.

THE FUTURE OF INDIA

The brightest elements of India's future rest on (1) the huge democracy that links together India's cultural diversity and (2) the economic rise of India. The democracy of India has brought many Indians, whether Hindu or Muslim, Sikh or Christian together. The country has a variety of official languages besides Hindi, including English and Sanskrit. The federal system has allowed local states as well as the national government political power. Individuals share and contribute to a common India. Although violent outbursts between different religious, ethnic, and linguistic groups occur, overall communities are integrated together into a shared identity—India. Out of plurality comes a unity (Kux 2007; Ganguly 2006).

The economic rise of India has relied on scientific expertise and a global diaspora that places a strong value on education. However that economic rise was also based on the new economic policy in 1991 to do away with the micromanaging of licenses and permits that confined the economy. The new economic regime embraced the market and led India to self-sustaining growth. A large domestic market, growing international market, lower wages, large scientific community, and fluency in English have brought India substantial growth in recent years (of course, the 2008 economic depression hit India as well) (Rothermund 2008).

The future challenges of India are many. In terms of development, there is a two-speed India: an area of high growth around Delhi, Mumbai, and Bangalore, and regions of low growth around Kolkatta and central India. There is stark contrast between impoverished villagers and a high-tech India. Unemployment in the countryside drives people to the city where, if they are lucky, they find jobs; if not they join the ranks of the poor and sleep on the streets or in vast slums of makeshift housing. Unemployment and underemployment are linked to another issue, population increase. As discussed earlier, environmental issues are related to the economic rise and the population growth. More people leads to greater consumption of scarce resources. India has protective laws on the books, but the power of large corporations and corrupt politicians often renders these laws ineffective. Inequality between men and women shows up in the unequal treatment of women and men, notably a lack of healthcare and education for women in India. A new emphasis on educational and economic opportunities for women needs to be in place. Finally, communal violence that places religious fundamentalism, whether Hindu or Muslim, above cultural and political unity, is a risky path for India to follow (Kristof and WuDunn 2009; Karan 2004; Thussu 2013).

ASIA MATTERS: GLOBAL CONNECTIONS

The historical challenges of Central Asia and the cultural complexities of South Asia are all a part of Asia's future. India is regionally dominant in

South Asia. In Central Asia, Kazakhstan holds more power because of its oil industry. Even in the midst of cultural diversity and population challenges, South Asia, with its rising economy, is an important component of the world.

South Asia is globally connected. Elements of South Asian culture are known and recognized worldwide. Indian yoga or Indian restaurants in US cities point to the globalization of India. Cultural connections such as Bollywood whose movies play in cinema houses across Asia, Africa, and the middle East, is entering into Europe and North America through hybrid films. One of these, *Slumdog Millionaire*, made in India in the slums of Mumbai in 2008 with a British director and Anglo and Indian actors, won Academy Awards (including Best Picture) in the United States to the tune of its theme song, "Jai Ho," by A. R. Rahman. In Scotland, a good fast-food meal is not McDonald's but kebab (possibly Afghani or Pakistani) or a good curry. Gandhi started his nonviolent movement in South Africa against British repression, but his ideas have influenced the American civil-rights movement and the Arab Spring. South Asian migration of Indian, Pakistani, or Bangladeshis to all corners of the world followed the path of the British Commonwealth to Canada, South Africa, Kenya, and of course to Britain. Pakistanis in the United Kingdom, Indians in the United States, Trinidad, Kenya, and Guyana are all examples of the migration of the South Asian diaspora (Luce 2007).

Central Asia has global connections as well but they occur through past histories and contemporary geographies. Uzbeks, Kyrgyz, and Kazakhs were part of the Russian Empire and then the Soviet Union for so long that the Russian language became a common tongue among the various ethnic groups in Central Asia. Connections in Central Asia link through Russia to Europe. The other global connection in Central Asia is through Islam and through Turkey to the Middle East. Most of the Central Asian languages are varieties of Turkish, albeit with a heavy Arab, Persian, and Russian vocabulary written in various Cyrillic-style scripts (Sengupta 2009).

Global transnational corporations have their production centers in South Asia. Indian firms such as Infosys, Tata, and Wipro represent the new wave of entrepreneurialism in Asia. The information technology sector in India has grown rapidly because of the large scientific community in India. Innovation in software, medical technology, and international films are growth areas. The liberalization of the Indian economy in 1991 points toward an India that is a global producer. By contrast Central Asia has focused its resource on primary products such as oil (Kazakhstan), natural gas (Uzbekistan, Turkmenistan), and cotton (Uzbekistan).

Political power and security issues also point toward the South Asian role in the world. Expansion of the Security Council includes discussion of India as a possible permanent member. After the Cold War ended in the early 1990s, India and Pakistan tested nuclear weapons in 1998. The rise of the Taliban in Afghanistan and Pakistan and the death of Osama bin Laden in Pakistan are two events that have maintained a global focus on South Asia. Politically and economically India has become a regional power in Asia and by extension a global power. Some observers think that India will surpass China's economic development in this century because of India's relative political freedom (Sen 2000).

In 2012 the shooting of Malala Yousafzai, a young girl in Swat, Pakistan, by the Taliban provoked international reaction and recognition. She was shot simply for campaigning for better rights for girls in Pakistan, including being able to go to school. Some areas of Pakistan are still under the domain of the Taliban. Luckily she was able to get medical care and has now moved to the United Kingdom. She has since coauthored a book, *I Am Malala*, and has won several awards, including the European Union's Sakharov Prize. Malala's experience shows the complexities of political, economic, and cultural issues in Pakistan today (Yousafzai and Lamb 2013).

Nehru, in his speech on India's independence in 1947, spoke of a "tryst with destiny." For South and Central Asia, that destiny is rapidly approaching (Kristof and WuDunn 2000). India represents the capacity of democracy to manage enormous cultural complexity and is soon to be the world's most populous country and a rising economic power. In contrast Afghanistan is in the midst of conflict. The overall trend, on the whole, is brighter for South Asia than Central Asia. In the metaphor of the movie *Crouching Tiger, Hidden Dragon*, India is the Tiger and China is the Dragon. The Tiger though, has leaped, and the Dragon is no longer hidden.

TIMELINE OF TWENTIETH-CENTURY
SOUTH AND CENTRAL ASIAN HISTORY

1876	Tsars annex Central Asia.
1880	Anglo-Afghan War.
1906	Muslim League formed in India.
1917	Russian Revolution; Communists extend control to Central Asia.
1918	Secularization campaign in Central Asia.
1919	Gandhi leads Indian National Congress.
1919	Amritsar massacre in India.
1921	Provincial self-rule in India.
1929	National Congress for Indian Independence.
1930s	Stalin's purge of Uzbek leaders.
1933	Zahir Shah King of Afghanistan.
1935	Government of India Act.
1937	Indian National Congress wins elections.
1940	Muslim League for Independent Pakistan.
1947	Indian independence and partition.
1947	Nehru Prime Minister of India.
1947–1948	India–Pakistan war.
1948	Mohandas Gandhi assassinated.
1950s	Cotton-production campaign in Central Asia.
1951	Indian federal constitution.
1954	Virgin lands campaign in Kazakhstan. Russian in-migration.
1955	Bandung Conference of non-aligned states.
1955	Baikonur Soviet space center in Kazakhstan built.
1959	Dalai Lama flees to India.
1962	Sino-Indian War.
1966	Tashkent earthquake.
1964	Death of Nehru.
1967	"Green Revolution" crops in India.
1971	Indo-Pakistan War, independence of Bangladesh.
1977	Military coup in Pakistan.
1979–1989	Soviet invasion of Afghanistan.
1981–1989	Pakistan aid to Afghan rebels.
1982	Sikh rebel against India.
1984	Indira Gandhi assassinated.

1988	Benazir Bhutto prime minister of Pakistan.
1989	Kashmiri Muslims rebel against India.
1989	Karimov in power in Uzbekistan.
1989	Nazarbayev in power in Kazakhstan.
1990	Indian economic reforms.
1991	Soviet Union collapses. Formation of Central Asian States.
1995	Taliban controls Afghanistan.
1998	India and Pakistan both have nuclear tests.
1999	Military coup in Pakistan.
2001	September 11 al Qaeda bombings in New York and DC.
2001	US and allies invade Afghanistan.
2001	Opening of pipelines from Kazakh oil fields to Russia.
2001	Shanghai Cooperation organization of China, Russia, Kazakhstan, Kyrgyzstan, Tajikistan, and Uzbekistan.
2004	Hamid Karzai elected President of Afghanistan.
2004	Indian Ocean tsunami.
2005	Kashmir earthquake.
2005	Andijan killings in Uzbekistan.
2007	Benazir Bhutto assassinated in Pakistan.
2008	Asif Ali Zardari (B. Bhutto's husband) elected president of Pakistan.
2008	Mumbai terrorist attack.
2011	Osama bin Laden killed.
2011	US Department of State articulates "New Silk Road."
2012	Malala wounded.
2014	NATO withdraws from Afghanistan.

272

Table 9.1 Population and Rate of Growth

Country	Population	RNI%	Country	Population	RNI%
South Asia:			**Central Asia:**		
Bangladesh	163,654,860	1.59	Afghanistan	31,108,077	2.25
Bhutan	725,296	1.15	Azerbaijan	9,590,159	1.01
India	1,220,800,359	1.28	Kazakhstan	17,736,896	1.20
Maldives	393,988	−0.11	Kyrgyzstan	5,548,042	0.97
Nepal	30,430,267	1.81	Mongolia	3,226,516	1.44
Pakistan	193,238,868	1.52	Tajikistan	7,910,041	1.79
Sri Lanka	21,675,648	0.89	Turkmenistan	5,113,040	1.15
			Uzbekistan	28,661,637	0.94

This chart shows the population and rate of population growth (natural increase) among the countries of South and Central Asia.

SOURCE: *CIA World Factbook 2013*

Table 9.2 Gross Domestic Product and GDP Real Growth

Country	GDPpc	GDP real growth	Country	GDPpc	GDP real growth
South Asia:			Central Asia:		
Bangladesh	$2,100	6.10%	Afghanistan	$1,100	10.20%
Bhutan	$6,800	9.70%	Azerbaijan	$10,700	2.20%
India	$3,900	6.50%	Kazakhstan	$14,100	5.00%
Maldives	$9,400	3.50%	Kyrgyzstan	$2,400	−0.90%
Nepal	$1,300	4.60%	Mongolia	$5,500	12.30%
Pakistan	$2,900	3.70%	Tajikistan	$2,300	7.50%
Sri Lanka	$6,200	6.40%	Turkmenistan	$8,900	11.00%
			Uzbekistan	$3,100	8.50%

This chart shows the GDP per capita and rate of GDPpc real growth among the countries of South and Central Asia.

SOURCE: *CIA World Factbook 2013*

Table 9.3 Literacy Rates and Life Expectancy

Country	Literacy	LE-years	Country	Literacy	LE-years
South Asia:			Central Asia:		
Bangladesh	58%	70	Afghanistan	28%	50
Bhutan	53%	68	Azerbaijan	99%	72
India	63%	67	Kazakhstan	100%	68
Maldives	98%	75	Kyrgyzstan	99%	70
Nepal	57%	67	Mongolia	98%	68
Pakistan	55%	67	Tajikistan	100%	67
Sri Lanka	91%	76	Turkmenistan	100%	69
			Uzbekistan	99%	73

This chart shows the Literacy Rates and Life Expectancy (In Years) among the countries of South and Central Asia.

SOURCE: *CIA World Factbook 2013*

Table 9.4 Major Religions

Country	Religion
Central Asia:	
Afghanistan	Sunni Muslim 80%, Shia Muslim 19%, other 1%
Azerbaijan	Muslim 93%, Russian Orthodox 2%, Armenian Orthodox 2%, other 2%
Kazakhstan	Muslim 70%, Russian Orthodox 24%, other Christian 2%, other 1%, atheist 3%
Kyrgyzstan	Muslim 75%, Russian Orthodox 20%, other 5%
Mongolia	Buddhist Lamaist 50%, Shamanist and Christian 6%, Muslim 4%, none 40%
Tajikistan	Sunni Muslim 85%, Shia Muslim 5%, other 10%
Turkmenistan	Muslim 89%, Eastern Orthodox 9%, unknown 2%
Uzbekistan	Muslim 88% (mostly Sunni), Eastern Orthodox 9%, other 3%
South Asia:	
Bangladesh	Muslim 90%, Hindu 9%, other 1%
Bhutan	Lamaistic Buddhist 75%, Hinduism 25%
India	Hindu 81%, Muslim 13%, Christian 2%, Sikh 2%, other 2%
Maldives	Sunni Muslim
Nepal	Hindu 81%, Buddhist 11%, Muslim 4%, Kirant 3%, other 1%
Pakistan	Muslim (official) 96% (Sunni 85–90%, Shia 10–15%), other 4%
Sri Lanka	Buddhist (official) 69%, Muslim 8%, Hindu 7%, Christian 6%, unspecified 10%

This chart shows the types of religions among the countries of South and Central Asia.

SOURCE: *CIA World Factbook 2013*

Table 9.5 Type of Government

Country	Government	Country	Government
South Asia:		**Central Asia:**	
Bangladesh	Parliamentary democracy	Afghanistan	Islamic republic
Bhutan	Constitutional monarchy	Azerbaijan	Republic
India	Federal republic	Kazakhstan	Republic, authoritarian rule
Maldives	Republic	Kyrgyzstan	Republic
Nepal	Federal democratic republic	Mongolia	Parliamentary
Pakistan	Federal republic	Tajikistan	Republic
Sri Lanka	Republic	Turkmenistan	Democracy/Presidential republic
		Uzbekistan	Republic, authoritarian rule

This chart shows the form of government among the countries of South and Central Asia.

SOURCE: *CIA World Factbook 2013*

References

Adeney, Katharine, and Andrew Wyatt. 2010. *Contemporary India*. Houndsmills, Basingstoke, Hampshire: Palgrave Macmillan.

Bissell, Tom. 2003. *Chasing the Sea: Lost Among the Ghosts of Empire in Central Asia*. New York: Pantheon Books.

Borthwick, M. 2013. *Pacific Century*. Boulder, CO: Westview Press.

Boulnois, Luce. 2004. *Silk Road: Monks, Warriors, and Merchants on the Silk Road*. Trans. by Helen Loveday. Hong Kong: Odyssey Guide.

Bradnock, Robert W., and Glyn Williams. 2002. *South Asia in a Globalising World: A Reconstructed Regional Geography*. Harlow, England: Prentice Hall.

Brower, Daniel R. 2005. *The World in the Twentieth Century*. 6th ed. Upper Saddle River, NJ: Prentice Hall.

Brunn, S., and S. Toops. 2012. *The Routledge Atlas of Central Eurasian Affairs*. London, NY: Routledge.

Davis, Elizabeth V. W, and Rouben Azizian. 2007. *Islam, Oil, and Geopolitics: Central Asia After September 11*. Lanham, MD: Rowman & Littlefield.

De Blij, H., et al. 2014. *Geography: Realms, Regions, and Concepts*. 16th ed. Hoboken NJ: John Wiley.

Engelmann, Kurt, and Vjeran Pavlakovic. 2001. *Rural Development in Eurasia and the Middle East*. Seattle: University of Washington.

Frank, A. G. 1998. *Reorient: Global Economy in the Asian Age*. Berkeley: University of California Press.

French, P. 1997. *Liberty or Death: India's Journey to Independence and Division*. London: Harper Collins, 1997.

Ganguly, Sumit. 2006. *South Asia*. New York: New York University Press.

Ganguly, Sumit, and Neil DeVotta. 2003. *Understanding Contemporary India*. Boulder, CO: Lynne Rienner.

Hanks, Reuel. 2013. "A Global Crossroads Reemerges in the Twenty-first Century: An Introduction to Central Asia." *Education About Asia*. Winter 18(3): 5–11.

Karan, P. P. 2004. *The Non-Western World*. New York: Routledge.

Kristof, Nicholas D., and Sheryl WuDunn. 2009. *Half the Sky: Turning Oppression into Opportunity for Women Worldwide*. New York: Knopf.

Kristof, Nicholas D., and Sheryl WuDunn. 2000. *Thunder from the East: Portrait of a Rising Asia*. New York: Knopf.

Kux, Dennis. 2007. *India at Sixty: A Positive Balance Sheet*. New York: Foreign Policy Association.

Lewis, R., ed. 1992. *Geographical Perspectives on Soviet Central Asia*. London: Routledge.

Luce, Edward. 2007 *In Spite of the Gods: The Strange Rise of Modern India*. New York: Doubleday.

Ma, Yo-yo, 2013. The Silk Road Project. www.sikroadproject.org. Accessed November 10, 2013.

Mazzarella, William. 2003. *Shoveling Smoke: Advertising and Globalization in Contemporary India*. Durham, NC: Duke University Press.

Megoran, Nick, and S. Sh Sharapova. 2013. *Central Asia in International Relations: The Legacies of Halford Mackinder*. New York: Columbia University Press.

Meyer, Karl Ernest. 2003. *The Dust of Empire: The Race for Mastery in the Asian Heartland*. New York: PublicAffairs.

Meyer, Karl Ernest, and Shareen Blair Brysac. 1999. *Tournament of Shadows: The Great Game and Race for Empire in Central Asia*. Washington, DC: Counterpoint.

Millward, James. 2013. *The Silk Road: A Very Short Introduction*. New York: Oxford University Press.

Nadkarni, Vidya, and Norma C. Noonan. 2013. *Emerging Powers in a Comparative Perspective: The Political and Economic Rise of the BRIC Countries*. New York: Bloomsbury.

Population Reference Bureau. 2013. *World Population Data Sheet 2013*, Washington, DC.

Rangan, Haripriya. 2000. *Of Myths and Movements: Rewriting Chipko into Himalayan History*. London: VERSO.

Robbins, P. 2012. *Political Ecology*. 2nd ed. Oxford: Blackwell.

Robbins, P., and J. Moritz. 1999. "Resourceful People and People's Resources: Teaching the Cultural Ecology of South Asia." *Education about Asia*. 4(2): 12–16.

Rocheleau, Dianne E., Barbara P. Thomas-Slayter, and Esther Wangari. 1996. *Feminist Political Ecology: Global Issues and Local Experiences*. London: Routledge.

Rothermund, Dietmar. 2008. *India: The Rise of an Asian Giant*. New Haven, CT: Yale University Press.

Rowntree, L., et al. 2014. *Globalization and Diversity*. Upper Saddle River, NJ: Prentice Hall.

Sen, Amartya Kumar. 2000. *Development as Freedom*. New York: Anchor Books.

Sengupta, Anita. 2009. *Heartlands of Eurasia: The Geopolitics of Political Space.* Lanham, MD: Lexington Books.

Shaw, D. 1995. *The Post-Soviet Republics.* New York: Wiley.

Sievers, Eric W. 2003. *The Post-Soviet Decline of Central Asia: Sustainable Development and Comprehensive Capital.* London: Routledge Curzon.

Thussu, Daya Kishan. 2013. *Communicating India's Soft Power: Buddha to Bollywood.* New York: Palgrave Macmillan.

Todaro, M. P., and S. C. Smith. 2012. *Economic Development.* 11th ed. Boston: Addison Wesley.

US Department of State. 2014. "U.S. Support for New Silk Road." http://www.state .gov/p/sca/ci/af/newsilkroad/index.htm. Accessed January 28, 2014.

Weightman, Barbara. 2011. *Dragons and Tigers, A Geography of South, East and Southeast Asia.* Hoboken, NJ: John Wiley.

Wolpert, S. 2004. *A New History of India.* New York: Oxford University Press.

Yousafzai, Malala, and Christina Lamb. 2013. *I Am Malala: The Girl Who Stood Up for Education and Was Shot by the Taliban.* New York: Little, Brown.

Further Reading

Dutt, A. 1987. *An Atlas of South Asia.* Boulder, CO: Westview.

Potter, R., et al. 1999. *Geographies of Development.* Harlow, UK: Pearson Education Limited.

Walcott, Susan, and Cory Johnson, eds. *Eurasian Corridors of Interconnection.* London, New York: Routledge.

Journals

Central Asian Survey
Contemporary South Asia
Education about Asia
Eurasian Geography and Economics
Journal of Asian Studies

Films

Earth (2000). Deepa Mehta, director. New York: New Yorker Video.
Fire (1998). Deepa Mehta, director. New York: New Yorker Video.

Monsoon Wedding (2001). Mira Nair, director (India).
Osama (2004). Siddiq Barmak, director. Santa Monica, CA: MGM Home
    Entertainment.
Slumdog Millionaire (2008). Danny Boyle and Loveleen Tandan, directors (India/
    UK).

Websites

Asian Times Online. http://www.atimes.com/
Association for Asian Studies. https://www.asian-studies.org/
International Institute for Asian Studies. http://www.iias.nl/
Silk Road Seattle. http://depts.washington.edu/uwch/silkroad/index.html
South Asia Resource Access on the Internet. http://library.columbia.edu/locations
    /global/virtual-libraries/sarai.html

10

Africa and the
International Community

Africa has long struggled to carve out an independent role in world affairs. More than any other continent, Africa has experienced illegitimate and corrupt rule, economic exploitation, and cultural assault on a large scale. During the Cold War, African countries were important to the United States and the Soviet Union solely for geopolitical reasons and strategic raw materials. Neither side prioritized democracy, peace, or prosperity for Africa. Furthermore, Africa's postcolonial leaders, for the most part, have not followed liberal democratic practices or adopted sound economic policies to raise standards of living. African experiences of poverty, disease, authoritarian regimes, and ethnic conflicts have been sadly similar. Most African countries lag behind in most categories of economic development and democratic freedoms.

While Africa still suffers from the legacy of **colonialism**, the superpower rivalry, and corrupt leadership, the continent is poised to enter a new age of positive political and economic development and greater integration into the world community. According to a Gallup poll, seven out of ten Africans view globalization favorably. Only one-third of North Americans and Europeans share this view (WPO 2006). Cell phone and Internet use is growing faster in Africa than any other continent, and more and more city dwellers enjoy all the amenities of any modern metropolis.

Africa's vast economic and human potential is already having an effect on the world marketplace. Africa has about one-third of the world's primary commodities. African countries have experienced robust economic

282

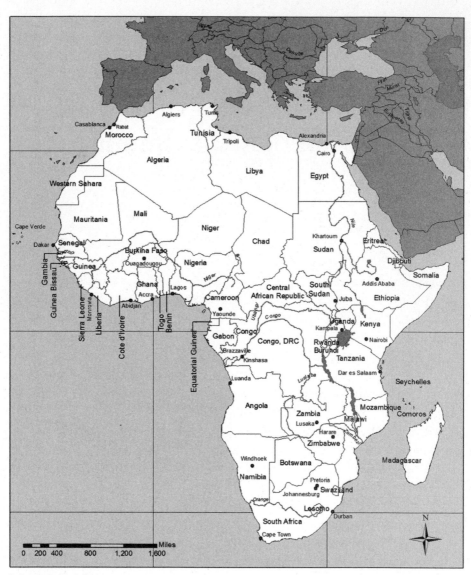

MAP 10.1 Africa.

growth in the past few years, and the world is fostering new commercial and political connections to the continent.

AFRICAN GEOGRAPHY AND CULTURE

Africa is more diverse than any of the other regions discussed in this book. Westerners often think of Africa as a country rather than a continent and ignore the vast differences among its countries and regions.

Europeans defined Africa as a continent surrounded by three great bodies of water, the Mediterranean Sea on the northern coast, the Atlantic Ocean in the west, and the Indian Ocean in the east. Africa is the second-largest continent, stretching five thousand miles from north to south and nearly as far from West Africa to the Horn of Africa in the east. It is more than three times the size of the United States.

Western geographers arbitrarily divided Europe from Asia at the Ural Mountains, but the Sahara, which is an even greater physical barrier, was not designated as a continental divide. There is no definitive description of sub-Saharan Africa. Many African countries, such as Mali, Niger, and Chad, sit astride the Sahara and have a mix of Arab and non-Arab peoples. South Africa is sometimes left out of the sub-Saharan Africa category.

There are, however, significant historical, political, climatic, and cultural differences between the areas north and south of the Sahara. The "Middle Eastern" countries in North Africa from Morocco in the west to Egypt in the east are predominantly Arab and Islamic and have as many connections to the Mediterranean area and to the Middle East as to sub-Saharan Africa (see Chapter 11 on the Middle East). Fifty-five African countries are members of the UN or the **African Union** (AU); forty-five or so make up sub-Saharan Africa. Chad, Sudan, Ethiopia, and Nigeria represent the transition between the two regions.

Africa is rich in various topographies and climates. It has some of the world's driest and largest deserts, highest mountain peaks, and densest rain forests. Tropical jungles in the coastal regions of West Africa transition into grasslands in the interior. The Congo River dominates the west central rain forests of equatorial Africa, while the Nile River is the lifeblood of northeast Africa. The East African landscape includes mountains, lakes, upland plateaus, and rich grasslands that are home to the wild animals that European colonists treasured as wall trophies. The southern regions of Africa are a mix of deserts, hills, and plateaus.

African political unity and economic development have been hindered by several geographic disadvantages. Africa has few natural harbors and navigable rivers to the interior. Rain is a precious commodity in Africa, and it tends to be seasonal. Dry seasons last for six to seven months, making sustainable agricultural production difficult. During the dry season in West Africa, many farmers in the north migrate to work on farms in the south. Most of the continent is in the tropical zone, but it has few tropical rain forests. Nearly one-third of Africa is savanna, and almost three-fifths is desert or steppe. The chief physical feature is the African plateau.

Beginning in the 1970s, recurrent drought has plagued the Sahel countries of Mali, Burkina Faso, and Chad, and the Horn of Africa (Sudan, Ethiopia, and Somalia). Expansion of the Sahara, deforestation, and a lack of rainfall have created repeated famine conditions in the area. The competition between **pastoralists** and nomadic herders for land has even resulted in ethnic conflict. Hundreds of thousands have died in Sudan's **Darfur** region as the result of a conflict that started in part because of competition for scarce resources. Many African countries are rich in natural resources, but colonial exploitation, corrupt leadership, and civil wars have left the majority in relative poverty.

Africa is home to over one billion people, about 890 million in sub-Saharan Africa. Population density on most of the continent is low, although people tend to be clustered around capital cities, coastlines, and areas of arable land. For example, only 12 percent of Niger's land can be tilled, but 90 percent of the country's 17 million people make their living from agriculture. The World Bank estimates that two-thirds of Africans are employed in the agricultural sector. In the developed world only one to two percent of the population is engaged in agriculture. According to the UN, however, a majority of Africans will live in cities by 2025. Although infant-mortality rates are high and life expectancies are low, the birthrate in most African countries is very high. Life expectancy in Zimbabwe is 54, South Africa 50, and Ghana 65. Life expectancy is a little over 55 years for sub-Saharan Africa as a whole, while the world average is just over 68 (web.worldbank.org; *CIA World Factbook*). (See Table 10.3.)

The UN recognizes the political borders between countries as they exist today. The legitimacy of African state boundaries, however, is disputed because Africans had little role in drawing them. Most lines of political demarcation are the constructions of European imperialists in the nineteenth century. At that time, British prime minister Lord Salisbury quipped that "we have been engaged in drawing lines upon maps where no white man's feet have ever trod; we have been giving away mountains and rivers and lakes to each other, only hindered by the small impediments that we never knew exactly where the mountains and rivers and lakes were." Salisbury might have added African peoples to his list. For the Europeans, as the old saying went, geography was about "maps not chaps" (Hargreaves 2004, 100–101). Africa, more than any other region, is a mosaic of different ethnicities, religions, cultures, and history.

Country borders tend to be less contested if they are clearly marked, do not cross densely populated areas, and follow mountain ranges. Because people often cluster around rivers, they form less stable borders. One scholar estimates that only about one-fifth of Africa's borders run across sparsely populated deserts, while many political boundaries divide ethnic groups (Zartman 2001, 66–67). The borders are incompatible with the Western notion of the nation-state. In the late-nineteenth century, one British colonial secretary commented that the division of chiefdoms and peoples was "a wretched system, unjust to the chiefs and their people, and a fruitful source of disputes and trouble to the dividing Powers" (Hargreaves 2004, 103).

Nation building in Africa after independence from the colonial powers was difficult because borders do not follow ethnic or physical boundaries. Traditional states such as the Ashanti in West Africa or the Bakongo in the Congo Basin included many different ethnic and linguistic groups, as did the states created by the **imperial borders**. The new historical African names that some indigenous leaders have given to their states do not reflect old traditional empires. For example, Benin today does not include the site of the ancient city-state of the same name (Fernandez-Armesto 1995, 588). Ghana (Gold Coast) encompasses little territory of medieval Ghana. Ghana's first leader, Kwame Nkrumah, claimed that "our people are fundamentally homogeneous, nor are we plagued with religious and tribal problems . . . we have hardly any color bar." In reality, Ghana has been riven by these divisions (von Laue 1987, 251).

African countries have fought over a dozen border wars since the 1950s, some as the result of poorly demarcated boundaries. For example, Somalia attacked Ethiopia in 1977, and rebels took over much of Eritrea from Ethiopia. The Ethiopian leaders who had overthrown Haile Selassie in 1974 turned to the Soviet Union and Cuba for weapons, expelling Somalian troops in 1978. The war, drought, and collectivization policies created famine conditions in the late 1970s (Kissi 2006, 65–66). According to US scholar William Zartman, "the 1998–2000 border war between Eritrea and Ethiopia was absolutely predictable, given the undemarcated nature of their shared boundary." Morocco and Algeria, Benin and Niger, Uganda and Tanzania, Chad and Libya, Senegal and Mauritania, Mali and Burkina Faso, and Nigeria and Cameroon have also fought border wars (Zartman 2001, 67).

Over the centuries, indigenous, colonial, and national influences have formed African identities. There is no one African culture, or even one Ethiopian or Nigerian culture. Ethiopia has seventy-six ethnic groups and 286 languages (Kennedy 1993, 215). Anthropologists identify approximately fifteen hundred different African languages, divided into five major groups: (1) Afro-Asiatic from roughly the Sahara north to the Mediterranean; (2) Niger-Congo (Bantu) in sub-Saharan Africa; (3) Khoisan in southern Africa; (4) Nilo-Saharan in pockets in north central Africa; and (5) Malagasy (Austronesian). Bantu speakers number over 200 million (Diamond 1999, 381–382). Africans often have greater allegiance to their ethnic group than to the central government, unless of course that ethnic group controls the government or is privileged by it. Ethiopia, Somalia, Angola, Sudan, Congo (formerly Zaire), and Rwanda have all experienced recent civil wars, as have most African countries in the last half-century.

Africa has historical links to the Middle East, South Asia, and Europe. Approximately one-third of all Africans are Muslims. In the seventh and eighth centuries, Arabs conquered northern Africa, bringing their language and religion with them. In the early sixteenth century, the Muslim Turks extended their Ottoman Empire into northern Africa, solidifying Islam in that region. Muslim traders brought Islam to Saharan and sub-Saharan Africa through commercial centers such as Timbuktu. Swahili Muslim gold traders from the region around what is Kenya today carried the religion down the east coast of Africa (Hanson 1995, 97–104).

In the fifteenth century, Portuguese ships began to ply African coastal waters, ushering in five hundred years of European influence on the continent. Muslim law forbade the enslavement of other Muslims, but Muslim traders were complicit in capturing non-Muslim Africans and selling them to European slavers. Until the Europeans took over most of Africa in the late-nineteenth century, Ottoman rulers and Omani sultans established coastal plantations in northeastern and eastern Africa. Europeans converted many Africans to Christianity. Ethiopia escaped colonial rule, but

FIGURE 10.1 British African Soldiers.
SOURCE: Library of Congress.

some 50 percent of Ethiopians adopted Christianity. About 40 percent are Muslim.

Since the end of **colonial rule**, traditional African societies have been challenged by Western political ideas emphasizing equal rights (e.g., for ethnic groups and for women) and individual rather than communal interests. The Western media has focused on practices in some countries that oppress women and deny others their human rights. Women have struggled in many countries to establish their legal equality. Forced marriages, polygamy, and clitoridectomy (removal of part or all of the clitoris) are not uncommon practices in some African countries. Women's educational opportunities in many countries in Africa are limited. Only one in five students at the higher education levels is female.

Because the definition of *modern* political, economic, and cultural development comes from foreign sources, many African societies face an identity crisis. For example, African writers have to overcome several obstacles to develop their work. The African written tradition is not as old as it is in Asia or Europe, and most sub-Saharan African societies passed down their histories orally. Only after the Europeans came did indigenous peoples develop written languages. African writers today face the dilemma of choosing to write in a European or a local language. If they use a European language they are often criticized for not writing authentic African works or of writing for African elites and non-African audiences. Only about 25 percent of West Africans are literate in a European language. Illiteracy, poverty, and lack of publishing opportunities restrict the circulation of books written in indigenous languages.

Africa has the highest average birthrate in the world and the lowest average life expectancy. The birthrate in war-torn Somalia, for example, averages at least 6 children per woman, and has a life expectancy of 51 years. Rwanda averages 4.7 children per woman and a life expectancy of 59. Although the population was reduced in 1994 tragically—by the genocide of 800,000 Tutsis and moderate Hutus—the government has launched a birth-control program, because Rwanda has one of the highest population densities in the world (CIA World Factbook).

Disease and malnutrition have hampered economic growth as well. Sub-Saharan countries spend about six percent of their GDP on healthcare (www.worldbank.org.) High infant-mortality rates, chronic malnutrition, AIDS, malaria, and civil strife have reduced life expectancies in some countries to barely two-thirds of those in developed countries. Life expectancy in Zambia is 51.5 years, Mozambique 52.3, and the Central African Republic 50.5 (CIA *World Factbook*).

AFRICA AS PART OF WORLD HISTORY

Africa is perhaps the least understood continent in the world. Misperceptions about African civilizations and peoples have abounded since European traders, slavers, and imperialists came into greater contact with Africans in the sixteenth century. Western domination of Africa in the last several hundred years has resulted in an image of a continent beset by disease, primitive tribal customs, rudimentary economies, and little technological development.

The record of African history has been dominated by Western accounts, which until recently ignored the political, cultural, and religious development of the region before Europeans began to explore the continent by sea in the fifteenth century. For hundreds of years before Europeans developed the means to explore and colonize Africa, African trade with Europe was peripheral to flourishing commerce with China, Persia, and India.

Ghana and Mali were among the great West African commercial states of the premodern period. The Mali king might have been the world's richest man in the fourteenth century. According to some reports, on his *hajj* (pilgrimage) to Mecca the Mali king caused inflation in Egypt because of his exorbitant spending in gold (Fernandez-Armesto 1995, 191–192). Ethiopia in the east and Zimbabwe in the south were flourishing agricultural and trading societies. The rich art, music, architecture, and literature of the premodern period attest to the sophistication of these civilizations.

Some of this history has been lost. Unlike the spread of European and Asian cultures, the majority of the sub-Saharan African diaspora in the West is made up of descendants of slaves, who over time were stripped of their language, religion, and history. Communities and families were torn apart, and the memories of shared regional African cultures faded. With few economic or educational opportunities, many Africans in other lands lost connection to their ancestral homes. Their voices, which would have constructed very different histories of Africa, were not heard.

When Western Europeans began to explore West Africa in the fifteenth century, the Mali Empire was already in decline. The Europeans had not witnessed the wealth or sophistication of this empire, and the political and economic troubles they found engendered in Europe an image of Africa as a less civilized place. A sixteenth-century Portuguese traveler could not believe that Africans could have built the sophisticated fortifications in Zimbabwe: "To say now how and by whom these buildings could have been made is an impossible thing, for the people of this land have no tradition of that sort of thing and no knowledge of letters: therefore they take it for a work of the devil, for when they compare it with other buildings they cannot believe that men could have made it" (Fernandez-Armesto 1995, 191–192).

Initially, Portuguese and Dutch traders were interested in gold and ivory. By the beginning of the eighteenth century, however, trade in slaves surpassed all other commerce with Africa. Slavery was not new to Africa, but the European slavers took the terrible practice to a new level. Between the sixteenth and the late-nineteenth century, approximately 12 million Africans were enslaved and taken to the Western Hemisphere and other places. More than 1 million died in passage.

The slave trade coincided with a decline of some African societies that have struggled to recover to this day. Europeans exploited and encouraged local rivalries to undermine Africans' control of the slave supply. These conflicts among African peoples made it easier for the Europeans—armed with quinine to combat malaria and technologies such as the repeating rifle and the steamboat—to penetrate the African interior.

Taking their cue from Great Britain—the greatest imperial power at the time—other European states began a frantic scramble for empire in Africa in the late nineteenth century. Darwin's theory of natural selection, or survival of the fittest, was now applied to nations. Even if some areas were not profitable, European states staked their claim to territories in Africa before someone else did. By the beginning of the twentieth century, the British, French, Portuguese, Italians, Spanish, Germans, and Belgians had established formal control over the entire continent, with the exception of Liberia and Ethiopia. The Berlin Conference of 1884–1885 finalized the imperial borders of Africa, most of which exist to this day.

Europeans exploited indigenous labor to tap Africa's abundant natural resources, which include rubber, timber, palm oil, cocoa, and various minerals. They gave countries names like Gold Coast (Ghana) and Ivory Coast. Edmund Morel, a British journalist, wrote about the exploitation of Africans in the Congo in *Black Man's Burden*, which was a direct reference to the hypocrisy of Rudyard Kipling's call for a "civilizing mission" in Africa in his poem "White Man's Burden." Morel charged that

> the Europeans managed to reduce all the varied and picturesque and stimulating episodes in "savage" life to a dull routine of endless toil for uncomprehended ends; to dislocate social ties and disrupt social institutions; to stifle nascent desires and crush mental development; to graft upon primitive passions the annihilating evils of scientific slavery, and the bestial imaginings of civilized man, unrestrained by convention or law; in fine, to kill the soul in a people—this is a crime which transcends physical murder. (Duiker and Spielvogel 2001, 674)

Europeans did improve transportation links, native health and nutrition, and sanitation. Average African life expectancies rose. But only a few African elites benefited from colonial rule. The vast majority of African people remained in subsistence agriculture or menial, poorly paid

FIGURE 10.2 Modernization of Africa. SOURCE: National Archives and Records Administration.

jobs. The best private- and public-sector positions went to the European colonists.

The end of colonial rule began in the late 1950s. Ghana, in 1957, was the first sub-Saharan country to break from British rule. When the Portuguese colonies of Mozambique and Angola gained their independence in 1975, the era of European rule in Africa was finally over. Southern Rhodesia declared independence from Britain in 1965 in order to maintain white rule, but African opposition movements forced Prime Minister Ian Smith to allow black majority rule in the country—renamed Zimbabwe—in 1980. South Africa abandoned **apartheid** and relinquished Namibia (formerly South West Africa) in 1990.

The transition to local African rule went peacefully except in those countries where Europeans had settled in greater numbers, such as Kenya, Algeria, Zimbabwe, and South Africa. The **Mau Mau rebellion** in Kenya from 1952 to 1959 was a particularly brutal conflict. The rebellion had its roots in the grievances of the Kikuyu people, whose lands had been confiscated by the British early in the twentieth century. The Kikuyu were relegated to small land reserves, which became overcrowded and impoverished. The Mau Mau were a radical militant Kikuyu element, many of whom were veterans of World War II. They demanded land reform and freedom for the Kikuyu lands.

In the early 1950s, British forces executed more than one thousand Mau Mau. One member of the all-white Kenya Police Reserve remembered killing Mau Mau captives immediately to avoid messy trials: "Killing prisoners? Well, it's not really the same thing, is it? I mean, I'd feel an awful shit if I thought I'd been killing prisoners" (Ascherson 2005, 26). The Mau Mau responded by brutally killing and terrorizing white settlers. They coerced the general Kikuyu population into joining the rebellion as well. The British press published photos and accounts of attacks on whites, but only thirty-two were killed. The Mau Mau slaughtered at least eighteen hundred fellow Africans. The British fostered the internecine conflict by recruiting "loyalist" Kikuyu into the Kikuyu Home Guard. About a third of Kikuyu society passed through detention camps, where the British tried to reindoctrinate them. British security forces lost about two hundred people, while approximately fifteen thousand Kenyans, alleged to be Mau Mau, were killed. Thousands more died in the detention camps. When Kenya gained its independence in 1963, a Kikuyu moderate, Jomo Kenyatta, became president. Although the British had imprisoned Kenyatta during the rebellion, he called the Mau Mau "a disease which has been eradicated, and must never be remembered again." (Elkins 2004; Anderson 2004).

Former Libyan leader Muammar Qaddafi labeled those who portrayed Africa as a war-torn continent "imbeciles and stupid," claiming that "Africa is the model continent in the world. Conflicts in Africa are a result of backwardness made by colonialism" (Lacey 2003, A1). While it is undeniable that **independent Africa** is burdened with a legacy of arbitrary and oppressive martial colonial regimes, some Africans themselves have made a mess of independent rule. Many African leaders adopted the imperialists' divide-and-conquer method to eliminate any political opposition and have exploited their countries' economies for personal self-aggrandizement.

As long as Europeans maintained advantageous economic relationships with their former colonies, they did not push for greater democratic rule or equitable economic development. Western technology and modern infrastructure had been introduced by the imperialists, but most of it was relegated to urban areas and barely reached most Africans. African economies remained dependent on exports of primary resources and Western imports of technologies and manufactured goods.

The model of the European nation-state did not fit African historical, political, or cultural realities. African political elites tended to establish **neo-patrimonial** systems in which leaders funneled government largesse to their own constituencies, often to the detriment of national political and economic development. Some Westerners might label this as corruption, but African leaders often argue that they are merely taking care of their own community or ethnic group. This communal character of political identity conflicts with development of transparent, rule-bound, formal democratic institutions and common national goals. As Africanist Patrick Chabal put it, African political elites "use their official position to fulfill their unofficial obligations to their clients and to meet the demands on which their power and standing as rulers rest" (Chabal 2005, 22–24).

The new African leaders were versed in progressive Western political values, although most African countries had no well-established political parties. Europeans trained few Africans in democratic practices or economic self-sufficiency; for example, when Belgium was forced to grant Congo its independence in 1960, Congolese held only three of the nearly five thousand senior administrative jobs. There were only thirty eligible Congolese college graduates to fill the remaining positions (Judt 2000, 66–69; Hochschild 2005, 40). At the beginning of their independence in 1961, Tanzania had two trained engineers and nine doctors in a country of 9 million people (Best et al. 2004, 397). While the number of college graduates in African countries has dramatically increased in the last few decades, Africa lags far behind other regions of the world.

In the first quarter century after the end of colonial rule, African governments were dominated by military regimes, and **military coups** were "Africa's revolutionary routine." From 1956 to 2001, thirty African nations had eighty successful coups. Almost 90 percent of these coup attempts tried to overthrow military regimes, which themselves had come to power through a coup (Collier 2004, 469). Some African leaders, in an attempt to legitimize extending their rule, have turned to rigging elections or amending their constitutions. After Kenya's presidential election of 2007, ethnic violence broke out in protest of the results. Although the election of Uhuru Kenyatta in the spring of 2013 was deemed fair,

Kenyatta is under indictment by the International Criminal Court for his support of the violence in the earlier election. In the spring of 2013, yet another coup in the Central African Republic continued this authoritarian political tradition. Supporters of the rebel leader, President Jichel Djotodia, have attacked and killed scores of people in towns backing the ousted President Francois Bozize.

The Cold War ensured that Africa would still have the attention of the great powers, but mainly as a battleground for allegiance to the free or communist world and as a source of valuable raw materials. When the West connived to assassinate Congo leader Patrice Lumumba in 1961 because of his leftist leanings, the continent began to take sides in the Cold War. Ghana's Kwame Nkrumah, one of the leaders of the pan-African movement, became involved in undermining other pro-Western governments in the region. Fearing that Africa might be fertile ground for communist takeovers, the United States supported any leader who did not nationalize foreign assets or partner with the Soviet Union. Most Western economic aid was a reward for political loyalty and went right into the coffers of corrupt elites and their cronies. The term to describe this was **kleptocracy** and described regimes such as Mobutu Sese Seko's in Zaire. In the 1980s, anti-Communist governments such as Zaire, Liberia, Sudan, and Somalia got 80 percent of US aid to sub-Saharan Africa. All of these countries descended into civil war in the 1990s. As foreign aid to sub-Saharan Africa increased in the last three decades of the twentieth century, poverty increased from 10 percent to over 65 percent (French 2010, 60). Corrupt regimes siphoned off monies and failed to build infrastructure and growing economies. The United States even backed South Africa, whose white-only government ran an apartheid system that deprived black Africans of their basic human and civil rights. South Africa has valuable deposits of gold, diamonds, and uranium, which can be used to build nuclear weapons.

Some Western scholars have called the Cold War a "long peace" because no war broke out between the superpowers, but as an old African aphorism goes, "When the elephants fight the grass suffers." Over 25 million people were killed in Third World conflicts during the Cold War. Not all of these casualties can be attributed to the Cold War directly, but the West and the Soviet bloc supplied their clients with sophisticated weapons that increased the length and lethality of civil conflicts in Ethiopia, Sudan, Somalia, Angola, and Mozambique. Furthermore, the superpowers plied African authoritarian leaders with the necessary military means to oppress their own people.

CHALLENGES TO AFRICAN POLITICAL AND ECONOMIC DEVELOPMENT

In the 1980s, many African countries seemed headed toward freer democratic governments and prosperous and growing economies. Military regimes collapsed, and the Cold War ended. But since the 1990s a disappointing number of African countries reverted to ethnic conflict and civil war: Ethiopia, Somalia, and Sudan in East Africa; Burundi, Uganda, Rwanda, and Congo in Central Africa; Mozambique and Angola in southern Africa; and Sierra Leone, Ivory Coast, Liberia, and Nigeria in West Africa. Freedom House reports that, of the 48 countries in sub-Saharan Africa, political and civil rights improved in 10 countries from 2005 to 2012, but got worse in 23. Freedom House rated 9 countries as "free," 21 "partly free," and 19 "not free." The political situation improved in such states as Niger, Cote d'Ivoire, and Zambia, and worsened in Gambia, Uganda, Ethiopia, and the Democratic Republic of Congo (Freedom House 2013).

Unstable governments and civil conflict have taken a heavy toll on African peoples. Almost half of African countries are experiencing or have recently ended civil conflicts (Gettleman 2010, 73). Millions have died in ongoing civil wars in Sudan, Somalia, Chad, and Congo. About a third of sub-Saharan countries are still suffering from violent civil wars. (Devarajan and Fengler 2013, 69). Furthermore, these **failed states** pose a threat to neighboring countries and can harbor terrorist organizations that seek to attack targets abroad. The UN reports that Africa has the most states that are susceptible to political and economic collapse.

World trade has boomed in the last several decades. Improved transportation networks, technological advances, and reduced trade barriers have brought economies together and spurred record economic growth. Developing countries such as China and India have opened their economies, lifting hundreds of millions of people out of poverty. Economic integration, exemplified by the European Union, has enabled regions to become important players in the world economic system.

Africa will not reach its full economic potential and fully integrate into the global economy until it achieves political stability and makes

FIGURE 10.3 Secretary Clinton with Morgan Tsvangirai, prime minister of Zimbabwe. SOURCE: US Department of State. PHOTO: Michael Gross.

significant improvements in education and healthcare. The imperialists left vast inequities in education levels and distribution of wealth, and since independence, corruption, bloated bureaucracies, protectionism, inadequate spending on education, civil conflicts, and high military spending have stunted economic development.

Of the 50 least-developed countries in the world, over 35 are located in Africa. Living standards in many sub-Saharan countries today are actually lower than they were in the 1980s. At the end of the 1950s, Ghana's per capita GDP was about the same as South Korea's. In 2012, Ghana's stood at $3,400 compared with $32,800 in South Korea (CIA *World Factbook*). Three of four Africans live on less than $2 a day, and in such countries as Mozambique, Malawi, and Tanzania, 90 percent of the population live on less than $2 a day (World Bank 2011). Excluding South Africa, sub-Saharan Africa has a smaller combined GDP than France (www.wto.org; www.usaid.gov; web.worldbank.org).

Although 42 of the 55 African countries are in the WTO, Africa is less connected to the global economy than any other continent. Africa accounted for about three percent of world trade in 2011. Africa has only two of the world's top 50 exporting countries; Nigeria ranks thirty-fifth, and South Africa forty-first. Of the leading importers, South Africa ranks thirty-second and Nigeria fiftieth (www.wto.org).

During colonial rule, African trade was directed toward the home country, and regional commercial links languished. African countries were predominantly raw-material exporters and importers of manufactured goods and technology. These trends persist. The EU, Asia, and the United States are Africa's top trading partners. Raw materials and commodities still make up over 90 percent of Africa's exports. Africa has 54 percent of the world's cobalt, 32 percent of its bauxite, 52 percent of its manganese, and 81 percent of its chromium stocks. Eighty-four percent of the world's platinum is in South Africa. Such mineral wealth has been a curse for some African countries. Mining has not brought more jobs, and brutal wars have erupted in western and southern Africa over gold and diamonds. Sierra Leone experienced a particularly awful civil conflict over diamonds in which child soldiers were enlisted to do the fighting. In this cruel conflict, rival militias cut the hands off of many of those they captured (Beah 2006).

Some economists argue that trade barriers between African countries stunt economic growth. Tariffs within the continent are higher than external duties. For example, the WTO estimates that it costs an African country $900 to import a container from Southeast Asia, but $2,500 from another African country. Intra-African trade can also reduce dependence on exports to the EU, the United States, and Japan. About two-thirds of African exports are fuels and minerals. When the economic crisis hit these developed countries in 2008 and demand dropped, African economies suffered as well (www.wto.org).

Extraction industries such as oil drilling provide few employment opportunities, and economic growth based on commodity exports is subject to price fluctuations. Most of the foreign direct investment (FDI) in Africa has gone to mine diamonds, platinum, and gold, and to drill for oil. Recent job growth has been dependent on higher prices on these and other commodities, foreign aid, and debt relief (UNECA 2010).

An increase in oil prices in the twenty-first century has been a rich source of revenue for some African countries, but few of the world's **petro-states** have been able to parlay oil exports into broad economic prosperity. Most African governments have not used their mineral wealth to rectify income inequalities or foster sustained economic growth. The unemployed and impoverished masses in many Middle East oil-exporting countries provide ample proof that oil reserves are no guarantee of long-term economic prosperity. Nigeria, sub-Saharan Africa's largest oil exporter, has a GDP of $2,800 per capita, ranking 180th in the world. Equatorial Guinea is the third-largest African oil exporter to the United States, and Washington, DC, has courted the corrupt regime of dictator Teodoro Obiang to keep the spigot open. Obiang has won three phony elections, garnering over 95 percent of the vote in 1996 and 2009. Teodorin Obiang, the dictator's son, paid $30 million for his mansion, $380 million for his yacht, and owns at least 25 luxury cars. The regime has been guilty of human-rights abuses and the population lives in poverty; one in three die before the age of 40 (CIA *World Factbook*; Silverstein 2011).

Foreign aid has often reduced incentives for African governments to reform economic and political policies. In the last sixty years, Africa has received over $1 trillion in aid. Sub-Saharan Africa received more than $300 billion from 1980 to 2000, but economic growth in much of the region declined (van de Walle 2005, 72–73). Corrupt officials have siphoned off fortunes, and governments have become dependent on foreign aid, reducing incentives to create rational tax structures and raise sufficient revenues. The AU estimates that corruption costs Africa $150 billion annually. Since 1972, dictators, many of them in Africa, have received an estimated one-third of international aid expenditures (democracies receive about one-fifth of all aid). Zaire's notorious despot Mobutu stole an estimated $5 billion from 1965 to 1997 (Moyo 2009). Paul Biya has received about $35 billion in aid in the three decades he has led Cameroon, but his country has seen no economic growth or reduction in poverty. In 2008 he brutally put down a protest against a hike in food prices, and added an amendment to the constitution to extend his rule until at least 2018. Other recipients of the West's largesse are Ethiopia's dictator Meles Zenawi, Chad's Idriss Deby, Uganda's Yoweri Museveni, and Rwanda's Paul Kagame (Easterly 2010, 37–38).

In many cases foreign aid has undermined local producers and skewed the local markets. It is not clear how much aid money is actually going to the people who need it. For example, as much as 60 percent of US foreign aid does not leave the United States because it is gobbled up by computers, travel, cars, salaries, and other overhead (Epstein 2005, 41). Some aid-receiving countries have thrived, however. Botswana and Mauritius received an average of over $150 per capita for three decades, and the governments used that money to build infrastructure and to improve the health and education systems. Another big aid recipient, Mozambique, has averaged over 7 percent growth for 20 years. Liberia has rebounded from a deadly civil war with the help of foreign aid, without which President Ellen Johnson-Sirleaf said that the conflict might not have ended. Liberia experienced double-digit growth rates at the end of the 2000s (*Time*, December 3, 2012; Radelet 2010, 98–99).

The economic outlook has improved in Africa in part because in the last decade the World Bank and the IMF have forgiven a significant portion of Africa's debt. In 2013, Brazil continued that trend by announcing that it was easing the $900 million debt burden on 12 African countries. Growth rates in Africa in the 2010s have rebounded to around 5 percent annually, and of the ten fastest-growing economies in the world, Africa is home to seven (www.voanews.com; www.oecd.org; www.usaid.gov). Ghana benefited from this debt forgiveness, registering a huge 14.4 percent rise in GDP in 2011 (*Time*, December 3, 2012).

Africa has great economic growth potential. In 2011 African attracted less than 5 percent of the world's foreign direct investment (investment made by a company or individual from one country into another); China alone received $124 billion in 2011, while Africa as a whole got $52 billion. The African Development Bank identifies infrastructure improvements as a key to improving economic opportunities. The Bank estimates that Africa spends only half of the necessary $93 billion annually on infrastructure projects (www.wto.org).

Economic development will not come without improvement in Africa's educational systems. A third of Africans are illiterate. A good indicator of modern economic and political development is female literacy, and here too African countries have trailed behind. African scholars produce only about two percent of the world's scientific knowledge. Unscrupulous officials often siphon off money that is supposed to go to teachers and schools. According a World Bank study of Ugandan public primary education, only 13 percent of the nonwage funds allocated to schools ever get there (Devarajan and Fengler 2013). If living standards do not improve, educated Africans will continue to leave for developed countries. Africa loses an estimated $2 billion annually because of "brain drain." Some African countries have lost more than half of their doctors. Half of Ghana's university graduates emigrate. Through "selective migration" policies, developed countries have welcomed these educated Africans. Over half of African immigrants in the United States have a graduate degree (*Time*, December 3, 2012; Lutulala 2012).

Scholars and politicians have spent as much time debating the causes of Africa's political and economic problems today as they have developing solutions. One school of thought blames the legacy of the slave trade, colonial rule, and the Cold War. Despite European efforts to shed the best light on the supposed civilizing elements of their colonial endeavors, on the whole the European imperialists exploited Africa's resources, brutalized its people, and fomented ethnic conflicts.

While not underestimating the damage done by colonial rule and Cold War conflicts, another school of African politicians and scholars acknowledges that African misrule since independence has contributed mightily to Africa's dismal human-rights record and slow economic development. Nigerian writer and political activist Wole Soyinka has been a particularly harsh critic of African leadership. While a student in Great Britain, he recalled that

> the nationalists, the first-generation elected leaders and legislators of our semi-independent nation, had begun to visit Great Britain in droves. We watched their preening, their ostentatious spending and their cultivated condescension, even disdain, toward the people they were supposed to represent. Some turned students into pimps, in return for either immediate rewards or influence in obtaining or extending scholarships. Visiting politicians financed lavish parties for one sole purpose—to bring on the girls! They appeared to have only one ambition on the brain: to sleep with a white woman. One scandal after another was hushed up by the British Home Office. (Rush 2006, 12)

Some African scholars blame the second generation of African leaders for not following the nation-building policies of their predecessors. This second generation often emptied their country's coffers and sent the continent barreling toward an economic dead end. These scholars point out that Africa is not the only continent that has experienced the oppression of imperialism and colonialism. They encourage African self-reliance and renewal on the premise that the former imperial powers are unwilling to provide the necessary aid or promote economic policies that would enable

African economies to compete in the world market (Houngnikpo 2000; Agonafer 1996).

During the Cold War, some African countries adopted the socialist economic strategies of their benefactors from the Soviet bloc. Ghana, Tanzania, Somalia, Benin, Madagascar, Mozambique, Angola, and Ethiopia also followed the socialist path, but they all failed to sustain economic growth. These are all among the poorest countries in the world. Some countries such as Kenya and Nigeria maintained freer market systems but experienced economic instability as well. African countries remained dependent on their European connections, exporting raw materials and importing value-added manufactured goods and technologies. Many states still rely on one main export—such as Zambia (copper), Cote d'Ivoire (cocoa), and Nigeria (oil)—and their economic growth is at the whim of global commodity prices. As the prices of oil, cocoa, coffee, and minerals have gone up in the 2010s, in part due to demand from China and India, Africa again has an opportunity to invest in more-balanced, manufacturing-based economies.

Economic development of African agriculture has suffered from a lack of infrastructure needed to profitably export commodities, as well as high protective tariffs levied by developed countries. During the 1960s, agricultural production was increasing about 3 percent a year, but it has declined since then. Africa produces less food now than it did in 1980. Famines in Somalia, Ethiopia, and Mozambique were exacerbated by war, disrupted distribution lines, corruption, mismanagement, and poverty. Approximately two-thirds of Africans make their living off the land. In contrast, less than two percent of Americans work in the agricultural sector. Impoverished Africans have flooded cities looking for work, creating vast slums and straining sanitation systems. Most Africans do not have running water or electricity, two benchmarks of modern economic development.

Many African economies still have structural weaknesses that could undermine sustainable economic development. African economies must grow at a high rate to provide jobs for the burgeoning population but disease stunts economic growth in the region. Africa has about 15 percent of the world's population, but 66 percent of the world's HIV/AIDS cases and 80 percent of the world's malaria cases. There has been some progress on the HIV/AID front: nearly two-thirds of those infected receive anti-AIDS drugs today, and Africa has seen a 25 percent decline in these cases from

2001 to 2011. Ninety percent of the malarial deaths still occur in Africa, but malaria cases fell by 33 percent from 2000 to 2010. (www.who.org).

Nonetheless, Africa is struggling to reach the goals of the UN **Millennium Development Project**. In 2000, 189 countries pledged to eliminate extreme poverty and hunger, reduce child mortality, and combat HIV/AIDS. The WTO estimates that Africa needs investments of $75 billion a year to fight diseases such as AIDS, malaria, tuberculosis, and river blindness. Corruption is rampant in the health sector as well; in 2013, Sierra Leone arrested top health officials for skimming off half a million dollars of grants provided by vaccine provider GAVI Alliance. "Doctors are meant to heal wounds," said one member of Sierra Leone's Anti-Corruption Commission. "Not bleed them" (*New York Times*, April 14, 2013).

AFRICAN STATE BUILDING AND GLOBAL ECONOMIC INTEGRATION: THE CASES OF NIGERIA AND THE DEMOCRATIC REPUBLIC OF CONGO

This section focuses on two African countries to illustrate some of the historical, geographical, economic, political, and cultural challenges the region faces in state building, economic development, and integration into the international community. Nigeria is an oil-rich country, but political corruption, political instability, and ethnic conflicts have stunted its growth. The Democratic Republic of Congo is another resource-rich African country whose economic progress has been blunted by a particularly onerous colonial legacy, poor leadership, civil war, disease, and inadequate spending on infrastructure and education.

Despite its oil wealth, Nigeria remains mired in political conflict and economic stagnation. It is the sixth-largest oil producer in the world, but has suffered the many deprivations of a country reliant on oil exports. With 175 million people, it has the largest population of the sub-Saharan countries. As a geographical entity, Nigeria is purely and simply a British imperial creation, and, like other postcolonial states in Africa, it has struggled to establish a national identity. The British formed this huge and unwieldy state by combining Lagos and South Nigeria in 1906 and adding the northern areas in 1914. Nigeria has some 250 different ethnic groups. The four largest are the mostly Christian Yoruba in the southwest (Lagos), the Igbo in the southeast, and the Muslim Hausa and Fulani in the north; these groups comprise about two-thirds of Nigeria's population. The other ethnic groups are usually subsumed into these groups. One African scholar observes that "what people actually call the North is the Hausa-Fulani, forgetting that there are non-Hausa-Fulani people living in the North. When you talk of the West, they say it is Yoruba. When you talk about the East, they think of the Igbo. What happens is that you have core groups and peripheral groups" (Ayoade 2005, 40).

The uneasy coexistence of these peoples changed into factional fighting after Nigeria achieved independence in 1960. British administrators favored the Muslim peoples in the north, and because they usually voted as a bloc, they dominated the government in Lagos. The Hausa and Fulani make up about 30 percent of the population, the Yoruba and the Igbo in the south comprise about 40 percent. About half of the population is Muslim, and 40 percent Christian. The Igbo became second-class citizens in the Muslim-run government, and their massacre at the hands of government forces prompted them to form the independent state of Biafra in 1967. The Yoruba and Hausa-Fulani were not about to let the Igbo get away with Nigerian oil in the region, and Lagos reestablished its hold in a bloody three-year civil war. At least a million Biafrans died in the fighting or starved to death. In this case, as has been all too common in Africa, the famine was the result of war and the poverty it caused.

The wartime alliance between the Yoruba and the Hausa-Fulani broke down after the war ended, and sporadic clashes among the four largest ethnic groups and smaller minorities have continued, resulting in thousands of dead, wounded, and homeless citizens. In the 1990s, serious communal clashes erupted after the annulment of an election of a Yoruba president. Over two hundred Hausa-Fulani and Yoruba were killed in fighting in Lagos in 2000 and 2002 (Bah 2005, 48–49).

Nigeria has had eleven different regimes and repeated military coups since independence in 1960. Its governments have changed about every five years. Ethnic divisions have certainly contributed to the political instability, and the failure of multiparty democracy to build the nation-state has given authoritarian leaders the excuse to run a one-party system. Nigeria's leaders tried to reconcile the country's ethnic differences in the constitutions of 1963, 1979, 1989, and 1999, but parties remain linked to ethnic groups, making consensus and compromise difficult and causing parliamentary gridlock (Bah 2005, 48–49). A decline in the standard of living, conflicts over scarce resources, ethnic favoritism, dominance of the north, and the threat of the northern Muslim leaders to impose Islamic law in the northern provinces have led to continued civil unrest. Attacks by the Islamist terrorist group Boko Haram has resulted in hundreds of deaths in the north, and brutal reprisals from the Nigerian army, with civilians caught in the crossfire. "When you burn down shops and massacre civilians," said the governor of Borno State, "you are pushing them to join the camp of Boko Haram" (*New York Times*, April 30, 2013).

Oil revenues buoyed the economy in the 1970s, but when the price of oil sank in the early 1980s, Nigeria suffered the same fate as other petro-states; Nigerian per capita income plummeted by nearly three-fourths by the middle of the decade. Today, 70 percent live below the poverty line. Nigeria ranks 31st in the world in GDP, but 180th in per capita GDP. The World Bank estimates that 80 percent of the oil revenues go to one percent of the population, and corruption is rampant. Because of its declining refining capacity, Nigeria actually has to import gasoline. The infrastructure serving the 10 million people in Lagos is in serious condition. Roads are pockmarked, electricity blackouts are regular, and crime is rampant. The UN Human Development Index ranks Nigeria's standard of living below Bangladesh; life expectancy is only 52.5 years, which ranks 211th in the world (*CIA World Factbook*).

This rapid economic decline and the expansion of disparity in wealth have exacerbated the divisions between the Muslim north and other ethnic groups in the south. People living in the oil-producing south and on the Niger delta have seen few of Nigeria's oil profits. The deadliest and most publicized incident of ethnic strife was the Ogoni uprising against government forces and Shell Oil in the 1990s, which left a thousand dead and tens of thousands homeless. Oil spills in the region are an environmental disaster. Unrest in the poor southern delta region, where foreign oil companies operate, costs about one thousand lives a year. Rebel groups in the south tap pipelines to sell oil on the black market. This dangerous practice has caused numerous accidents, but the incentives are too great: a single can of oil can bring in the equivalent of two weeks' wages. Local militias have hijacked the government's attempts to develop the region.

In a survey conducted in 2004, Nigerians had less faith in their politicians than any other Africans. Only 7 percent trusted the government (Dowden 2009, 451). The political outlook has improved in the 2010s, however. The international community did not deem the April 2007 elections for a new president credible, but it was the first nonviolent transfer of power in Nigerian history. In the spring of 2011, Goodluck Jonathan defeated Mahammadu Buhari, a Muslim from the north, which sparked riots in which 800 people died. A Human Rights Watch researcher observed that "the April elections were heralded as among the fairest in Nigeria's history, but they also were among the bloodiest." Jonathan, a Christian from the Niger Delta, has brought a semblance of stability to the country. Nigeria achieved robust growth rates of 7 percent from 2010 to 2012, but these figures are highly dependent on world oil prices (*CIA World Factbook*).

The history of the Democratic Republic of the Congo (DRC, formerly Zaire) illustrates the many obstacles that have stood in the way of African development and greater integration into the global economy. The DRC comprises one-thirteenth of the African landmass and possesses some of Africa's most valuable natural resources, such as oil, rubber, gold, diamonds, copper, and zinc. Belgian King Leopold II made Congo his personal property in the late-nineteenth century, and he accumulated a vast fortune from sales of ivory, rubber, and minerals. The Belgians had little regard for African lives and exploited them ruthlessly. The barbarism of Belgian rule was laid bare in Joseph Conrad's famous novel, *The Heart of Darkness*. Through forced labor, disease, and killing, scholars estimate that Congo lost nearly 50 percent of its population during Belgian colonial rule—approximately 10 million people (Hochschild 2005, 42).

Congo has confronted formidable impediments to stable, legitimate, and unified governance. It has a population of 75.5 million people who speak more than seventy-five different languages. The majority of the people are Bantu, but Congo has over two hundred other ethnic groups. The literacy rate is 67 percent, with wide disparity between men (77 percent) and women (57 percent). Life expectancy is 56.1 years, ranking 200th in the world (*CIA World Factbook*).

Patrice Lumumba was the first prime minister of Congo after achieving independence in 1960. But his socialist leanings, and Western fears that Congo would fall into the Soviet sphere of influence prompted the US and Belgian governments to assist the political opposition to assassinate him (see De Witte 2001). His successor, Mobutu Sese Seko, established one of the most corrupt dictatorships in Africa. Mobutu, who changed the name of Congo to Zaire, was supported by the United States and Europe during the Cold War for his staunch anti-communism. Mobutu's thievery imitated the Belgians'. By the time he was forced out of office in 1997,

Figure 10.4 Nixon and President Mobutu Sese Seko of Zaire meeting in the Oval Office, October 10, 1973. SOURCE: US National Archives and Records Administration.

Mobutu had homes in Switzerland and France and hundreds of millions of dollars stashed in foreign bank accounts.

Longtime opposition leader Laurent Kabila mobilized rebel forces in eastern Congo and overthrew Mobutu's government in 1997. Congo descended into what some have called Africa's First World War. Eight countries in the region became involved in the conflict. Rwanda, Burundi, and Uganda backed the opposition to Kabila, and Angola, Zimbabwe, Namibia, Chad, and Sudan sent troops to support Kabila's embattled regime and to steal the country's mineral wealth. An estimated 5.4 million people have died in the fighting, and over 2 million Congolese have been displaced. It is the deadliest war since World War II (French 2009, 44).

Unlike the rebel leaders who had fought the colonialists or corrupt regimes, the new generation of fighters in the Congo and neighboring Uganda have made plunder their end rather than political goals. These hoodlums have recruited children into their militias. About one-third of the rebel fighters in Congo are under eighteen. These gangs have used rape as pure sadism rather than as a terror tactic. This complete lack of morality has made political solutions to these conflicts impossible. The only way to defeat these groups, according to journalist Jeffrey Gettleman, is to kill the leaders (Gettleman 2010, 73, 75).

In 2001, Kabila was assassinated and his son, Joseph Kabila, has been in power since. In late 2002, the younger Kabila was able to negotiate the withdrawal of the Rwandan Army from eastern Congo, and the warring parties in Congo agreed to a government of national unity. In November 2006, Congo held its first multiparty election in forty years, which the international community deemed fair and impartial. Kabila won nearly 60 percent of the vote. The United Nations has some 14,000 troops on the ground to keep the uneasy peace (Gettleman and Mwassi 2006, 3).

Congo's civil war, weak central government, and rampant corruption have left the infrastructure in total disrepair. As one local Congolese official asked of a *New York Times* journalist, "How will you get anything to the market?" There's only so much you can carry on your head." A gaping divide between rich and poor is reflected in its per capita GDP of $400, which ranks 228th in the world. In a country with an estimated $24 trillion in mineral wealth over 70 percent live below the poverty line. There is some hope for this war-torn country; the global recession of 2008–2009 cut Congo's growth rate in half, but the country rebounded to a healthy 7 percent in 2012 (*CIA World Factbook*; *New York Times*, December 15, 2012).

AFRICA AND GLOBALIZATION:
RELATIONS WITH THE UNITED STATES, EUROPE, AND ASIA

The international community has vital economic, security, and humanitarian interests in peace and prosperity in Africa. Africa is becoming an important exporter of crude oil, holding 9 percent of the world's oil reserves. Demand from Asia and concerns about the stability of African and Middle Eastern suppliers such as Libya, Iraq, and Iran have increased the significance of the oil-rich countries of Nigeria, Chad, Angola, Sudan, Equatorial Guinea, Congo, and Gabon. The United States and Canada import about one-third of sub-Saharan crude oil, China another third, and Europe about 20 percent. Africa supplies 10 percent of US oil imports (CFR 2011l; Flintoff 2012).

The United States has steadily expanded trade through the Africa Growth and Opportunity Act (AGOA) of 2000, which gave 38 (now 39) African countries duty-free access to US markets. Through AGOA's Third Country Fabric Provision, African textile manufacturers using materials from outside of the continent can export textile products to the United States duty free. Some 6,400 items now have no import duty. US imports from sub-Saharan Africa shot up 177 percent from 2002 to 2012, although oil made up the bulk of them. US exports to the region grew 6.3 percent from 2011 to 2012, and a third of those went to South Africa. In 2012 legislation was passed to extend the Third Country Fabric Provision to 2015 (www.ustr.gov).

In the 2000s, the United States pledged $15 billion for an Emergency Plan for AIDS Relief, and in 2003 launched the Millennium Challenge Corporation for long-term economic development to those countries that displayed solid democratic practices, such as a commitment to women's rights. In 2010 the United States made grants of over $400 million each to Mali and Burkina Faso, over $500 million to Senegal, Ghana, Mozambique, and almost $700 million to Tanzania (MCC 2010). In conjunction with President Obama's visit to Africa in the summer of 2013, the United States pledged $7 billion for an ambitious plan to double access to electricity in sub-Subharan Africa (Minneapolis *Star Tribune*, July 2, 2013).

The United States is also very concerned about the upsurge in terrorist activity in East Africa. In August 1998, the terrorist organization al Qaeda claimed responsibility for bombing two US embassies in Dar es Salaam, Tanzania, and Nairobi, Kenya, killing over 250 people and injuring another 4,000. US President Bill Clinton responded by bombing suspected terrorist training camps in Afghanistan and a pharmaceutical plant in Khartoum, which was allegedly making chemical weapons for terrorists. No solid evidence has been found that this was true. In recent years several Somalis living in America have returned to Somalia to engage in the fighting against the government or to carry out terrorist attacks. The new US African command (AFRICOM) is part of the effort to head off these terrorist and piracy acts, to protect US economic interests, and to counter Chinese influence in the region. In the fall of 2013, Al Shabab, the Somali Islamist group, conducted a deadly terrorist attack on an upscale mall in Nairobi in retaliation for Kenya's incursion into Somalia in 2011 to support the anti-Islamist government. Over 60 people were killed, a stark reminder that security in the region is still fragile.

Europe is twenty miles away from Africa, and their modern histories are inextricably linked. In 2007, the United Kingdom marked the bicentennial of the abolition of the slave trade. Britain was the first major colonial power to end the slave trade (although slavery in British colonies continued), and British prime minister Tony Blair invoked Britain's moral stand two centuries ago as a way to challenge the EU and the rest of the developed world to eradicate African poverty, disease, and debt (M2 Presswire 2006).

The EU is making new efforts to increase trade with Africa. It now has consular and trade offices in nearly every African capital. In 2007 the EU signed interim economic partnerships (EPAs) with several African countries that opened the EU market to African goods without tariffs. For example, textiles from Kenya and Tanzania, and beef from Botswana are sold in the EU under EPAs. Africa's trade with the EU steadily increased from 2004 to 2008, but the global economic downturn in 2009 resulted in a 10 percent drop. The European Union, like the United States, imports mainly African oil. In the wake of the 2011 revolt against Libyan dictator Muammar Qaddafi and the disruption of that country's oil supplies, Nigeria and Angola stepped up their oil exports to Europe (Eurostat 2011).

As of 2013, however, African countries have not ratified the EPAs, much to the dismay of the EU. Some African leaders are focusing on increasing trade within the continent, and they see the EPAs as detrimental to that effort. Some observers—such as Abdoulie Janneh, the UN under-secretary general and executive secretary of the Economic Commission for Africa—recommend that Africa concentrate first on strengthening its economies through regional trade and at the same time entering into phased-in freer trade agreements with Europe and the rest of the more developed world. Some Latin American and other developing countries have protested the EPAs, arguing that the agreements violate WTO rules prohibiting unilateral trade agreements that afford a country special treatment (www.theguardian.com). African countries have been particularly critical of European agricultural subsidies, which the Africans feel have undercut this potential export sector.

While the jury may still be out about the long-term safety of genetically modified crops, Europe's opposition to them has had a detrimental short-term effect on the African agricultural sector. During the famine of 2003, some African governments refused shipments of genetically modified grains from the United States for fear that Europe would not accept future exports from Africa (Love 2005, 151ff).

Africa's heavy dependency on the West has prompted some African countries to look elsewhere for economic connections. The region is rapidly becoming an important trading partner to Asia, especially India and

China. India and eastern and southern Africa have centuries-old connections that are being rekindled today. Many people of Indian ancestry live in East African countries, some of whom came in the late-nineteenth century to work on construction projects such as the Kenyan-Ugandan railroad. The father of Indian independence, Mohandas Gandhi, spent many of his early years in South Africa.

India's high economic growth rates and geographical position hold great promise for the future. Indians also speak English, which is a big advantage over the Chinese in doing business in Africa. At the Indian-African Partnership Conference in New Delhi in the fall of 2006, an Indian Foreign Ministry official declared that "there is a new expectation and optimism as modern India seeks to enhance its relationship with a resurgent Africa to contribute to the development of a new international order." Hundreds of African and Indian businesspeople at the conference discussed more than 300 projects worth approximately $17 billion. India's trade with Africa jumped from $1 billion in 2001 to about $50 billion in 2011–2012. From 2008 to 2011, India's trade with Africa grew 32.4 percent, faster than China's at 27 percent. India is now Africa's fourth-largest market (www.business-standard.com).

The new Export-Import Bank of India and the Indian Africa Fund have facilitated this trade, and India has granted credits to many African countries for technology transfers, rural electrification, manufacturing plants, potable water facilities, and other development projects. India has also tapped Africa's energy resources. In 2003, India's largest company, the Oil and Natural Gas Corporation Ltd. (ONGC), bought a 45-percent stake in Greater Nile Petroleum Oil Company in Sudan. ONGC has also been involved in oil and natural gas deals in Ivory Coast, Gabon, and Egypt.

In 2009 China surpassed the United States as Africa's largest trade partner. China's trade with Africa amounted to $200 billion in 2012, outpacing the $100 billion in trade with the United States and India's $65 billion (Khare 2103; www.census.gov). China's exports to Africa are up nearly 40 percent since 2007, and China wants and needs vital African raw materials, particularly oil. Ninety percent of China's imports from Africa are primary commodities; fuels are over two-thirds of that amount (Danchie 2010). In the last decade China has made more loans to Africa than the World Bank (*Economist* 2011b). Chinese companies have signed big mining contracts in such countries as Zambia, Gabon, and the Democratic Republic of Congo. In 2008, China offered Congo a $6 billion investment deal for copper and cobalt mines, railways and roads, and clinics, schools, universities, and hospitals. China has invested heavily in infrastructure to extract oil and minerals from the interior of the continent. Beijing has launched sixty-three aid projects in forty-eight African countries and regions, primarily for the agricultural sector, infrastructure projects, and health initiatives. China also has granted zero-tariff treatment for many imports from more than twenty-five of the least-developed countries in Africa (French 2010, 60–68).

Still, there is some doubt whether China will do better by Africa than developed Western countries. A Congolese legal scholar complained that the Chinese do not make use of local talent in management and technical positions: "They hire laborers, and that's it. . . . When they pack up and go, the Congo will be left with nothing, not even an upgrade in our human resources. Our earth will be dug up, emptied, and left that way" (French 2010, 60–68). In 2013 the Niger government renounced some provisions of its oil contracts with China, charging the Chinese with environmental degradation. Gabon confiscated oil areas from the Chinese and gave them to its state company. Niger's oil minister Foumakoye Gado reflects this new African concern about sustainable development: "This is all we've got. . . . We've got to fight to get full value for these resources . . . to bring something to our people." In neighboring Chad, the oil minister halted the work of Chinese companies because they were making unprotected Chadian workers clean up excess oil they had dumped into ditches. The oil minister threw the company's local director and his assistant out of the country (*New York Times*, September 18, 2013).

In 2013, Ghanaian officials shut down gold mines run by the Chinese and jailed more than 200, charging them with pollution and mistreatment of Ghanaian workers. Local residents even attacked some of the Chinese workers. One Chinese family had borrowed almost $490,000 to invest in the venture in Ghana, and stood to lose it all. "My son might be killed in Ghana," lamented the mother. "But if he comes back he's dead [from debt] anyway" (*New York Times*, June 30, 2013).

China is also interested in the fruits of African agriculture, although purchase of land is a sensitive issue. China has encouraged emigration among the approximately 12 million farmers who have been displaced by China's Three Gorges Dam project. But as one scholar points out, "For many, land is at the heart of a nation's identity, and it is especially easy to raise emotions about outsiders when land is involved" (French 2010, 64).

International pressure on African countries to strengthen their liberal democratic systems and grant citizens basic human rights will be complicated in the near future by China's economic boom. The Chinese leadership has ignored undemocratic practices from their suppliers. The UN has failed to act decisively in Darfur, for example, because of Chinese opposition to Security Council sanctions on Sudan, an important oil exporter to China.

African Prospects

In the spring of 2013, *The Economist* ran a special report, "Emerging Africa: A Hopeful Continent." The report declared that "African lives have already greatly improved over the past decade. The next 10 years will be even better" (Christiaensen and Devarajan 2013). The West African country of Senegal has been a model of political stability since independence, and its president, Macky Sail, sees a bright future for the continent: "I am very optimistic, because I am aware that Africa today has every chance to catch up. Africa has a young population, natural resources, and, now, democracy. Africa is stable, democratic, and secure, and its natural resources are better managed thanks to transparency in the extractive industries. . . . Development has gone around the world, to Europe, America, to Asia. It's Africa's turn now" (Sall 2013).

Sail might be exaggerating Africa's prospects, but Africans themselves agree with him. Polls often show that Africans are more hopeful about the future than people in other regions. A 2010 Pew Forum survey found that 76 percent of sub-Saharan Africans believed that life would be better in five years (Pew Forum 2010). Perhaps some Africans feel that they have reached rock bottom and that their lives can only improve. Some scholars point to Africans' strong religious beliefs. "We have our faith, if nothing else," observed one Nigerian pastor. "We can find hope in faith even if there is darkness all around." Africans are clearly committed to democracy and desire strong, competent, and just leaders. According to one Gallup poll, 87 percent of Africans—tied at the top with North Americans—thought that democracy was the best form of government. Africans prove this again and again by voting in droves any time a truly free election is held (Palgreen 2007, 4).

Several indicators point to better days for African economic development, political stability, and full integration into the global political and economic community. The debt burden that had retarded growth for two decades has eased. Cell phone and Internet use is growing fast in Africa, increasing productivity and expanding local and regional markets. African growth rates have averaged a healthy 5 percent in the 2010s, although the UN Millennium Development Project targets growth rates of 7 percent in order to halve African poverty by 2015. Poverty rates (living on less than $1.25 a day) have declined from 58 percent in 1999 to 48.5 percent in 2012, but this rate is still far too high (MDG Report 2013). Some economists have suggested that these rates can be dramatically reduced in the resource-rich countries with a simple transfer to its citizens of 10 percent of the resource revenues (Christiaensen and Devarajan 2013).

Civil wars in Rwanda, Angola, Sierra Leone, Burundi, and Liberia have ended, and all have conducted elections. Africa has the most violent conflicts in the world, but in the last five years the continent has made the most progress toward ending war. In January 2006, Liberia conducted its first peaceful elections in a decade, and Ellen Johnson-Sirleaf became the continent's first female president. Many African countries are trying to integrate their complex web of political actors—ethnic groups, religious identities, and classes—into national governments based on accepted democratic norms of political behavior.

Africa today has more democratic regimes than ever before. Since 1990 most African leaders have left office voluntarily. Zimbabwe's despotic President Robert Mugabe, who has run that country's economy into the ground, is a glaring exception. This new generation of leaders is often Western educated and comes from the private sector. Most realize that Mugabe's dogmatic anticolonial rhetoric—however well-grounded in historical realities—does nothing to build a country and improve relations with needed economic partners in Europe. Africans are generally in favor of Western aid and loan packages that have been tied to better governance (French 2010, 69). Some African intellectuals also praise the International Criminal Court in The Hague for indicting perpetrators of human-rights abuses: "The ICC has contributed to the diminution of violence," says Richard Pituwa, the head of a Congolese radio station. "I know people in the armed groups. I grew up with some of them. Now they begin to fear: *If I become a big chief, they might come for me*" (Hochschild 2010, 82).

Many African countries are eschewing the tradition of using extralegal means to exact retribution from previous regimes. Countries are holding former leaders accountable by establishing transparent and fair political and judicial systems. A dozen countries, such as Sierra Leone and Zambia, have indicted former leaders for corruption and crimes against humanity. In early 2007 Ethiopian courts sentenced former dictator Mengistu Haile Mariam to life in prison for genocide during his military rule from 1974 to 1991. Forty-seven other officials in his government received sentences as well. Mengistu lives in Zimbabwe, however, and Mugabe has refused to deport him (Timburg 2006, 13).

Progress is also being made in stemming the tide of desertification. In the last fifty years, the Sahara has grown by an area about the size of Somalia. The UN estimates that fourteen African countries have water shortages, and another ten or so will have water scarcity by 2025. The UN also reports that nearly 50 percent of Africa's land is "threatened by degradation." Niger has led a program to plant millions of trees to stop desertification. In the last two decades Niger has "regreened" approximately 12 million acres. Niger has seen an increase in rainfall, and farmers can grow vegetables in the shadows of the trees. One environmental researcher found that conflicts between farmers and herders over scarce land have decreased by 80 percent (Perry 2010, 70–73).

Africans are getting healthier and better educated, both prerequisites of political stability and sustainable economic growth. The mortality rate of African children under five years has declined 47 percent from 1990 to 2011, and maternal mortality is down 42 percent. In the 29 countries where data is available, primary-school enrollment is up from 64 percent to 2000 to almost 90 percent today. Much still needs to be done to achieve gender equality, however. Less than 20 percent of women in sub-Saharan Africa are paid for their work (MDG Report 2013).

The greatest success story in recent African history is the end of apartheid in South Africa and the relatively peaceful transition from white to black majority rule in 1994. The collapse of communism in Europe from 1989 to 1991 overshadowed this monumental political development. After decades of apartheid run by a seemingly intransigent white government, few scholars predicted its demise or a peaceful transition to majority rule.

The inspirational story of **Nelson Mandela** and the African National Congress attests to the importance of enlightened leadership to human progress. Mandela's courageous and peaceful opposition to apartheid

FIGURE 10.5 President William J. Clinton with Nelson Mandela, Philadelphia Freedom Festival, July 4, 1993. SOURCE: US National Archives and Records Administration.

eventually persuaded the white South African leadership to do the right thing. In 1990, President F. W. de Klerk released Mandela after twenty-seven years in prison and agreed to end apartheid and to grant all South Africans full rights of citizenship.

South Africa is the richest and most industrialized country in subSaharan Africa. Since South African democracy emerged in 1994, the literacy rate for black men has jumped from 63 to 94 percent (92 percent for women). After initial hardships, the economy has rebounded to rank twenty-sixth in the world (McLaughlin 2005; *CIA World Factbook* 2013). South Africa promises to be the engine of the region's economic expansion.

Ghana's first president, Kwame Nkrumah, dreamed of an all-African state that would overcome its cultural and ethnic differences to create a powerful counterpart to the rest of the world's powers. In part as a result of US and Belgian intrigue to overthrow Lumumba in Congo, thirty-two African states formed the **Organization of African Unity** (OAU) in 1963. The OAU hoped to maintain the independence of African states in the wake of immense Soviet and American pressure to take sides in the Cold War. It was also an attempt to find a common African bond of freedom, justice, and equality. The original charter read that it is "desirous that all African States should henceforth unite so that the welfare and well-being of their peoples can be assured" (Duiker and Spielvogel 2001, 914).

The OAU was a loose grouping that could not overcome competing national and regional interests that were exacerbated by Cold War rivalries. Like pan-Arabism, pan-Africanism foundered because of the myriad African languages, ethnic groups, histories, and traditions. Geographical proximity and the common experience of colonialism were the main unifiers, while war, political instability, and poverty were the great dividers.

After the end of the Cold War, Africa renewed efforts to create a greater continental community. In 1991, the OAU formed an African Economic Community to promote trade within the region. But lack of economic growth and protectionist policies have thwarted greater integration. Leaders of any country are loath to reduce tariff barriers or open borders to imports when so many of their own people are out of work. Ten West African nations formed the Economic Community of West African States in 1975, but its members saw little benefit. Growth rates for these ten countries fell precipitously in the 1980s. Although extenuating global economic factors and local political instability were often to blame for the downturn in economic fortunes, politicians had no incentive to further economic integration.

In 2001, African leaders formed the **African Union** (AU), and agreed to the **New Partnership for Africa's Development** (NEPAD), which called for a thorough examination and rectification of the policies that have stunted African economic growth for so long. As one scholar of Africa has observed, it remains to be seen whether African leaders are willing to admit their role in misguided economic policies and whether there really exists a new set of circumstances to send Africa on a path of prolonged peace and prosperity. African leaders, their bureaucracies, and their militaries must be committed to end armed conflict, corruption, and patronage, and instead practice democratic principles and adopt economic policies that benefit all of their people (Chabal 2005, 447–478). Nonetheless, it is clear that African governments are operating in a new and more open environment. Continued political and economic progress is dependent on a freer press, incorruptible civil servants, and powerful watchdog legislatures and judiciaries (van de Walle 2005, 82).

The AU's Peace and Security Council has played a key role in resolving and preventing conflicts. NEPAD has implemented an African Peer

Review Mechanism to monitor government practices. Twenty-five African countries have signed on to the initiative, which mobilizes regional organizations to monitor government practices and suggest improvements (M2 Presswire 2006).

Mandela once said that, "I am fundamentally an optimist. Whether that comes from nature or nurture, I cannot say. Part of being optimistic is keeping one's head pointed toward the sun, one's feet moving forward. There were many dark moments when my faith in humanity was sorely tested, but I would not and could not give myself up to despair. That way lays defeat and death" (Mandela 1994). Mandela captured the heart and soul of most African peoples, who remain sanguine about their future despite all of their years of suffering and heartache.

TIMELINE OF TWENTIETH-CENTURY AFRICAN HISTORY

1884–1885	Congress of Berlin delineates European empires in Africa.
1898–1902	Boer War in South Africa.
1919	After Germany's defeat in World War I, Great Britain takes over German colonies in Tanzania and Namibia; France takes mandates in Togo and Cameroon.
1957–1975	African states gain independence.
1963	Organization of African Unity created.
1975	Economic Community of West African States created.
1980	White rule ends in Rhodesia.
1991	African Economic Community created.
1994	White rule ends in South Africa.
1994	Genocide in Rwanda.
1997	Mobutu Sese Seko deposed; Congo civil war.
1998	Bombings of US embassies in Tanzania and Kenya.
2001	African Union formed.
2001	The New Partnership for Africa's Development created.
2007	Nigerian president Umaru Musa Yar'Adua elected in a disputed vote.
2007	Chinese premier Hu Jintao visits eight African countries.
2011	Free and fair Nigerian presidential election of Goodluck Jonathan.
2013	Somali terrorist group al-Shabab attack on Kenyan shopping mall.

Table 10.1 Population and Rate of Growth

Country	Population	RNI%	Country	Population	RNI%
West Africa:			**East Africa:**		
Benin	9,877,292	2.84	Burundi	10,888,321	3.08
Burkina Faso	17,812,961	3.06	Djibouti	792,198	2.26
Cape Verde	531,046	1.41	Eritrea	6,233,682	2.36
Côte d'Ivoire	22,400,835	2.00	Ethiopia	93,877,025	2.90
Gambia	1,883,051	2.29	Kenya	44,037,656	2.27
Ghana	25,199,609	2.19	Rwanda	12,012,589	2.70
Guinea	11,176,026	2.64	Somalia	10,251,568	1.67
Guinea Bissau	1,660,870	1.95	South Sudan	11,090,104	4.23
Liberia	3,989,703	2.56	Tanzania	48,261,942	2.82
Mali	15,968,882	3.01	Uganda	34,758,809	3.32
Niger	16,899,327	3.32			
Nigeria	174,507,539	2.54	**North Africa:**		
Senegal	13,300,410	2.51	Algeria	38,087,812	1.90
Sierra Leone	5,612,685	2.30	Egypt	85,294,388	1.88
Togo	7,154,237	2.73	Libya	6,002,347	4.85
			Mauritania	3,437,610	2.29
Southern Africa:			Morocco	32,649,130	1.04
Angola	18,565,269	2.78	Sudan	34,847,910	1.83
Botswana	2,127,825	1.35	Tunisia	10,835,873	0.95
Comoros	752,288	1.97	Western Sahara	538,811	2.96
Lesotho	1,936,181	0.34			
Madagascar	22,599,098	2.65	**Central Africa:**		
Malawi	16,777,547	2.74	Cameroon	20,549,221	2.04
Mauritius	1,322,238	0.68	Central African Republic	5,166,510	2.14
Mozambique	24,096,669	2.44	Chad	11,193,452	1.95
Namibia	2,182,852	0.75	Congo	4,492,689	2.86
South Africa	48,601,098	−0.45	Democratic Republic of the Congo	75,507,308	2.54
Swaziland	1,403,362	1.17	Equatorial Guinea	704,001	2.58
Zambia	14,222,233	2.89	Gabon	1,640,286	1.96
Zimbabwe	13,182,908	4.38	São Tomé and Principe	186,817	1.94

This chart shows the population and rate of population growth (natural increase) among the countries of Africa.

SOURCE: *CIA World Factbook 2013*

Table 10.2 Gross Domestic Product and GDP Real Growth

Country	GDPpc	GDP real growth	Country	GDPpc	GDP real growth
West Africa:			**East Africa:**		
Benin	$1,700	3.8%	Burundi	$600	4.0%
Burkina Faso	$1,400	8.0%	Djibouti	$2,700	4.8%
Cape Verde	$4,200	4.3%	Eritrea	$800	7.0%
Côte d'Ivoire	$1,800	9.8%	Ethiopia	$1,200	7.0%
Gambia	$1,900	3.9%	Kenya	$1,800	4.7%
Ghana	$3,400	7.0%	Rwanda	$1,500	7.7%
Guinea	$1,100	3.9%	Somalia	$600	2.6%
Guinea Bissau	$1,200	−1.5%	South Sudan	$1,000	−53.0%
Liberia	$700	8.3%	Tanzania	$1,600	6.9%
Mali	$1,100	−1.2%	Uganda	$1,400	2.6%
Niger	$800	11.2%			
Nigeria	$2,800	6.3%	**North Africa:**		
Senegal	$2,100	3.5%	Algeria	$7,600	2.5%
Sierra Leone	$1,400	19.8%	Egypt	$6,700	2.2%
Togo	$1,100	5.0%	Libya	$12,300	104.5%
			Mauritania	$2,200	6.4%
Southern Africa:			Morocco	$5,400	3.0%
Angola	$6,500	8.4%	Sudan	$2,600	−4.4%
Botswana	$17,100	3.8%	Tunisia	$9,900	3.6%
Comoros	$1,300	2.5%	Western Sahara	$2,500	N/A
Lesotho	$2,200	4.0%			
Madagascar	$1,000	1.9%	**Central Africa:**		
Malawi	$900	1.9%	Cameroon	$2,400	4.7%
Mauritius	$15,800	3.3%	Central African Republic	$800	4.1%
Mozambique	$1,200	7.5%	Chad	$2,000	5.5%
Namibia	$7,900	4.0%	Congo	$4,700	3.8%
South Africa	$11,600	2.5%	Democratic Republic of the Congo	$400	7.1%
Swaziland	$5,900	−1.5%			
Zambia	$1,700	7.3%	Equatorial Guinea	$26,400	2.0%
Zimbabwe	$600	4.4%	Gabon	$16,800	6.2%
			São Tomé and Principe	$2,400	4.0%

This chart shows the GDP per capita and rate of GDPpc real growth among the countries of Africa.

SOURCE: *CIA World Factbook 2013*

Table 10.3 Literacy Rates and Life Expectancy

Country	Literacy	LE-years	Country	Literacy	LE-years
West Africa:			**East Africa:**		
Benin	42%	61	Burundi	67%	60
Burkina Faso	29%	54	Djibouti	68%	62
Cape Verde	85%	71	Eritrea	69%	63
Côte d'Ivoire	57%	58	Ethiopia	39%	60
Gambia	51%	64	Kenya	71%	59
Ghana	72%	65	Rwanda	70%	57
Guinea	41%	59	Somalia	38%	51
Guinea-Bissau	55%	50	South Sudan	27%	NA
Liberia	61%	58	Tanzania	68%	61
Mali	33%	55	Uganda	73%	54
Niger	29%	54			
Nigeria	61%	52	**North Africa:**		
Senegal	50%	61	Algeria	73%	76
Sierra Leone	43%	57	Egypt	74%	73
Togo	60%	64	Libya	90%	76
			Mauritania	59%	62
Southern Africa:			Morocco	67%	76
Angola	70%	55	Sudan	72%	63
Botswana	85%	55	Tunisia	79%	75
Comoros	76%	63	Western Sahara	N/A	62
Lesotho	90%	52			
Madagascar	65%	65	**Central Africa:**		
Malawi	75%	53	Cameroon	71%	55
Mauritius	89%	75	Central African Republic	57%	51
Mozambique	56%	52	Chad	35%	49
Namibia	89%	52	Congo	84%	56
South Africa	93%	49	Dem Rep of Congo	67%	56
Swaziland	88%	50	Equitorial Guinea	94%	63
Zambia	61%	52	Gabon	89%	52
Zimbabwe	84%	54	Sâo Tomé & Principe	70%	64

This chart shows the Literacy Rates (2011) and Life Expectancy (In Years) (2013) among the countries of Africa.

SOURCE: *CIA World Factbook 2013*

Table 10.4 Major Religions

Country	Religion
West Africa:	
Benin	Catholic 27.1%, Muslim 24.4%, Vodoun 17.3%, Protestant 10.4%, other Christian 5.3%, other 15.5%
Burkina Faso	Muslim 60.5%, Catholic 19%, indigenous 15.3%, Protestant 4.2%, other 0.6%, none 0.4%
Cape Verde	Mostly Christians, Roman Catholic and Protestant
Côte d'Ivoire	Muslim 38.6%, Christian 32.8%, indigenous 11.9%, none 16.7%
Gambia	Muslim 90%, Christian 8%, indigenous 2%
Ghana	Christian 71.2%, Muslim 17.6%, traditional 5.2%, other 0.8%, none 5.2%
Guinea	Muslim 85%, Christian 8%, indigenous 7%
Guinea-Bissau	Muslim 50%, indigenous beliefs 40%, Christian 10%
Liberia	Christian 85.6%, Muslim 12.2%, indigneous 0.6%, other 0.2%, none 1.4%
Mali	Muslim 94.8%, Christian 2.4%, Animist 2%, none 0.5%, unspecified 0.3%
Niger	Muslim 80%, other (includes indigenous and Christian) 20%
Nigeria	Muslim 50%, Christian 40%, indigenous 10%
Senegal	Muslim 94%, Christian 5%, indigenous 1%
Sierra Leone	Muslim 60%, Christian 10%, indigenous 30%
Togo	Christian 29%, Muslim 20%, indigenous 51%
Southern Africa:	
Angola	Indigenous beliefs 47%, Roman Catholic 38%, Protestant 15%
Botswana	Christian 71.6%, Badimo 6%, other 1.4%, unspecified 0.4%, none 20.6%
Comoros	Sunni Muslim 98%, Roman Catholic 2%
Lesotho	Christian 80%, indigenous 20%
Madagascar	Indigenous beliefs 52%, Christian 41%, Muslim 7%
Malawi	Christian 82.7%, Muslim 13%, other 1.9%, none 2.5%
Mauritius	Hindu 48%, Roman Catholic 23.6%, Muslim 16.6%, other Christian 8.6%, other 3.2%
Namibia	Christian 80–90%, indigenous 10–20%
Mozambique	Catholic 28.4%, Protestant 27.7%, Muslim 17.9%, other 7.2%, none 18.7%
South Africa	Protestant 36.6%, Catholic 7.1%, Muslim 1.5%, other Christan 36%, other and none 18.8%
Swaziland	Zionist 40%, Roman Catholic 20%, Muslim 10%, other 30%
Zambia	Christian 50%–75%, Muslim and Hindu 24%–49%, indigenous 1%
Zimbabwe	Syncretic 50%, Christian 25%, indigenous 24%, Muslim and other 1%

continues

Table 10.4 Major Religions *continued*

Country	Religion
East Africa:	
Burundi	Christian 82.8%, Muslim 2.5%, Adventist 2.3%, other 6.5%, unknown 5.9%
Djibouti	Muslim 94%, Christian 6%
Eritrea	Muslim, Coptic Christian, Roman Catholic, Protestant
Ethiopia	Ethiopian Orthodox 43.5%, Muslim 33.9%, Protestant 18.6%, traditional 2.6%, Catholic 0.7%, other 0.7%
Kenya	Christian 82.5%, Muslim 11.1%, traditionalists 1.6%, other 1.7%, none 2.4%, unspecified 0.7%
Rwanda	Roman Catholic 56.5%, Protestant 26%, Adventist 11.1%, Muslim 4.6%, indigenous 0.1%, none 1.7%
Somalia	Sunni Muslim
South Sudan	Animist, Christian
Tanzania	mainland - Christian 30%, Muslim 35%, indigenous 35%; Zanzibar - more than 99% Muslim
Uganda	Roman Catholic 41.9%, Protestant 42%, Muslim 12.1%, other 3.1%, none 0.9%
North Africa:	
Algeria	Sunni Muslim 99%, Christian and Jewish 1%
Egypt	Muslim (mostly Sunni) 90%, Coptic 9%, other Christian 1%
Libya	Sunni Muslim 97%, other 3%
Mauritania	Muslim 100%
Morocco	Muslim 99%, Christian 1%, Jewish about 6,000
Sudan	Sunni Muslim, small Christian minority
Tunisia	Muslim 98%, Christian 1%, Jewish and other 1%
Western Sahara	Muslim
Central Africa:	
Cameroon	Indigenous beliefs 40%, Christian 40%, Muslim 20%
Central African Republic	Indigenous beliefs 35%, Protestant 25%, Roman Catholic 25%, Muslim 15%
Chad	Muslim 53.1%, Catholic 20.1%, Protestant 14.2%, animist 7.3%, other 0.5%, unknown 1.7%, atheist 3.1%
Democratic Republic of the Congo	Roman Catholic 50%, Protestant 20%, Kimbanguist 10%, Muslim 10%, other 10%
Equitorial Guinea	nominally Christian and predominantly Roman Catholic, indigenous
Gabon	Christian 55%–75%, indigenous, Muslim less than 1%
Republic of Congo	Christian 50%, indigenous 48%, Muslim 2%
São Tomé and Principe	Catholic 70.3%, Evangelical 3.4%, New Apostolic 2%, Adventist 1.8%, other 3.1%, none 19.4%

This chart shows the types of religion among the countries of Africa.

SOURCE: *CIA World Factbook 2013*

Table 10.5 Type of Government

Country	Government	Country	Government
West Africa		**East Africa:**	
Benin	Republic	Burundi	Republic
Burkina Faso	Parliamentary republic	Djibouti	Republic
Cape Verde	Republic	Eritrea	Transitional government
Côte d'Ivoire	Republic, multiparty	Ethiopia	Federal republic
Gambia	Republic	Kenya	Republic
Ghana	Constitutional democracy	Rwanda	Republic, multiparty
Guinea	Republic	Somalia	Transitional government
Guinea-Bissau	Republic	South Sudan	Republic
Liberia	Republic	Tanzania	Republic
Mali	Republic	Uganda	Republic
Niger	Republic		
Nigeria	Federal republic	**North Africa:**	
Senegal	Republic	Algeria	Republic
Sierra Leone	Constitutional democracy	Egypt	Republic
Togo	Rep., transition to multiparty	Libya	Transitional government
		Mauritania	Military Junta
Southern Africa:		Morocco	Constitutional monarchy
Angola	Republic, multiparty	Sudan	Shared-power government
Botswana	Parliamentary republic	Tunisia	Republic
Comoros	Republic	Western Sahara	Contested Territory
Lesotho	Parliamentary consitutional monarchy		
		Central Africa:	
Madagascar	Republic	Cameroon	Republic, multiparty
Malawi	Multiparty democracy	Central African Republic	Republic
Mauritius	Parliamentary democracy	Chad	Republic
Mozambique	Republic	Congo	Republic
Namibia	Republic	Democratic Republic of the Congo	Republic
South Africa	Republic		
Swaziland	Monarchy	Equatorial Guinea	Republic
Zambia	Republic	Gabon	Republic, multiparty
Zimbabwe	Parliamentary democracy	São Tomé and Principe	Republic

This chart shows the form of government among the countries of Africa.

SOURCE: *CIA World Factbook 2013*

References

AfricaFocus. 2007. "Europe/Africa: Partnership Reality Check." *AfricaFocus Bulletin*. February 4. http://www.africafocus.org/docs07/epa0702.php.

Agonafer, M., ed. 1996. *Africa in the Contemporary International Disorder: Crises and Possibilities*. New York: University Press of America.

AllAfrica. 2006. "The Most Effective Vaccine Against Child Death in Africa is a Glass of Clean Water." Interview with Kevin Watkins. November 10. Available at http://allafrica.com/stories/200611100001.html.

Anderson, David. 2004. *Histories of the Hanged: The Dirty War in Kenya and the End of Empire*. New York: Norton.

Ascherson, Neal. 2005. "The Breaking of the Mau Mau." *New York Review of Books*. April 7.

AVERT. 2011. "HIV and AIDS in Africa." www.avert.org/hiv-aids-africa.htm.

Ayoade, J.A.A. 2005. Quoted in Abu Bakarr Bah, *Breakdown and Reconstitution: Democracy, the Nation-State, and Ehtnicity in Nigeria*. Lanham, MD: Lexington Books.

Bah, Abu Bakarr. 2005. *Breakdown and Reconstitution: Democracy, the Nation-State, and Ethnicity in Nigeria*. Lanham, MD: Lexington Books.

Basu, Nayanima. 2011. "India, Africa Trade Ties Take Quantum Leap." *Business Standard*. May 23. http://www.business-standard.com/india/news/india-africa-trade-ties-take-quantum-leap-/436390/.

BBC News. 2006. "Summit Shows China's Africa Clout." November 6. http://news.bbc.co.uk/2/hi/business/6120500.stm.

Beah, Ishmael. 2006. *A Long Way Gone: Memoirs of a Boy Soldier*. New York: Farrar, Straus and Giroux.

Best, Antony, Jussi M. Hanhimäki, Joseph A. Maiolo, and Kirsten E. Schulze. 2004. *International History of the Twentieth Century*. New York: Routledge.

CFR (Council on Foreign Relations). 2011. www.cfr.org.

Chabal, Patrick. 2005. "Power in Africa Reconsidered." In *The African Exception*, edited by Ulf Engel and Gorm Olsen, 17–34. Burlington, VT: Ashgate.

Christiaensen, Luc, and Shantayanan Devarajan. 2013. "Making the Most of Africa's Growth." *Current History* (May): 181–187.

CIA (Central Intelligence Agency). 2009. "Country Comparison: GDP Per Capita (PPP)." *The World Factbook*. Washington, DC: Central Intelligence Agency. https://www.cia.gov/library/publications/the-world-factbook/index.html.

Collier, Paul. 2004. "Africa's Revolutionary Routine." *Foreign Policy* (May–June): 82–83.

Danchie, S. J. 2010. "Towards a More Balanced Trade Within the Framework of the Forum for China-Africa Cooperation: The Impact of China on Africa's Trade." African Center for Economic Transformation. http://www.global tradealert.org/sites/default/files/GTA5_danchie.pdf.

Devarajan, Shantayanan, and Wolfgang Fengler. 2013. "Africa's Economic Boom." *Foreign Affairs* 92, no. 3 (May/June 2013): 68–81.

De Witte, Ludo. 2001. *The Assassination of Lumumba.* New York: Verso.

Diamond, Jared. 1999. *Guns, Germs, and Steel: The Fates of Human Societies.* New York: Norton.

Dowden, Richard. 2009. *Africa: Altered States, Ordinary Miracles.* New York: PublicAffairs.

Duiker, William J., and Jackson J. Spielvogel. 2001. *World History.* Belmont, CA: Wadsworth.

Easterly, William. 2010. "Foreign Aid for Scoundrels." *New York Review of Books* (November 25): 37–38.

Economist. 2011a. "No Stopping Them." February 3. http://www.economist.com /node/18061574.

———. 2011b. "The Chinese Are Coming to Africa." April 22. http://www .economist.com/blogs/dailychart/2011/04/chinese_africa.

———. 2011c. "Hunger in the Horn of Africa." July 7. http://www.economist .com/node/18929467.

———. 2011d. "Africa Rising: After Decades of Slow Growth, Africa Has a Real Chance to Follow in the Footsteps of Asia." December 3. http://www .economist.com/node/21541015.

Elkins, Caroline. 2004. *Imperial Reckoning: The Untold Story.* New York: Henry Holt.

Epstein, Helen. 2005. "The Lost Children of AIDS." *New York Review of Books.* November 3.

Eurostat. 2011. "Africa-EU–Economic Indicators, Trade and Investment." European Union. http://epp.eurostat.ec.europa.eu/statistics_explained/index .php/Africa-EU_-_economic_indicators,_trade_and_investment.

Fernandez-Armesto, Felipe. 1995. *Millennium: A History of the Last Thousand Years.* New York: Scribner.

Flintoff, Cory. 2012. "Where Does the U.S. Get Its Oil?" NRP.

Fosu, Joseph. 2011. "Sub-Saharan Africa: The Challenge of Integration into the Global Trading System." *Current History* (May): 115–126.

Freedom House. 2011. "Freedom in the World 2012: The Arab Uprisings and Their Global Repercussions." http://www.freedomhouse.org.

Freedom House, 2012. "Perilous State of Freedom in Sub-Saharan Africa." www
       .freedomhouse.org.
Freedom House. 2013. http://www.freedomhouse.org.
French, Howard W. 2009. "Kagame's Hidden War in the Congo." *New York Re-
       view of Books* (September 24): 44–47.
———. 2010. "The Next Empire?" *The Atlantic* (May): 59–69.
Gettleman, Jeffrey. 2007. "The Other Somalia: An Island of Stability in a Sea of
       Armed Chaos." *New York Times*. March 7.
———. 2010. "Africa's Forever Wars." *Foreign Policy* (March–April), 178.
Gettleman, Jeffrey, and Mossi Mwassi. 2006. "Challenger in Congo Says He'll
       Contest Results." *New York Times*. November 17.
Gordon, David F., and Howard Wolpe. 1998. "The Other Africa: An End to
       Afro-Pessimism." *World Policy Journal* (Spring).
Hanson, John H. 1995. "Islam and African Societies." In *Africa*, edited by Phyl-
       lis M. Martin and Patrick O'Meara, 97–114. Bloomington: Indiana Univer-
       sity Press.
Hargreaves, J. D. 2004. "West African Boundary Making." In *Borders and Border
       Politics in a Globalizing World*, edited by Paul Ganster and David E. Lorey,
       97–106. Wilmington, DE: Scholarly Resources.
Hochschild, Adam. 2005. "In the Heart of Darkness." *New York Review of Books*
       (October 6): 39–42.
———. 2010. "The Trial of Thomas Lubanga." *The Atlantic* (December): 77–82.
Houngnikpo, Mathurin. 2000. "Stuck at the Runway: Africa's Distress Call." *Af-
       rica Insight* (May): 5–12.
ITA (International Trade Administration). 2009. US Department of Commerce.
       "US-Africa Trade Profile 2009." http://agoa.gov/resources/US_African
       _Trade_Profile_2009.pdf.
Judt, Tony. 2000. "The Story of Everything." *New York Review of Books*. Septem-
       ber 21.
Keller, Edmond J. 1995. "Decolonization, Independence, and the Failure of Poli-
       tics." In *Africa*, edited by Phyllis M. Martin and Patrick O'Meara, 156–172.
       Bloomington: Indiana University Press.
Kennedy, Paul. 1993. *Preparing for the Twenty-first Century*. New York: Random
       House.
Khare, Vineet. 2013. "China and India: The Scramble for Business in Africa."
       August 4. www.bbc.co.uk.
Kissi, Edward. 2006. *Revolution and Genocide in Ethiopia and Cambodia*. Lanham,
       MD: Lexington Books.

Kotch, Nick. 2005. "African Oil: Whose Bonanza?" *National Geographic* (September): 50–65.

Lacey, Mark. 2003. "New Name, Similar Struggles for Group of African Nations." *New York Times*. February 5. Available at www.nytimes.com.

Lutulala, Bernard. 2012. "Brain Drain in Africa." www.wilsoncenter.org.

Love, Janice. 2005. *Southern Africa in World Politics*. Boulder, CO: Westview Press.

M2 Presswire. 2006. "UN: New Partnership for Africa's Development." October 16. http://goliath.ecnext.com/coms2/gi_0199–5849016/New-Partnership -for-Africa-s.html.

Mandela, Nelson. 1994. *Long Walk to Freedom: The Autobiography of Nelson Mandela*. Boston: Little, Brown.

MCC (Millennium Challenge Corporation). 2010. "A New Vision for Development." Millennium Challenge Corporation Annual Report. http://www.mcc .gov/documents/reports/report-2011001049801–2010annual.pdf.

MDG (Millennium Development Goals) Report: Assuring Progress in Africa to the MDG. 2013. www.un.org.millenniumgoals.

McLaughlin, Abraham. 2005. "Africans Ask: 'Why Isn't Anyone Telling the Good News?" *Christian Science Monitor*. May 25.

McNulty, Robert L. 1995. "The Contemporary Map of Africa." In *Africa*, edited by Phyllis M. Martin and Patrick O'Meara. Bloomington: Indiana University Press.

MDG (Millennium Development Goal Indicators). 2011. http://mdgs.un.org /unsd/mdg/Default.aspx.

Moyo, Dambisa. 2009. "Why Foreign Aid Is Hurting Africa." *Wall Street Journal– Africa*. March 22. http://online.wsj.com/article/SB123758895999200083 .html.

New York Times. 2007. "Hu heads for South Africa–Asia–Pacific." February 7.

Palgreen, Linda. 2007. "In Niger, Trees and Crops Turn Back the Desert." *New York Times*. February 11.

Perry, Alex. 2010. "Land of Hope." *Time* (December 13): 68–73.

Pew Forum on Religious and Public Life. 2010. "Tolerance and Tension: Islam and Christianity in Sub-Saharan Africa." April 15. http://www.pewforum.org /uploadedFiles/Topics/Belief_and_Practices/sub-saharan-africa-chapter-5.pdf.

Radelet, Steven. 2010. *Emerging Africa: How 17 Countries Are Leading the Way*. Washington, DC: Center for Global Development.

Refugees International. 2010. "Somalis in Kenya: Invest in the Long-Term." http:// www.refugeesinternational.org/policy/field-report/somalis-kenya-invest -long-term.

Rush, Norman. 2006. "Exile's Return." *New York Review of Books*. April 23.

Sall, Macky. "Africa's Turn: A Conversation with Macky Sall." *Foreign Affairs* 92, no. 5: 2–8.

Sieff, Michelle. 2008. "Africa: Many Hills to Climb." *World Policy Institute* (Fall): 185–195.

Silverstein, Ken. 2011. "Teodorin's World." *Foreign Policy* (March/April): 54–62.

Sorbora, Mark. 2007. "India and Africa—It's Old Friends, New Game and Rules." *The Nation*. February 9.

South Bulletin. 2007. "China Follows Up on Beijing Summit with Africa Leaders." *South Bulletin* 141: 113. http://www.southcentre.org/index.php?option =com_content&view=article&id=511%3Asouth-bulletin-141-15 -march-2007&catid=80%3Asouth-bulletin-2007&Itemid=107&lang=en.

Tayler, Jeffrey. 2006. "Worse Than Iraq?" *Atlantic Monthly* (April): 34–35.

Timburg, Craig. 2006. "African Justice." *Washington Post*. May 6.

UNECA (United Nations Economic Commission for Africa). 2010. "Economic Report on Africa." http://www.uneca.org/era2010/overview.pdf.

USAfrica. 2011. www.usafricaonline.com.

van de Walle, Nicholas. 2005. "The Donors and the State in Africa: How Much Has Changed?" In *The African Exception,* edited by Ulf Engel and Gorm Olsen, 69–86. Burlington, VT: Ashgate.

von Laue, Theodore H. 1987. *The World Revolution of Westernization: The Twentieth Century in Global Perspective.* New York: Oxford University Press.

WHO (World Health Organization). 2011. "Vector-Borne Diseases." http:// www.who.int/vaccine_research/documents/Chapter3_Vector-borne_New .pdf.

World Bank. 2011. *World Development Report 2011.* http://go.worldbank.org /G83FOS3GW0.

WPO (World Public Opinion). 2006. "Africans and Asians Tend to View Globalization Favorably; Europeans and Americans Are More Skeptical." http://www.worldpublicopinion.org/pipa/articles/btglobalizationtradera/273 .php?nid=&id=&pnt=273&lb=btgl.

WTO (World Trade Organization). 2010. "World Trade Developments." http:// www.wto.org/english/res_e/statis_e/its2011_e/its11_highlights1_e.pdf.

Zartman, I. William. 2001. "Bordering on War." *Foreign Policy* (May–June): 66–67.

Further Reading

Fage, J. D. 2002. *A History of Africa.* London: Routledge.

Hartman, Saidiya. 2006. *Lose Your Mother: A Journey Along the Atlantic Slave Route*. New York: Farrar, Straus, and Giroux.

Kristof, Nicholas D. 2006. "Genocide in Slow Motion." *New York Review of Books* (February 9): 14–17.

Meredith, Martin. 2005. *The Fate of Africa: From the Hopes of Freedom to the Heart of Despair*. New York: PublicAffairs.

Milan, William B., and Jennifer G. Jones. 2011. "Ivory Coast: Another Asterisk for Africa's Democratization." *Current History* (May): 177–183.

Murithi, Timothy. 2005. *The African Union: Pan-Africanism, Peacebuilding and Development*. Burlington, VT: Ashgate.

Nugent, Paul. 2004. *Africa Since Independence: A Comparative History*. New York: Palgrave.

Journals

Africa Today. muse.jhu.edu/journals/at

African Affairs. afraf.oxfordjournals.org

African Studies Review. journals.cambridge.org/action/displayJournal

Journal of African History. journals.cambri dge.org/action/displayJournal?jid=AFH

Journal of Contemporary African Studies. www.tandfonline.com

Films

Blood Diamond (2006). Edward Zwick, director.

Hotel Rwanda (2004). Terry George, director.

The Last King of Scotland (2006). Kevin MacDonald, director.

Lumumba (2000). Raoul Peck, director.

A World Apart (1988). Chris Menges, director.

Websites

African News Network. www.allafrica.com

African Studies Programs links. www.africanstudies.org

African Union. www.africa-union.org

Links to sources on Africa. www.u.s-africa.tripod.com

United Nations Economic Commission for Africa. www.uneca.org

11

The Middle East

For thousands of years, the region we now call the Middle East has been a cradle of civilizations, a crossroads of vast trading networks, a place of holiness and conflict. Linking Africa, Asia, and Europe, encircling half the Mediterranean Sea, the Middle East has for millennia played a crucial economic role on all three continents, dominating the trade in gold and slaves from Africa, spices and fabrics from Asia, and glass and other manufactured goods from Europe. In the twentieth century it literally fueled globalization as the primary source of the oil that powers the ships, planes, trains, and trucks that make it possible for bananas from El Salvador or manufactured goods from China to reach the shelves of stores in Europe and the United States at astonishingly low costs.

Since the invention of agriculture, the Middle East has been the site of great empires, from the rise of Pharaonic Egypt more than six thousand years ago to the fall of the Ottoman Empire in the twentieth century. It is the birthplace of at least a half dozen world religions, from Judaism, Christianity, and Islam to Bahai, Druze, and Zoroastrianism, and dozens more that flourished for centuries or even millennia but have since passed away. Geographically, the Middle East is often conceived as a hodgepodge, an arbitrary and shifting blend of western Asia, North Africa, and parts of South and Central Asia. But the cultural, economic, and geopolitical importance of the region throughout history requires that the Middle East be considered a distinct center of global significance.

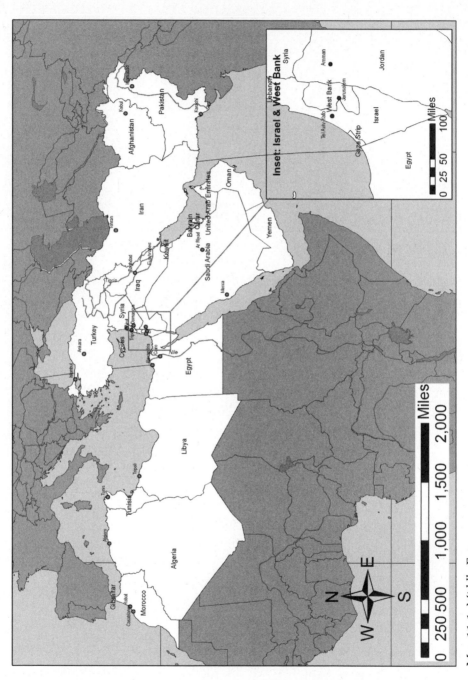

MAP 11.1 Middle East.

THE MIDDLE OF WHERE?

In 2001, when the United States began its invasion of Afghanistan because of the Taliban regime's refusal to turn over the leaders of the al Qaeda movement, dozens of American students at the American Universities in Cairo and Beirut received e-mails and phone calls from their parents ordering them home. To these students living abroad, Afghanistan was a dangerous country a thousand miles away. To their parents, Cairo in North Africa, Beirut on the Mediterranean coast, and Kabul in Central Asia were somehow the same place, the Middle East, so that military conflict in one part had to mean dangers in other parts.

Where is the Middle East? What is it in the middle of? By the time of Napoleon those areas east of Europe were often lumped together as a generic Orient, a Latin term that literally means "east." To Europeans, Orientals included Bedouin tribes guiding the expanding tourist trade in Palestine, women of an *Arabian Nights* harem, Turkish troops parading in Western-style military uniforms, Persian dervishes, Hindu holy men, Chinese intellectuals, and Japanese Samurai swordsmen. The only thing all these people had in common was that they were east of Europe. For many in Western civilization this meant they were inferior or even uncivilized.

There is no indigenous term in Arabic or Persian or Pashtun or any other language of the region for the area stretching from the Atlantic coast of North Africa to the Iran-Afghan border that Europeans and Americans call the Middle East. North Africa, especially the Western half, is the **Maghreb**. Iran and Iraq were Persia, and the areas farther east were labeled by many different names. The term *Middle East* was created by an American military historian writing in a British military journal to help label and talk about European—and later American—geopolitical concerns centered in the Persian Gulf. Because of this, the geographical area constituted by the term *Middle East* changes with the changing interests of Western journalists, scholars, and politicians (Scheffler 2003). Before September 11, 2001, Afghanistan and Pakistan were usually considered South Asian countries and were rarely included in maps of the Middle East; since then, they are included in most American textbooks and maps of the region. The G8 countries (Canada, France, Germany, Italy, Japan, Russia, the United Kingdom, and the United States) recently adopted the terms *Middle East* and *Greater Middle East* to differentiate between the core of Arabic and Persian countries around the Persian Gulf and the broader range of countries from North Africa to South and Central Asia.

Even the borders of most contemporary Middle Eastern states, including Iraq, are still those established by European governments more than half a century ago. With the fall of the Ottoman Empire at the end of World War I, the colonial powers of Europe divided up the Middle East and established arbitrary borders where none had previously existed. The European concern with borders exhibits a different concept of space and power than that historically held by Middle Eastern geographers. Precolonial maps drawn by Arab and Persian cartographers rarely show borders or boundaries; instead they mapped centers—seats of power and spheres of influence. The idea of culturally distinct peoples inhabiting geographically exclusive space did not become widespread in the region until the colonial rulers brought it in.

Today, European concepts of geographical space have largely come to replace Arab and Persian concepts. People living in the region routinely use translations of the European term *Middle East* (*al-Sharq al-Awsat*) in writing and communicating with the international community. Nationalism of various kinds has become very important in local and regional politics. All of these modern nation-states have a flag, a national anthem, and a seat at the United Nations.

Yet there are also strong supernational affinities tied to linguistic, cultural, ethnic, and religious similarities that transcend borders. In the 1960s and 1970s, political leaders like Egypt's Gamel Abdel Nasser spoke of an Arab superstate linking many important Arabic-speaking lands into a single political and economic unit (Dawisha 2005). While this dream is dead as a realistic political goal in the contemporary Middle East, Arab nationalism continues to live on in the popular imagination. The Arab League is only one of several regional institutions that continue to emphasize and build common economic, cultural, and political goals among Arabic-speaking countries. The term **Arab world** is often used to describe the twenty-two Arabic-speaking countries of the world as a single geopolitical unit. Stretching from Morocco to Iraq, and including several sub-Saharan African countries, the combined population of this Arab world is 325 million.

Other border-crossing affinities also exist. Since its revolution in 1979, Iran has inspired two generations of political Muslims and also significantly raised the profile of Shia Islam. Although Shiites make up only about 15 percent of the world's Muslims, they are a majority in Iran and

Iraq, and many countries have sizable minority Shiite communities. The rise of Iran, the fall of Saddam Hussein's Sunni-dominated government in Iraq in 2002, and the success of the militant arm of the Shiite Lebanese group Hezbollah against Israel in 2006, have led some to speak of a Shiite resurgence in the world (Moubayed 2005; Nasr 2006). Shiite minorities in countries where they suffer political and economic marginalization, like Saudi Arabia, may well look to the successes of their coreligionists with greater pride and affinity than they feel for their own nations.

The largest and most encompassing of transnational identities centered in the Middle East is that of Islam. Although the ways Muslims practice their religion may differ significantly from Africa to the Arabian peninsula to Asia, most Muslims have a strong sense of themselves as members of a worldwide community of believers, or *ummah*. The term **Islamic world** is usually used to refer to the total number of the world's Muslim majority countries in Asia, Africa, the Middle East, and Europe. Some, however, conceive of an even more-encompassing concept. As the world's fastest growing religion, Islam is now the second largest religion in most Christian majority nations. The term **Muslim world** is frequently used in a cultural sense to refer to the worldwide community of Muslims and also in a geographical and political sense to include Muslim enclaves in non-Muslim majority countries, such as Yinchuan in China, Southall in London, and Dearborn, Michigan. Although the majority of the world's Muslims live in Asia and the religion is growing fastest in Africa, the Middle East looms large in the Islamic imagination throughout the world as the geographic location of Islam's sacred historical sites, as the place toward which prayer is directed, and as the destination for the pilgrimage all Muslims seek to make during their lifetimes. These terms thus remind us that the Middle East is the center of global cultural networks as well as economic and political ones.

FROM PAST TO PRESENT

The Middle East includes three of the world's major early river valley civilizations—the Nile, the Jordan, and the land between the Tigris and Euphrates. Together, these form what historians call the **Fertile Crescent**, a region where the invention of agriculture led to the early rise of some of the world's first cities and empires. Along this broad stretch, civilizations rose and fell, camels and horses were domesticated, and vast trading

336 INTERNATIONAL STUDIES

networks developed. Later European empires like those of Macedonia and Rome conquered vast stretches of North Africa and Asia Mino, where they clashed with indigenous empires like those of Egypt and Persia.

For the first thousand years following the birth of Jesus, Christianity's history is the history of the Middle East. Christianity originated in Palestine, then spread outward along trade routes throughout the Middle East and North Africa. When early Christianity came into conflict with the official religions of the Roman Empire, it was in the Middle East that most martyrdoms occurred. Even after Christianity became the state religion of the Roman Empire it continued for centuries to be considered an Eastern religion, and its influence extended into neighboring non-Christian realms. In fourth-century Sassanid Persia, for example, the emperors copied the Roman Christian model in establishing Zoroastrianism as a state religion.

By the seventh century CE, the Arabian peninsula was being squeezed between the Christian Roman Empire, based in Constantinople, and the Zoroastrian Sassanid Empire, based in Ctesiphon (now a nearly forgotten ruin located twenty kilometers south of Baghdad). Most of Arabia's wealth came from camel caravans that could transport goods across Arabia, from the Red Sea to the Gulf, more rapidly than ships could sail around the peninsula. Cities that lay along trading routes, like Mecca, grew large and wealthy. The tribes who controlled the overland trade were in continual states of warfare, however, and the cities were often divided by internal disputes and under political and military pressure from Persia and Rome.

Into this seething cauldron, Muhammad, an orphan who rose to become a successful businessman and then a prophet, brought a message of unity and egalitarianism, of a brotherhood greater than that of the tribe, that encompasses all people who submit to God (which is what the term *Muslim* means). As his message spread, Muhammad forged the tribes of Arabia into a single community of believers, using trade agreements and political alliances as well as religious conversion.

Muhammad died in 632 CE, by which time his message had spread across trade routes, and small communities of believers had appeared in many lands. Muhammad was succeeded by a series of **caliphs**, who sent out military forces to defend Muslim communities from persecution. These expeditions rapidly turned into outright conquests. The Sassanian Empire, already beset by internal problems, fell to Muslim forces by 650 CE, as did most of the North African provinces of Rome.

The rapid expansion of Islam as both a faith and an empire brought vast wealth to the caliphs. Factionalism began to divide the Muslim community. A dispute in the seventh century over the succession to the caliphate led to a division of the Muslim community into **Shia** (or Shiites), who followed the biological descendants of the prophet (whom they called *imams*), and the majority **Sunni**, who accepted the authority of the caliph. The former, who have probably never numbered more than one-fifth of the world's Muslims, settled largely in what are today Iran, Iraq, Lebanon, and India.

Under a series of caliphal dynasties the Muslim world eventually stretched from the Atlantic coast to India and beyond. Vast mercantile networks carried the wealth of the known world from Asia to the Mediterranean, and from Africa to the Black Sea. Arab merchants profited from trade on the Red Sea and Indian Ocean trading network. Great centers of learning were established, and the region enjoyed an efflorescence of art and science. For several centuries, the Middle East seemed to be the center of the world. When Marco Polo traveled through the region at the end of the thirteenth century, it was still one of the most important in the world.

The dominance of Arabs over this center of world trade began to decline with the rise of Turkish empires in the eleventh and twelfth centuries. The first of these arose at the beginning of the eleventh century in what is today eastern Iran, Afghanistan, and Pakistan. These areas on the outskirts of the empire had increasingly been governed by slave-soldiers. Taking advantage of their positions on the outskirts of the empire, powerful slave-soldiers created semiautonomous dynastic kingdoms. Subsequently the Seljuk Turks from Central Asia seized much of the rest of the Middle East and defeated the Byzantine army to conquer Anatolia (in modern-day Turkey), which became their political base.

These political and economic disruptions paved the way for, and were exacerbated by, a series of invasions by so-called foreign barbarians. The first series of invasions came from Western Europe, beginning in 1095 when Pope Urban II called for a crusade against Muslim domination of Christian holy places and pilgrimage routes. A series of raids by warriors from the central Asian steppes was even more devastating. Led by Hulegu Khan in the thirteenth century and Timur Leng in the fourteenth, the Mongols laid waste to entire cities, killing millions.[1] They were finally stopped when a succession struggle back in Asia forced the splitting of

FIGURE 11.1 After the conquest of Constantinople, the great Christian church Hagia Sophia became a mosque. Today the building is a museum. PHOTO: Mark Allen Peterson.

their forces just as they faced unexpected resistance from the Mamluk rulers of Egypt.

In the meantime, a new power emerged in Anatolia when the Ottoman emirs ("*commanders*"), inheritors of the Seljuks, conquered Constantinople and made themselves rulers in 1453. At the beginning of the sixteenth century, the Ottoman Turks began conquering adjoining territories. In the Middle East they conquered Iraq in 1515, Syria in 1516, and Egypt in 1517, uniting the whole region under one rule for the first time since the reign of the Abbasid caliphs of the tenth century. In Europe, they extended their dominion to the Danube River, conquering Greece, the Balkans, and most of Hungary.

The leaders of this new Ottoman Empire took the title **sultan** (from an Arab word for "authority") and quickly established their control over almost the entire Muslim world. Under strong rulers like Suleyman the Magnificent, the Ottomans pushed their political influence into Asia and

Europe, beyond the territories of the caliphal dynasties. Under weak rulers, provincial governors ruled almost as independent kings.

A century of weak administrators and a failure to keep up with changing technologies of production, transportation, and communication eventually reduced the Ottoman Empire to "the sick man of Europe," in the words of Czar Nicholas I of Russia. From 1700 to 1900, first Hungary, and then Greece, Serbia, Romania, and Bulgaria, established independence from the empire. France, Italy, and Britain were able to wrest colonies in North Africa away from the Ottomans and to increase their influence in Middle Eastern provinces that remained nominally Ottoman controlled. These actions played a critical role in inducing the empire to join World War I on the side of Germany in 1914. When Germany and its allies eventually lost that war, the Ottoman Empire fell apart.

A strong leader, Mustafa Kemal Ataturk, seized control of Turkey and turned it into a Western-style nation-state. The rest of the empire was quickly divided up by the colonial powers. Great Britain created the kingdoms of Iraq and Kuwait out of the Ottoman provinces of Mosul, Baghdad, and Basra, and took control of Palestine. France assumed control of Lebanon and Syria.

Colonialism—the political, economic, and cultural domination of Middle Eastern societies by European powers—transformed the Middle East in many ways. Increased demand for agricultural products on the world market, coupled with better medical care, led to a population explosion. International corporations were brought in to better exploit natural resources and ship them to Europe to fuel its industries. Borders between states, established by Europeans without regard for the geographies of local communities, were given force of law. Tribal, religious, ethnic, and other cultural distinctions that had often been fluid and negotiable were enumerated in laws and censuses, making them more rigid and often exacerbating tensions between groups as they competed for power and resources under colonial administrations.

World War II, however, effectively bankrupted the European colonial system. In addition, the United States pressured its European allies to abandon their colonies to reduce incentives for locals to turn to its rival, the Soviet Union, for assistance in throwing off the colonial yoke. The transition from colonies to states was difficult. In many new states, the populations had no particular sense of themselves as members of a common nation; even the names of their countries had often been imposed by foreign rulers. Local leaders seized control of administrative apparatuses, which had been designed not to govern but to rule, and to remove natural resources and sell them abroad. Whatever the original intentions of the new governments, these colonial legacies made easy the development of paternalistic central authorities and allocation states that sell their resources abroad and distribute the proceeds. These historical legacies contribute to contemporary problems in the Middle East.

DIVERSITY AND DIVISION

One of the things that puzzles many people who have lived and worked in the region we call the Middle East is the tendency by those outside the region to imagine it as all of a piece, understanding the entire vast area in terms of a handful of stereotypes. The late critical theorist Edward Said suggested that these stereotypes originated during the colonial era as a way to justify European economic, political, and cultural domination. They have survived, he argued, because journalists, politicians, and scholars have continued to find them useful (Said 1979 and 1997). Whatever the reasons, the heterogeneity of the peoples living in the Middle East often goes unrecognized. People who see Spain, France, and England as very different from one another will nonetheless often imagine Egypt, Saudi Arabia, and Iran to be much the same. Yet these countries not only differ significantly from one another in economy, social organization, and cultural practices, they also have considerable internal diversity as well.

The Middle East is a land of considerable linguistic diversity. Major languages spoken in the region include Afghan, Arabic, Aramaic, Armenian, Assyrian, Baluchi, Bari, Berber, Circassian, Coptic, English, Farsi, French, Greek, Hebrew, Hindi, Italian, Kurdish, Nubian, Pashtu, Russian, Turkic, Turkish, Turkmen, and Urdu. Some of these, like Arabic, Farsi, and Berber, are regional languages that cut across state boundaries. Others are national languages, spoken primarily within a particular country, like Turkish and Hebrew. Some, like Nubian in Egypt and Bari in the Sudan (and Bari is only one of a dozen such Hamitic-Nilotic tongues in the Sudan) are languages of minority communities within state boundaries. Others, like English, French, Italian, and Russian, are languages of political and economic elites. And still others, like Hindi in the United Arab Emirates and Urdu in Oman are spoken by the South Asian guest workers who make up more than 15 percent of the population. A few, like Coptic in Egypt, are strictly liturgical languages.

Simply listing languages barely touches on the complexities of communication in the Middle East. Arabic is the most widely spoken language throughout the region, but how it is spoken differs dramatically. Proper Arabic, or *fusha* (pronounced foos-ha), refers to the classical Arabic of the **Quran** and of medieval literature, and to the **Modern Standard Arabic** of newspapers, television news programs, schools, and contemporary literature. Except on formal occasions, though, almost nobody speaks *fusha*. Instead, they speak a variety of dialects, some of which are mutually unintelligible. Other dialects are widely understood. Egypt itself has several different dialects, but the dialect of Cairo is widely understood throughout North Africa and the Middle East because Egypt is the center for most regional movie and television production. Even Disney films and cartoons are dubbed into Egyptian dialect.

As the language of the Quran, classical Arabic is the language of prayer for all Muslims. But Muslim religious leaders traveling from Afghanistan or Kyrgyz to Cairo or Mecca for theological training will often attend special courses in which the lectures are in English, because while they can read Arabic, they cannot speak or understand it fluently. Similarly, many members of the political and economic elites across the region are illiterate in their native tongues, speaking local dialects but being more comfortable reading and writing in English, French, or Russian than literate Arabic.

Moreover, ways of using Arabic continue to evolve, for example, in computer-mediated communication. While Arabic character sets and Arabic versions of Microsoft Windows are in widespread use regionally, the vast majority of global Internet and Web tools utilize ASCII characters based on the twenty-six characters of the Roman alphabet. The Arabic alphabet features twenty-eight characters, including several that represent sounds that do not occur in English. To facilitate computer-mediated communication in Arabic, many high school and college students have developed a form of ASCII-Arabic that uses standard ASCII characters to represent Arabic sounds, such as 2 for the glottal stop and 5 for the unvoiced fricative (Palfreyman and al-Khalil 2003). With this system, Arab speakers can use e-mail or instant messaging from any computer or cell phone anywhere in the world.

The region also has much greater religious diversity than many people realize. While Islam is far and away the dominant religion of the Middle East, it is by no means the only faith. The Middle East has been the birthplace of many religions, from the now extinct religions of the Sumerians, Babylonians, and Pharaonic Egyptians, to the world religions of Judaism, Christianity, Islam, and Bahai, to religions whose adherents number only a few million or less, like Zoroastrianism (India, Pakistan, Iran, and Afghanistan), Yazidism (Iraq, Syria, Turkey, Iran, Georgia, and Armenia), and Druze (Syria, Lebanon, Israel, Turkey, and Jordan). Many Middle Eastern countries have sizable Christian minorities.

Many of these religions are strongly related by similar beliefs (one God, angels, devils), shared ethical values, and a common prophetic tradition. Christianity has roots in Judaism, and Islam has roots in both. Muhammad's revelation makes clear that the God of Islam is the God of the Jews and the Christians. For Muslims, Muhammad is the last of a line of prophets, beginning with Adam, who have brought God's message to humankind. Bahais agree, but teach that the line of prophets did not end with Mohammed. The Druze also emerged from a post-Muhammadan prophetic tradition. Zoroastrianism, in its long history, has both influenced and been influenced by Judaism, Christianity, and Islam. Yazidi religious traditions probably predate the Christian era, but they have clearly been influenced by Christianity, Zoroastrianism, and Islam.

Today, Islam is the dominant religion throughout the region, and the second largest religion in the world after Christianity. The word **Islam** means "submission"; a Muslim is one who submits to the will of God. The message of Islam is that God is one and indivisible, the Christian Trinity being seen as a distortion of God's revelation. God is at once great beyond human comprehension and closer to us than our jugular vein, according to the Quran.

Submitting to God begins with the *arkaan,* a set of practices sometimes called the Five Pillars of Islam, which shape people's minds and bodies into those of good Muslims. The first of these is the *shahada,* or declaration of faith: "There is no god but God, and Muhammad is his prophet." This declaration implies a commitment to the absolute priority of God and an acceptance of the authority of the revelation of Muhammad as contained in the **Quran** (the written record of Muhammad's revelation) and the *hadith* (collected accounts of sayings and actions of the prophet and his companions). The second is prayer. Muslim prayer involves the

FIGURE 11.2 The Quran is the written record of God's revelation to mankind through the prophet Muhammad. PHOTO: Natalia Sui.

entire body: standing, kneeling, bowing, prostrating oneself. Every Muslim is expected to pray five times each day unless circumstances make it impossible. The prayers at dawn, noon, mid-afternoon, dusk, and night are intended to break up the day, reminding Muslims that the unseen, eternal world of God takes precedence over the visible, mundane world of human activity.

The third orthodox practice is fasting. During the month of Ramadan, the entire Muslim world collectively fasts from dawn to dusk. The fourth practice is charity. Every Muslim is required each year to give 2 percent of his or her entire net worth, less the amount necessary to live at a subsistence level. Charity can be given as a personal act or it can be given to a mosque, bank, or other institution for redistribution to various charities. Finally, every Muslim who is physically and financially able is expected to make a pilgrimage (*hajj*) to the city of Mecca (in modern-day Saudi Arabia) at least once in his or her life. Mecca is the city where Muhammad lived when he received his prophetic revelation, and it is believed to have been visited through history by many other prophets, including Adam and Ibrahim (Abraham). Millions of Muslims make the hajj each year, and millions more around the world celebrate the feast that culminates the event in communion with them.

In spite of the universality of these practices, Islam is not understood or practiced everywhere in the same ways. The most significant difference is between Shia and Sunni Muslims. Although they accept the orthodox principles described above, the Shia also venerate saints and make pilgrimages to their tombs, invest their clerics with special authority, and appeal to a different body of hadith in interpreting Sharia law. Other communities like the Alevis of Turkey, Syria, Iraq, and Lebanon may deviate even from the Five Pillars, so that they are regarded as non-Muslims by most Sunni and Shia Muslims.

But even members of the Sunni majority do not practice their faith everywhere in the same way. There are many ways orthodox Muslims in the Middle East and around the world differ in performing even such required acts as daily prayers, although every community tends to assume the ways it prays are the closest to those of the prophet and his companions. The same is true of interpretations of the Quran and of the hadith. Western journalists often write of **Sharia** law as if the code of law derived from the Quran and hadith were a coherent body of rules all Muslims agreed on. But it is not. A law must be interpreted, and within orthodox Islam there are a number of accepted schools of legal interpretation, which can differ in the ways they address everyday behavior.

Taqlid is the position that authoritative interpretation for almost any position already exists in centuries of accumulated work by theologians and jurors. Those who call themselves *salafis* believe the Quran must be interpreted in the light of the collected sayings of Muhammad and the first three generations of Muslims. Many other Muslims, particularly in Europe and the Americas, call for *ijtihad*, the use of good judgment in applying the word of God to contemporary situations. Although they strive for consistency, different authorities may in good faith issue contradictory *fatwas*, or juridical decrees, on the same topic. In the thirteenth century, for example, debates raged over whether the newly discovered drink coffee was permitted or prohibited by the prophet's ban on intoxicants, and similar debates later emerged over tobacco. Although the view that coffee and tobacco were not forbidden won out, and both are now widely enjoyed throughout the Islamic world, some Muslims choose to follow stricter interpretations and avoid both.

Some scholars believe the current era may be a time of tremendous transformation in Islam, comparable to the Protestant Reformation in Europe in the sixteenth century. Several generations of public schooling in Islamic countries have transformed Islam from something one simply did as a member of a community to an object of scrutiny. Students around the world have begun to discover that many of the religious conventions their community took for granted were not practiced in other Muslim communities and may not be supported by the Quran or hadith. The possibility has emerged that individuals can diverge from their community's practice on the basis of their personal study, not only of sacred texts and schoolbooks, but also of published commentaries, radio, television, cassette tape, and podcast sermons, and other sources of knowledge. The World Wide Web and other new media technologies have opened up tremendous possibilities for divergent opinions about Islam to be disseminated worldwide, not only in Arabic but in every language. People with educations in engineering, business administration, or nursing who might never dream of disagreeing with a learned sheikh or *da'wa* (religious teacher) in a traditional setting like a mosque or school often have no compunctions about authoritatively presenting their interpretations of Islam in blogs or on websites. The term **Public Islam** is being used to describe these diverse invocations of Islam by "religious scholars, self-ascribed religious authorities, secular intellectuals, Sufi orders, mothers, students, workers, engineers, consumers and many others" in public life (Eickelman and Salvatore 2006).

From Empires to Nation-States

As befits a region of such extraordinary cultural diversity, political relations in the Middle East are complex. The history of the twentieth century is, as historian Daniel Brower points out, the history of a transformation from empires to nation-states (2002). But this transformation has been less successful in the Middle East than in Western Europe and North America. For thousands of years, most of the Middle East was comprised of communities under more-or-less loose rule by distant authorities. Outside urban centers of power, and to some extent even within them, people went about their lives with only minimal regulation by the state. Employment, marriage, banking, and living arrangements were all largely organized by informal networks of people related by blood, religion, or co-residence.

The creation of nation-states was a process that, in most cases, involved political and economic elites taking over the apparatuses of power previously held by foreign empires. Since the boundaries of the state encompassed diverse peoples with different languages, ethnicities, religious beliefs, and ways of life, it was often difficult for these myriad peoples to see themselves as forming a common nation. Instead, they continued to rely on the same informal networks they had under the empires.

One of the most important of these is tribal structure. It is often as difficult for people from nontribal societies to understand the concept of tribe as it is for oppressed or conquered people to understand patriotic sentiment for one's country. Yet the two are in some ways similar. **Tribes** are large groups of people who share a common identity based on an assumption of common ancestry. They are, in a sense, extended families who may number in the tens of thousands. Common membership in a tribe can be the basis for mutual support—someone traveling to a strange city in a foreign country would certainly expect to find help from other members of their tribe who had already settled there. But tribes can also call on their members to make sacrifices for the good of the tribe, just as nations can call on their members to serve their country.

Like patriotic sentiment, people's tribal sentiments wax and wane according to personal experience and current political, social, and economic conditions. Tribal members can rely on help and protection from their tribe in the absence of external law and order. When the Taliban fell in Afghanistan in 2001, many people turned to tribal leaders for economic aid and protection. Tribal leaders moved rapidly into poppy cultivation to maximize their economic gains so they would have money to feed and house people, and to buy weapons. Likewise in Algeria, when civil society all but collapsed in the 1990s, after the government refused to accept the results of an election that would have put Islamist parties in power, ties of reciprocity and obligation organized in part around tribal identity allowed much of everyday life to continue without the assistance of police, courts, and bureaucratic structures.

Tribal organization can become the basis for state power. The classic example is Saudi Arabia, in which one tribe essentially established hegemony over most of the other tribes of the Arabian peninsula and declared a kingdom. Tribal politics can also crosscut political organization in both democracies and dictatorships. During the reign of Saddam Hussein in Iraq (1979–2003), the dictator appointed many members of his own tribe to positions of power as a way to maximize the loyalty of those surrounding him. But tribal politics can also play a crucial role in democratization. During the legislative elections in Iraq in 2005, most of the parties were salted with tribal leaders, and many people voted as their tribal leaders recommended. In addition, some tribes had members in several parties simultaneously, ensuring that no matter which parties won, there would be tribal members in positions of power. This should not be seen only as a power grab—tribal organizations can play important roles in any political system. For example, tribal membership is a powerful way to cut across bureaucratic restrictions; the citizen who needs a favor and can't get at his or her representative through the government bureaucracy may well be able to get attention from politicians through tribal connections.

Because the borders of many states are a colonial legacy, there is often no territorial connection between state boundaries and community tribal and ethnic identities. Sizable minorities exist in many Middle Eastern countries whose primary affiliation is not to the state but to linguistic, religious, ethnic, or tribal fellows who live in other states. These communities can number in the hundreds of thousands or even millions.

In some cases, such as that of the Kurds, these communities are spatially coherent. That is, although the Kurds live as minority communities in Iraq, Turkey, Syria, and Iran, the primary area in which they dwell is the land in which Kurds have lived for centuries. From the popular Kurdish perspective, the contemporary borders of these states arbitrarily cut up the Kurdish homeland. It should not be surprising then, that a majority of Kurds in these states support the creation of a new state, Kurdistan, to be carved out of pieces of each of these countries.

Communities like the Kurds are often referred to as **proto-states**. Other well-known examples in the Middle East include Armenians and Palestinians. Armenians now have a state, but its borders are not what they were before it was absorbed by the Soviet Union. Armenia lays claim to sizable, mostly Christian Armenian minorities in the neighboring Muslim-majority states of Turkey and Azerbaijan and has occupied nearly one-quarter of Azerbaijan in an effort to reclaim territory Armenians see as part of their historical homeland.

The Palestinian situation is especially complex. When the region of Palestine controlled by Great Britain was divided to create the new state of Israel in 1948, hundreds of thousands of Palestinians fled from the violence of clashes between the Israelis and invading armies from Syria,

Egypt, Jordan, Arabia, and Lebanon. Although a Palestinian territorial authority now exists, most of these refugees and their descendants have been refused the right to return by Israel because of fears they would fuel the violent clashes between Israelis and Palestinians that have become part of everyday in Israel and the Palestinian territories, and fears that an Arab majority in a democratic state would cause Israel to lose its Jewish character. The result is more than 4 million exiles living mostly in the Arab states bordering Israel whose primary allegiance is to a country many have never seen and that, in fact, no longer exists. Ironically, Israel itself is proof to the Palestinians that lost homelands can be recreated.

THE RICHEST AND THE POOREST

Economists often divide the states of the Middle East into *production* and *allocation* states. **Production states** derive the bulk of their revenues from the labor of their citizens in agriculture, herding, manufacturing, or trade. A productive state has a centralized bureaucracy to collect taxes and other charges from the citizens. An **allocation state** does not derive its revenues by taxing its citizens but rather by directly selling key resources to the rest of the world (Luciani 1987). Most of the major oil-producing states—Saudi Arabia, Kuwait, Libya, Oman, Qatar, and the United Arab Emirates—are allocation states. Allocation states are often dependent on foreign companies and workers for everything from mining the resources to delivering services to citizens. Allocation states attract labor migration both from within the region and from elsewhere in the world. This is why in countries like Kuwait foreign workers can outnumber citizens.

The region we call the Middle East is marked by extreme economic disparities because of the irregular distribution of resources—both arable land and minerals, including oil. The region includes some states whose GDP per capita puts them among the wealthiest nations in the world. Qatar's mean average GDP per person is $28,300, and Kuwait's is $20,300. But the Middle East also includes some of the world's poorest states, like Yemen ($900) and Afghanistan ($800). Countries like Egypt ($3,900) and Jordan ($4,700) belong to the world's middle class. The key factor is oil—Qatar and Kuwait are oil rich, Yemen and Afghanistan have few oil reserves, and Egypt and Jordan have mixed economies in which oil and natural gas play a large but not dominant role.

Figures indicating average GDP per capita are misleading; the hypo-thetical average Jordanian does not earn $4,700 per year, nor does a typi-cal resident of Saudi Arabia earn $13,100 per year. An average is just that: for every millionaire in Saudi Arabia or Syria, there must be millions of people who earn substantially less than these sums. Although Yemen has approximately one hundred billionaires and twenty thousand millionaires, the World Bank estimates that 42 percent of the people live in poverty and one in five is malnourished. Some 40 percent of the country's pop-ulation is unemployed. Economic disparities are thus just as great within states as among them.

Economic disparities are exacerbated by massive population growth. For example, Egypt had a total population of about six hundred thousand at the dawn of the twentieth century but had some 60 million people by the dawn of the twenty-first century. Egyptian officials estimate that a baby is born within its borders every three minutes.

Population growth has been accompanied by a huge upswing in ur-banization. One hundred years ago, less than 10 percent of the peoples of the Middle East lived in cities. By 2000, cities accounted for more than 60 percent of the population of the region. There are many reasons for this. In some countries, like Egypt, there is simply insufficient arable land to create work for people living in rural communities. In some allocation states, the agricultural sector of the economy has been allowed to atrophy because of oil revenues. In yet other cases, poor agricultural planning by colonial and national rulers has led to desertification and left thousands of farmers homeless. In each case, unemployed rural peasants have sought a better life by moving to cities. Between 1800 and 2000, Cairo's popula-tion rose from about 200,000 to more than 12 million. Tehran went from about 10,000 to more than 8 million. Istanbul rose from 300,000 to more than 6 million. Casablanca had only 20,000 people in 1900, and by 2000 its population was approaching 3 million.

Some Middle Eastern nations have also experienced massive labor mi-gration. The tremendous wealth available in oil-rich countries such as Saudi Arabia, Kuwait, and Qatar attracts millions of workers. From highly trained technicians and managers to unskilled laborers to domestic ser-vants, workers flow from the United States, Europe, India, the Philippines, and elsewhere to oil-rich countries in the Arabian peninsula. In some of these countries, such as Kuwait, foreign workers make up as much as 70

FIGURE 11.3 Under constant population pressure, cities like Cairo continue to grow even at the expense of valuable farmland. PHOTO: Mark Allen Peterson.

percent of the population. Arab countries are also major exporters of labor, especially Egypt and Yemen, which benefit from the cash remittances sent back into their local economies (Sarageldin et al. 1983).

All these problems have been exacerbated by a half century of growing international debt and fiscal mismanagement by governments, local business elites, multinational corporations, and international agencies. In the aftermath of World War II, the United States and its allies in Western Europe, and the USSR and its allies in Eastern Europe, sought to offer economic aid to developing countries in the Middle East and elsewhere, primarily to extend their spheres of influence. Through organizations like the World Bank and the International Monetary Fund, huge loans were arranged to assist countries in developing their economic infrastructures. Often these projects failed to achieve their projected outcomes, producing low returns on investments so that the recipient countries found themselves unable to pay back the loans. Additional loans, including loans to pay the interest on previous loans, led to ever-higher levels of debt. So-called **structural adjustment programs** (SAPs) imposed on recipient countries to make them abandon nonmarket practices like food subsidies often led to riots and increasingly desperate living conditions among the poor.

International investment has also sometimes contributed to economic problems. Multinational corporations have naturally preferred to partner with local elites, people who have capital to invest and knowledge of how to work with local bureaucracies. These Middle Eastern elites in return have often preferred to put their shares of profits into reliable American, Asian, or European investments, leading to **capital flight**—the tendency for wealth to leave poor countries rather than trickle down from the wealthy to the middle classes. Although these investments bring jobs to local economies, they are often unskilled, low-paying jobs, and foreigners are often brought in to serve as management. And they can have unforeseen consequences: in the five years leading up to the Iranian Revolution, inflation caused by foreign corporate investment caused rental prices to double every year (Beeman 2004). Allocation states are less affected by many of these problems, but they face severe levels of resource extraction that cannot be indefinitely sustained.

There are many explanations offered for the failure of development strategies in the Middle East. Some have argued that the centralized, bureaucratically controlled economies of most Middle Eastern states make it difficult for them to participate in organizations like the World Trade Organization because these institutions assume European and North American open-market philosophies. Others blame the region's colonial heritage. They argue that borders were established for administrative purposes rather than designed for national viability and that colonial economic structures were designed to extract wealth, not to nurture its growth. These legacies left a crippling burden on emergent nations as they won their freedom. Still others have argued that the theory of development—the idea that wealthy countries can assist poor countries in becoming productive—is itself flawed. Interestingly, such critiques come from both the political left and the right. The former argues that it is simply impossible for wealthy countries to offer economic assistance to poorer countries on a for-profit or even a break-even basis, since more often than not aid recipients just end up further in debt. The latter argues that the problem lies in the centralized nature of many development projects, but if bolstered by the world market, international investment, and microloans to encourage entrepreneurship, foundering Middle Eastern economies can still transform themselves.

At the dawn of the twenty-first century, all of the countries of the Middle East and North Africa face similar challenges: rapid population growth, unequal distribution of resources, economic distortions caused by the enormous flow of oil revenues into the region, international debt, poor economic management by a relatively small elite, conflicts between community identities and nation building, and often unwelcome political attention from powerful states outside the region. People survive these conditions as best they can, often relying on informal social and economic networks to get by. Such informal economies can include everything from barter to street vending to private loans to smuggling and black market activities. The International Labor Organization has estimated that the informal economies in Algeria, Morocco, Tunisia, and Egypt may exceed 4 percent of these countries' total economic activity (ILO 2002). But while they may help many people get by, informal economic activities do little to solve larger economic issues and often exacerbate them. Most people are desperate for more permanent solutions to these problems.

THE PROBLEM OF PALESTINE

Perhaps the most significant of these historical and contemporary issues in the Middle East is that of the establishment of the state of Israel in the former British colony of Palestine. The roots of this lie in the rise of secularism and nationalism in Europe during the seventeenth and eighteenth centuries, which transformed the ways many Jews conceived of themselves as a people. Traditionally, Jewish identity had been rooted in pre-Christian Rome's expulsion of thousands of Jews from the province of Palestine in 136 CE, following a revolt against imperial domination. The subsequent travels of these Jews and their descendants into Europe, North Africa, South and West Asia, and elsewhere is called the Jewish *diaspora*, a term used to describe transnational communities of peoples who maintain a distinct identity inside the host communities in which they settle, usually through a sense of connection to a common homeland, often one that most members of the community have never seen (Sheffer 1986).

Although Jewish communities around the world developed disparate identities and cultures, even evolving new languages like Yiddish and Ladino, their common commitment to their lost homeland was deeply embedded in shared religious doctrines and ritual practices. Jews were met with different receptions in different places and times, but Jewish communities in Europe mostly experienced prejudice and oppression. Beginning with England in 1290, many states expelled Jews from their borders. Jews who had grown wealthy under the tolerant rule of the Fatimids in Spain and Portugal found themselves forced to convert to Christianity or face losing their property after the peninsula was reconquered by Christian rulers. In other states walled communities called *ghettos* were established to seal Jews off from the larger community. Traditional religious teaching had it that someday a Messiah would come who would reestablish a Jewish kingdom centered in Jerusalem. Until then, the homeland was remembered in prayer and ritual, for example on Yom Kippur and Passover, with the traditional hopeful toast, "next year in Jerusalem."

European **nationalism**, with its ideal of the nation-state, strongly affected the ways many Jews in Europe conceived of their collective identity. Jewish intellectuals like Leo Pinsker, Moses Hess, and Theodore Herzl began to describe Jews as a nation, a distinct people united by some common origin and character. The belief that Jews constitute a sovereign people and nation and that they should have the right to establish and maintain a state in their ancestral homeland became known as **Zionism**. Zionist clubs and study groups sprang up across Europe in the 1870s and 1880s, and adventurous Jews were inspired to travel to Palestine, then a province of the Ottoman Empire, and settle there (Avineri 1981). A series of pogroms and waves of anti-Semitism in Russia and Eastern Europe between 1882 and 1914 induced another seventy-five thousand Jews to emigrate to Palestine. A central concept of Zionism was *aliyah* (ascent), which refers to both voluntary immigration and the flight of persecuted populations of Jews to Palestine. Nonetheless, by the outbreak of World War I, only about 7 percent of Palestine's population was Jewish, smaller than its Christian Arab population and much smaller than its Muslim Arab population (Shlaim 2001).

In 1917, Great Britain, in order to obtain war loan guarantees from several Jewish banks, issued the Balfour Declaration. This was a letter from the British secretary of state to Lord Rothschild that stated that if Britain won the war and took control of Palestine from the Ottomans, the government would "view with favour the establishment in Palestine of a national home for the Jewish people, and will use their best endeavours to facilitate the achievement of this object, it being clearly understood that nothing shall be done which may prejudice the civil and religious rights of existing non-Jewish communities in Palestine, or the rights and

354 INTERNATIONAL STUDIES

political status enjoyed by Jews in any other country." After several initial defeats, British forces captured Palestine in December 1918, and in 1920 the newly formed League of Nations passed the British Mandate for Palestine, which gave England direct administration of the region.

More than 150,000 Jews, mostly from Russia and Eastern Europe, emigrated to Palestine over the next seventeen years, sparking Arab riots in 1929 and again in 1933–1936 (Sherman 2001). Great Britain restricted immigration in response, but Jews continued to come illegally in the tens of thousands to flee the rise of Nazism in Germany. Increasingly violent Arab hostility and Jewish anger at Britain's refusal to enforce the Balfour Declaration, in the way many settlers interpreted it, led to the formation of Jewish terrorist organizations like Irgun Tzvei Leumi, and the Stern Gang (Vest 2001). After World War II, European survivors of the Holocaust swelled the numbers of illegal immigrants to Palestine, and Britain established internment camps to hold those they captured while they considered where to send them.

The international community grew increasingly dissatisfied with Britain's handling of its mandate. On November 29, 1947, the United Nations voted thirty-three to thirteen to partition Palestine into two states, one predominantly Jewish and one predominantly Muslim, in the land that had been Palestine. In order to ensure that all the Jewish majority settlements would be in Israel, a UN commission had recommended a patchwork partitioning of the country into seven interlocked sections, three controlled by Jews, three by Muslim Arabs, and one (which included Jerusalem and Bethlehem) by the United Nations. On May 14, 1948, the day set for the British mandate to expire, Israel declared its existence and independence. The following day, military forces from Egypt, Syria, Lebanon, Transjordan, and Iraq attacked the new state. In the face of this external threat, internal divisions within the Israeli independence movement vanished. Arab forces, on the other hand, were hampered by just the opposite problem: states failed to commit promised troop levels, and troops resisted following orders from commanders of other Arab states. Israel defeated the Arab armies, and an armistice was signed in 1949 (Goldschmidt and Davidson 2005). Almost simultaneously, Jordan seized a large tract of land west of the Jordan River reaching to East Jerusalem, which became known as the West Bank territory.

The establishment of the state of Israel is known to Palestinian Arabs as the *nakba*, or catastrophe, because it left the majority of them without a homeland. During the war, more than half a million Palestinian Arabs—Muslim and Christian—fled Palestine for neighboring Arab countries. Others were expelled from their homes in the early days of independence. In 1948, there were approximately 150,000 Arab Israelis, 400,000 Arabs who had become "Jordanians" through the seizure of the West Bank, and some 550,000 to 800,000 refugees. Israel refused to allow the refugees to return, claiming that they had fled under orders from the Arab high command and so abandoned any claim to Israeli citizenship.[2] Arab countries responded by expelling Jews from their own countries. These Jews were welcomed by Israel, and today only a few Jewish communities exist in most other Middle Eastern states.[3]

In 1956, members of this refugee community formed the Palestinian Liberation Organization (PLO), to fight for the reestablishment of a Palestinian homeland. A second organization, al-Fatah, organized along Marxist principles, was founded in 1965. Four years later they merged, and Yasir Arafat became head of the PLO. Lacking an organized, well-funded military, the PLO relied primarily on guerrilla strategies, including terrorist strategies targeting civilians. In 1972, the PLO grabbed international headlines when it killed eleven Israeli Olympic athletes in Munich, Germany, after negotiations for the return of captured PLO leaders failed. In addition to dealing with terrorist attacks by the PLO and similar groups, the state of Israel fought two more wars with its Arab neighbors: the 1967 Six-Day War, which established Israel as the preeminent military power in the region, and the 1973 Yom Kippur War, which had international consequences. It was settled at a peace conference in Geneva and was followed by UN recognition of the PLO as a legitimate political agency for the Palestinian diaspora. In 1979, following a visit by Egypt's president Anwar Sadat to Israel's Knesset (parliament), US president Jimmy Carter organized the historic Camp David Accord between Egypt and Israel, the first treaty to conclude with an acknowledgment of Israel's existence by an Arab state.

In fulfillment of these treaty obligations, Israel in 1982 returned lands to Egypt that it had captured in the 1967 war, most prominently the Sinai peninsula. That same year, Israel invaded Lebanon to put an end to terrorist organizations operating out of refugee camps, and to chase Arafat and the PLO out of Beirut. The occupation lasted eighteen years, establishing Israel as the undisputed military power in the region. However, the occupation not only failed to meet its objective of stamping out terrorists, it also produced a new anti-Israeli terrorist organization, Hezbollah,

FIGURE 11.4 The wall built by Israel to separate itself from the Palestinian territories—and seen by many Arabs as an effort to grab additional Palestinian land—stands as a monument to the intractable problems of just and peaceful coexistence. PHOTO: Brad Bailey.

comprised primarily of Lebanese Shiites committed to resisting what it called Israel's colonization of Lebanon. In 1987, Palestinians declared the First Intifada (resistance) against Israel. All celebrations ceased—people still married, but no parties were held. Resistance, both passive and militant, increased dramatically. The following year, the PLO said it would agree to a two-state solution—the formation of an independent Palestinian state coexisting with Israel. This has been the basis for all subsequent peace negotiations, including the ambitious Oslo Accords signed in 1993. In 1994, a government—the Palestinian Authority—was established for the Palestinian state, which did not yet exist and whose boundaries were not yet agreed upon.

Peace has proven elusive. On the Israeli side, continued construction of Israeli settlements on what was, under the treaty, supposed to become Palestinian land, led most Palestinians to doubt Israel's sincerity. Targeted assassinations of Palestinian leaders accused of terrorism, the deaths of large numbers of Palestinian noncombatants, and the refusal of Israel to consider the rights of refugees to return to their former homes or receive compensation for their losses, exacerbated tensions. On the Palestinian side, the inability of the Palestinian Authority to represent all Palestinian factions, demonstrated particularly by its incapacity to enforce cease-fire agreements or to control terrorist groups, made any negotiations unreliable at best.

In 2000, the visit of Israeli prime minister Ariel Sharon to the Dome of the Rock in Jerusalem surrounded by hundreds of police sparked riots that turned into the Second Intifada, or "uprising," a period of extended violence and noncooperation. Palestinian anger was exacerbated by Sharon's subsequent decision to build a wall separating the two states. The wall did not follow the established border, and many Palestinians saw it as a further effort by Israel to expropriate Arab land.

In 2006, the militant anti-Israeli organization Hamas was elected to lead the Palestinian Authority. The rival Fatah organization assumed power in the West Bank, and Hamas-controlled Gaza was subjected to an economic blockade that led to the suspension of an estimated 95 percent of Gaza's factories and created more than 40 percent unemployment (Oxfam 2010), which continues to this day. The Palestinian Authority remains split and thus ineffective at representing the Palestinian cause as a whole, although Egypt brokered a fragile cooperation agreement in 2011. Efforts to move forward on peace talks were renewed in 2008, 2010, and 2013 but quickly foundered each time. Although polls show that a majority of both Israelis and Palestinians believe a two-state solution is a just and workable possibility (Yaar and Hermann 2007), the problems of borders, settlements, and refugees remain seemingly intractable obstacles to peace in the foreseeable future.

POLITICAL CHANGE IN THE MIDDLE EAST

"The people want to bring down the regime!" Chanted by tens of thousands of voices, this slogan was raised in late 2010 and much of 2011 by protesters in a score of countries as people of all walks of life gathered in public places to demand political change: Tunisia, Egypt, Yemen, Libya, Syria, Bahrain, Algeria, Jordan, Oman, Morocco, and Iraq. The news media named it the **Arab Spring**, although not all those taking part in the protests identify as Arabs. Popular, peaceful, and persistent in the face of violent reprisals by the government and pro-government counterdemonstrators, the Arab uprisings shared both common techniques of civil resistance (demonstrations, marches, rallies, strikes) and the use of social media to communicate among protesters and with the outside world, circumventing attempts at censorship by the state.

This regional wave of antigovernment protests began December 18, 2010, when an Algerian street vendor named Mohammed Bouazizi set himself on fire to protest his ill treatment at the hands of the police. The incident sparked continued protests by hundreds of thousands of Tunisians of all walks of life, culminating in the flight of Tunisian president Zine El Abidine Ben Ali on January 14, 2011. The success of the Tunisian revolt sparked a wave of similar protests in Algeria, Egypt, Jordan, and Yemen, then spread to other countries. Egypt, the largest Arab state, was particularly successful: after eighteen days of protests, President Hosni Mubarak resigned February 11, ending his thirty-year reign. Mubarak and his sons were subsequently prosecuted for their part in the deaths of protesters.

Not all protests were successful. Governments in Jordan, Kuwait, Lebanon, Morocco, and Oman quelled major protests by implementing political and economic reforms. But in Syria and Yemen, government troops met protesters with force, resulting sometimes in hundreds of reported deaths and injuries. Another violent site was Libya, where protests against the government of Muammar Qaddafi turned into civil war, with a NATO-imposed "no fly zone" and air strikes, culminating in the death of the dictator. In contrast, relatively small protests in Sudan and Saudi Arabia led to little or no significant change.

The Arab Spring was the culmination of years of protest movements. Egypt, for example, had had more than 3,000 strikes and demonstrations since 2000. These protests were driven in part by economic concerns. Most Middle Eastern states face rising poverty, inflation, and failing infrastructure (especially schools and public hospitals). These issues were exacerbated by a sense of helplessness in the face of autocratic governments, often supported by Western powers. Protesters complained of endemic corruption, rigged elections, and censorship of the media; they criticized police brutality, and "Emergency Laws" that render the police safe from reprisals.

Social movements against ruling regimes date back to the colonial era. Most European colonial powers were democracies at home but imperialists

FIGURE 11.5 Protests in Egypt, inspired by an uprising in Tunisia, brought down a dictator and inspired other protests throughout the region. PHOTO: Malak Rouchdy.

in their colonies. Resistance to this imperialism led to the emergence of many insurgent groups throughout the late nineteenth and early twentieth centuries. The most wide-ranging terrorist movement was that of the anarchists, a global network of mostly European intellectuals and militants organized into independent cells and committed to a common utopian political vision—not unlike al Qaeda is today (Bergesen and Han 2005). Early uses of terrorism in the Middle East developed during the late colonial era, between and after the world wars (Vest 2001), when organizations like the Muslim Brotherhood sought to reform political systems dominated by foreign powers. This organization began as an effort to meet civil society needs—such as clinics, schools, loan programs, and employment opportunities for rural migrants—that were not taken care of by the British-controlled Egyptian government. Their criticisms of the government's failures to take care of the Egyptian people led to the establishment of a political arm, and the government's periodic crackdowns on the society led to the creation of a militant arm. The outlawing of the organization was a direct result of the militant arm's role in the 1981 assassination of Egyptian president Anwar Sadat.

After World War II, inspiration for revolutionary movements was drawn primarily from Marxist ideologies, in solidarity with similar groups throughout the world, drawing inspiration from Soviet models of revolution and employing terrorism as a tool. **Terrorism** is a strategy by which subnational groups, not recognized as legitimate by the states they oppose, seek to resist those states by targeting nonstate actors, disrupting the flow of everyday life, and spreading generalized fear among the populations of those states.[4] As an act of political communication, terrorism can be extremely effective. As Eqbal Ahmed points out, in 1970 Golda Meier could say "there are no Palestinians" because they had no state and Israel refused to recognize them as a people or a nation. By the 1980s, everyone acknowledged that the Palestinians existed, even if only as a "problem" (Ahmed 2001).

However, terrorism has proven historically ineffective at achieving specific political goals. Such high-profile crimes as the murder of the Israeli Olympic athletes in 1972, the 1975 OPEC hostage taking, and the hijacking of the *Achille Lauro* in 1985 did little to advance the specific political goals of these organizations.

Instead, the first successful overthrow of a Western-backed regime was masterminded by Islamic clerics and their followers. The success of the Iranian Revolution in 1979 led to the rise of Islamic political movements. From the viewpoint of those seeking political change in the Middle East, Iran was a watershed—a relatively bloodless coup that replaced a dictatorship with a semi-democratic government and put an elected parliament in place within months of the revolution. It seized US diplomats and successfully traded them after more than a year for arms with which to fight against invasion by another Western-backed dictatorship, that of Iraq. Iran inspired the rise of "political Islam."

Political Islam refers to the invocation of Islam in contemporary political and economic life, both by political actors within states and by groups opposed to existing governments. In most parts of the Middle East, this represents a new trend that has been growing since the early 1980s. For the most part, it represents a disillusionment with the secularization that has marked most Middle Eastern political economies since the end of World War II. The failure of Western economic models—socialist or capitalist—to bring about the prosperity once promised and the lack of democratization by governments who enjoy the support of the United States and European nations have led to doubts, disappointments, and anger. In the face of what many regard as a complete failure of Westernization in the region, the politicization of Islam promises new models and offers many Muslims new hope for the future. The recent success of Islamic parties in elections in Turkey, Tunisia, and Egypt, reflects popular support for political Islam, although the subsequent popular protests and removal of the Islamist president in Egypt demonstrates ongoing concerns about balancing religious reform with national interests.

Although political Islam is a relatively recent phenomenon, its roots can be traced back at least to the nineteenth century, to thinkers like Jama al-Afghani, Sayyid Abul Ala Maududi, and Sayyid Qutb, and to groups like the Muslim Brotherhood in Egypt. Shortsighted policies by the international community have also contributed to the creation of Islamist groups. For example, the United States strongly encouraged political Islam in Afghanistan and provided strong support for the Afghans fighting a military jihad against Soviet invaders in the 1980s. Under Presidents Carter and Reagan, the United States spent over $5 billion to arm, supply, and train Afghan freedom fighters—including many of those who went on to create al Qaeda. But when the Soviets finally withdrew in 1989, the United States effectively abandoned its Afghan allies, leaving them with a collapsed economy, the second highest saturation of land mines in the world, and the highest percentage of weapons per person in the world. Power was seized by the only two groups that still had international connections—the Taliban, with ties to Pakistan, and al Qaeda, with its international financial networks. Afghanistan quickly became a training ground for terrorists. The September 11 terrorist attacks in New York were examples of what some political scientists call "blowback"—situations in which foreign policies and interventions that seem like good ideas at the time have unforeseen consequences years later.

Muslim militants often invoke the concept of *jihad*, which has come to mean "holy war" in many international contexts, and especially in international news media. For Muslims, though, jihad is a much more complex concept. The term means "struggle," and Islamic scholars have long distinguished between the greater jihad of one's personal struggle to submit to God's will in the face of worldly temptations, and the lesser jihad of militant struggle against injustice—including, but not limited to, just war.

Because war is a public undertaking fraught with possibilities for abuse, theologians have devoted far more attention to working out the rules for the lesser jihad that many terrorists claim defines their actions. Most mainstream Muslim theologians of all schools denounced the September

11 attacks. "The killing of innocent men, women and children is a horrible and hideous act against all religion and against rational thinking," pronounced Sheikh Mohammed Sayyid Tantawi, grand imam of Cairo's Al-Azhar University, the world's foremost center of Islamic learning. His fatwa is based on traditional interpretations that limit the use of violent force to soldiers and political officials. But Tantawi, like most Muslim clerics, does not denounce Palestinian terrorism, since the right to use violence against occupiers is well testified to in Islamic jurisprudence, and the right of Israel to exist as an exclusively Jewish state on what was once Palestinian Arab land is not recognized by most theologians.

In spite of this clerical rejection of their actions, the messages the September 11 attackers left behind show that many of them saw themselves as true believers. They quoted verses from the Quran and vowed to overcome their fears of death by saying prayers and calling on God's name right to the end. Al Qaeda's justification of jihad against civilians is particularly modern, since it derives from taking democracy seriously. In essence, the argument is that in a democracy, citizens govern themselves and therefore all citizens are political actors and hence subject to violent reprisals for the acts of their government. This point of view has been embraced by some other terrorist groups, such as Islamic Jihad, but rejected by many, including Hamas. The US invasion of Iraq increased sympathy for such anti-Western interpretations of jihad throughout the Islamic world. On the other hand, the callous disregard for the lives not only of collaborators but innocent bystanders in Iraq has sparked debates even within al Qaeda over the proper limits of jihad.

The Arab uprisings marked a dramatic new shift in the politics of the region that challenged two decades of political Islam and contradicted the narratives of groups like al Qaeda. These movements drew on people of all walks of life—across religious, age, gender, and class boundaries. They employed highly sophisticated technologies, as well as traditional means of communication. They were primarily nonviolent, although self-defense against violent attacks by government forces sometimes escalated into civil war. They sought not to attack the outside powers that supported the regimes they sought to overthrow, but to confront them and demand that they support the values of democracy they professed. In some countries, these movements failed; in others, they led to political reform, or even the overthrow of political regimes; in others they led to civil war. The final outcome of these movements on the region, and the world, will not be clear for many years.

CONCLUSION

Located at the intersection of three continents, the Middle East remains today, as in the past, an international center of economic activity, social transformation, religious revitalization, and political struggle. As we enter the twenty-first century, the peoples of the region continue to seek good governance, productive economies, and the right to live according to their own cultural systems and traditions. As always, the devil is in the details. What kinds of democracies are appropriate for these diverse peoples? How can economies become productive in the face of burdensome international debts and global market pressures? Which traditions will have force of law, and how will multiple traditions coexist within states? The coming decades will see the peoples and states of this region struggle for answers, with global ramifications. A multidisciplinary lens offers our best opportunity to understand events as these struggles play out.

TIMELINE OF TWENTIETH-CENTURY MIDDLE EASTERN HISTORY

1914	World War I breaks out; the Ottoman Empire enters the war on the side of Germany.
1917	Britain issues the Balfour Declaration.
1918	British forces capture Palestine.
1920	League of Nations issues British Mandate for Palestine.
1922	Mustafa Kemal Ataturk establishes an independent Turkey and abolishes the Sultanate.
1925	Reza Shah establishes the Pahlavi dynasty in Iran.
1926	Ibn Saud proclaims himself King of the Hijaz and, in 1932, proclaims the Kingdom of Saudi Arabia.
1932	Independence of Iraq.
1947	United Nations appoints the Special Commission on Palestine (UNSCOP) to deal with the fate of Palestine; UN votes for partition.
1948	Establishment of Israel; first Arab-Israeli war between Israel and its neighbors.
1953	Egypt establishes a republic.

1956	President Nasser of Egypt nationalizes the Suez Canal; Sudan, Morocco, and Tunisia become independent; Palestinian Liberation Organization formed.
1958	Iraq becomes a republic.
1962	Algeria becomes independent from France.
1965	Fatah formed.
1967	Second Arab-Israeli war (Six-Day War), between Egypt and Israel.
1971	Formation of the Union of Arab Emirates.
1973	Yom Kippur War (or October War), Israel against Syria and Egypt.
1975	Lebanese civil war begins.
1979	Iran expels the shah and declares itself an Islamic Republic; Egyptian president Anwar Sadat visits Israel; Egypt and Israel sign the Camp David Accords; Saddam Hussein seizes control of Iraq; Soviet forces invade Afghanistan.
1980–1988	Iran-Iraq War.
1982	Israel invades Lebanon; Israel will occupy southern Lebanon until 2000.
1987	First Intifada ("resistance") declared by Palestinians against Israel.
1989	Soviet troops withdraw from Afghanistan.
1990–1991	Iraq invades Kuwait, sparking the first Gulf War.
1992–2002	Algerian Civil War.
1994	Palestinian Authority established.
2000	Second Intifada (or Al-Aqsa Intifada) against Israel.
2001	Al Qaeda terrorists attack New York City; United States and allies invade Afghanistan.
2003	United States and allies invade Iraq.
2005	Elections held in US-occupied Iraq.
2006	Israeli-Hezbollah conflict in southern Syria; Saddam Hussein executed; Hamas wins Palestinian national elections and takes control of Gaza; Israel establishes economic blockade of Gaza.
2009	Large-scale protests in Iran over alleged election fraud.
2010	Israeli commandos attack a flotilla of "freedom activists" seeking to break the Gaza embargo; nine protesters are killed and ten commandos wounded.
2010–2013	The "Arab Spring" popular revolutions in Tunisia, Egypt, Libya, Yemen, Syria, and elsewhere in the region.

Table 11.1 Population and Rate of Growth

Country	Population	RNI%	Country	Population	RNI%
Algeria	38,087,812	1.90	Oman	3,154,134	2.06
Bahrain	1,281,332	2.57	Qatar	2,042,444	4.19
Egypt	85,294,388	1.88	Saudi Arabia	26,939,583	1.51
Iran	79,853,900	1.22	Sudan	34,847,910	1.83
Iraq	31,858,481	2.29	Syria	22,457,336	0.15
Israel	7,707,042	1.50	Tunisia	10,835,873	0.95
Jordan	6,482,081	0.14	Turkey	80,694,485	1.16
Kuwait	2,695,316	1.79	United Arab Emirates	5,473,972	2.87
Lebanon	4,131,583	−0.04	West Bank	2,676,740	2.03
Libya	6,002,347	4.85	West Sahara	538,811	2.96
Mauritania	3,437,610	2.29	Yemen	25,408,288	2.50
Morocco	32,649,130	1.04			

This chart shows the population and rate of population growth (natural increase) among the countries of the Middle East.

SOURCE: *CIA World Factbook 2013*

Table 11.2 Gross Domestic Product and GDP Real Growth

Country	GDPpc	GDP real growth	Country	GDPpc	GDP real growth
Algeria	$7,600	2.5%	Oman	$29,600	5%
Bahrain	$29,200	2.9%	Qatar	$103,900	6.6%
Egypt	$6,700	2.2%	Saudi Arabia	$31,800	6.8%
Iran	$13,300	−1.9%	Sudan	$2,600	−4.4%
Iraq	$7,200	8.4%	Syria	$5,100	NA
Israel	$32,800	3.1%	Tunisia	$9,900	3.6%
Jordan	$6,100	2.8%	Turkey	$15,200	2.6%
Kuwait	$40,500	5.1%	United Arab Emirates	$49,800	3.9%
Lebanon	$16,000	1.5%	West Bank	$2,900	6%
Libya	$12,300	104.5%	West Sahara	$2,500	N/A
Mauritania	$2,200	6.4%	Yemen	$2,300	0.1%
Morocco	$5,400	3.0%			

This chart shows the GDP per capita and rate of GDPpc real growth among the countries of the Middle East.
SOURCE: *CIA World Factbook 2013*

Table 11.3 Literacy Rates and Life Expectancy

Country	Literacy	LE-years	Country	Literacy	LE-years
Algeria	73%	76	Oman	87%	75
Bahrain	95%	78	Qatar	96%	78
Egypt	74%	73	Saudi Arabia	87%	75
Iran	85%	71	Sudan	72%	63
Iraq	79%	71	Syria	84%	75
Israel	97%	81	Tunisia	79%	75
Jordan	96%	80	Turkey	94%	73
Kuwait	94%	77	United Arab Emirates	90%	77
Lebanon	90%	75	West Bank	95%	75
Libya	90%	76	West Sahara	N/A	62
Mauritania	59%	62	Yemen	65%	64
Morocco	67%	76			

This chart shows the Literacy Rates and Life Expectancy (In Years) among the countries of the Middle East.

SOURCE: *CIA World Factbook 2013*

Table 11.4 Major Religions

Country	Religion
Algeria	Sunni Muslim (state religion) 99%, Christian and Jewish 1%
Bahrain	Muslim (Shia and Sunni) 81.2%, Christian 9%, other 9.8%
Egypt	Muslim (mostly Sunni) 90%, Coptic 9%, other Christian 1%
Iran	Muslim (official) 98% (Shia 89%, Sunni 9%), other 2%
Iraq	Muslim 97% (Shia 60%–65%, Sunni 32%–37%), Christian or other 3%
Israel	Jewish 75.6%, Muslim 16.9%, Christian 2%, Druze 1.7%, other 3.8%
Jordan	Sunni Muslim 92%, Christian 6%
Kuwait	Muslim 85% (Sunni 70%, Shi'a 30%), other 15%
Lebanon	Muslim 60%, Christian 39%, other 1.3%
Libya	Sunni Muslim (official) 97%, other 3%
Mauritania	Muslim 100%
Morocco	Muslim 99%, Christian 1%, Jewish about 6,000
Oman	Ibadhi Muslim 75%, other 25%
Qatar	Muslim 77.5%, Christian 8.5%, other 14%
Saudi Arabia	Muslim 100%
Sudan	Sunni Muslim, small Christian minority
Syria	Sunni Muslim 74%, other Muslim 16%, Christian 10%, Jewish
Tunisia	Muslim 98%, Christian 1%, Jewish and other 1%
Turkey	Muslim 99.8% (mostly Sunni), other 0.2%
United Arab Emirates	Muslim 96%, other (includes Christian, Hindu) 4%
West Bank	Muslim 75% (predominantly Sunni), Jewish 17%, Christian and other 8%
West Sahara	Muslim
Yemen	Muslim (Shia and Sunni)

This chart shows the percentage of major religions among the countries of the Middle East.

SOURCE: *CIA World Factbook 2013*

Table 11.5 Type of Government

Country	Government	Country	Government
Algeria	Republic	Oman	Monarchy
Bahrain	Constitutional monarchy	Qatar	Emirate
Egypt	Republic	Saudi Arabia	Monarchy
Iran	Theocratic republic	Sudan	Shared-power government
Iraq	Parliamentary democracy	Syria	Republic, authoritarian rule
Israel	Parliamentary democracy	Tunisia	Republic
Jordan	Constitutional monarchy	Turkey	Republican parliamentary democracy
Kuwait	Constitutional emirate	United Arab Emirates	Federation
Lebanon	Republic	West Bank	NA
Libya	Transitional government	West Sahara	Contested territory
Mauritania	Military junta	Yemen	Republic
Morocco	Constitutional monarchy		

This chart shows the form of government among the countries of the Middle East.

SOURCE: *CIA World Factbook 2013*

Sudan: Federal republic ruled by the National Congress Party the (NCP), which came to power by military coup in 1989; the CPA-mandated Government of National Unity, which since 2005 provided a percentage of leadership posts to the south Sudan-based Sudan People's Liberation Movement (SPLM), was disbanded following the secession of South Sudan.

Notes

1. Timur himself was not a Mongol. He was actually from a town near Samarkand, in modern-day Uzbekistan. He is usually called a Mongol because he arose as a general within the Mongol empire and because he claimed descent from Genghis Khan.

2. Although Israeli histories generally present this as established historical fact, some European and US historians have questioned the lack of primary evidence that Arab broadcasts ordering Palestinians to flee occurred (Hitchens 2001).

3. An exception is Iran, which has a thriving Jewish community of some 35,000 people who have their own synagogues, kosher butchers, and Hebrew schools (Theodoulou 1998).

4. This is not the only possible definition. The term was originally coined by British statesmen and journalists to describe terrorizing methods used by governments on their own people, a form of terrorism this definition excludes. See Global Issue #1 "International Terrorism" elsewhere in this text for a more thorough discussion of definitions.

References

Ahmed, Eqbal. 2001. *Terrorism: Theirs and Ours*. New York: Seven Stories Press.

Avineri, Shlomo. 1981. *The Making of Modern Zionism*. New York: Basic Books.

Beeman, William O. 2004. *The "Great Satan" vs. the "Mad Mullahs": How the United States and Iran Demonize Each Other*. Westport, CT: Praeger.

Bergesen, Albert J., and Yi Han. 2005. "New Directions for Terrorism Research." *International Journal of Comparative Sociology* 46, no. 1–2: 133–151.

Brower, Daniel R. 2002. *The World in the Twentieth Century: From Empires to Nation States*. 5th ed. Upper Saddle River, NJ: Prentice Hall.

Dawisha, Adeed. 2005. *Arab Nationalism in the Twentieth Century: From Triumph to Despair*. Princeton, NJ: Princeton University Press.

Eickelman, Dale F., and Armando Salvatore. 2006. "Public Islam and the Common Good." *Etnográfica* 10, no. 1: 97–105, www.scielo.oces.mctes.pt.

Goldschmidt, Arthur, Jr., and Lawrence Davidson. 2005. *A Concise History of the Middle East*. Boulder, CO: Westview Press.

Hitchens, Christopher. 2001. "Broadcasts." In *Blaming the Victims: Spurious Scholarship and the Palestinian Question*, edited by Edward Said and Christopher Hitchens, 73–84. London: Verso.

ILO (International Labour Organization). 2002. "Men and Women in the Informal Economy: A Statistical Picture." Geneva: International Labour Office, www.ilo.org/public/english/employment/gems/download/women.pdf.

Luciani, Giacomo. 1987. "Allocation vs. Production States: A Theoretical Framework." In *The Rentier State*, edited by Hazem Beblawi and Giacomo Luciani. New York: Croom Helm.

Moubayed, Sami. 2005. "The Waxing of the Shi'ite Crescent." asiatimes.com, April 20, www.atimes.com/atimes/Middle_East/GD20Ak01.html.

Nasr, Vali. 2006. "When the Shiites Rise." *Foreign Affairs*, July/August 2006. http://www.foreignaffairs.org/20060701faessay85405/vali-nasr/when-the -shiites-rise.html.

Oxfam. 2010. *The Gaza Strip: A Humanitarian Explosion*. Oxford, UK: Oxfam International.

Palfreyman, David, and Muhamed al-Khalil. 2003. "'A Funky Language for Teenzz to Use': Representing Gulf Arabic in Instant Messaging." *Journal of Computer Mediated Communication* 9, no. 1 (November): jcmc.indiana.edu/vol9 /issue1/palfreyman.html.

Said, Edward W. 1979. *Orientalism*. New York: Vintage.

———. 1997. *Covering Islam: How the Media and the Experts Determine How We See the Rest of the World*. Rev. ed. New York: Vintage.

Sarageldin, Ismail, et al. 1983. *Manpower and International Labor Migration in the Middle East and North Africa*. New York: Oxford University Press.

Scheffler, Thomas. 2003. "'Fertile Crescent,' 'Orient,' 'Middle East': The Changing Mental Maps of Southwest Asia." *European Review of History* 10, no. 2: 253–72.

Sheffer, G., ed. 1986. *Modern Diasporas in International Politics*. London: Croom Helm.

Sherman, A. J. 2001. *Mandate Days: British Lives in Palestine 1918–1948*. Baltimore: Johns Hopkins University Press.

Shlaim, Avi. 2001. *The Iron Wall: Israel and the Arab World*. New York: Norton.

Theodoulou, Michael. 1998. "Jews in Iran Describe a Life of Freedom Despite Anti-Israel Actions by Tehran." *Christian Science Monitor*, February 3. www.csmonitor.com/durable/1998/02/03/intl/intl.3.html.

Vest, Jason. 2001. "Oy McVey: From the Irv Rubin Bust to the Stern Gang: The Rich History of Jewish Terrorism." *Village Voice*, December 19–21. www .villagevoice.com/news/0151,vest,30862,1.html.

Yaar, Ephraim, and Tamar S. Hermann. 2007. *The Peace Index, November 2007.* The Peace Index Project. http://www.peaceindex.org/files/peaceindex2007 _9_3.pdf.

Further Reading

Ahmed, Eqbal. 2001. *Terrorism: Theirs and Ours.* New York: Seven Stories Press.
Bowen, Donna Lee, and Evelyn A. Early, eds. 2002. *Everyday Life in the Muslim Middle East.* 2nd ed. Bloomington: Indiana University Press.
Fernea, Elizabeth. 2002. "The Veiled Revolution." In *Everyday Life in the Muslim Middle East,* edited by Donna Lee Bowen and Evelyn A. Early. Bloomington: Indiana University Press.
Ghannam, Farha. 2002. *Remaking the Modern: Space, Relocation, and the Politics of Identity in a Global Cairo.* Berkeley: University of California Press.
Halliday, Fred. 2002. *Two Hours that Shook the World: September 11, 2001: Causes and Consequences.* London: Saqi Books.
Mamdani, Mahmood. 2004. *Good Muslim, Bad Muslim.* New York: Pantheon.
Mernissi, Fatima. 2001. *Scheherazade Goes West: Different Harems, Different Customs.* New York: Washington Square Press.
Peterson, Mark Allen. 2011. *Connected in Cairo: Growing Up Cosmopolitan in the Modern Middle East.* Bloomington, IN: Indiana University Press.
Telhami, Shibley. 2002. *The Stakes: America and the Middle East.* Boulder, CO: Westview Press.

Journals

International Journal of Middle East Studies
Middle East Journal
Middle East Studies
Middle East Report
Oxford Journal of Middle East Studies

Films

Battle of Algiers (1966). Gillo Pontecorvo, director.
Control Room (2004). Jehane Noujame, director.
The English Sheik and the Yemeni Gentleman (2000). Bader Ben Hirsi, director.

The Message: The Story of Islam (1976). Moustapha Akkad, director.
Paradise Now (2005). Hany Abu-Assad, director.

Websites

Al-Jazeera (English edition). english.aljazeera.net
Arab Media & Society. www.arabmediasociety.com
Global Connections: The Middle East. www.pbs.org/wgbh/globalconnections/
    mideast/index.html
Middle East Research and Information Project. merip.org/index.html
Tabsir: Insight on Islam and the Middle East. www.tabsir.net

12

Latin America

Latin America is poised to take its place among the most prosperous regions of the world. Great progress has been made in recent years toward freer markets and the formation of governments that are truly working in the interests of their peoples. Brazil is one of the so called BRICs (Brazil, Russia, India, and China), countries that are bidding to take a place at the table of the most developed nations.

The key concept to keep in mind when thinking about Latin America is diversity. As in all regions discussed in this book, Latin America has as much to differentiate it as to bind it. The region's physical geography does indeed include the hot climates of the tropical lowlands. Yet cool temperatures are more common for the millions who live in the Andean highlands and distant latitudes in Argentina and Chile. Many a tourist has traveled to the capital of Ecuador (Spanish for "equator") expecting the hot climates that a latitude of zero degrees would seem to promise. Yet Quito stands at over nine thousand feet in the Andes, nearly twice the altitude of Denver, and is therefore never hot.

Latin Americans speak Spanish, Portuguese, Dutch, English, and French, as well as dozens of indigenous languages such as Quechua and Yucatec. Latin America's political history ranges from long-standing democracies to brutal military dictatorships. So although this chapter treats Latin America as a unit and discusses trends within the region, it is crucial to remember that all generalizations are tempered by the region's many dissimilarities.

WHAT IS LATIN AMERICA?

How did Latin America get its name? The answer points to a theme that dominates the explanation of many of Latin America's social, political, and economic traits today: colonialism. Europe's colonization of the Western Hemisphere left its imprint on all aspects of society. The French coined the term *Latin America* in the mid-nineteenth century as a means to assert French influence in a region where the Spanish and Portuguese were so dominant (Skidmore and Smith 2005, 3). France shared with Spain and Portugal a language and culture that drew on Latin. The effort largely failed, because France never gained a strong foothold outside of the Caribbean. Yet the *Latin America* appellation remained. It is important to note that the name by which an entire region is known, both by outsiders and by its own inhabitants, derives from Western European linguistic and colonial power games.

The region we call Latin America begins in the deserts of the US-Mexico border and stretches south to the tumultuous waters of Tierra del Fuego in Argentina and Chile. Longitudinally, it begins as far west as Mexico's Baja Peninsula and stretches to the eastern coast of Brazil. It encompasses the high peaks of the **Andes**, the lush lowlands of the Amazon basin, and the microhabitats of endangered species in the Caribbean.

There is a rough consensus that Latin America has three distinct geographical territories: South America, Central America, and the islands of the Caribbean Sea. Geographically and historically, the Caribbean differs in significant ways from the mainland. There are, nonetheless, enough similarities, not the least of which is simply that the mainland and the Caribbean share roughly the same location on the earth's surface, to discuss them together.

South America is for many the most recognizable piece of territory in Latin America. A huge landmass that emerges from a tiny land bridge known as Panama, the South American continent is clearly distinguishable from the other parts of the Western Hemisphere. Social scientists divide South America into four major regions. The **Southern Cone** refers to the states that form the conical southern part of the continent: Chile, Argentina, Paraguay, and Uruguay. The Andean nations are Peru, Ecuador, Colombia, and Venezuela. Brazil stands alone, distinguished by its Portuguese colonial history and its massive territory. The final group consists of the small states of Guyana, Suriname, and French Guiana in the

377

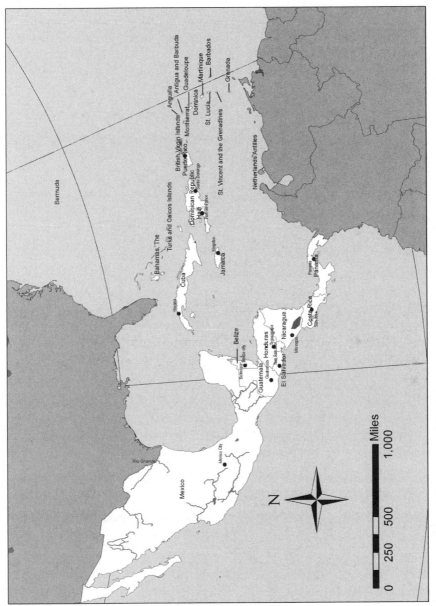

MAP 12.1 Central America and Caribbean.

MAP 12.2 South America.

northwest corner of the continent. South America's political history helps us think about it as a unit. Spain and Portugal overwhelmed all other colonizers' efforts in South America, and Spanish and Portuguese remain the dominant languages on the continent. Only three small states in northeast South America escaped Spanish-Portuguese control, though they did not escape the domination of other European powers: Guyana (British), Suriname (Dutch), and French Guiana (French).

South American physical geography encompasses the extremes of the frigid temperatures of the Andean peaks to the sweltering temperatures of the rain forest lowlands. The Amazon River is the world's largest by volume, and it accounts for one-fifth of the world's freshwater that flows into oceans. South America is also home to the world's driest desert, the Atacama in Chile. A traveler to Ecuador could in one week experience the thin air and sparse vegetation of the highlands, the lush greenery in the lowland and coastal areas, and the exquisite and unique biodiversity of the Galapagos Islands.

Although it is physically much smaller than South America, Central America shares the same kind of geographic diversity: mountains, highlands, fertile lowlands, and widespread coastal regions teeming with agricultural activity. Central America is slightly less understood than South America. Central America ranges from Guatemala in the north to the Panama-Colombia border in the south and comprises the Central American states of Guatemala, El Salvador, Nicaragua, Honduras, and Costa Rica, in addition to Belize and Panama.

Mexico is a partner of the **North American Free Trade Agreement (NAFTA),** but in terms of history, geography, and culture it is more akin to Latin America than to its English-speaking power to the north. Spain colonized Mexico and left its linguistic, political, and to a certain extent, economic and social legacy.

What are the differences between Central and South America, and why do we maintain a distinction that a physical map suggests is an artificial one? The answer lies largely in the history of the different states. After most of Central and South America gained independence from Spain in the early nineteenth century, the region was organized in large political units such as Gran Colombia (modern-day Colombia, Ecuador, and Venezuela). Today's Central America is the modern manifestation of the post-independence entity known as the United Provinces of Central

America. Mexico has been its own political entity since the end of the colonial era.

And what of Panama and Belize? A glance at a map suggests that Panama geographically belongs in Central America because it so clearly covers that thin strip of land that unites the two continents. Belize, tucked under the Yucatan peninsula, seemingly could go to either Mexico or Central America. Again, history is the answer. Until 1903, Panama was a northwestern province of Colombia. The United States engineered Panamanian independence from Colombia in order to ensure that the United States could build and control a canal on the isthmus. Panama was a US protectorate until 1924 and did not win sovereignty over the canal until December 31, 1999. Finally, Belize differs from the rest of Central America in that its colonial power was the United Kingdom, not Spain. In distinct contrast to its neighbors, British Honduras did not gain independence until 1964, a full century and a half century after the Spanish colonies. Its language is English, and its official name became Belize in 1973.

Social scientists generally divide the Caribbean into two subunits: the Greater and Lesser Antilles. The former include Cuba, Jamaica, Puerto Rico, and Hispaniola (home to the Dominican Republic and Haiti). These islands are much larger than the Lesser Antilles, which include islands such as Barbuda, Grenada, Trinidad, the Caymans, Dominica, and St. Lucia. In terms of history and culture, the Caribbean encompasses as much diversity within its relatively small population as all the mainland countries combined. Spain, France, and Britain were the main colonizers here, Spain mainly in the Greater Antilles, and France and Britain generally in the Lesser Antilles. Jamaica was a British holding, and Haiti a French colony. From a physical standpoint, the Caribbean is much more diverse than most tourist posters suggest. Indeed, the magnificent beaches that attract visitors from around the world typify much of the region's landscape, but the Caribbean islands are in fact mountains under the sea. The islands are the mountaintops, and therefore they contain steep slopes and cooler temperatures outside of the coastal regions. This concentrated ecological diversity makes the Caribbean one of the world's most important sites for species protection, as many organisms are adapted only to this unique environment.

We think of these three regions together as Latin America because they share important traits that transcend their many differences: their location in the Western Hemisphere, their colonial history, and their modern economies, which are characterized by an enormous gap in the distribution of wealth between the small group of haves and the large group of have-nots.

A Shared History

Latin American studies define the entire region's history by the voyage of Christopher Columbus (*Cristóbal Colón* in Spanish). The region's history, culture, and art are always described as either pre- or post-Columbian. The 1992 quincentennial celebration of Columbus's voyage changed many attitudes among those in the United States who grew up learning that "Columbus discovered America." Students today are more likely to learn about the encounter of Europeans and American indigenous peoples, as opposed to one's discovery of the other. Columbus and his conquistador successors are known as much for their launching the age of European imperialism in Latin America as for their prowess as explorers.

Although anthropologists and archeologists find pre-Columbian Latin America among the most fascinating places to study human history, the typical Westerner knows little of the indigenous peoples who thrived in the region before 1492. We think of these cultures largely through stories and artifacts. The Incas left the glorious mountain city of Machu Picchu, a monument to their master engineering skills. Their legacy is that of a thriving empire that enslaved other cultures and constructed vast and intricate road and irrigation systems. Among the Aztecs, the story is much the same. Magnificent pyramids, the human sacrifices sometimes practiced there, and the great city of Tenochtitlan upon which Mexico City is built are the few reminders of a long-defeated empire. It is important to remember that while Inca and Maya ruins remain fascinating tourist attractions today, indigenous populations have not disappeared. Descendants of the Incas, Aztecs, Mayas, Caribs, and others remain in the region, in many cases speaking their native language and practicing indigenous customs. As in the United States and elsewhere throughout the colonized world, native peoples in Latin America find themselves at the bottom of the social and economic ladder.

When the Iberian powers of Spain and Portugal looked west for colonial expansion, they were equipped in a way that the indigenous Americans could not match. They had superior technology (including weaponry), greater resources for establishing and maintaining control of settlements, and a sense of mission to dominate the "Indians," who are

FIGURE 12.1 Machu Picchu, Peru. Before the Europeans came in the early sixteenth century, Latin America had many sophisticated civilizations. PHOTO: Alicia Gomez.

to this day known as such because Columbus mistakenly thought that he had found India, when in fact he had landed in the modern-day Bahamas. That sense of mission was both political and religious. The so-called New World gave the Iberians a vast colonial opportunity they were sure to exploit. If the Europeans had any concern over the moral validity of their enterprise, their mission to convert any heathens they "discovered" satisfied their conscience. This combination of mission, technological superiority, and abundance of resources resulted in the Iberians conquering the mighty American empires in only a few years.

Colonialism in Latin America lasted over 300 years. Between the fifteenth and eighteenth centuries, the Europeans established political, social, geographical, and economic systems that remain remarkably intact today. Modern Latin American nations' borders largely mirror the vice-royalties demarcated by the Spanish and Portuguese. The mix of racial groups—African, indigenous, European, and a mix of all of these—paint a picture of colonial Latin America. African populations are found largely on the coastal areas and in the Caribbean, where they were transported as slaves to do plantation work. Indigenous peoples are more common in the interiors and highlands where their ancestors flourished. Those of European descent are found throughout the region, reflecting the widespread reach the colonial enterprise achieved. Furthermore, modern Latin America's social structure parallels that of the colonial era. Those with European ancestry and skin color disproportionately dominate the institutions and benefits of wealth and power.

By the eighteenth century, Spanish and Portuguese power in Europe was waning. European competitors took advantage of their weakness to wrest territory from the American colonies, claiming, for example, Haiti for the French, Curacao for the Dutch, and Jamaica for the British. Simultaneously, the tension in the colonies between the European-born *peninsulares*, who were loyal to the Crown, and the American-born *criollos* grew so that by the dawn of the nineteenth century, Spain and Portugal found that they could little afford to keep control of their American colonial empire. The colonies' independence movements were an elite enterprise that cared nothing for the rights of the indigenous people or slaves living under colonial rule. Instead, the *criollos* increasingly chafed under the Crown's government and sought independence in order to gain control of Latin America for themselves. In this sense, Latin American independence was much like North American independence; the *criollos* wanted political freedom from Europe while maintaining domination over indigenous peoples and African slaves at home.

Whereas representatives of the Iberian Crowns had arrived in the Americas in the late-fifteenth century at a great strategic advantage, by the early-nineteenth century the royals faced a trio of obstacles to their continued colonial rule in the Americas: (1) their own waning power in Europe; (2) incursions from other colonial powers, especially the United Kingdom, on their American holdings; and (3) revolts by colonist elites. Thus, Latin America, except for much of the Caribbean, has been independent since the early nineteenth century. This distinguishes Latin America from other former colonies in Africa, Asia, and the Middle East, most of which did not gain independence from their colonial powers until well into the twentieth century.

During the first 150 years of independence, these features of social and political life cemented themselves in Latin America: (1) caudillismo,

(2) unequal land distribution, (3) a racist social hierarchy, and (4) a neo-colonial trading structure. The dominant political model was caudillismo. During both the colonial and independence periods, the nominal heads of government (monarch, viceroy, president, governor) rarely had effective power outside the major cities. Latin America's vast and difficult terrain made central control nearly impossible. The *caudillo* filled the political void. *Caudillo* is a Spanish word for "leader" or "political chief." The Latin American caudillo was typically a wealthy landowner with dominion over dozens or hundreds of workers tilling vast plots of land. His power as a landowner gave him local political power. Most caudillos were the un-elected, de facto local sheriffs and judges, administering their own law with the help of private militias. The caudillo tradition laid the foundation for modern Latin American dictators such as Nicaragua's infamous An-astasio Somoza and super powerful drug lords such as Colombia's Pablo Escobar.

The caudillo's power emerged from his wealth and armed prepared-ness, which are now firmly rooted in Latin America's patriarchal tradition. Peasants who revolted rarely succeeded against a caudillo's army, just as peasants who revolted against corrupt presidents rarely won more than a jail cell (or worse). Latin American political culture has made significant strides toward democracy since the 1980s, especially at the national level. Yet the caudillo tradition remains in some pockets of the region where na-tional governments are weak. Furthermore, modern-day private militias, whether they are leftist guerrilla groups or right-wing paramilitaries, find their origins in the caudillo private armies. In Colombia, such groups re-main extraordinarily powerful and hold effective, and often brutal, control of large swaths of land.

A second feature of independent Latin America concerns the concen-tration of land holdings in the hands of a very few caudillos and the state. Early in the nineteenth century, newly "independent" political leaders seized peasant and church landholdings and sold them cheaply to criollos sympathetic to the government. These enormous plantations became not only a center of power and wealth for the caudillos, but established the landholding and agricultural patterns that persist to this day. Plantation owners controlled the most important source of wealth in Latin America: land. Furthermore, they became the bosses of the peasants who had typi-cally farmed the land communally before it was expropriated. Those same peasants then became debt peons, unable to search for independent work because of their inability to pay off their debts to the plantation company store (Keen and Haynes 2000, 217–218).

The plantations are crucial to understanding the distribution of wealth in the primary export economy that has dominated Latin America since independence. Landowners controlled all the profits and decisions over wages, healthcare, and education on their farms. They frequently left hundreds of thousands of acres fallow. As the peasant population grew throughout the nineteenth and twentieth centuries, peasant workers argued for greater access to land for themselves and their families. Political leaders were typically either the plantation owners or indebted to them for political support. Politicians therefore had little incentive to break up the landholdings to allow peasants to farm or break out of the system that kept them as poor laborers.

The nineteenth-century plantations transformed into twentieth-century corporate farms which were often controlled by foreign interests. The best known of these is the United Fruit Company (UFC), a US-based corporation that grew to be the largest landholding "family" in Guatemala by the 1950s. UFC's control of the Guatemalan economy, its treatment of peasant workers, and its refusal to allow unemployed peasants to farm its uncultivated holdings led to a national revolt in 1954. The company abandoned the UFC label and is today known by the popular Chiquita brand, headquartered in Cincinnati, Ohio.

A third feature of modern Latin America is its racial hierarchy. The social ladder is rooted in Latin America's history of European racism, the devastation of the indigenous peoples, and the importation of African slaves. Indigenous and African populations occupy the lowest branches in the social tree. They are the most likely to live in poverty, have poor educational opportunities, work menial jobs, and suffer from poor healthcare. Few indigenous or black people hold political office, though it is important to note that grassroots indigenous movements have gained considerable recognition in recent years in countries where they have significant populations. In Ecuador, for example, the indigenous political movement known as CONAIE has succeeded in shutting down the government, closing off access to major cities, suing global oil companies for environmental damage, and electing members to the Ecuadoran Congress. An indigenous leader, Evo Morales, was elected president of Bolivia in early 2006 and has placed indigenous interests high on the national agenda. This progress is notable but does not erase the trend of indigenous poverty and discrimination in Latin America. Native Americans' progress in political halls also outstrips their advances in industry and commerce.

Blacks also suffer many of the same difficulties as the indigenous peoples. In some parts of the coastal mainland and in most of the Caribbean, people of African descent are the majority of the population. In these areas, they have managed to share wealth and power with the whites. This does not change the fact that the whitest people are still those with the most power and wealth in Latin America. Colombia and Ecuador illustrate this point. Both have significant European, indigenous, mestizo (indigenous-European mix), and African populations. Yet a survey of political leaders at the national and regional level, as well as of landholders and major business figures, reveals that they are overwhelmingly of European ancestry. Brazil has the largest African-descendent population in mainland Latin America. The 2010 census revealed that a plurality of the population self-identify as black or mulatto (mix of white and black), yet the Brazilian legislature, courts, and state governments remain overwhelmingly dominated by Brazilians of European ancestry (BIGS 2011).

Finally, Latin America's international trading patterns in modern times exhibit a classic export-import strategy for economic growth (Skidmore and Smith 2006). Following the model established during colonial times, Latin American countries after independence continued to sell primary products to Europe and North America while importing finished goods from those same areas. Exports included copper from Chile, bananas from Central America, coffee from Colombia and Brazil, bauxite from Jamaica, industrial minerals from Bolivia, beef and wheat from Argentina, sugar from the Caribbean, and rubber from Brazil. In return for such raw materials, the developed world has sent products such as appliances, finished textiles, and automobiles. For decades, this export-import model fueled Latin American growth, including that of a small middle class. But this economic strategy carries important risks and consequences, including dependence on trade partners, vulnerability to price fluctuations, and a failure to deliver development to the majority of the working class. Even today, most of Latin America's exports are primary products, although finished products requiring low-skill labor are increasing.

This review of historical themes and their modern-day consequences reveals that many of Latin America's social problems are rooted in European imperialism and colonialism and the concentration of wealth that those systems produced. Over a third of the region still lives in poverty.

(CFR). Poverty, racism, and violence are harsh realities in Latin American life. They help to explain twentieth-century Latin America's history of rebellion and armed struggle. Numerous, mostly mainland, Latin American countries have seen revolutionary guerrilla groups rise up against the economic and political elites. In most cases, such as in Chile, Guatemala, and El Salvador, these rebellions were quashed by the national militaries with significant aid from the United States. In others, such as Cuba and Nicaragua, revolutionary forces succeeded at ousting corrupt dictators and assuming governmental power. In the main, revolutionary Latin America has seen little success. Cuba's experiment with communist dictatorship has maintained control at home, but ultimately it has not acted as a model for regional neighbors. Colombia's formidable revolutionary forces have never threatened a true government takeover. Furthermore, they have recently become corrupted by drug trafficking. Despite these setbacks for truly revolutionary governments in Latin America, recent political events show a marked turn to the left.

Latin American Economic and Political Development

Our discussion now turns to two themes that define much of Latin American history and modern society: sluggish economic development and the challenge of democratic rule. In addition to their importance to understanding the region, these themes reflect the same issues that international studies scholars focus on in other less-developed regions of the world.

Latin America joined the free-market global trading order much earlier than most other less-developed regions. While most of Africa, Asia, and the Middle East remained colonies with economies directly tied to their European "masters," Latin Americans traded from a purportedly independent position, owing to their early status as sovereign states. Yet throughout the nineteenth century and well into the twentieth, Latin America remained poor and underdeveloped when compared with Europe and North America. A small and wealthy elite controlled land, resources, and wealth, just as it had during the colonial era. Latin America thus poses a fascinating question to students of international studies: Why does its poverty persist when it achieved independence shortly after the United States did and when the region is well endowed with resources?

This question, and policies aimed at enhancing development in the region, became a focus for Latin American leaders in the second half of the twentieth century. In essence, their answer was that even though Latin American countries were independent politically, they had never wrested their economic choices from colonial structures. Post–World War II Latin American development strategy has its genesis in a United Nations body known as the Economic Commission for Latin America (ECLA). The ECLA's policy recommendations, developed in the late 1940s and early 1950s, were adopted by most Latin American states over the following thirty years. At the heart of ECLA's policy proposals is **dependency theory**. Dependency theorists argue that the global marketplace is an unfair trading ground for most former colonies. They disagree with liberal economic theory, which holds that all economies benefit if they specialize national production in comparative advantage goods for export, and import all their other needs from abroad.

ECLA economists argued that there were three primary faults in the liberal, free-trade, economic model. First, the modern global economy was simply not an even playing field among equal trading partners. Instead, it was a neocolonial world in which former colonies participated in a trading structure that had been imposed by the colonial powers for their own benefit, not that of the colony. Second, the liberal model was one of "dependent development" for developing countries. The destination of Latin American exports, and the source of the region's imports, was not truly a global market but instead almost exclusively the United States. After independence, Latin America shifted its trade away from Europe and toward its more natural trading partner to the north. This made the region vulnerable to US economic health, a truth that had been demonstrated tragically during the Great Depression of the 1930s. Demand and prices of Latin American exports to the United States fell, causing an economic crisis in Latin America (Skidmore and Smith 2006). Third, primary products of the type in which Latin America specialized were at a structural disadvantage to finished products produced in the wealthy countries. Compared to their finished counterparts, agricultural and mining goods suffer relatively low prices, experience greater price fluctuation, and are easier to substitute (e.g., synthetic rubber substitutes for natural rubber, tea substitutes for coffee). This put the primary producer at a permanent disadvantage.

The ECLA argued that Latin America could not hope to develop if it remained in this so-called free-market system. It called for an entirely new strategy to allow the region to break out of the cycle of importing expensive goods while exporting cheap ones. The new prescription was **import substitution industrialization,** or ISI. ISI was fundamentally a nationalist strategy in that it prioritized national development goals over participation in a global economy. The nationalist sentiment surrounding this economic development scheme was crucial in justifying it to the local population and to the world.

The industrialization component of ISI called for Latin America to minimize its status as an agricultural and extractive economy, and to develop strategies like those of the industrialized United States and Europe. The region's new commitment to industrial development meant significant adjustments in state planning and behavior. It required government spending and borrowing from international lenders to finance infrastructural enhancement, technological investment, and construction. Latin American leaders established state-owned industries in key sectors from automobiles to appliances to steel. Workers moved from the rural areas to the cities for new jobs in manufacturing.

The import-substitution half of ISI was equally as important as the industrial development itself. Import substitution meant that the driving force behind industrialization was to eliminate Latin America's dependence on imported finished goods. Instead, Latin Americans would use goods for their own domestic consumption, thereby substituting locally produced commodities for the more expensive foreign ones. How did policymakers achieve this? First, they placed stiff tariffs and other trade barriers on foreign imports. They taxed foreign direct investment and required foreign investors to reinvest their profits in Latin America, rather than repatriate them to Europe or the United States. They promoted national industries to consumers and worked to develop a nationalist pride around domestic industries. It was not unlike what we see in the United States today in "Buy American" advertising campaigns and private industry's efforts to impose tariffs on imported steel, automobiles, and other areas in which US companies have stiff foreign competition.

Was the ISI experiment a success? The initial results were impressive. Between 1950 and the mid-1970s, manufacturing growth averaged 6.9 percent in Latin America, much higher than in the United States or Europe at the time. Manufacturing's share of total economic output reached nearly 25 percent by 1975, an enormous change for what had been an exclusively agrarian and extractive economy (Weaver 2000, 129). Furthermore, these years saw the increasing growth of the middle class. Industrial labor unions formed and gained political power. Education rates grew as more peasant families came to the cities.

In the long term, however, ISI was largely a failure. Its structural defects became the undoing of the very gains it had achieved. First, Latin American industry never became fully independent of imports. Tools, machinery, technology, and other inputs on which manufacturing relied continued to be produced abroad. The balance of payments problem that dependency theory predicted under the neocolonial trading structure reemerged in industrial technology. Second, domestic consumption was insufficient for sustained economic growth. Because Latin American industry was not oriented toward export, it could not benefit from purchases abroad. At home, many Latin Americans remained too poor to buy all the goods that domestic industry wanted to sell. Complicating this problem was the fact that domestic goods never gained the reputation for quality that foreign imports enjoyed. Middle- and upper-class consumers frequently preferred to pay more for everything from imported cigarettes to tractors. Third, because domestic industries were so protected, and often state-owned, they had little incentive to produce cost-efficient and high-quality goods. They had few if any international competitors and often enjoyed monopoly status at home. Finally, much of ISI's growth was achieved on borrowed money, especially in the late 1960s and early 1970s. Heavy borrowing from eager lenders in the West saw Latin American debts explode in the latter ISI years. At the time, the borrowing seemed a wise choice given that it would pay off in expansive economic growth in the future. As Latin American leaders soon discovered, the lavish trips to European and US banks soon caused a regional nightmare.

The Debt Crisis and the Lost Decade

The 1980s saw Latin America's debt burden reach into the hundreds of billions of dollars, owed primarily to commercial banks in the United States and Europe but also to intergovernmental development bodies such as the World Bank and the Inter-American Development Bank. For example, between 1970 and 1990, Argentina's external debt rose from $5 billion to $62 billion, Mexico's from $6 billion to $104 billion, and Brazil's from $5 billion to a staggering $120 billion (Weaver 2000, 174). By 1990, the region's total debt exceeded $400 billion and became the source of enormous suffering in Latin America (Sherman 2000, 162).

How did this happen? Latin American leaders borrowed heavily for the industrial and infrastructural projects associated with ISI. Buoyed by overly rosy growth forecasts, the region's economic ministers signed the loan notes to finance current development. All too often, government corruption played a role as well. Many Latin American countries in the 1970s were ruled by military dictatorships whose leaders were sometimes corrupt and rarely accountable to the electorate. Because repayment of the loans was left to future governments, there was little incentive to borrow responsibly. The oil price shock of the early 1970s also contributed. Most of Latin America had to import petroleum, the price of which multiplied during this decade. Many of the capital-intensive development projects similarly relied on imported materials, which had become more expensive than ever.

As important as the behavior of the borrowers, however, was the behavior of the lenders. As early as the 1950s, cash-flush US banks looked to Latin America to lend to from their coffers. In the 1970s, their incentive to lend globally increased for two reasons. First, inflation in the United States (and the Carter administration's decision to print more dollars) made the US dollar less valuable on the world market. In order to service their deposits, banks had to lend more than before (Sherman 2000, 155). Second, Western banks suddenly found themselves the recipients of large **petrodollar** deposits. When oil prices soared, in part because of the global oil embargo, oil exporters in the Middle East and elsewhere became fabulously rich almost overnight. They placed their money in the most reputable banks, especially in the United States and Europe. Once again, the banks lent those funds to Third World countries in order to pay the interest on the petrodollar deposits.

Events in the 1970s set the stage for the economic crises of the 1980s, the so-called lost decade in Latin America. Everything bad that could happen to the region's economies did. Inflation soared, the debt figures burgeoned, interest rates increased, economic growth rates went into negative figures, state industries collapsed, international competition for exports increased, poverty rates grew, and states' ability to pay for public services, employment, and projects dwindled. Under such dramatic economic contraction, Latin America's ISI strategy fell apart completely. Domestic markets could not sustain industry, and the enormous debt made it impossible to finance improvements that would make Latin American manufacturing globally competitive. In South America during this decade, only Colombia and Chile escaped negative growth, and their growth rates averaged less than a paltry 2 percent, nowhere near what was needed to pay the public debt, much less finance development at home (Weaver 2000, 175).

Structural Adjustment and Neoliberalism

The lost decade removed Latin America's ability to create its own economic strategy. The nationalism that had fueled ISI gave way to the reality of total economic vulnerability. The poor and indebted region's economic policy was now in the hands of the international financial institutions (IFIs), including the **International Monetary Fund (IMF)**, the **World Bank**, the Inter-American Development Bank, major government lenders such as the United States, and private banks. The IFIs prescribed **structural adjustment programs (SAPs)**, which are part of a broader approach to economic policy known as **neoliberalism**. The imposition of SAPs typically occurred in the following manner (using Ecuador as an illustrative example). As the date to make a payment on the external debt neared, Ecuadoran policymakers alerted the IFIs that they had insufficient funds to cover the scheduled sum. Representatives from the IMF visited Ecuador to arrange an agreement by which the IMF would make a fresh loan to cover the immediate payment in exchange for Ecuador's promise to implement a SAP. Once Ecuador agreed to the terms, the IMF not only made the "cover" loan but also gave Ecuador the IMF seal of approval, making Ecuador eligible for the much larger loans available from Western private banks. There are two important points to note here. First, this was a robbing-Peter-to-pay-Paul scheme: the IFIs did not reduce Latin America's debt. Second, this arrangement leaves very little decision making in the hands of democratically elected officials in Latin America, and instead puts it in the hands of international bankers who may not have the best interests of Latin American populations in mind.

What did the SAPs entail? In short, they were a shock therapy designed to balance national budgets and reinsert Latin America into global commerce. These may be laudable goals, but the SAPs imposed enormous hardship on the Latin American people. The poor suffered the most. SAPs varied slightly depending on national circumstances, but all of them essentially included the following policy prescriptions: devalue national currency to promote exports, slash government spending, eliminate trade barriers, privatize national industries, and create a climate favorable to foreign investment. The effects were as predictable as they were harsh: triple-digit inflation, escalated poverty rates, an even wider rich-poor gap, massive unemployment as public employees were laid off, crumbling infrastructure, cuts in subsidies (on food, transportation, and education), and the inability of local industry to compete with foreign firms.

One might ask why such hardship would be imposed or accepted by entities such as the World Bank and IMF, whose missions are economic development in the Third World. Some critics argue that the IMF, the World Bank, and other IFIs care little about Latin Americans' suffering and simply want to impose policies that make Latin America a safe and profitable place for multinational corporations. Certainly, Latin America today is a happier place for foreign investors than it was in the 1970s. Even absent such nefarious intentions, however, the IFIs argue that the shock therapy was a necessary but short-term alternative to Latin America's disastrous experiment with nationalistic economic policy in the form of ISI. They further argue that the SAPs, while incurring short-term inflation, reduced inflation rates over the long term.

SAPs are the first stage in the larger economic development model of neoliberalism. Neoliberalism is the modern version of the traditional liberal economic model that values free global trade, comparative advantage, low government spending and interference in the economy, and private enterprise. It is capitalism on a global scale. Nearly all Latin American leaders today have embraced neoliberalism, though doing so often puts them at odds with their own constituencies. The Latin American economic development experience illustrates how much this still-poor region remains a weak player in the global economy. The triumph of neoliberalism and its hardship on the poorest Latin Americans reveals the extent to which Latin America has to play by the rules set by the wealthiest nations.

That said, Latin Americans resist the wholesale neo-liberal model when they can. A recent example is the failure of the Free Trade Area of the Americas (FTAA) to gain support outside of the United States and a few Latin American countries. The FTAA envisions a Western Hemisphere free-trade area (minus Cuba), an enormous expansion of the North American Free Trade Agreement (NAFTA) that would compete with the EU. Presidents Bill Clinton and George W. Bush strongly advocated for the FTAA, yet it has failed to emerge. In November 2005, Bush traveled to

FIGURE 12.2 The poverty in some Latin American countries is crushing. Here girls walk through a village built on a garbage dump near Rio de Janeiro. PHOTO: Jennifer Setters.

South America in hopes of achieving an agreement on the FTAA. He came home empty-handed. A combination of popular protests and Latin American leaders' unwillingness to sign the FTAA revealed the extent to which many Latin Americans are frustrated with the neoliberal model. Having accepted SAPs and neoliberalism for decades now, they reject the idea of deepening that model in a hemispheric free-trade agreement. Because President Barack Obama made a so-called "pivot" to East Asia to further US interests there, he did not press the issue of free trade in Latin America. The failure to create an FTAA is a blow to the US-led model of Latin American development, but in no way indicates that it has lost the battle against nationalist policy. In fact, the US Congress recently approved bilateral free-trade agreements with Colombia and Panama. The United States now has trade agreements with a third of the countries in the Western Hemisphere. Neoliberalism remains the dominant development paradigm in the region, and, indeed, the world (Regenstreif 2013).

China's recent interest in Latin America has enabled the region to chart a more independent course away from the United States and the EU, however. In the 1990s, China began to import raw materials from Latin America, especially energy products. From 2005 to 2012 China invested $43 billion in Latin America's energy industries, and $47 billion in other sectors. Brazil, Mexico, Argentina, Ecuador, and Venezuela have been particular targets of Chinese trade and investment. Still, the United States does more than $800 million in trade with Latin America annually, about three times of China's business there. China is even making inroads into Latin America's high-tech market, which is particularly concerning to the EU's high-quality goods. Germany's trade with Latin America, for example, grew by 16.3 percent from 2005 to 2009. Latin American expert Michael Shifter points out that Latin America now has more options: "The U.S. relationship comes with more complications. The Chinese one comes strictly on the economic question. They're very targeted, strategic in areas they want to support. They have a specific agenda. The U.S. agenda is more diffuse. Latin America welcomes both" (Regenstreif 2013; O'Donnell 2013).

The Challenge of Democracy

Just as Latin America is a laboratory for studying and testing development policy, it is a model for what can go wrong and right in the quest for democratic government. Modern Latin American history shows us stunning democratic successes and also horrific dictatorial abuses. The path to democracy has been full of obstacles and often circuitous, but the region has made impressive strides in recent years.

Recall that modern Latin America's beginnings were anything but democratic. The criollos who ousted the Europeans did so not out of a desire for a truly "people's republic," but rather to impose themselves as leaders of a wholly antidemocratic society. At the time of independence and for decades thereafter, legal slavery thrived and indigenous populations worked in indentured servitude. Enormous landholdings, and the profits that came from their abundance, lay firmly in the hands of Europeans. Courts, legislatures, and other public institutions were populated by and largely served the white elite.

Latin America, however, was not immune to the democratic wave that swept across the globe after World War II. Indeed, some Latin American states instigated that wave. Many Latin American constitutions are among the oldest democratic founding documents in the world. The Mexican revolution succeeded in ousting a dictator of thirty-five years in 1911. Colombia and Venezuela were among the twentieth century's most democratic countries, at least as measured by constitutionally sanctioned transfers of power. Most of the region's countries gave at least lip service to popular democracy in their constitutions, and experienced varying success with it from their founding through the post–World War II era.

The Cold War had a profound impact on US relations with Latin America. The United States supported a myriad of right-wing, anti-communist dictatorships in the name of preventing Soviet influence in the region. In 1954 the United States directly supported the overthrow of the democratically elected government of Jacobo Arbenz because he had expropriated property owned by the United Fruit Company. Arbenz later captured the essence of US interventionist policy throughout the Cold War: "They have used the pretext of anti-communism. The truth is very different. The truth is to be found in the financial interests of the fruit company and the other US monopolies which have invested great amounts of money in Latin America and fear that the example of Guatemala would be followed by other Latin countries" (Schlessinger and Kinzer 1999, 200).

Although Washington exaggerated the threat of communist takeovers in the Western Hemisphere, the revolution of Fidel Castro in Cuba in 1959 sent shock waves through US foreign-policy establishment. Cuba became a Soviet client, and in 1961, President John F. Kennedy launched a CIA-backed attack by Cuban exiles. The Bay of Pigs invasion was an utter failure, and the Cuba's communist regime has been in power ever since. The United States still has an embargo on Cuba.

The Cuban revolution inspired anti-American leftists throughout the region. Ernesto "Che" Guevara, a young Marxist from Argentina, was in Guatemala during the CIA-coup in 1954, and then joined Castro's revolution. In 1967, Che was executed in Bolivia for trying to foment revolution there, and his face became the symbol of the anti-American revolution throughout the region.

The United States was determined to prevent another Cuba. In 1973 the CIA was again involved in a coup against Chilean President Salvador Allende, and in the 1980s the United States backed the right-wing thugs of former Nicaraguan dictator Anastasio Somoza in their effort to topple the leftist government of President Daniel Ortega.

FIGURE **12.3** Typical street mural in Valparaiso, Chile, depicts Salvador Allende, the left-leaning Chilean leader who was overthrown in 1973 by Augusto Pinochet, with the help of the CIA. PHOTO: Alicia Gomez.

Chile is an ideal case to illustrate Latin America's fall of democracy and rise to military dictatorship. Chile's resources lay mostly in primary products—fish, copper, and agricultural products. Allende, a pro-ISI candidate, typical of that era in Latin America, won the presidential election in 1970 and began to implement policies antagonistic to international corporate interests. Allende nationalized Chile's copper industry, effectively ousting US-based Anaconda Copper from Chilean mines. Allende also looked to communist countries such as the Soviet Union and Cuba for trade and aid. In what became one of the most criticized elements of US

Cold War policy, the CIA undermined Allende politically and economically. In 1973 the United States supported a military coup that killed the president and established the military dictatorship of General Augusto Pinochet, a staunchly pro-US, pro–free market strongman.

Eighteen years of military dictatorship followed in Chile. Pinochet's regime was notable for successes and failures. The successes were largely economic and administrative: Chile became known as a favorable site for foreign investment, Western aid flowed in, and the government became known for running the trains on time, no small achievement in a poor region. The costs, however, were high. Political opponents, perceived or real, were exiled, removed from their jobs, tortured, imprisoned, and killed. Pinochet made no pretense at democratic institutions, so citizens learned to stay quiet and passive or risk imprisonment or worse. By the mid-1980s, however, international pressure against such obviously anti-democratic regimes such as Chile's was strong enough to force Pinochet to transition to a constitutionally elected government. In 1990, he left office after a national plebiscite rejected the continuation of his presidency.

Latin America gained notoriety as the model for military dictatorship in the 1960s and 1970s. Excepting Mexico, the "big" mainland states of Argentina, Chile, and Brazil all saw military takeovers and brutal political repression. Torture, intimidation, and murder of political opponents became commonplace while elections were either eliminated or open only to pro-military candidates. Military governments took control in nearly every mainland Latin American country during this period (most of the Caribbean was only just gaining independence), typically funded by national coffers and aid from the United States. The rationale behind the generals' takeover typically came in the form of "national security" and "economic development." In other words, civilian leaders could not be trusted to protect the homeland from (usually) communist interests or to guide it out of poverty. In the end, the outrage of the population combined with international pressure and in some cases a desire by the generals to return to civilian rule to bring an end to the Latin American military experiment by the mid-1980s. Since then, no military government has endured more than a few weeks in any mainland country in the region.

The United States came under considerable criticism in the 1970s for its indifference to the suffering of Latin American peoples living under these brutal military regimes. In the 1970s, President Jimmy Carter tried

to base US foreign relations on other governments' human-rights policies, but that effort was short-lived. The Ronald Reagan administration
responded to this criticism of US support of "our thugs" in the region by
positing the theory that it was easier to transition from an authoritarian,
anti-communist government to a liberal democracy and a free-market
economy than it was from a communist dictatorship. The rapid transition
of the East European communist states from communism to capitalism
and liberal democracy in the 1990s belied this theory.

The United States is still intolerant of leftist leaders, even if they are
elected democratically. In 2002 Washington tacitly approved of a coup attempt against the late Venezuelan President Hugo Chavez because of his
socialist domestic policies and anti-American foreign policy. In 2009 the
United States did not protest the illegal removal of democratically elected
Honduran President Manuel Zelaya.

Latin American Prospects

Latin American liberal democracy is still fragile, but it is more robust
than most other so-called less-developed regions such as the Middle East,
Africa, and Asia. Furthermore, the region is experiencing a fascinating
change brought on at the ballot box. After twenty years in which Latin
American leaders embraced (or had forced upon them) the neoliberal
economic model, and with few exceptions sought a strong relationship
with Washington, Latin American presidents increasingly favor a more
left-leaning stance that is leery of the United States and free-market economics. The electoral success of leftist candidates in Venezuela, Argentina, Bolivia, Chile, and Ecuador reveals a notable dissatisfaction among
the South American electorate with neoliberal economics. This is not to
say that there will be a socialist revolution sweeping across the region, although so-called Bolivarist and Chavist movements use Marxist rhetoric.
Instead, we will likely see isolated yet important acts of rebellion aimed at
wresting economic control away from private actors' hands and putting it
into those of the nation. Bolivian President Evo Morales's nationalization
of the natural gas industry in 2006 was perhaps the beginning of a series
of such acts, barely imaginable just fifteen years ago. What distinguishes
these acts of rebellion from those in the past is that they happen within a
constitutional framework.

Furthermore, politicians are being held responsible by an increasingly vocal citizenry. Grassroots protests around the world in the last decade, facilitated by the social media, have changed the way governments operate. For example, Brazil is putting on the 2014 World Cup Soccer Finals, and Rio de Janeiro is hosting the 2016 Olympic Games. The budget for the World Cup is $13.3 billion and $18 billion for the Olympics. This does not include billions more spent on infrastructure needs for these events. Concerned about security for the tourists coming to Rio, the government has begun to crack down on the vast, lawless *favelas* (squatter communities). In 2013, over a million Brazilians took to the streets to protest political corruption, the lack of government spending on basic infrastructure, and poor government services in general (Zimbalist 2013). This increasing engagement of Latin America's people in the conduct of their political and economic systems bodes well for a region that will see more peace and prosperity in this century than the last.

TIMELINE OF MODERN
LATIN AMERICAN HISTORY

Early 1800s	Most Latin American countries gain independence from Europe.
1823	United States declares Monroe Doctrine, warning Europe to stay out of Western Hemisphere.
1846–1848	Mexico loses American west in Mexican-American War.
1888	Brazil abolishes slavery.
1898	Spain ousted from Cuba and Puerto Rico in the Spanish-American War.
1902	Cuba gains independence. United States keeps base at Guantanamo Bay.
1903–1914	United States oversees Panamanian independence from Colombia and builds Panama Canal.
1910–1920	Mexican Revolution.
1938	Mexico nationalizes petroleum industry.
1948	Organization of American States (OAS) created.
1948	Costa Rica abolishes army.
1954	CIA-backed overthrow of Guatemalan President Jacobo Arbenz.
1959	Cuban revolution and beginning of the Castro era.

1962	Failed US-backed Bay of Pigs invasion of Cuba to overthrow communist regime.
1973	CIA-backed overthrow of Chilean President Salvador Allende.
1979	Nicaraguan leftist revolution.
1982	Great Britain defeats Argentina in Falklands War.
1983	US invasion of Grenada to oust Cubans.
1984	United States mines Nicaraguan harbors.
1989	US invasion of Panama to overthrow dictator Manuel Norieg.
1994	North American Free Trade Agreement (NAFTA) takes effect.
1999	Panama Canal Zone transferred to Panamanian sovereignty.
1999	Populist Hugo Chavez assumes presidency of Venezuela.
2001	First non-PRI candidate Vicente Fox wins Mexican election for president.
2006	Leftist indigenous candidate Evo Morales wins Bolivian presidency.
2008	Fidel Castro retires and hands power to his brother Raul Castro.
2011	Brazil becomes the world's sixth-largest economy.
2013	Hugo Chavez dies.

402

Table 12.1 Population and Rate of Growth

Country	Population	RNI%	Country	Population	RNI%
Caribbean:			**South America:**		
Anguilla	15,754	2.11	Argentina	42,610,981	0.98
Antigua and Barbuda	90,156	1.26	Bolivia	10,461,053	1.63
Aruba	109,153	1.39	Brazil	201,009,622	0.83
Bahamas	319,031	0.89	Chile	17,216,945	0.86
Barbados	288,725	0.34	Colombia	45,745,783	1.10
Cayman Islands	53,737	2.19	Ecuador	15,439,429	1.40
Cuba	11,061,886	−0.13	French Guiana	239,450	N/A
Dominica	73,286	0.22	Guyana	739,903	−0.21
Dominican Republic	10,219,630	1.28	Paraguay	6,623,252	1.23
Grenada	109,590	0.52	Peru	29,849,303	1.00
Guadeloupe	N/A	N/A	Suriname	566,846	1.15
Haiti	9,893,934	0.99	Uruguay	3,324,460	0.25
Jamaica	2,909,714	0.70	Venezuela	28,459,085	1.44
Martinique	N/A	N/A			
Montserrat	5,189	0.48	**Middle America:**		
Puerto Rico	3,674,209	−0.47	Belize	334,297	1.97
St. Barts	7,298	N/A	Costa Rica	4,695,942	1.27
St. Kitts and Nevis	51,134	0.80	El Salvador	6,108,590	0.29
St. Lucia	162,781	0.36	Guatemala	14,373,472	1.91
St. Martin	31,264	N/A	Honduras	8,448,465	1.79
St Vincent and the Grenadines	103,220	−0.30	Mexico	116,220,947	1.07
			Nicaragua	5,788,531	1.05
Trinidad and Tobago	1,225,225	−0.09	Panama	3,559,408	1.38
Turks and Caicos	47,754	2.87			
Virgin Islands (Brit.)	31,912	2.40			
Virgin Islands (US)	104,737	−0.53			

This chart shows the population and rate of population growth (natural increase) among the countries of Latin America.

SOURCE: *CIA World Factbook 2013*

Table 12.2 Gross Domestic Product and GDP Real Growth

Country	GDPpc	GDPpc growth	Country	GDPpc	GDPpc growth
Caribbean:			**South America:**		
Anguilla	$12,200	−8.50%	Argentina	$18,400	1.90%
Antigua and Barbuda	$18,300	1.60%	Bolivia	$5,200	5.20%
Aruba	$25,300	2.40%	Brazil	$12,100	0.90%
Bahamas	$31,900	2.50%	Chile	$18,700	5.50%
Barbados	$25,800	0.00%	Colombia	$11,000	4.00%
Cayman Islands	$43,800	1.10%	Ecuador	$10,200	5.00%
Cuba	$10,200	3.10%	French Guiana	$8,300	0.00%
Dominica	$14,400	0.40%	Guyana	$8,100	3.30%
Dominican Republic	$9,800	3.90%	Paraguay	$6,200	−1.20%
Grenada	$13,900	−0.80%	Peru	$10,900	6.30%
Guadeloupe	N/A	N/A	Suriname	$12,600	5.00%
Haiti	$1,300	2.80%	Uruguay	$16,200	3.80%
Jamaica	$9,300	0.10%	Venezuela	$13,800	5.50%
Martinique	N/A	N/A			
Montserrat	$8,500	3.50%	**Middle America:**		
Puerto Rico	$16,300	−0.58%	Belize	$8,900	5.30%
St. Barts	N/A	N/A	Costa Rica	$12,800	5.00%
St. Kitts and Nevis	$16,500	−0.90%	El Salvador	$7,600	1.60%
St. Lucia	$13,300	−0.40%	Guatemala	$5,300	3.00%
St. Martin/Sint Maarten	$19,300	N/A	Honduras	$4,700	3.30%
St Vincent and the Grenadines	$12,000	0.50%	Mexico	$15,600	3.90%
			Nicaragua	$4,500	5.20%
Trinidad and Tobago	$20,400	0.40%	Panama	$15,900	10.70%
Turks and Caicos	$29,100	11.20%			
Virgin Islands (Brit.)	$42,300	1.30%			
Virgin Islands (US)	$14,500	2.00%			

This chart shows the GDP per capita and rate of GDPpc real growth among the countries of Latin America.

SOURCE: *CIA World Factbook 2013*

Table 12.3 Literacy Rates and Life Expectancy

Country	Literacy	LE-years	Country	Literacy	LE-years
Caribbean:			**South America:**		
Anguilla	95.00%	81.09	Argentina	97.90%	77.32
Antigua and Barbuda	99.00%	75.91	Bolivia	91.20%	68.22
Aruba	96.80%	76.14	Brazil	90.40%	73.02
Bahamas	95.60%	71.69	Chile	98.60%	78.27
Barbados	99.70%	74.75	Colombia	93.60%	75.02
Cayman Islands	98.90%	80.91	Ecuador	92.00%	76.15
Cuba	99.80%	78.05	French Guiana	83.00%	77.27
Dominica	94.00%	76.39	Guyana	91.80%	67.68
Dominican Republic	90%	77.62	Paraguay	93.90%	76.60
Grenada	96.00%	73.55	Peru	89.60%	72.98
Guadeloupe	90.00%	N/A	Suriname	94.70%	71.41
Haiti	48.70%	62.85	Uruguay	98.10%	76.61
Jamaica	87.00%	73.53	Venezuela	96.00%	74.23
Martinique	N/A	N/A			
Montserrat	97.00%	73.65	**Middle America:**		
Puerto Rico	90.30%	79.07	Belize	76.90%	68.40
St. Barts	N/A	N/A	Costa Rica	96.30%	78.06
St. Kitts and Nevis	97.80%	75.07	El Salvador	84.50%	73.93
St. Lucia	90.10%	77.22	Guatemala	75.90%	71.46
St. Martin/Sint Maarten	N/A	N/A	Honduras	85.00%	70.81
St Vincent and the Grenadines	96.00%	74.62	Mexico	93.50%	72.00
			Nicaragua	78.00%	72.45
Trinidad and Tobago	98.80%	71.96	Panama	94.10%	78.13
Turks and Caicos	98.00%	79.40			
Virgin Islands (Brit.)	97.80%	78.12			
Virgin Islands (US)	90–95%	79.61			

This chart shows the Literacy Rates and Life Expectancy (In Years) among the countries of Latin America.
Source: CIA World Factbook 2013

Table 12.4 Major Religions

Country	Religion
Caribbean:	
Anguilla	Protestant 83.1%, Roman Catholic 5.7%
Antigua and Barbuda	Protestant 76.4%, Roman Catholic 10.4%
Aruba	Roman Catholic 80.8%, Protestant 7.8%
Bahamas	Protestant 67.6%, Roman Catholic 13.5%
Barbados	Protestant 63.4%
Cayman Islands	Protestant 67.7%
Cuba	Before Castro: Roman Catholic 85%
Dominica	Roman Catholic 61.4%, Protestant 20.6%
Dominican Republic	Roman Catholic 95%
Grenada	Roman Catholic 53%, Anglican 13.8%, other Protestant 33.2%
Guadeloupe	Roman Catholic
Haiti	Roman Catholic 80%, Protestant 16%, Voodoo
Jamaica	Protestant 62.5%
Martinique	Roman Catholic
Montserrat	Protestant, Roman Catholic
Puerto Rico	Roman Catholic 85%
St. Barts	Roman Catholic, Protestant, Jehovah's Witnesses
St. Kitts and Nevis	Anglican, Protestant, Roman Catholic
St. Lucia	Roman Catholic 67.5%, Protestant 18.2%
St. Martin	Roman Catholic, Jehovah's Witness, Protestant, Hindu
St Vincent and the Grenadines	Protestant 75%
Trinidad and Tobago	Roman Catholic 26%, Protestant 32%, Hindu 18%, Muslim 5%
Turks and Caicos	Protestant 72.8%
Virgin Islands (Brit.)	Protestant 84%
Virgin Islands (U.S.)	Protestant 59%, Roman Catholic 34%

continues

Table 12.4 Major Religions *continued*

Country	Religion
South America:	
Argentina	Roman Catholic 92%
Bolivia	Roman Catholic 95%
Brazil	Roman Catholic 73.6%, Protestant 15.4%
Chile	Roman Catholic 70%, Evangelical 15.1%
Colombia	Roman Catholic 90%
Ecuador	Roman Catholic 95%
French Guiana	N/A
Guyana	Protestant 30.5%, Hindu 28.4%
Paraguay	Roman Catholic 89.6%
Peru	Roman Catholic 81.3%
Suriname	Hindu 27.4%, Protestant 25.2%
Uruguay	Roman Catholic 47.1%, non-Catholic Christians 11.1%, nondenominational 23.2%
Venezuela	Roman Catholic 96%
Middle America:	
Belize	Roman Catholic 39.3%
Costa Rica	Roman Catholic 76.3%
El Salvador	Roman Catholic 57.1%, Protestant 21.2%
Guatemala	Roman Catholic, indigenous Mayan beliefs
Honduras	Roman Catholic 97%
Mexico	Roman Catholic 82.7%
Nicaragua	Roman Catholic 58.5%, Protestant 23.2%
Panama	Roman Catholic 85%, Protestant 15%

This chart shows the percentage of major religions among the countries of Latin America.

SOURCE: *CIA World Factbook 2013*

Table 12.5 Type of Government

Country	Government	Country	Government
Caribbean:		**South America:**	
Anguilla	British territory	Argentina	Republic
Antigua and Barbuda	Constitutional monarchy, parliamentary system of government	Bolivia	Republic
		Brazil	Federal republic
		Chile	Republic
Aruba	Parliamentary democracy	Colombia	Republic
Bahamas	Constitutional parliamentary democracy	Ecuador	Republic
		French Guiana	French territory
Barbados	Parliamentary democracy	Guyana	Republic
Cayman Islands	Parliamentary democracy	Paraguay	Constitutional republic
Cuba	Communist state	Peru	Constitutional republic
Dominica	Parliamentary democracy	Suriname	Constitutional democracy
Dominican Republic	Democratic republic	Uruguay	Constitutional republic
Grenada	Parliamentary democracy	Venezuela	Federal republic
Guadeloupe	French territory		
Haiti	Republic	**Middle America:**	
Jamaica	Constitutional parliamentary democracy	Belize	Parliamentary democracy
Martinique	French territory	Costa Rica	Democratic republic
Montserrat	French territory	El Salvador	Republic
Puerto Rico	US Commonwealth	Guatemala	Constitutional democratic republic
St. Barts	French territory	Honduras	Constitutional democratic republic
St. Kitts and Nevis	Parliamentary democracy		
St. Lucia	Parliamentary democracy	Mexico	Federal republic
St. Martin/ Sint Maarten	Overseas collectivity of France	Nicaragua	Republic
St Vincent and the Grenadines	Parliamentary democracy	Panama	Constitutional democracy
Trinidad and Tobago	Parliamentary democracy		
Turks and Caicos	British territory		
Virgin Islands (Brit.)	British territory		
Virgin Islands (U.S.)	US territory		

This chart shows the form of government among the countries of Latin America.

Source: CIA World Factbook 2013

References

BIGS (Brazilian Institute of Geography and Statistics). 2011. http://www.ibge.gov
.br/english/.

(CFR) Council on Foreign Relations. "U.S.-Latin American Relations: A New
Direction for a New Reality." www.cfr.org.

Keen, Benjamin, and Keith Haynes. 2000. *A History of Latin America,* vol. 2. Boston: Houghton-Mifflin.

O'Donnell, Thomas W. 2013. "Competing with China in Latin America." *IP Journal,* August 19. German Council on Foreign Relations. https://ip-journal
.dgap.org.

Regenstreif, Gary. 2013. "The Looming U.S.–China Rivalry over Latin America."
June 12. http://blogs.reuters.com/great-debate.

Schlessinger, Stephen, and Stephen Kinzer. 1999. *Bitter Fruit: The Story of the
American Coup in Guatemala.* Cambridge: Harvard University Press.

Sherman, John W. 2000. *Latin America in Crisis.* Boulder, CO: Westview Press.

Skidmore, Thomas E., and Peter H. Smith. 2005. *Modern Latin America,* 6th ed.
New York: Oxford University Press.

Weaver, Frederick Stirton. 2000. *Latin America in the World Economy.* Boulder,
CO: Westview Press.

Zimbalist, Andrew. 2013. "Brazil's Long To-Do List." *America's Quarterly* (Summer).

Further Reading

Atkins, G. Pope. 1999. *Latin America and the Caribbean in the International System.*
Boulder, CO: Westview Press.

Guimarães, Roberto P. 2001. "The Environment, Population, and Urbanization."
In *Understanding Contemporary Latin America,* edited by Richard S. Hill-
man, 197–228. Boulder, CO: Lynne Rienner.

Gwynne, Robert N., and Cristóbal Kay, eds. 2004. *Latin America Transformed:
Globalization and Modernity.* London: Arnold.

Potter, Robert B., et al. 2004. *The Contemporary Caribbean.* New York: Prentice
Hall.

Skidmore, Thomas E., and Peter H. Smith. 2005. *Modern Latin America,* 6th ed.
New York: Oxford University Press.

Journals

Canadian Journal of Latin American and Caribbean Studies. http://uofcpress.com/
    canadian-journal-latin-american-and-caribbean-studies

Journal of Interamerican and World Affairs. onlinelibrary.wiley.com/journal/10
    .1111/(ISSN)1548–2456a/issues

Journal of Latin American Cultural Studies. www.tandfonline.com

Journal of Latin American Studies. journals.cambridge.org/action/displayJournal
    ?jid=LAS

Latin American Perspectives. www.lap.sagepub.com

North American Congress on Latin America. http://nacla.org/naclareport

Films

Central Station (Brazil, 1998)
El Norte (Guatemala, 1984)
Life and Debt (Jamaica, 2001)
Memories of Underdevelopment (Cuba, 1968)
The Two Escobars (Colombia, 2010)

Websites

Inter-American Development Bank. www.iadb.org

Latin American Network Information Center. lanic.utexas.edu/la/region/statistics

Latin American Studies Association. lasa.international.pitt.edu

University of Manchester Centre for Latin American Cultural Studies.
www.llc.manchester.ac.uk/Research/Centres/CentreforLatinAmericanCultural
    Studies

PART THREE
CONTEMPORARY GLOBAL ISSUES

13

Global Issue 1

International Terrorism

On November 26, 2008, members of the Pakistani-based militant organization Lashkar-i-Taiba entered the Indian city of Mumbai by sea and carried out a terrorist attack. Fanning through the city, ten heavily armed militants attacked luxury hotels and restaurants, a women's hospital, a Jewish community center, a train station, a movie theater, and a college building. One hundred sixty-six civilians and Indian security personnel were killed in the three-day rampage, which ended in the deaths of nine of the terrorists and the capture of the last one.

In spite of the Mumbai attacks, in his national address to the people of India the following year, Prime Minister Manmohan Singh said that the greatest single threat to India was not Islamic terrorists from abroad but the Naxalite terrorist threat within. The Naxalites are Marxist insurgents who, allied with local anti-globalization groups and indigenous-rights activists, operate in ten Indian states, particularly the so-called red corridor, an area of 92,000 square kilometers under Naxalite control.

The attention paid by Western media to the Mumbai attacks, and the paucity of international news about the Naxalites, points to the inherent bias in people's understanding of the threats of global terrorism. Americans have understandably tended to see terrorism everywhere through the lens of September 11. But understanding terrorism exclusively in these terms fails to take into account either the historical depth or geographical breadth of terrorism. Worse, it creates a tendency to conflate all terrorism into a single entity against which we can imagine ourselves at war. To call for a war on terror is to group together such diverse terrorists as al Qaeda, Chechens fighting for a separate state from Russia, the rival Palestinian groups Hamas and Fatah, the United Wa State Army in Burma, the Liberation Tigers of Tamil Eelam in Sri Lanka, Colombia's Fuerzas Armadas Revolucionarias de Colombia (FARC), Ejercito del Pueblo and drug cartel militias, Peru's Sendero Luminoso, the Irish Republican Army (IRA), the Basque Euskadi Ta Askatasuna (ETA) in Spain, the Israeli Irgun and Stern Gang, the Kurdistan Workers Party in Turkey, the Japanese AUM sect and Red Army, and the United States' Timothy McVeigh and the Unabomber. All these groups and individuals have used terrorism, but they believe in very different things and seek very different goals. A realistic assessment of terrorism requires consideration of historical and contemporary political and economic conditions in which terrorism operates.

Terrorism is a strategy by which subnational groups not recognized as legitimate by the states they oppose seek to resist those states by targeting nonstate actors, disrupting the flow of everyday life, and spreading generalized fear among the populations of those states.[1] Terrorism is primarily a communicative act, not a strategic one. It is a technique through which groups seek to force states to acknowledge them. In many cases, terrorists seek to provoke a military or political response as a form of recognition. Terrorism may also seek to demoralize the citizens of a state and so undermine support for the regimes they oppose. The technologies of globalization create greater opportunities for terrorists to expand those messages, for example by posting videos to websites. Terrorism on the scale of the September 11 attacks may also inflict real damage on economic infrastructures, at least in the short run.

A great deal of misunderstanding stems from rhetorical misuses of the term *terrorism* in political speech and news reporting. The activity of terrorism—the use of violence against noncombatants and civil institutions—is often confused with terrorists' motives. In part, this is because states generally do not like to describe their allies as terrorists. For example, the British praised and supported the Malayan People's Anti-Japanese Army during World War II even though it targeted civilian collaborators as much as Japanese occupiers. When these same groups turned on the British colonial administration of Malaya after the war, assassinating civil administrators and plantation owners, the British relabeled them terrorists (Bayly and Harper 2004). Sometimes it is difficult to tell whether an organization is terrorist or engaged in a legitimate fight for freedom. In Canada, two members of the same Pakistani political organization were given completely different judgments by the country's Immigration and

Refugee Board in 2007. One was declared a refugee and the other a terrorist (Humphreys 2007). "There is the famous statement: 'One man's terrorist is another man's freedom fighter.' But that is grossly misleading," said Martin Rudner, director of the Canadian Centre of Intelligence and Security Studies at Ottawa's Carleton University. "It assesses the validity of the cause when terrorism is an act. One can have a perfectly beautiful cause and yet if one commits terrorist acts, it is terrorism regardless" (Humphreys 2007).

Terrorism has a long history, but it is primarily associated with the rise of colonialism. Most European colonial powers were liberal democracies at home but imperialists in their colonies. Local insurgencies arose to combat them, often targeting civilians as part of their resistance. Early uses of terrorism in the Middle East—Jewish terrorists like Irgun and the Stern Gang against British power, and Arab and Jewish groups against one another—developed at this time (Vest 2001). The most global terrorist movement of the colonial era was that of the anarchists, a network of loosely affiliated European intellectuals and militants committed to a common utopian political vision—not unlike al Qaeda today (Bergesen and Han 2005). Between the 1870s and World War I, anarchist terrorists assassinated three kings, two presidents, and two prime ministers, and they bombed cafés, railway cars, and financial districts in North America and Europe.

In 2012, nearly 15,500 people were killed in more than 8,500 terrorist attacks spread across Africa, Asia, and the Middle East, with most of the violence committed in Muslim majority countries, and with primarily Muslim victims (National Consortium for the Study of Terrorism and Responses to Terrorism 2013). Latin America (especially Colombia, Chile, and Venezuela) and Asia (particularly Afghanistan, India, Bangladesh, Indonesia, and the Philippines) are also sites of large numbers of terrorist attacks. The shift of terrorism primarily to Middle Eastern countries has occurred in the last ten years, coinciding with the US invasions of Afghanistan and Iraq. Previously, Latin America and Africa were the centers of global terrorism. In 2001, for example, Colombia alone accounted for 191 terrorist incidents, more than all of Asia and the Middle East combined. Africa accounted for 48 incidents, while the Israel-Palestine conflict fell into the 8–10 range (US State Department 2002). Prior to 2002, terrorism had been on the decline; the number of terrorist incidents worldwide peaked in 1987 and had been declining. The total number of terrorist attacks in the first five years of the new millennium was less than half the total number of terrorist incidents between 1985 and 1990. Recent years are seeing unprecedented numbers of victims of terrorism. Prior to 2010, the highest number of casualties in one year from terrorist incidents was 5,379 in Africa in 1998. Because of the September 11 attacks, North America took second place, with 4,465 casualties in 2001 (US State Department 2004).

This rise in terrorism is linked to a number of factors. Wars, the collapse of the Soviet Union, and ongoing political and economic crises in Africa have created many new states that are seen as weak and unstable, and hence vulnerable. Weak states and wars means that more people have access to increasingly lethal weaponry. The global economic decline exacerbated already existing problems of poverty and high unemployment, particularly among young men who make up the primary demographic from which terrorists are recruited. Shrinking economic opportunities worldwide have also increased competition for scarce resources and have exacerbated sectarian tensions.

Finally, the use of rape, mass killing, drone strikes, assassinations, and similar tactics by military forces as tactics of war has led many people in the world to see these as forms of state terrorism that call for similar kinds of retaliation. Many experts emphasize that terrorism is closely related to activities by states: terrorists define themselves in opposition to states and exist in a dynamic relationship to oppression by those states (Lauderdale and Oliverio 2005). One of the earliest uses of the term *terrorists* is by British statesman Edmund Burke to describe the French revolutionary government and philosophers like Jean-Jacques Rousseau and Voltaire, whose ideas inspired the revolution. The contemporary use by states of retaliatory bombing, death squads, torture, and other such actions is sometimes referred to as **state terrorism**.

A classic example occurred in the 1970s when six Latin American governments led by Chile formed a military alliance called Operation Condor to carry out kidnappings, torture, and political assassinations against leftist opponents they deemed "terrorists." Operation Condor carried out activities not only in South America but also North America and Europe, initially with support and training from the United States (Dinges 2012). Although these states justify their actions as fighting fire with fire, many experts argue that being able to occupy a higher moral ground than their opponents is crucial for states seeking to defeat terrorism.

State terrorism should not be confused with **state-sponsored terrorism**, in which a state harbors, and sometimes supports, the terrorist enemies of another state. This concept is also highly controversial, since states rarely acknowledge that the paramilitaries and insurgents they support are terrorists. Afghanistan, Argentina, Belgium, Chile, Cuba, Iran, Iraq, Italy, Libya, Pakistan, the Palestinian Authority, South Africa, the Soviet Union, Spain, Syria, the United Kingdom, and the United States have all at various times been accused by other states of sponsoring terrorism. The United States has the distinction of being the only state to have been convicted for this offense by the World Court because of its support for the paramilitary Contras in Nicaragua in the 1980s (International Court of Justice 1986).

But state-sponsored terrorism may well be declining. Globalization has opened up unexpected new opportunities for terrorists. Global communication networks have made it easier for terrorist organizations to communicate directly with their publics, as when Iraqi insurgents have posted videos of beheadings on the Internet. In an era where a billion people every year are moving across national borders for tourism, work, or flight from disaster, the movements of a few handfuls of terrorists are relatively easy to mask.

Moreover, as the international community seeks to crack down on terrorists, organizations with very different ideologies and goals are increasingly sharing knowledge, technology, and other resources. In 2001, three members of the Provisional Irish Republican Army were arrested in Bogota, Colombia, after spending five weeks training FARC insurgents in advanced uses of explosives, particularly homemade mortars. In Southeast Asia, a network of explosive technology exchanges is emerging among terrorist organizations in the Philippines, Indonesia, Malaysia, Brunei, and the southern Malay provinces of Thailand. Resource sharing between Lebanon's Hezbollah and Palestine's Hamas is becoming commonplace even though Sunni Hamas ideologues officially consider Shiite Hezbollah to be heretics (Cragin et al. 2007).

Another key area of global interconnectedness in which international terrorism plays a significant role is drug trafficking. Traffickers and terrorists have similar logistic needs to covertly move goods, people, and money across national borders. Cooperation thus benefits both: drug traffickers benefit from terrorists' military skills, weapons supply, and access to clandestine organizations, while terrorists gain a source of revenue and expertise in transferring and laundering of money from illicit transactions. Both groups can call on networks of corrupt officials whose services provide such mutual benefits as greater access to fraudulent documents, including passports and customs papers. Terrorist organizations and drug traffickers take many forms, ranging from facilitation—protection, transportation, and taxation—to direct trafficking by the terrorist organization itself in order to finance its activities (Beers and Taylor 2002).

One of the consequences of September 11 and subsequent political terrorism by Islamic groups, such as the Madrid and London bombings, is that it has created a popular equation between Islam and terrorism in many parts of the world, especially North America and Europe. Previously, groups like the Palestinian Liberation Organization were no more referred to as Islamic terrorists than members of the Irish Republican Army were referred to as Christian terrorists. Since September 11 there has been a growing tendency in the West to see terrorism less in political and more in religious terms. This has been exacerbated by the murder of Dutch filmmaker Theo van Gogh by a Dutch Muslim man, and by the often violent protests around the world that took place in response to caricatures of Muhammad published in a Danish newspaper, neither of which were terrorist acts.

Terrorism, however, is not an inherently religious act, nor is Islam, or any other religion, especially prone to producing terrorists. Atheist, Buddhist, Christian, Hindu, Islamic, and Jewish terrorists are all part of the historical record. Until very recently, the majority of terrorists in the world have been some variety of Marxist, and even today Marxist groups are responsible for the majority of terrorist acts. More important, over-attention to the religion or ideology of terrorist organizations can blind us to the economic and political realities that motivate many terrorists. Contemporary terrorism seems to be directly related to changes in international and intercultural relations, especially the growing integration of markets, political structures, images, technologies, and environmental concerns around the world. Globalization, in the words of one terrorism scholar, exports dreams of freedom and affluence. The failure of these dreams, and their contrast with the grim realities of global disparity, can lead to "the migration of nightmares" (Nassar 2005).

Norwegian anthropologist Unni Wikan lived and worked in an Egyptian neighborhood next to the one where September 11 terrorist Mohammed Atta grew up. Although she does not think she ever met Atta, she understands his story through the lens of another young man's journey into **political Islam**. Sayyid, like Atta, was a smart boy who excelled in school, tested into college, received a teaching degree, and completed his mandatory military service. He then became an elementary school teacher. Sayyid's downfall, suggests Wikan, was his honesty. Unwilling to force his pupils to pay him for private lessons the way most of Egypt's poorly paid teachers do, he could not make enough money to get married. Many poor Egyptian teachers emigrate to Saudi Arabia to receive better wages. Sayyid refused to pay bribes to the officials in charge of this ex-change program and went abroad privately. As a result, when he returned two years later and married his sweetheart, he found himself blacklisted from teaching. He was forced to make a living peddling used clothing.

"The recruits to Islamic fundamentalist movements generally come from backgrounds like Sayyid's: they are educated, intelligent, disillu-sioned men of middle and lower middle class who have been denied their place in the sun" (Wikan 2002, 125). They are looking for a way out of the hopelessness of what they see as unjust, corrupt, and repressive societies—societies immune to democratic change because they know that their gov-ernments are backed by foreign powers like the United States. Many turn to forms of Islam that reassure them that their souls are better than those of the wicked who prosper in this world. Some come to believe in the possibility of a political solution that would bring about a just, free, and peaceful new world order guaranteed by God. A few are willing to sacrifice their lives, and take the lives of others, to make this vision a reality.

In fact, this absence of hope that life will get better seems to be a more common denominator for terrorist motives than religion. For example, while the Islamist terrorist organization Hamas emphasizes the religious fervor of the young suicide bombers it recruits, the secular Fatah group also fields suicide bombers whose motivations may not involve religious faith at all. In her conversations with Sikh militants in Asia, anthropol-ogist Cynthia Keppley Mahmood found that economic collapse and vio-lence by Indian national military forces created a climate in which many men and women saw militancy, including terrorism, as the only mean-ingful option open for them (Mahmood 1996). Similarly, investigations into the motivations of captured suicide bombers in Israel suggests that the effort to escape from a hopeless present by doing something decisive and dramatic is more significant than personal faith in either religion or political ideology (Moghadam 2003). There is a great danger, writes Mah-mood, "in insisting that physically exterminating terrorists is the way to eradicate terrorism. A lethal game of one-upmanship ensues, which feeds the appetite for power on both sides and injures many innocent bystanders in the process" (Mahmood 1996, 273). The most realistic way to end the threat of terrorism is to transform the socioeconomic conditions that give rise to it, as World War I and the postwar changes in the global political economy ended organized anarchist terrorism.

At the turn of the twenty-first century, as at the turn of the twentieth century, we find ourselves in an age of terrorism. Whether the sweeping changes posed by such trends as the rise of Asian economies, the continuing population explosion, increased mobility and communication around the globe, and economic shifts due to climate change will exacerbate the use of terrorism by nonstate actors unhappy with the changes in the world around them, or whether the success of alternative modes of civil resistance such as those used in the Arab Spring will mitigate it, remains to be seen.

Note

1. For other definitions, see Chomsky 2001, Enders and Sandler 2002, Ruby 2002, Stern 1999.

References

Bayly, Christopher Alan, and Timothy Norman Harper. 2004. *Forgotten Armies: The Fall of British Asia, 1941–1945*. Cambridge, MA: Belknap Press.

Beers, Rand, and Francis X. Taylor. 2002. "Narco-Terror: The Worldwide Connection Between Drugs and Terror." Testimony before the Senate Committee on the Judiciary Subcommittee on Technology, Terrorism and Government Information. Washington, DC. March 13. www.state.gov/p/inl/rls/rm/2002/8743.htm.

Bergesen, Albert J., and Yi Han. 2005. "New Directions for Terrorism Research." *International Journal of Comparative Sociology* 46, no. 1–2: 133–151.

Chomsky, Noam. 2001. "U.S.—A Leading Terrorist State." *Monthly Review* 53: 10–19.

Cragin, Kim, Peter Chalk, Sara A. Daly, and Brian A. Jackson. 2007. *Sharing the Dragon's Teeth: Terrorist Groups and Exchanges of New Technologies*. Santa Monica, CA: Rand Corporation.

Dinges, John. 2012. *The Condor Years: How Pinochet and His Allies Brought Terrorism to Three Continents*. New York: New Press.

Enders, Walter, and Todd Sandler. 2002. "Patterns of Transnational Terrorism, 1970–1999: Alternative Time-Series Estimates." *International Studies Quarterly* 46: 145 65.

Humphreys, Adrian. 2007. "One Official's 'Refugee' Is Another's 'Terrorist': IRB Criticized for Dissimilar Rulings on Similar Cases." *National Post.* January 17. www.canada.com/nationalpost/news/story.html?id=a64f73d2-f672–4bd0 -abb3–2584029db496.

International Court of Justice. 1986. "Summary of the Judgment of 27 June 1986 in the Case Concerning the Military and Paramilitary Activities in and against Nicaragua." www.icj-cij.org/docket/index.php?sum=367&code =nus&p1=3&p2=3&case=70&k=66&p3=5.

Lauderdale, Pat, and Annamarie Oliverio. 2005. "Critical Perspectives on Terror." *International Journal of Comparative Sociology* 46, no. 1–2: 3–10.

Mahmood, Cynthia Keppley. 1996. *Fighting for Faith and Nation: Dialogues with Sikh Militants.* Philadelphia: University of Pennsylvania Press.

Mamdani, Mahmood. 2004. *Good Muslim, Bad Muslim.* New York: Pantheon.

Moghadam, Assaf. 2003. "Palestinian Suicide Terrorism in the Second Intifada: Motivations and Organizational Aspects." *Studies in Conflict and Terrorism* 26, no. 1: 65–92.

Nassar, Jamal. 2005. *Globalization and Terrorism: The Migration of Dreams and Realities.* Lanham, MD: Rowman and Littlefield.

National Consortium for the Study of Terrorism and Responses to Terrorism. 2013. Global Terrorism Database. http://www.start.umd.edu/gtd/.

Ruby, Charles L. 2002. "The Definitions of Terrorism" *Analysis of Social Issues and Public Policy* 2, no. 1: 9–14.

Stern, Jessica. 1999. *The Ultimate Terrorists.* Cambridge, MA: Harvard University Press.

United States State Department. 2002. *Patterns of Global Terrorism 2001.* www.state .gov/s/ct/rls/crt/2001.

———. 2004. *Patterns of Global Terrorism 2003, Appendix G.* www.state.gov/s/ct /rls/crt/2003/33777.htm.

Vest, Jason. 2001. "Oy McVey: From the Irv Rubin Bust to the Stern Gang: The Rich History of Jewish Terrorism." *Village Voice,* December 19–25. www .villagevoice.com/news/0151,vest,30862,1.html.

Wikan, Uni. 2002. "'My Son—A Terrorist?' (He was such a gentle boy)" *Anthropological Quarterly* 75(1): 117–128.

14

Global Issue 2
Turkey and the European Union

The Crossroad from Europe to Asia

Turkey began accession talks with the European Union (EU) in December 2005. Bulgaria and Romania joined the EU in 2007, and Croatia in 2013, but Turkey is still on the outside looking in. Turkey is the only predominantly Muslim country in the Middle East with a liberal democratic system. Turkey's geopolitical position as a bridge between Asia and Europe assures that Ankara will assume a greater role in resolving issues related to the Israeli-Palestinian conflict, the Syrian civil war, sectarian strife in Iraq, and Iran's nuclear program and support of Shiite groups such as Hezbollah. If Turkey is admitted into the EU, the ramifications for the organization's character, mission, and future expansion will be profound. Turkey's application illustrates the controversies over what it means to be European. Many Europeans do not want a poorer, Muslim-majority, Asian country in the union. Furthermore, the Syrian civil war on Turkey's southern border adds to the EU's fear of being dragged into Middle Eastern conflicts.

Turkey has historic, geographic, political, cultural, and ethnic arguments for inclusion in the EU. The Ottoman Turkish Empire was one of the world's great powers until the end of the seventeenth century. It stretched from the western reaches of North Africa to Mesopotamia (today Iraq) in the east. Speculation that Turkey could be a Muslim model of modern political and economic development in the Middle East could founder on the imperial history of this non-Arab country. In the fourteenth century, the Ottoman Empire expanded into the Balkans, and by the early sixteenth century was laying siege to Vienna, the capital of the Hapsburg Empire and the seat of the Holy Roman Empire. The Christian world lived in fear of the armies of an Islamic empire, but Vienna survived that assault.

In the sixteenth century, Europe began modernizing its political, economic, and social institutions while the Ottoman Empire stagnated. Europe's superior weaponry, armies, and political organization enabled it to roll back Ottoman rule in southeast Europe in the eighteenth and nineteenth centuries. Two years before the beginning of World War I in 1914, the Turks lost the First Balkan War to the Serbs, Bulgarians, and Greeks, who grabbed the last of the Ottoman Empire in Europe. Over five centuries of Ottoman rule in the Balkans was over, but strong Turkish influences remain in the region. Another historical argument for Ankara's inclusion in the EU is Turkey's role in the Cold War. President Harry S Truman's speech to Congress in March 1947 called for millions of dollars in aid for Turkey and Greece to combat communist influence and threats from the Soviet Union. The speech launched the Truman Doctrine, which enunciated US containment policies during the Cold War. Turkey became an important US military ally on the Soviet Union's strategic southern flank and was invited to join NATO in 1952. The United States deployed nuclear weapons in Turkey, and Soviet premier Nikita Khrushchev responded by putting nuclear missiles in Cuba in 1962, which brought the two Cold War rivals close to nuclear war. Although removing the missiles from Turkey was not officially part of the deal to resolve the Cuban Missile Crisis, it was an indirect quid pro quo for Khrushchev's withdrawal of the missiles from Cuba.

History also works against Turkey's application. The Turkish government refuses to acknowledge the genocide of Armenians during World War I. Armenians today demand an official apology from Turkey for the massacre of hundreds of thousands of their compatriots in 1915. They want Turks to admit that the killings constituted genocide, and were not, as most Turks claim, part of a battle against an enemy combatant in World War I. Key EU member Germany has long since made official apologies. In 2005 Germany acknowledged its own "inglorious role" for failing to try to stop their Ottoman allies from committing the extermination of Armenians, and it paid retribution for the Holocaust. Until Turkish officials and scholars deal honestly with this tragic episode in their history, skepticism about the viability of Turkey's EU application continues.

The geographic separation of Asia and Europe is the most artificial of all continental designations. Asia Minor is historically, geographically, and culturally closer to the heart of Europe than some regions on the far reaches of eastern Europe. The defeat of the Ottoman Turks in the First Balkan War left them with a small piece of territory on the European continent with part of Istanbul at its tip, some 850 miles from Rome. Constantinople (now Istanbul) was the center of the Catholic Church under Constantine in the fourth century, and was the capital of the Eastern Orthodox Church when the Christian church split seven hundred years later. Greek Orthodox communities flourished in Asia Minor until most were expelled after World War I.

The EU has already expanded its connections to Turkey's Black Sea neighbors to the north and to the South Caucasus to the east. The EU's European Neighborhood Policy in Ukraine, Moldova, Armenia, Azerbaijan, and Georgia calls for expanded economic and political partnerships. Turkey as an EU member would be a key player in drawing these former Soviet republics toward the West. Russian President Vladimir Putin has made it clear that he opposes these inroads into what he considers to be Moscow's sphere of interest. Turkey's economic connections and linguistic affinity with the former Soviet Republics in central Asia (Kazakhstan, Uzbekistan, Turkmenistan, and Kyrgyzstan) could be another source of friction with Russia.

Some Europeans argue that culturally Muslim Turks do not belong in the EU, but the five-century Ottoman presence in southeast Europe left behind a deep footprint. For example, the Ottomans introduced innovative architecture, silks, painted tile artwork, and ornamental rugs. Turkish rugs featured a complicated knot that originated in the Turkish town of Gordes, from which the term *Gordian knot*—which means an intractable problem—derives. Coffee came by way of the Ottomans, as did coffeehouse culture, where patrons could enjoy musicians, storytellers, and good conversation. The Ottoman authorities became so concerned with the frivolity of coffeehouses and the time people took away from their work that they were banned for a time in the seventeenth century (Duiker et al. 2001, 468–469).

The Ottomans allowed the Jewish and Christian communities confessional autonomy, although Albanians and some Bosnian Slavs converted to Islam. Almost 3 million Turks live in Germany today. Most of these families migrated to Germany as *Gastarbeiter* (guest workers) in the 1960s and early 1970s. Along with Muslims who have emigrated from the former European empires in North Africa and Asia, at least 18 million Muslims now live in Western Europe. France has approximately 5 million Muslim residents, most of them Algerian (Vaïsse 2010, 88). Europe is already a colorful and intricate ethnic, religious, and linguistic quilt, and Turks argue that ethnicity and religion should have no bearing on their entry into the EU, whose laws prohibit discrimination on the basis of national and religious identity.

Europe's worries about the economic effects of Turkey's admission to the EU could trump all other factors. Some EU observers caution against admitting another poor country. Turkey has over 80 million people, which would make it the second-largest country in the EU, the first being Germany. It has the second-largest army in NATO. However, in many ways, Turkey is still a developing country. Over 25 percent of Turkish workers are employed in the agricultural sector, and women make up less than a quarter of the workforce, while over 60 percent of adult women in the EU are employed (CIA World Factbook; Fowler 2011). Average per capita income in Turkey was $15,200 in 2012, compared with the EU average of over $35,000. Although inflation and unemployment have hovered around 9 percent, Turkey has reduced government control of some important industries, and its entry into the EU Customs Union in 1995 has facilitated a boom in trade with Europe (CIA World Factbook, EC 2011). New EU members Bulgaria and Romania are among the poorest countries in Europe. Their annual per capita income is $14,500 and $13,000 respectively, lower than Turkey's. Some EU countries such as Greece, Portugal, and Italy are facing serious budget deficits and the EU is reluctant to provide even more development funds for Turkey.

Europeans fear a massive influx of Turks seeking work and opening borders with a country so close to the volatile Middle East. Many opponents of Turkey's application point to the negligible influence the **North American Free Trade Agreement (NAFTA)** had on stemming the tide of Mexican immigration into the United States. A 2011 Pew Research Center poll found that 52 percent of Europeans want to keep Turkey out of the EU, with only 35 percent in favor of admission. Seventy-one percent of Germans opposed Turkey's membership, and 61 percent of French respondents. Turks are becoming disgruntled with the EU's feet of clay: only 52 percent of Turks say they want EU membership now, down from 68 percent in 2005 (PRC 2011). Furthermore, nearly half of the Turks in

Germany want to return to Turkey, even those who were born in Germany or have lived there for over thirty years. Forty-five percent felt they were not wanted in Germany (*Der Spiegel* 2009). Nonetheless, most Turkish parties have pressed to join the EU.

Turkey's democratic credentials predate those of many current EU members. After World War I, Mustafa Kemal Ataturk established the Republic of Turkey and instituted a strict separation of religion and state. The Turks have a parliamentary system with an independent judiciary, and Turkey has been a member of the Council of Europe since 1949 and NATO since 1952.

Turkey has made significant reforms to synchronize its political system with the rest of the EU countries. On the surface, Turkey's democracy is stable, but the role of the Turkish military in political affairs is a stumbling block to EU membership. Periodically, the Turkish military has intervened to maintain the secular character of the republic. Until recently, even the wearing of the **hijab** in the Turkish Parliament was prohibited, which led to the expulsion of a female representative in 2003. The current prime minister, Recep Tayyip Erdogan, is a member of the Justice and Development Party, which has Islamic leanings. Erdogan has won three straight elections (2003, 2007, 2011). During the 2007 elections, one Turkish woman opposed to Erdogan's party said that "we don't want to become another Iran, another Afghanistan," and another denounced the idea of adding three letters to the Turkish alphabet to accommodate Arabic sounds: "I've done pretty well with 29 [letters] so far" (Reuters 2007, 4; Tavernise 2007, 13). So far, though, the party has made few efforts to Islamicize Turkish law, although the ban on the *hijab* in state offices was lifted in 2013. In fact, Erdogan has encouraged Islamic groups in Egypt and Tunisia to create secular governments rather than overtly Islamic states.

Turkey has made great strides toward ending criticism of its human rights record and falling into line with the EU's criminal-justice system. Turkey eliminated the death penalty in 2004, and it has renounced the use of torture as an interrogation tactic. Ankara has curtailed its brutal treatment of Kurdish insurgents in the southeast of the country, although the EU has still been critical of Turkey for not doing more to find a political solution to the conflict.

Accession talks were held up in the summer of 2013 after the Erdogan government brutally suppressed a popular protest against a development project in Istanbul. The demonstrations that spread to over 70 Turkish cities were in part directed against Erdogan's increased authoritarianism. Four people were killed and over 8000 injured (*New York Times*, July 3, 2013).

Cyprus is another political obstacle to Turkey's entry into the EU. Relations between Turkey and Greece have been tense since the Greek-Turkish War in the early 1920s, in which tens of thousands on both sides were killed, and approximately 1.5 million Greeks were expelled from Turkey and about half a million Turks were forced out of Greece. In 1974, the Turkish army invaded Cyprus, claiming the northern half of the island. The Greeks maintained control of the southern half and, despite Greece's membership in NATO, Greece and Turkey have not been able to unify the island. The Greek part of Cyprus was admitted to the EU in 2004. Talks for a Cypriot federal state have taken place since then, but the strength of right-wing nationalists in parliamentary and presidential elections in northern Cyprus in recent years has put negotiations on hold. If Turkey does not bend on Cyprus, the EU, and especially Greece, will place roadblocks in the way of its membership. Accession talks resumed in the fall of 2013 after Turkey promised a resolution to the impasse over Cyprus.

Those who favor Turkish entry into the EU argue that Ankara will be a valuable bridge between the democratic West and the Islamic countries in North Africa and the Middle East, both politically and culturally. As the Arab uprisings began in the early 2010s, some pointed to Turkey as a model of modern political and economic development in the region. Arab, Iranian, and other peoples in the Islamic world might see otherwise. At first Prime Minister Erdogan supported Libyan dictator Muammar Qaddafi against the rebel opposition, but he quickly backed off that position when NATO went to the aid of the rebels. Turkey has been at odds with the United States, Saudi Arabia, and Qatar over which Syrian rebel groups to support. In 2013, Turkey also opposed the Egyptian military's overthrow of democratically elected Prime Minister Mohammed Morsi and the Muslim Brotherhood, a move tacitly accepted by the United States and its Arab allies (*New York Times*, October 3, 2013).

The Syrian civil war has put great strain on the Turkish government. As of late 2013 some two million Syrians had fled into neighboring countries, about 500,000 into Turkey. Complicating the situation is the presence of al Qaeda–affiliated rebel groups in northern Syria, and the fate of over 2 million Syrian Kurds who look for refuge from their brothers and sisters in Turkey—some 16 million strong. The Syrian conflict has emboldened European opponents of Turkey's EU membership who see Turkey as a conduit for poor immigrants and extremist Islamic influences. Turkey's application is certainly complicated by the borders it shares not only with Syria, but with Iraq, which has also experienced an uptick in sectarian violence in 2014. Another neighbor, Iran, is at odds with the West over its nuclear weapons program. Until these issues on Turkey's borders are resolved, Turkey's entry into the EU is unlikely.

References

Central Intelligence Agency. CIA World Factbook.

Der Spiegel. 2011. "Not at Home in Germany: Almost Half of Turkish Migrants Want to Leave." November 20. http://www.spiegel.de/international /germany/0,1518,662520,00.html.

Duiker, William J., et al. 2001. *World History.* Belmont, CA: Wadsworth.

EC (European Commission). 2011. "EU-Turkey Relations." http://ec.europa.eu /enlargement/candidate-countries/turkey/relation/index_en.htm.

Economist. 2007. "Economic Data." April 22.

Fowler, Suzanne. 2011. "Women Still an Untapped Labor Force in Turkey." *New York Times.* May 4.

PRC (Pew Research Center). 2011. "China Seen Overtaking US as Global Superpower." Pew Global Attitudes Project. Chapter 8. July 13. http://www.pew global.org/2011/07/13/chapter-8-rating-countries-and-institutions/.

Reuters. 2007. "Thousands Protest Religion in Turkish Government." *New York Times.* May 6.

Tavernise, Sabrina. 2007. "300,000 Protest Islamic Hue of Turkish System." *New York Times.* April 15.

Vaïsse, Justin. 2010. "Eurabian Follies." *Foreign Policy* (January/February): 86–88.

15

Global Issue 3

New Global Players in the Twenty-First Century

Who has power globally? For international studies we can approach this question in various ways. Are there historical trends of global power? What are the cultures of the global powers? Where are the global powers of the world? What are the political systems of the global powers? What are the economic systems of the global powers?

Much has changed in two thousand years; with the exception of China, the global powers are vastly different from those in 100 CE. A long history of the world's global powers of the past two millennia might begin with the Roman Empire (centered in Rome and spreading from England to Egypt), the Kushan Empire (including Afghanistan, Pakistan, and Northern India), the Eastern Han Dynasty (China but not Tibet), Axum in Ethiopia, and the Maya in modern Mexico and Guatemala in 100 CE. By 700 CE the Roman Empire had become the Byzantine Empire and shrank to modern Turkey and Greece, an Arab empire (the Umayyad Caliphate) covered the Middle East, India was split into a number of kingdoms, the Tang Dynasty ruled China, Axum and Ghana ruled territory in Africa, and Maya kingdoms ruled southern Mexico. By 1500 CE the Ming Dynasty ruled China; the Delhi Sultanate controlled northern India; the Mamluk Sultanate controlled Egypt and the Levant; the Ottoman Sultanate controlled Turkey and Greece; the kingdoms of France, Spain, Portugal, and Britain expanded to the Americas and met the Incas, Mayas, and Aztecs; and Mali and Songhay had kingdoms in West Africa (Barraclough and Overy 1999; O'Brien 1999).

Empires of the early twentieth century gave way to the republics and federations of today's world. After World War II, the allied powers formed the United Nations in 1945. The permanent members (P5) of the UN Security Council are the People's Republic of China, France, Russia, the United Kingdom, and the United States of America. The Security Council deliberates on international security issues. The five permanent members of the Security Council have veto power over any substantive measure. Ten other rotating members are elected from the general assembly. The other members vote but do not have veto power. As discussed in Chapter 9 on the Asia Pacific, countries such as India, Japan, Brazil, South Africa, and Germany have expressed their goal to join the Security Council permanently, but it is unlikely that the P5 will change the Security Council any time soon. All the P5 have nuclear weapons (as do India, Pakistan, and probably Israel), strengthening their power in global affairs (Bosco 2009; Hassler 2013).

Power is represented in several organizations beyond the UN Security Council. The Organisation for Economic Co-operation and Development (OECD) was established in 1961. The OECD began with 18 countries, mostly in Europe, including the United States and Canada. Today the group includes 34 countries in Europe, North and South America, and the Asia Pacific. While the members are mostly developed counties, Chile, Mexico, and Turkey have also joined. The focus of the OECD is on the improvement of economic and social well-being of countries around the world; the OECD has also worked with China, India, and Brazil, among others (OECD 2005, 2013).

A number of governmental forums have focused on economic matters, such as the Group of 7 (G7), the Group of 8 (G8), and the Group of 20 (G20). The first meetings were rather informal among finance ministers of western democracies in the early 1970s. By 1976 the forum was known as G7 and included France, West Germany, Italy, Japan, the United Kingdom, the United States, and Canada. After the end of the Cold War, the forum became the G8 with the inclusion of Russia. The EU also attended the meetings. There was no formal structure like the UN or World Bank. In 2000, the G8 invited South Africa to the summit. By 2003, regular attendees to the summits included Brazil, China, India, Mexico, and South Africa (G8+5) (Hajnal 2007).

Since 1999, finance ministers from 19 states and the EU have formed the G20. The first meeting was in response to financial crises of the late

1990s. Since 2008, the heads of the G20 states have met annually. The members include the United States, Canada, Mexico, Brazil, Argentina, South Africa, China, Japan, South Korea, India, Indonesia, Russia, the European Union, Germany, France, the United Kingdom, Italy, Turkey, Saudi Arabia, and Australia. The G20 is the broadest economic grouping of states and accounts for a substantial majority of the world's economy, 90 percent of Global GDP, 80 percent of international trade, and 66 percent of the world's population. While the states do not agree on everything, they have held talks on a wide variety of economic topics including food, energy, resources, population, and finances (G20 2013). Issues to consider about the G20 are the members of the G20, the exclusion of European countries such as Norway and Switzerland which are not in the EU, the exclusion of Taiwan (as in many international bodies), as well as Singapore, Malaysia, and other newly industrialized countries. Other issues have to deal with the deliberations of the G20 and the lack of a formal charter (Cooper and Thakur 2013; Bremmer 2012).

Table 15.1 shows the major characteristics of the G20 countries, including their membership in P5, G8, OECD, or their status as one of the BRICS (Brazil, Russia, India, China, South Africa). The Human Development Index (HDI) brings together statistics on life expectancy, mean years of schooling, expected years of schooling, and gross national income per capita into an index ranging from 0 (poor) to 1 (wonderful)—0.7 is a high rating.

A subset of the G20 has developed in recent years. In 2001, Jim O'Neil of Goldman Sachs coined the term BRIC to consider the situation of the emerging economies of Brazil, Russia, India, and China (O'Neill 2001). In 2010 the acronym was extended to "BRICS" to include South Africa. These countries are characterized by higher rates of annual average growth of gross domestic product, large territories, large populations, and large economies in contrast to countries with advanced economies, which may have slower rates of growth as well as smaller populations and economies. The BRICS have been holding summits among heads of state since 2009, discussing in part the global financial situation and how the countries could have greater involvement globally, a counterpoint to the US and European leadership of G8, G20, and OECD. At the Durban summit in 2013, the heads of state agreed to establish a new Development Bank, a possible alternative to the World Bank (BRICS Fifth Summit 2013). The BRICS have a number of issues to consider; one is that in recent years the

Table 15.1 World Economic Powers

Country	GNI pc 2012	GDP growth 2012	HDI 2012	P5	G8	BRICS	OECD	G20
US	50,120	2.2	0.937	Yes	Yes	No	Yes	Yes
Canada	50,970	1.7	0.911	No	Yes	No	Yes	Yes
Mexico	9,600	3.9	0.775	No	No	No	Yes	Yes
Brazil	11,630	0.9	0.730	No	No	Yes	No	Yes
Argentina	NA	NA	0.811	No	No	No	No	Yes
China	5,680	7.8	0.699	Yes	No	Yes	No	Yes
Japan	47,870	1.9	0.912	No	Yes	No	Yes	Yes
South Korea	22,670	2.0	0.909	No	No	No	Yes	Yes
India	1,530	3.2	0.554	No	No	Yes	No	Yes
Indonesia	3,420	6.2	0.629	No	No	No	No	Yes
Russia	12,700	3.4	0.778	Yes	Yes	Yes	No	Yes
EU	33,598	−0.3	NA	NA	NA	NA	NA	Yes
Germany	44,010	0.7	0.920	No	Yes	No	Yes	Yes
France	41,750	0	0.893	Yes	Yes	No	Yes	Yes
UK	38,250	0.3	0.875	Yes	Yes	No	Yes	Yes
Italy	33,840	−2.4	0.881	No	Yes	No	Yes	Yes
Turkey	10,830	2.2	0.722	No	No	No	Yes	Yes
Saudi Arabia	21,210	5.1	0.782	No	No	No	No	Yes
South Africa	7,610	2.1	0.629	No	No	Yes	No	Yes
Australia	59,570	3.4	0.938	No	No	No	Yes	Yes

GNI pc: Gross National Income (US$) per capita

HDI: Human Development Index

P5: Permanent members of UN Security Council

SOURCE: CIA World Factbook 2013

rate of GDP growth has declined. Another is the relationship of BRICS to the G20, the OECD, and to such other emerging economies as Mexico and Turkey, as well as to the less-developed countries in Asia, Africa, and Latin America. Potentials for cooperation among the members are also increasing in areas beyond finances. Since China and Russia already have P5 status in the UN Security Council and are founding members of the Shanghai Cooperation Organization, a new political as well as economic bloc may be forming.

What role will China, Russia, India, Brazil, and South Africa play in years to come? Will they be CRIBS, homes to emerging economics? Will they be able to continue their growth or be joined by Indonesia, Iran, Mexico, Turkey, Egypt, and Philippines? Birdsall and Fukuyama (2011) see the BRICS as both donors and recipients of resources for development. Castañeda (2010) points out that the positions of the BRICS on global issues such as human rights, nuclear non-proliferation, and carbon dioxide emissions may not be the best for the world. Of course, one also wonders about the positions taken by other global leaders such as the United States and the UK. The BRICS are currently regional players in Europe, Latin America, Africa, and Asia. The twenty-first century will see if the BRICS will be global powers in the decades to come.

References

Antholis, William. 2013. "New Players on the World Stage: Chinese Provinces and Indian States." Brookings Institution. http://www.brookings.edu/research/essays/2013/new-players-on-the-world-stage-b?utm_expid=23328448–8.GYoNBylAQWSauglvjW_cLg.1&utm_

BRICS Information Centre. 2013. http://www.brics.utoronto.ca/

BRICS Fifth Summit. 2013. http://www.brics5.co.za/

Barraclough, Geoffrey, and R. J. Overy. 1999. *Hammond Atlas of World History*. Maplewood, NJ: Hammond.

Birdsall, Nancy, and Francis Fukuyama. 2011. "The Post–Washington Consensus: Development after the Crisis." *Foreign Affairs*. March/April, 45–53.

Bosco, David L. 2009. *Five to Rule Them All: The UN Security Council and the Making of the Modern World*. Oxford, UK: Oxford University Press.

Bremmer, Ian. 2012. "Welcome to the New World Disorder." *Foreign Policy*. May 14. http://www.foreignpolicy.com/articles/2012/05/14/welcome_to_the_new_world_order.

Castañeda, Jorge. 2010. "Not Ready for Prime Time: Why Including Emerging Powers at the Helm Would Hurt Global Governance." *Foreign Affairs*. September/October, 109–122.

Cooper, Andrew Fenton, and Ramesh Chandra Thakur. 2013. *The Group of Twenty (G20)*. Abingdon, Oxon: Routledge.

Group of Twenty (G20). 2013. http://www.g20.org/en

Hajnal, Peter I. 2007. *The G8 System and the G20: Evolution, Role and Documentation*. Aldershot, England: Ashgate.

Hassler, Sabine. 2013. *Reforming the UN Security Council Membership: The Illusion of Representativeness*. Abingdon, Oxon: Routledge.

———. 2013. http://www.oecd.org/

Organisation for Economic Co-operation and Development (OECD). 2005. OECD Factbook. Paris: Organisation for Economic Co-operation and Development.

O'Brien, Patrick Karl. 1999. *Oxford Atlas of World History*. New York: Oxford University Press.

O'Neill, Jim. 2011. *The Growth Map: Economic Opportunity in the BRICs and Beyond*. New York: Portfolio / Penguin.

O'Neill, Jim. 2001. "Building Better Global Economic BRICs." Global Economic Papers No. 66. Goldman, Sachs. http://www.goldmansachs.com/our-thinking/archive/archive-pdfs/build-better-brics.pdf

Popper, Nathaniel. 2013. "Old Economies Rise as Growing Markets Begin to Falter." *New York Times*. August 15. http://www.nytimes.com/2013/08/15/business/global/old-economies-rise-as-emerging-markets-growth-falters.html

Sidaway, James. 2012. "Geographies of Development: New Maps, New Visions?" *The Professional Geographer*, 64:1, 49–62, DOI: 10.1080/00330124.2011.586878

United Nations Development Programme (UNDP). 2013. "Human Development Index." http://hdr.undp.org/en/data/map/

United Nations (UN). 2013. http://www.un.org/en/

World Bank (WB). 2013. "GNI per capita." http://data.worldbank.org/indicator/NY.GNP.PCAP.CD

16

Global Issue 4

The Arab Uprisings

In 2011 a series of popular uprisings and protests swept North Africa and the Arab world. Quickly dubbed the **Arab Spring** by Western journalists, these protests swept from Tunisia to Algeria, Jordan, Oman, Egypt, Yemen, Iraq, Sudan, Bahrain, Libya, Kuwait, Morocco, Lebanon, and Syria. Minor protests also occurred in Djibouti, Mauritania, Somalia, and Saudi Arabia. Five governments were overthrown as a result of these protests (Lynch 2012).

The uprisings began 17 December 2010 in Tunisia, when a fruit seller named Mohammed Bouazizi set himself on fire to protest his humiliation and abuse by police. Protests began the next day calling Bouazizi a martyr and protesting widespread corruption at all levels of the government. Tunisia's President Zine El Abidine Ben Ali fled to Saudi Arabia on 14 January 2011.

The events in Tunisia sparked similar protests across the region. Protests began in Algeria on 29 December 2010, ending a month later after the government lifted the state of emergency law that gave police and courts the power to ignore constitutional protections. Protests began in Jordan on 14 January, leading King Abdullah to reform the government twice, hold early elections, and make other political concessions. In Oman, five months of protest led to economic concessions by Sultan Qabus, and more power was granted to the elected parliament (Gelvin 2013).

Among the most significant protests were those in Egypt. On 25 January 2011, National Police Day, thousands of Egyptians took to the streets to protest police and government corruption, and marched to Midan Tahrir ("Liberty Square") in the center of Cairo. The protesters were initially dispersed by authorities, but they returned the following day in greater numbers, braving water cannons and police blockades, and occupying the square for 18 days. Efforts by police to dislodge the protesters led to hundreds of deaths. Similar protests broke out in cities across Egypt, until President Hosni Mubarak resigned on 11 February, turning the reins of government over to the Armed Forces until elections could be held.

Major protests in Yemen beginning 27 January were met with violent reprisals, resulting in 200 deaths, but they compelled President Ali Abdullah Saleh to sign a power-transfer that led to elections; a new president was installed the following spring.

In other countries, leaders learned from the fates of the Tunisian, Egyptian, and Yemeni leaders and either made concessions to stay in power, or entrenched themselves. This had disastrous consequences in Libya and Syria.

In Libya, protests against the authoritarian regime of President Muammar Qaddafi began on 15 February and within three days protesters controlled most of Benghazi, Libya's second-largest city. A week later protests spread to the country's capital, Tripoli. Government forces violently suppressed protests and began to retake the Mediterranean coast while the rebels formed a shadow government to lead the country after Qaddafi's ouster.

On 17 March, a UN Security Resolution authorized a no-fly zone over Libya, and "all necessary measures" to protect civilians. Two days later, France, the United States, and the United Kingdom began a bombing campaign against pro-Qaddafi forces. A coalition of 27 states from Europe and the Middle East soon joined the intervention, over the protests of countries like Russia, which claimed the bombings exceeded the UN mandate. With coalition aid, rebels were able to push back government forces, eventually taking Tripoli in August, and in October capturing the final government stronghold of Sirte, where Gaddafi died in the fighting (Gelvin 2013).

Protests in Syria started on 26 January 2011 to demand the freedom of a man arrested for filing a complaint against a police officer who had assaulted him in public. This was followed by other peaceful protests, which intensified in early March after Syrian security forces arrested and reportedly abused 15 children for writing anti-government graffiti. By mid-March, thousands of protestors had gathered in the cities of Damascus, Aleppo, al-Hasakah, Daraa, Deir ez-Zor, and Hama. The government arrested approximately 3,000 people, and several were killed. On 18 April 2011, approximately 100,000 protesters sat in the central Square of Homs calling for the resignation of President Bashar al-Assad. Protests continued throughout the country in spite of harsh security clampdowns and military operations.

In July and August, Syrian army tanks stormed several cities killing at least 136 people, and security forces began firing on armed protesters. Rebels armed themselves, first to resist military assaults, then to actively revolt against the government. In early December, the district of Homs fell under armed Syrian opposition control. Battles between rebel forces and the Syrian military escalated in spite of an April 2012 ceasefire, and by June 2012, the chief UN peacekeeper in Syria acknowledged that the country was in a state of civil war. The pressure on the outside world to intervene to stop the killing increased in the fall of 2013 when Syrian government forces used chemical weapons on rebel-held areas (Muasher 2014).

The uprisings had several things in common. First, most took place in countries that claimed commitment to democratic principles but whose actual operations were autocratic. Second, even though many countries had growing economies when measured by the standards economists use, the wealth distribution was skewed to create huge gaps not only between rich and poor, but rural and urban, and, perhaps most significantly, between age groups. Most countries had growing numbers of young people who, regardless of education, were unemployed or underemployed, and had little expectation of prosperous futures. Third, integration into the global economy, guided by principles of neoliberalism, saw the decline and dismantling of state-run institutions that had eased these economic frictions. Even as jobs became harder to find, people watched public schools, free clinics and state-run hospitals, parks and public works decline, while fabulous new shopping malls and gated communities were built for the wealthy elites. Fourth, WikiLeaks revelations confirmed rumors about government corruption to pro-democratic bloggers, who used cell phones and Facebook pages to organize protests. These new information and communication technologies provide ways for disgruntled citizens to connect and share information, and to help organize protests, avoiding state-controlled media and telecommunications.

The Arab uprisings wrought enormous change across the region. The leaders of Tunisia, Yemen, and Egypt resigned; the leader of Libya was killed; and leaders in several countries, including Sudan and Iraq, announced that they would step down when their current terms ended.

Protests in Jordan, Kuwait, and Morocco led the kings of those countries to reform their governments. In December 2011, *Time* magazine named "The Protester" its "Person of the Year," and Yemeni protest leader Tawakel Karman was one of the three recipients of the 2011 Nobel Peace Prize.

The uprisings posed an immediate problem for Western allies, especially the United States. Although officially promoting democracy around the world, the United States had long since forged close alliances with authoritarian regimes who could maintain stability in the region. Official responses from the United States tended to be ambiguous, leading rulers to believe they were being abandoned and protesters to believe the United States was supporting their dictators (Nouheid and Warren 2013).

As countries with interests in the region chose sides in the uprisings, it not only highlighted traditional differences but disrupted traditional alliances. The decision of UN forces to actively aid rebels in Libya led Russia to refuse to allow a similar UN resolution for Syria. The US decision to support the new elected government of Egypt, dominated by Islamists, infuriated not only millions of Egyptians who wanted secular democracy, but put the United States in opposition to Saudi Arabia. Qatar and Saudi Arabia also found themselves on opposite sides in Egypt, each pouring billions of dollars into the coffers of the contesting parties (Tschirgi 2012). In the summer of 2013, the Egyptian military ousted the democratically elected Islamist government, further complicating Washington's stance.

Taken as a whole, the Arab uprisings had significance far beyond their regional transformations and their policy implications for Western nations. The protests had a regional aspect, but global significance. They could not be reduced to religious sectarianism, left-right politics, or anti-globalization explanations, and their consequences on a global scale are irrevocable. The symbolism of millions of people demanding the end of oppressive regimes inspired protesters and demonstrations around the world during a time of financial crises and unpopular corporate bailouts. The mix of traditional protest signs and techno-savvy young people organizing and connecting both locally and globally through new media underscored the growing significance of new technologies in political and social change (Christensen and Christensen 2013).

Although they wrought unprecedented political transformations, none of the revolutions has yet led to successful economic and political reforms that clearly benefit the working- and middle-class people who turned out in the millions to push for these changes (although the recent constitutional referendum in Tunisia is a hopeful sign). Many countries saw a rise of Islamic political activity, others saw merely superficial changes, and in many political unrest continues. The ultimate outcome of these uprisings will not be clear for many years.

References

Christensen, Miyase, and Christian Christensen. 2013. The Arab Spring as Meta-Event and Communicative Spaces. *Television & New Media* 14(4): 351–364.

Gelvin, James. 2013. *The Arab Revolutions: What Everyone Needs to Know*. Oxford, UK: Oxford University Press.

Haas, Mark L., and David W. Lesch, eds. 2012. *The Arab Spring: Change and Resistance in the Middle East*. Boulder, CO: Westview Press.

Lynch, Marc. 2012. *The Arab Uprising: The Unfinished Revolutions of the New Middle East*. New York: Public Affairs.

Muasher, Marwan. 2014. *The Second Arab Awakening and the Battle for Pluralism*. New Haven, CT: Yale University Press.

Nouheid, Lin, and Alex Warren. 2013. *The Battle for the Arab Spring: Revolution, Counter-Revolution and the Making of a New Era*. New Haven, CT: Yale University Press.

Tschirgi, Dan. 2012. "The United States and the Tahrir Revolution." In *Egypt's Tahrir Revolution*, edited by Dan Tschirgi, Walid Kazziha, and Sean F. McMahon, 233–256. Boulder, CO: Lynne Rienner.

17

Global Issue 5

The Veil Controversy

The practice of Muslim women to wear head coverings—ranging from head scarfs, to gowns and veils that cover the entire body—has become extremely controversial throughout the world. Belgium, France, Germany, Indonesia, the Netherlands, Tajikistan, Tunisia, and Turkey have all instituted bans on some forms of Islamic dress in schools or other public places. Veiling has also sparked recent public debates in Canada, Denmark, Egypt, Italy, and the United Kingdom, and unveiling movements have sparked controversy in Iran and Saudi Arabia. Rather than being understood as a matter of cultural style—as jeans, saris, robes, and business suits usually are—these forms of dress have become symbols to much of the world of backwardness and oppression of women or, in some cases, as part of a clash of civilizations (Huntington 1993) between the West and the Islamic world. Getting an understanding of this worldwide debate requires a multidisciplinary approach.

There are many different kinds of face and head coverings that Western writers tend to collectively call "the veil." The simplest and most common is the *hijab*, a head scarf that covers the hair and neck. Some Middle Eastern Muslim women—wishing to distinguish themselves from Christian women, many of whom also wear the hijab—have begun adopting the *khimar*, a head-to-midriff covering with an oval for the face. The most thorough form of modest dress is the *niqab*, a dress that covers the entire body, accompanied by a face veil, gloves, and, in some places, an eye screen or sunglasses. A variation of this, the *burqa,* a head-to-foot pleated gown with an eye screen, is worn in parts of Afghanistan and Pakistan.

Although some Eastern European and Baltic countries have indigenous Muslim minorities, throughout most of Europe Islamic dress is inextricably linked with cultural concerns about immigration and pluralism. The most common concerns expressed about veiling involve secularism, integration, and security. In France, for example, *l'affaire du voile* ("the affair of the veil") banning Islamic head coverings from public places split the traditional political spectrum of right and left. Many side with the government's argument that the nation is inherently secular and that ostentatious displays of religion like the veil disrupt this principle. Others insist that religious freedom must include the right to dress as one wishes.

But for many, Islamic dress represents a deeper divide, one between secular Enlightenment values and something alien and backward. Some European feminists, for example, have argued that women are not truly free to choose the veil because they are oppressed by social pressures within their religious communities. Veiling advocates respond that social pressures for European and American women to dress seductively for men are just as strong and that banning the veil is just as oppressive as requiring it. Others decry a double standard that allows nuns to wear their habits in public spaces but refuses Muslim women the right to veil.

Another criticism is that Islamic dress represents a refusal by migrants to integrate into their host societies. Even in countries like England, where the majority support the right of citizens to dress however they please as a civil-liberties issue, the veil is widely seen as a "mark of separation," as former British prime minister Tony Blair put it, segregating Muslims from the British shared national culture (BBC News 2006). Others have insisted that speaking to someone whose face is concealed is inherently undemocratic.

A major accusation leveled by anti-veiling activists in Europe and North America is that veiling is backward. In European history, Christian women wore veils or other head coverings in church, in accordance with a biblical injunction (1 Corinthians 11:4–10). Veils and head coverings were common in the European Middle Ages and the Renaissance. American and European notions of historical progress often draw on this history to see contemporary veiling by Muslims as an inappropriate remnant of history. But the history of veiling in the Middle East is quite different, and very complex. Historically, most of the world's Muslims have adopted whatever constituted modest dress in the areas in which they lived. Certainly this is true of the Middle East: head coverings and face veils were worn by Jews, Christians, and Zoroastrians before Islam. Ironically, veiling in the Islamic world seems to be rising in popularity largely through the influence of conservative Wahhabi and Salafi interpretations of Islam disseminated through global media using Saudi Arabian oil money, as a consequence of modern global migration patterns, and also as a result of twentieth-century economic patterns.

In many parts of the Middle East, veiling has long been a politically charged activity. In the 1920s and 1930s, Western-educated upper-class women in many Middle Eastern states scandalized convention by publicly unveiling. At the same time, in Turkey and Iran, the government sought to ban veiling as a way to impose Western modernity on the populace. By the 1970s, in many parts of the region, the *hijab* and *niqab* were largely confined to older women and to Islamist students on college campuses. However, as the economic structural adjustment policies of the 1980s began to have financial consequences for middle- and working-class families, more and more women were forced into the workplace. For these women, adopting the veil was a way of showing that a woman could hold a job without compromising her morality as wife and mother (Macleod 1991). Moroccan author Fatimah Mernissi reminds us that the *niqab* is like a one-way mirror. It conceals women from the gaze of the world, but it does not conceal the world from their gaze (Mernissi 2001). Many women who wear the *niqab*, or *burqa*, say that it offers them a sense of privacy in the most crowded conditions. Working women in particular say that it helps force men to pay attention to their minds rather than their bodies and allows them to be able to work with men without getting hit on. However, veiling has also been enforced on women by Islamist men through various means of coercion, including the horrific activity of throwing acid in the face of a Muslim woman who does not veil.

But many Westernized Arab governments were displeased with the widespread adoption of the veil in the 1980s and sought to curb it, seeing it as out of step with the modern secular ideologies they wanted to present. Egypt, for example, banned head scarfs from college campuses (Eickelman and Piscatori 1996). This led to a protest in which large numbers of women began wearing head scarfs to show solidarity with their fellow students and to send a message to the government not to meddle in domestic and religious issues. In the 1990s, the government tried again with regard to the *niqab*, only to achieve similar results. In Algeria, Tunisia, and Turkey "the new veiling" has also become an issue of political contention.

Why veiling? In Islam, the **Quran** requires men and women to dress modestly except in the presence of family members. What constitutes modest dress, and at what age it should be adopted, varies from community to community, and sometimes among people within a community. Worldwide, male modest dress has produced little or no controversy. It is only female modest dress that has sparked debate across parts of North America, Europe, Asia, and the Middle East.

The Quran itself is ambiguous about veiling. The term *hijab* is used only to refer to a curtain that provides privacy for the prophet's wives when guests were in the home. The text refers to neck scarfs and cloaks (*jilbab*) for Muslim women when they go out so that they will be recognized as Muslims by nonmembers of the community. Several **hadith** extend the rules for women's modesty, but scholars are divided in their interpretations of these verses (Saleem 1996). Since Arab women of the prophet's era did not veil, many scholars believe that Arabs adopted veiling garments from the Zoroastrian Persians and Byzantine Christians in the decades following Muhammad's death (Esposito 2005, 98).

Saudi Arabia and Iran legally require veiling. Among Saudis, Muslim women must wear a loose robe called an *abaya*, a *hijab*, and *niqab*. Under the monarchy from the 1930s until 1979, it was illegal for Iranian women to wear veils or head coverings in public; since the revolution, it is illegal *not* to wear a *chador*, a loose-fitting cloak, and the *hijab*. Such laws are not the norm across the Middle East, however, and women choose to wear some form of head covering, or not, for any number of reasons.

There are practical reasons for wearing a head covering. Most people live in unheated and uncooled homes, and when they travel they are exposed to hot sunlight. The veil, like the traditional Arabian male head coverings, regulates the temperature of the head, keeping the sun off it and keeping it warm on cool nights and chilly mornings. Face veils protect the skin from sun and wind and keep dust off the face and out of the nose and mouth.

Many contemporary religious movements in the Middle East urge women to adopt the *hijab*, *khimar*, or *niqab* as a religious obligation. Among women whose families have not traditionally veiled, the decision to assume a head covering is often an important expression of religious piety. Adopting modest dress does not just show others you are devout; according to many teachers, it helps you become more devout by practicing discipline in your life.

Women who don't wear a veil because of personal piety may do so to reflect their family's respectability or to improve their chances of getting a husband in a conservative community. Many women begin to cover during specific life transitions: after first menses to show that a girl has become a marriageable woman, after marriage, after the birth of a first child, or after the death of a husband. And while women draw on family and community traditions in making these decisions, they are often also influenced by the twists and turns their own lives take.

Some women also argue that veiling is part of the erotic relationship between husbands and wives. When your husband is the only man who sees your hair and body (and, if he is faithful, yours is the *only* female body he sees) the act of unveiling at home becomes sexually charged. Certainly, Victoria's Secret does a thriving business in Riyadh (although men are banned from working there), and even decades-old regional department stores like Cairo's Omar Effendi have erotic lingerie sections.

Veiling also has significant economic advantages. Secular middle- and working-class women in Muslim countries may wear the *hijab* simply because it is cheaper than having their hair done. The shampoos, conditioners, blow dryers, and other home hair-care equipment Americans and Europeans take for granted are out of reach for all but a small percentage of most of the world's population. Yet if secular women may wear the veil for economic reasons, many religious leaders tout the *niqab* as offering a spiritual liberation from materialism. When every woman wears identical garb, they claim, women meet one another as equals, without external signs of wealth or status.

In many places, though, this logic completely fails. As the *hijab* and *khimar* have become more popular among upper classes throughout the Muslim world, they are increasingly seen as stylish. Many women choose their head scarfs as carefully as they do their purses, shoes, belts, and other accessories. Chanel and other global fashion designers have begun offering elegant designer veils for Muslim women who can afford them. Islamic fashion for women is rapidly becoming a global industry.

Why do women veil? The reasons are many, and there is no universal meaning of veiling throughout the Middle East or in the Islamic world. Nor do European, American, and Asian governments agree about what the veil means and if they should do something about it. Many apologists of veiling in the Middle East and elsewhere ask why governments think they should *do* anything. Why, they ask, is the custom so arresting to Americans and Europeans that they talk of "liberating" Muslim women from the veil but rarely about liberating women from poverty, illness, and malnutrition—serious problems throughout the Islamic world (Abu-Lughod 2002)?

References

Abu-Lughod, Lila. 2002. "Do Muslim Women Really Need Saving?" *American Anthropologist* 104, no. 3: 783–90.

BBC. 2006. "Blair's Concerns over Face Veils." BBC News. October 17. http://news.bbc.co.uk/1/hi/uk_politics/6058672.stm.

Eickelman, Dale, and James Piscatori. 1996. *Muslim Politics.* Princeton, NJ: Princeton University Press.

Esposito, John. 2005. *Islam: The Straight Path.* 3rd ed. New York: Oxford University Press.

Huntington, Samuel P. 1993. "The Clash of Civilizations?" *Foreign Affairs* 72, no. 3: 22–49.

Macleod, Arlene. 1991. *Accommodating Protest: Working Women, the New Veiling, and Change in Cairo.* New York: Columbia University Press.

Mernissi, Fatimah. 2001. *Scheherazade Goes West: Different Cultures, Different Harems.* New York: Simon and Schuster.

Saleem, Shehzad. 1996. "The Qur'anic Concept of Hijâb." *Renaissance* 6, no. 11: http://www.renaissance.com.pk/index.html.

18

Global Issue 6
The Responsibility to Protect

In the early 2000s, the Sudanese government of Omar as-Bashir began supporting militias that were committing atrocities against mostly non-Arab groups in the western Darfur region. Shocked by the wanton violence and Khartoum's indifference to the suffering of the Darfur people, in 2004 the UN Security Country formed an International Commission of Inquiry on Darfur.

The crisis in Darfur was an impetus for the UN to formalize the protocols for a policy called "the responsibility to protect" (R2P). R2P would obligate and legitimize international intervention to protect innocents from atrocities committed by their own government. In 2005, the UN World Summit issued Paragraph 139 of the Outcome Document of the World Summit:

> The international community, through the United Nations, also has the responsibility to use appropriate diplomatic, humanitarian and other peaceful means, in accordance with Chapters VI and VIII of the Charter, to help to protect populations from genocide, war crimes, ethnic cleansing and crimes against humanity. In this context, we are prepared to take collective action, in a timely and decisive manner, through the Security Council, in accordance with the Charter, including Chapter VII, on a case-by-case basis and in cooperation with relevant regional organizations as appropriate, should peaceful means be inadequate and national authorities are manifestly failing to protect their populations from genocide, war crimes, ethnic cleansing and crimes against humanity. We stress the need for the General Assembly to continue consideration of the *responsibility to*

protect populations from genocide, war crimes, ethnic cleansing and crimes against humanity and its implications, bearing in mind the principles of the Charter and international law. (emphasis added)

In 2006, UN Secretary General Ban Ki-Moon issued a report on "Implementing the Responsibility to Protect," which recommended that the UN codify the "Outcome Document" above. In 2007, the UN General Assembly created the UN Human Rights Council (HRC) to monitor human rights violations and issue reports on the possible invocation of R2P. In 2007, the HRC's High Level Mission issued this report on Darfur (Ueda 2013, 78):

The Mission . . . concludes that the Government of the Sudan has manifestly failed to protect the population of Darfur from large scale international crimes, and has itself orchestrated and participated in these crimes. As such, the solemn obligation of the international community to exercise its *responsibility to protect* has become evident and urgent. (original emphasis)

No action was taken in Sudan because of Chinese opposition in the UN Security Council and US preoccupation in Iraq and Afghanistan. But the UN's R2P is the culmination of a long effort to regularize the rules of war and to protect innocent civilian populations. Western enlightened thinking in the late seventeenth and the eighteenth centuries raised sensibilities about a government's humane treatment of its citizens and wounded and imprisoned combatants in war. New rational and humane norms of behavior were introduced into an endeavor that was inherently destructive. Much like the guillotine was invented to provide a painless way of execution, the Geneva Conventions (1864, 1907, 1929) were supposed to bring decorum to the battlefield and on the high seas, and called for the humane treatment of POWs. The Hague Convention of 1899 further established laws and customs of warfare.

The Germans ignored these norms in World War I by using poison gas and by unleashing unrestricted U-boat warfare on neutral ships. In World War II, the Third Reich's war on civilian populations made a mockery of the Geneva and Hague conventions. The bombing of civilian populations by both sides in the war was justified on the basis that in total war industry in urban areas was a legitimate target. The Germans' use of gas again in the death chambers, and the utter horror and magnitude of the Holocaust elicited cries of "never again!" The top Nazi leaders were brought before the dock at the Nuremberg Trials for "crimes against humanity," and most were executed.

In 1948, the newly formed UN adopted the Universal Declaration on Human Rights, which was an important development in the evolution of R2P. Article 3 asserted that "everyone has the right to life, liberty and security of person," and Article 5 stipulated that "no one shall be subjected to torture or to cruel, inhuman or degrading treatment or punishment." Two years later 195 countries agreed to the Fourth Geneva Protocol, which protected the rights of noncombatants in wartime.

Tragically, the promise of "never again" has rung hollow as the world has remained silent in the face of repeated genocides. The United States, which might have led military action to stop atrocities in Cambodia and Iraq, for example, was focused on the Soviet challenge in the Cold War. Washington was often indifferent to the suffering, or was even complicit in some cases. In 1971, the United States supported Cold War ally West Pakistan in its brutal war against East Pakistan, which was vying to become the independent state of Bangladesh. Hundreds of thousands were slaughtered, and the flood of refugees to India prompted that country to go to war against West Pakistan. India leaned toward the Soviet Union in the Cold War, and US President Richard Nixon revealed his racist hatred for the Indians: "What they really need is a mass famine." Nixon's National Security Advisor Henry Kissinger agreed: "They are such bastards." Nixon also had nothing but contempt for the Pakistanis. "Pakistan," he said, "they're just a bunch of brown goddam Moslems" (quoted in Mishra 2013, 109–114).

The United States used napalm and carpet bombing in the Vietnam War with little concern for civilian deaths and turned a blind eye to the genocide in Cambodia in the late 1970s. From 1975 to 1979 the Khmer Rouge killed 1.7 million people, 21 percent of the entire population. It was not the West that intervened, but the United States' erstwhile enemy Vietnam that finally invaded in 1979 and stopped the madness.

In the early 1980s, Iraqi dictator Saddam Hussein used chemical weapons on his own people and in his war against Iran. Remembering the American diplomats who had been held hostage in Iran in 1979–1980, and fearing the spread of more fundamentalist Islamic states, the United States backed Hussein in this war.

Even after the end of the Cold War genocides continued. One of the most horrific genocides of the twentieth century occurred in Rwanda in 1994. In the course of a few months Hutus slaughtered 800,000 Tutsis without any reaction from the United States or other Western powers. At the same time Yugoslavia was breaking up in a civil war that would take over 200,000 lives. As Yugoslavia disintegrated and descended into civil war between Serbs, Croats, and Bosnian Muslims in the early 1990s, neither the EU nor the United States made any move to intervene militarily until Serbs massacred thousands of Bosnian Muslims in a supposed UN "safe haven" in Srebrenica in 1995. The UN was hamstrung by Russia's veto in the UN Security council of any action against its ally Serbia. US President Bill Clinton, embarrassed by his inaction in Rwanda, finally decided to bomb Bosnian Serb positions, and a deal was made to divide up Bosnia with NATO and the UN sending in peacekeepers to enforce it. When Serbia began to ethnically cleanse Albanians from the Serb province of Kosovo in 1999, NATO bombed Serbia for 78 days before Belgrade agreed to end the operation. These actions to protect innocent populations in the former Yugoslavia set a precedent for the deliberations that led to R2P.

There is no doubt that the media's coverage of this region in Western Europe's backyard influenced NATO's decisions to intervene in Bosnia and Kosovo. Without Western journalists writing about Rwanda, Congo, and Darfur, there was less urgency to act. An argument can also be made that the West does not value lives of non-Western peoples in the developing world, or the so-called "South."

The civil war in the eastern part of the Democratic Republic of Congo has claimed an estimated five million lives in the last decade, but no one is paying attention. Few Western journalists venture into the no-man's-land in the east. The transportation system into the vast interior of the country is in shambles. The central government in Kinshasa, in the far west of the country, has little control over the east, where all of the neighboring countries have been involved in the fighting and have been looting Congo's abundant mineral resources. Some have called it Africa's First World War. Ironically, an important player in fomenting the anarchy in eastern Congo is the Rwandan Army, which invaded the country in 1996. The Rwandan Army supports Tutsis in the region, in part as revenge for the genocide of Tutsis in Rwanda in 1994.

The carnage in Darfur has also begged for Western response. In 2005, at about the same time that a civil war between the north and the south

Sudan was winding down (South Sudan gained its independence in 2011), conflict broke out in the western province of Darfur. British colonial administrators were unconcerned with the economic development of the province, which is home to more than ninety different ethnic groups. Before World War II, Darfur had one elementary school and no maternity clinics. By the time Sudan gained independence in 1956, Darfur was the poorest and least-developed area of the country.

The Arab-dominated government in Khartoum continued the British policy of neglect in Darfur. The province endured a severe drought and famine in 1984, but Khartoum ignored the suffering and may have even exacerbated it. Perhaps two hundred thousand died in the famine, adding to the feeling among the peoples of Darfur that the Sudanese government has been conducting a policy of gradual eradication (Kristof 2006, 14–17; Ryle 2004, 55–58).

The drought prompted nomads in the north, mostly Arabs, to drive farther and farther south to seek pasturage for their livestock, where they encroached on southern farmers, mostly black Africans. According to a UN Environmental Program report, "there is a very strong link between land degradation, desertification and conflict in Darfur" (Polgreen 2007). In the mid-1990s Khartoum decided to back local militias to quell unrest in the region. They killed several thousand members of the Masaliti tribe, one of the three indigenous non-Arab tribes in Darfur. In the same decade, the militias conducted more attacks on the other tribes, the Fur and Zaghawa. The three tribes organized self-defense militias (some say that they are backed by Chad and Eritrea), and they began attacking government installations in 2003. Khartoum again unleashed its militias, dubbed the *janjaweed*, meaning "man on a horse." One survivor recalled a massacre on his village: "The *janjaweed* were accompanied by soldiers. They attacked the people, saying: 'You are opposed to the regime, we must crush you. As you are Black, you are like slaves. Then the entire Darfur region will be in the hands of the Arabs. The government is on our side.'" Another survivor witnessed the murder of his entire family: "[The attackers] took a knife and cut my mother's throat and threw her into the well. Then they took my oldest sister and began to rape her, one by one. My father was kneeling, crying and begging them for mercy. After that they killed my brother and finally my father. They threw all the bodies in the well" (Kristof 2006, 15).

These atrocities have been widespread: some estimates count two hundred thousand dead and another 2 million refugees in camps near cities or in neighboring Chad. Chad's president, Idriss Deby, has tried to stay out of the fray, although some of the affected people in Darfur are Zaghawans, people from his own ethnic group, and both Chad and Sudan have accused the other of cross-border raids.

The killing and raping continued in 2007, despite a token but ineffective peacekeeping force sent by the African Union (AU). Once again the call for strong diplomatic intervention by the international community has gone unheeded. The situation is muddled by the anti-Khartoum, anti-Arab sentiments of the Darfur rebels and by the central government's disingenuous denial of any support for the *janjaweed*. Since Khartoum gave the *janjaweed* free rein, however, the government has been hard-pressed to control them. Hundreds of people were killed in the fighting in the last half of 2010, and in 2013 the *New York Times* reported that the atrocities are beginning again. According to the UN, some 300,000 Darfuris have been displaced in the first part of the year, about the same number as in all of 2010–2011 (*New York Times*, July 21, 2013).

The UN has yet to act decisively, and the United States, which might lead such a mission, is still winding down operations in Afghanistan and dealing with Iran and North Korea over their nuclear weapons programs. The UN has had little leverage in Sudan because China, a UN Security Council member, has been making deals for Sudan's oil. China is by far Sudan's largest trading partner, taking 60 percent of Sudan's exports. Sudan supplies 7 percent of China's oil (CIA 2009). Beijing has had little interest in pressuring Sudan on human-rights issues when China faces criticism on this front as well. The World Court's indictment of al-Bashir in 2009 for human-rights violations in Darfur might change the equation for China. In June 2011, Bashir met Chinese President Hu Jintao, whom Bashir called his "friend and brother." As the international community increasingly isolates Bashir, however, China will find it more difficult to maintain normal relations with Khartoum.

The first action under the UN's R2P came in 2011 in reaction to Muammar Qaddafi's brutal campaign to suppress Libyan rebel groups. For the first time in its history the UN Security Council authorized military action to protect civilians against their own government. Resolution 1973 was influenced by past discussions of R2P, and was possible because even China and Russia, Security Council members that had blocked UN sanctions and military actions in Sudan, found Qaddafi's methods abhorrent. The resolution did not call for regime change, however, and when the

Western powers did just that, Russia and China felt they had been too quick to give the West the green light to intervene. This has become a problem for authorizing future operations under R2P, especially in Syria.

In 2013, the Syrian regime of Bashar al-Assad used chemical weapons on civilians in rebel-held areas. Over three decades earlier, Bashir's father, Hafaz al-Assad, had obliterated a Sunni insurrection in the city of Hama, leveling the city and killing an estimated 20,000 Syrians. The al-Assad family comes from the Shiite Alawite sect, and the communal violence in Syria mirrored the Sunni-Shiite violence in neighboring Iraq. By the end of 2013, some 120,000 Syrians had been killed and millions were externally or internally displaced.

In 2012 a special Human Rights Council Commission reported that Syrian "forces have committed widespread, systematic and gross human rights violations, amounting to crimes against humanity, with the apparent knowledge and consent of the highest levels of the State." The commission did not call for military action, however, recommending a political solution (Ueda 2013, 84). China and Russia would have blocked UN action against Syria under R2P anyway, in part because the Western powers went beyond the mandate of the UN's resolution on Libya. The West's no-fly zone evolved into an active bombing campaign against Qaddafi's forces and helped bring down the regime. China and Russia, and many other countries, wonder if R2P is just a guise for the United States and its allies to intervene into conflicts for their own national interests, ostensibly in a legal manner under international law.

In 2013, President Obama appointed Samantha Power US ambassador to the United Nations. As a journalist in the former Yugoslavia when that state descended into civil war, Power saw firsthand the human-rights atrocities that the world largely ignored until 1995. Shocked by these events, she published a Pulitzer Prize–winning book on the genocides in Cambodia, Rwanda, and Bosnia (*A Problem from Hell*, 2003). As a senior aide in Obama's National Security Council, Power was a strong advocate for action in Libya in 2011. Power was appointed US ambassador to the UN in 2013, and was confronted with Russian opposition to another UN intervention, even after it became known that the Syrian regime had used chemical weapons against the opposition. Obama was fortunate that Russia stepped in with a deal to disarm Syria of its chemical weapons, although the civil war continues (Ignatieff 2013). The Syrian government has been slow to relinquish all of its chemical weapons, and as it gained the upper hand in the civil war in early 2014, it is not clear whether Damascus will fully comply.

Certainly the UN's follow-through on enforcing the R2P has been spotty, and, by invoking this mandate too often without taking action, it can make the declaration meaningless. However, as one scholar argues, the strategy is a "habit former," not only for the UN to act to protect innocents, but as a warning to governments not to commit human-rights violations (Bellamy 2013, 333, 338).

References

Bellamy, Alex J. 2013. "The Responsibility to Protect: Added Value or Hot Air?" *Cooperation and Conflict* 48 (no. 3): 333–357.

CIA (Central Intelligence Agency). 2013. *The World Factbook.* Washington, DC: Central Intelligence Agency. https://www.cia.gov/library/publications/the -world-factbook/index.html.

Gettleman, Jeffrey. 2011a. "UN Officials Warn of a Growing 'Panic' in Central Sudan as Violence Spreads." *New York Times.* June 16.

———. 2011b. "Struggle Over, Independent South Sudan Rejoices." *New York Times.* July 10.

Ignatieff, Michael. 2013. "The Duty to Protect, Still Urgent." *New York Times.* Sept. 13.

Kristof, Nicholas D. 2006. "Genocide in Slow Motion." *New York Review of Books* (February 9): 14–17.

MacFarquhar, Neil. 2010. "Sudan: International Prosecutor Says Darfur Violence Has Continued." *New York Times.* December 9.

———. 2011. "Sudan Strikes Could Be War Crimes." *New York Times.* July 15.

Mishra, Pankaj. 2013. "Unholy Alliances." *The New Yorker* (September 23): 109–114.

Perry, Alex. 2011. "Can Sudan Split Without Falling Apart?" *Time* (January 10): 43–49.

Polgreen, Lydia. 2007. "New Depth: A Godsend for Darfur, Or a Curse?" *New York Times.* July 22.

Ryle, John. 2004. "Disaster in Darfur." *New York Review of Books* (August 12): 55–58.

Ueda, Akihiro. 2013. "UN Human Rights Council and the Responsibility to Protect." *Journal of Political Science* (no. 8): 71–91.

Williamson, Richard S. 2011. "Sudan on the Cusp." *Current History* (May): 171–176.

19

Global Issue 7

Global Population Projections

We do not know exactly what the world will be like in 2020 much less in 2050. If the UN's Millennium Development Goals are met, the world will be a better place. But prognostications on the economy ("If I had only bought Microsoft stock, rather than Worldcom"), political forecasting ("Who will win the next election in country X?"), and other efforts to use social science to look ahead are difficult. The most we can do is look at current trends and imagine how they might shape the near future.

Demographic trends give us clues as to future populations. The world's current population is about 7,137,000,000. We reached the first billion in 1850. The world reached two billion in 1929, three billion in 1959, four billion in 1974, five billion in 1987, and six billion in 1998. By 2050 we will probably have between nine and ten billion. In the time it has taken you to read this paragraph, perhaps another 1,000 babies will have been born (Cohen 2011).

For international studies, we have various questions about this rapid population growth. What are the demographic projections; what social classes are affected (sociology)? What political groups are touched by this growth; what countries will maintain power (political science)? What cultures are impacted by this growth; how will our sense of each other change (anthropology)? How will our spatial relations change; will we be more urban, how will our environment change (geography)? Can we provide for this larger population; can we handle the costs of this rising population (economics)? Can people handle this rise in population; how does this unprecedented change affect our lives (history)?

How Many People Will There Be?

Demographic projections provide probable clues to some aspects of our global future. The world's population is growing at a rate of 1.2 percent per year. Table 19.1 lists the top ten countries in size. Of those top ten, six are in Asia. China and India have huge populations with over one billion each. Only the United States, Japan, and Russia have developed economies. All continents are represented in this top ten list. Fertility trends are key to projections of future world population (CIA 2013; PRB 2013; O'Neill and Balk 2001).

Table 19.1 Most Populous Countries, 2013

Country	Millions
China	1,357
India	1,277
United States	316
Indonesia	249
Brazil	196
Pakistan	191
Nigeria	174
Bangladesh	157
Russia	143
Japan	127

SOURCE: *Population Reference Bureau 2013*

Table 19.2 Most Populous Countries, 2050

Country	Millions
India	1,652
China	1,314
Nigeria	440
United States	400
Indonesia	366
Pakistan	363
Bangladesh	226
Brazil	227
Dem. Rep. of Congo	182
Ethiopia	178

SOURCE: *Population Reference Bureau 2013*

The Population Reference Bureau estimates that by 2050 the global population will be 9,727,000, 000 and Table 19.2 lists the likely ten most-populous countries. Assuming current growth rates hold steady, India will have surpassed China in size. The only developed economy on the list is the United States (although Brazil and China may be considered developed by that time). Asia has five countries in the top ten. Africa has three countries in the top ten, led by Nigeria. Brazil and the United States represent the Americas. There is no country from Europe, unless one considers the EU in aggregate (projected at 517 million). That EU superstate would surpass the United States, but still have only one-third the population of India (PRB 2013).

Where are the world's people today? Table 19.3 shows the 2013 global distribution of the world's population. Of the 7,137,000,000 people in the world, Asia has 60 percent, Africa 15 percent, Europe 10 percent, Latin America 8 percent, Middle East 7.5 percent, North America 5 percent, and Oceania 0.5 percent (The Middle East includes Southwest Asia and North Africa, for present purposes.) Most (82.5 percent) of the world's population lives in the less-developed countries. Population growth rates higher than the world average are present in Africa and the Middle East. Note that Europe has a zero population growth rate.

Table 19.3 World Population 2013

	Millions	Rate of Natural Increase	Infant Mortality Rate	Urban %
World	7137	1.2	40	52
More Developed	1246	0.1	5	76
Less Developed	5891	1.4	44	47
Africa	1100	2.6	68	40
North America	352	0.4	6	81
Latin America	606	1.3	19	79
Asia	4302	1.1	35	46
Europe	740	0	5	71
Middle East	536	1.9	29	63
Oceania	38	1.1	20	66

SOURCE: *Population Reference Bureau 2013*

The infant-mortality rate is the number of infant deaths per 1,000 live births. This offers an excellent indicator of the overall health of a population. Based on this statistic, Africa, Asia, and the Middle East are regions with poorer health. These areas are important target regions for the Millennium Development Goals. North America and Europe have low infant-mortality rates. But health and mortality rates are also tied to urbanization. At present, about half of the world's population live in cities. In North America, Latin America, and Europe over 70 percent of the population is urban. Asia and Africa have lower rates of urbanism. So today we have two worlds: an urban world with low infant mortality and low rate of natural increase, and the other, in which most of the world's population lives, a more rural world (but rapidly urbanizing) with higher infant-mortality rates and higher rates of natural increase (PRB 2013).

What will the world's population look like by the mid-twenty-first century? Estimates indicate a global population that is 36 percent larger, or 9,727,000,000. Some analysts argue that the globe cannot sustain almost *ten billion* human beings. Further projections keep the top range at under eleven billion, simply because we will have to adjust our behavior and begin to have fewer children or face devastating ecological and economic consequences. Overall we will have a lower rate of natural increase (less than 1 percent), lower infant-mortality rate, and a higher urbanization rate (60–70% globally). Most population growth will occur in urban areas. The regional balance will shift over time. Asia will still be the largest with 54 percent of the world's people. Africa will have 25 percent, the Middle East 8.5 percent, Latin America 8 percent, Europe 7.5 percent, North America 4.5 percent, and Oceania 0.5 percent. Between 2013 and 2050, Africa will add more population than any other region, and most of that growth will be in sub-Saharan Africa. Europe's population will actually decline. Of course, these figures are made assuming no natural or human-made disasters like wars, plagues, or pestilences (PRB 2013).

Global population projections are complicated. If fertility rates do not decline, then the situation in Africa, Middle East, and parts of Asia in 2050 will be truly difficult, with hundreds of millions in grinding poverty. An increased population density would then mean declining healthcare. Demographic problems quickly become economic and then political problems as well. To keep the global population below ten billion assumes we will have adequate family planning and sex education. Women play a key

Table 19.4 World Population 2050

	Millions
World	9727
More Developed	1311
Less Developed	8416
Africa	2431
North America	448
Latin America	780
Asia	5284
Europe	820
Middle East	721
Oceania	58

SOURCE: *Population Reference Bureau 2013*

role and the empowerment of women is critical to a responsible healthy demography (Tucker 2006). Given these population projections, the basic elements of the Millennium Development Goals are not just wishful or wistful thinking—they may be necessary for our continued survival (PRB 2013; O'Neill and Balk 2001; United Nations 2013).

References

CIA (Central Intelligence Agency). 2013. *The World Factbook*. Washington, DC. www.cia.gov/library/publications/the-world-factbook/

Cohen, Joel. 2011. "7 Billion." *New York Times*. October 24, A10.

O'Neil, Brian, and Deborah Balk. 2001. "World Population Futures." *Population Bulletin* 56, No. 3 (September).

PRB (Population Reference Bureau). 2013. "World Population Data Sheet, 2013." http://www.prb.org/pdf13/2013-population-data-sheet_eng.pdf.

Tucker, Patrick. 2006. "Strategies for Containing Population Growth," *The Futurist* 40, no. 5, (Sept/Oct): 13–14.

United Nations. 2013. *UN Millennium Development Goals*. www.un.org/millennium goals 2013.

Conclusion

In 2000 the United Nations established a set of eight Millennium Development Goals to improve the future by harnessing globalization as a positive force in the world. All 189 United Nations member states committed to help achieve these goals, as did many international development agencies.

Table C.1

Goal 1: Eradicate extreme poverty and hunger

Goal 2: Achieve universal primary education

Goal 3: Promote gender equality and empower women

Goal 4: Reduce child mortality rates

Goal 5: Improve maternal health

Goal 6: Combat HIV/AIDS, malaria, and other diseases

Goal 7: Ensure environmental sustainability

Goal 8: Develop a global partnership for development

These goals range from eradicating extreme poverty to combating the spread of HIV/AIDS and achieving universal primary education—all by 2015 (United Nations 2007). As we approach the target date, we see that progress toward these goals has been spotty at best.

The United Nations reaffirmed, as part of the Millennium Goals debate, a goal that highly developed countries should commit 0.07 percent of their GNP to the needs of developing countries. While the European Union (EU) has agreed to this goal, and four EU countries have exceeded it, other wealthy nations have set their own goals. Australia, for example, set a goal of giving 0.05 percent of GNP. Still other countries, led by the United States, have balked at setting any specific targets.

The reluctance of developed countries to commit large sums to global development has been exacerbated by the global economic crisis, and the social and political unrest that has arisen as political parties find themselves unable to meet the economic expectations of their constituents. The complexity of the problems they address will require sustained efforts over many years. For example, achieving universal primary education requires an understanding of the historical trends, spatial organization, economic costs and benefits, political mechanisms, and cultural variables of education, both internationally and locally in each country and region. Achieving this level of understanding requires an interdisciplinary approach.

ADOPTING THE INTERDISCIPLINARY APPROACH

An interdisciplinary approach to global issues requires the application of basic methodological and theoretical assumptions of several disciplines to the understanding of an issue. It seeks a holistic approach that borrows the strengths of all the constituent disciplines.

Because we often think about global issues in terms of real or potential conflict, political science often seems the most relevant discipline. Political science assumes that all social units are political—not only countries but families, communities, enterprises, alliances, and all others. They are political in that their members organize and disagree around issues of resource allocation, behavioral norms, and ownership of authority. Political science teaches us to put conflict at the center of understanding an issue, and seeks to analyze relations of conflict and power.

Political science urges us to ask the question: How is power distributed and used to manage conflict? Following the political science approach means locating stakeholders in an event or situation, determining what each has at risk, and analyzing how relations of power are distributed and used to manage conflict.

The economic approach supplements these descriptions by offering effective explanatory mechanisms for the behaviors of the stakeholders in the situation you are trying to understand. Economics assumes that all social units act rationally, and that individuals, groups, and states will always seek to maximize their gains and minimize their losses as best they can, given their understanding of the situation.

The economic approach seeks to understand the behavior of stake-holders in a situation—and predict how they will act in the future—by describing what each stakeholder risks and what they stand to gain. An economic perspective prompts us to ask: What are the costs and benefits of particular courses of action for the various stakeholders?

Anthropology offers an important series of correctives for this political-economic framework. First, anthropology reminds us that knowledge of how the system works can differ according to different perspectives, so that what appears irrational from an analytical point of view may appear quite rational to actors operating according to different cultural logics. Second, anthropology suggests that in addition to power and wealth, social actors may view principles and values as significant. A social actor might act quite rationally to maximize *symbolic* capital (values, principles, religious beliefs) or *social* capital (status, reputation, honor, belonging) in addition to, or even instead of, economic (wealth) and political (power) capital. Anthro-pology urges us to ask: What do these events mean to the peoples involved in them, and how do these beliefs and values shape their interactions?

Geography and history add important dimensions to analysis of global issues by expanding the scope of inquiry to consider the past, and environ-mental capacities and constraints. Geography assumes the importance of the relationships between groups of people and the places where they live. It emphasizes the description and analysis of the relations between people, space, and environment, and urges us to broaden our analysis from the actors in a conflict to broader contexts: population shifts, environmental changes, ecological impacts. It also calls on us to look at constraints that might not occur to us when looking strictly at the actions of the people involved. How might a dam built in one country create further problems for the nations downriver? Are there enough consumers to make a free-market solution feasible? How can international groups be resettled if their traditional lands can no longer support them because of environmental degradation? Many apparently political conflicts have important spatial and environmental contexts. Geography, then, urges us to ask: How are the events I'm analyzing shaped by spatial environments—and vice versa?

History adds a temporal context that is crucial for understanding con-temporary conflicts and even more important for developing solutions. The historical approach reminds us that every people has a past, and they draw on that past to understand who they are, and to explain and inter-pret current events. History seeks to create chronological description and analysis of events in the development of a people or institution, including explanation of, and commentary on, those events. Historical approaches thus teach us to ask: How did things get to where they are now?

This set of key questions brings together the five international studies disciplines described in this book.

But the disciplines described in this textbook are not the only ones that can be brought to bear on understanding international problems. Other interdisciplinary approaches might include environmental studies, sociology, gender studies, comparative religions, or other disciplines in addition to, or in place of, some of those discussed in this book. What is important is developing a holistic approach that encourages us to look at the ways power, wealth, culture, and physical environments interact in complex international issues, and how these relations have changed over time, so that we can begin thinking about solutions.

SOLUTION-ORIENTED ANALYSIS

Using interdisciplinary thinking to analyze global issues usually takes place in three basic stages. The first is identification and description of the issue, usually focused on some form of conflict between social groups; second, a description of how those concerned in the problem have tried to fix it, and why these solutions haven't worked; finally, recommendations for a way forward that might successfully overcome the obstacles that caused those earlier efforts to fail. Following these three steps can help produce analyses of issues that can be expressed in many ways, from short, eight-hundred-word op-ed pieces to twenty-page reports to lengthy, detailed policy-analysis papers running more than seventy-five pages.

The first step is identification of a global issue. This can be a global issue such as one of the millennial goals, or an issue of international foreign policy such as Turkey's membership in the European Union, or a relatively small-scale problem of social inequity such as reducing cholera outbreaks in a Brazilian *favela* (squatter community).

Once you have identified the issue, you need to begin to unpack it, asking to whom the issue is a problem and why. You need to identify the stakeholders, and explain what rewards and risks each of them face, and how power relations are organized between them. You need to examine the wider political, cultural, and geographical contexts in which the issue is embedded.

Table C.2 POLITICAL SCIENCE

- **Key Assumption:** All social units form families to organize around and disagree about issues of resource allocation, behavioral norms, and ownership of authority.
- **Definition:** Description and analysis of relations of conflict and power.
- **Key Question:** *How is power distributed and used to manage conflict?*

ECONOMICS

- **Key Assumption:** All societies must transform nature through labor into goods that they can exchange or consume.
- **Definition:** Description and analysis of the production, distribution, and consumption of goods.
- **Key Question:** *What are the costs and benefits of particular courses of action for the various stakeholders?*

ANTHROPOLOGY

- **Key Assumption:** All human social action makes sense when understood within its own contexts.
- **Definition:** Description and analysis of the shared, learned systems of meaning members of societies use to orient themselves in the world and to render human action predictable.
- **Key Question:** *What do these events mean to the peoples involved in them and how do these beliefs and values shape their interactions?*

GEOGRAPHY

- **Key Assumption:** Every group of people lives in a place and interacts with the features of that place.
- **Definition:** The description and analysis of the relations between people, space, and environment.
- **Key Question:** *How are the events I'm analyzing shaped by ecologies and environments—and vice versa?*

HISTORY

- **Key Assumption:** Every people has a past, and they draw on that past to understand who they are, and to explain and interpret current events.
- **Definition:** Chronological description and analysis of events in the development of a people or institution, including explanation of or commentary on those events.
- **Key Question:** *How did things get to where they are now?*

Appropriate technologies refers to the low-cost technologies using local materials to create technologies useful in specific social and environmental contexts.

Fair Trade is a system of international exchange that seeks to intervene in the market by setting a minimum price for paying producers of export goods.

Microfinancing involves providing small-scale financial services including loans, savings accounts, funds transfers, and insurance to low-income clients or groups, who traditionally lack access to banking services.

Social entrepreneurship refers to the use of entrepreneurial principles to create, organize, and manage ventures designed to produce social change.

In the second stage, you need to describe the history of the issue, paying special attention to efforts at solutions. Again, it will take interdisciplinary thinking to explore why each possible solution tried in the past has failed. Many of your sources may give different reasons for the failure of a solution based on their own disciplinary assumptions. By reading these accounts against each other, you can come to a broader, more comprehensive understanding.

The third stage requires you to define a clear goal for your solution, including the criteria used for choosing the recommended solution. A specific course of action for implementing the solution should be spelled out along with, if possible, strategies for managing those problems, and any consequences you can foresee on the basis of your analysis.

Often, as you begin to analyze a global issue, you will find that it is just too big. In this case, it is useful to pare it down to manageable size. There are two common ways to do this. First, you can reduce the scale of the problem—instead of tackling the entire Palestinian-Israeli conflict, focus on one piece such as school parity in Jerusalem, conflict between Israeli settlers and the Palestinian villages on whose land the new building projects encroach, or the inability of Hamas to control armed gangs within Gaza. Second, you can choose one stakeholder as your "client" and focus on the issue from their perspective—in what aspects of the problem is this group interested, and does it have agency for resolving part of the issue?

One of the biggest problems with finding solutions for global problems is that most people seek to replicate such common solutions as new regulation, specialized education, or international dialogue, envisioning top-down programs administered through national government agencies or global agencies like the World Bank or United Nations. While there is an important place for these solutions, increasingly successful solutions involve creativity and innovation.

Sources of Innovative Solutions

In 2007, a team of four undergraduates from Miami University in Ohio won an international competition open to professionals and graduate students. The Massachusetts' Institute of Technology's Just Jerusalem 2050 competition (http://web.mit.edu/cis/jerusalem2050/) challenged competitors to imagine small projects that could make a positive change toward a just and sustainable future Jerusalem. The students entered in the "economic" category and focused on the city's rapidly dwindling water resources.

Initially, every solution they imagined from better wastewater management to water conservation regulations had already been implemented by the Israeli state, with indifferent results. And these solutions relied on top-down implementation by the Israeli state—which risked making water a political flashpoint. At last they began to research bottom-up strategies, water-management techniques that had worked successfully without state regulation. They found one in water harvesting—a simple technology involving collection of rainwater by households through cisterns that could dramatically alter stress on Jerusalem's water system, and one that could be managed through training and microloans from the UN Environmental Programme, which has extensive experience with the technology.

These kinds of low-cost, high-impact bottom-up solutions to manageable pieces of larger problems are increasingly the direction toward which solution-oriented analysis aims. There are many sources of innovative solutions, including leveraging inequities, fair trade, social entrepreneurship, appropriate technologies, and microfinancing.

Leveraging Inequities

In 1999, a first grader in Canada named Ryan Hreljac learned that many people in Africa do not have clean drinking water. Ryan began saving up the $2,000 it would take to pay for a well. His devotion to this cause, over several months, attracted the attention of a local newspaper, then a local television station, and soon donations came in and Ryan was able to team with an NGO called Water Can (www.watercan.com) to build a well.

Today, as a college student, Hreljac runs the Ryan's Well Foundation (www.ryanswell.ca), which has raised millions of dollars and helped build over 680 wells and 820 latrines bringing safe water and improved sanitation to over 723,000 people, mostly in Africa.

Hreljac's success depends on two fundamental principles. The first is that global inequities in the distribution of wealth mean that a middle-class Canadian boy has access to resources undreamed of by most adults in the world's poorest countries. In addition to the fact that money buys more in poorer countries than in wealthy ones (drilling a well in Canada would typically cost more than five times what it does in rural Africa), people in developed countries enjoy advantages of infrastructure. Access to media outlets, educational opportunities, automobile ownership, good roads, frequent flyer miles, personal computers, reliable telephone service, leisure time—can all serve as multipliers that make the work of philanthropic organizations easier and more effective.

In interviews, Hreljac has also insisted on a second lesson, which he calls "the power of one"—one person who devotes part of his or her time consistently to a cause can accomplish significant things while still leading a normal life. Hreljac himself has traveled internationally, met popes and presidents, and appeared on talk shows promoting the foundation, while also maintaining a healthy social life and extracurricular activities in school.

This principle is increasingly being used not only by philanthropies in the developed world but by people in developing countries seeking to improve conditions at home. For example, while struggling with school and the famine conditions that destroyed many families in Malawi, fourteen-year-old William Kamkwamba figured out how to build a windmill out of discarded engine components, PVC pipe, and bicycle parts to provide free electricity to his family's house. Teaming with philanthropists and entrepreneurs both in Africa and the developed world, he has begun working toward developing small windmills for use in his village and elsewhere in Malawi (Kamkwamba and Mealer 2009).

Fair Trade

While leveraging global inequities to fund assistance to the international poor is a classic component of philanthropic approaches, another rising approach is to transform the trade system to make it more equitable, and improve the lives of small producers within the market system. The most common example of this is **fair trade**, a system of trading partnerships that seeks to intervene in the market by setting a minimum price for paying producers of export goods. The extra cost of this minimum price is shared by the fair-trade wholesalers (using practices such as maximum wages for executives) and consumers, who often pay a small premium for fair-trade commodities.

Knowing how much they can expect to earn for their produce regardless of global market fluctuations allows local farmers in developing countries to plan ahead, expand their businesses, and take out loans. Many form cooperatives and pool their money to build schools or clinics, or create projects (like coffee roasteries) that add value to their product.

Fair trade has become a small but important part of global trade, especially in such commodities as bananas and other fresh fruits, cocoa and chocolate, coffee, cotton, flowers, handicrafts, honey, sugar, tea, and wine. As of 2010, roughly 27,000 certified fair-trade products were being sold in over seventy countries, with estimated sales amounting to $4.6 billion (FTLO 2010).

One common criticism of fair trade is that it reduces market efficiency. This is not always true. Some fair-trade practices recover efficiencies by creating more direct relationships between producers and retailers and cutting out middlemen (in the coffee trade, for example, there will sometimes be as many as seven middlemen from local bulk buyers to shippers to roasters, each adding their expenses and profit margin to the retail price). Another study argued that fair trade actually creates efficiencies by bringing exploitative conditions in developing countries more closely in line with the ideal market conditions assumed in most economic analyses (Hayes and Moore 2005).

Social Entrepreneurship

Social entrepreneurship refers to the use of entrepreneurial principles to create, organize, and manage ventures designed to produce social change. Successful entrepreneurship is understood to involve innovative, risky, solution-oriented activities that can further social and environmental goals. Social entrepreneurship is held up by advocates as a counter to the principles that get in the way of typical government and NGO-run projects: brief political cycles, demands for instant results, a desire to minimize risk and avoid blame, and an unwillingness to make difficult decisions that might be seen as unfair.

Most social entrepreneurship starts with building relationships in local communities, and identifying innovative and energetic individuals who can be provided with the means to establish sustainable social projects. Once established, these ventures are operated by committed and capable teams with vested interests in the outcomes, rewarded on the basis of measurable performance (Mawson 2008).

Appropriate Technologies

Many philanthropic projects seek to improve technological access in communities with underdeveloped infrastructures so that they can use these to improve their opportunities. The One Laptop per Child trade association, a US-based nonprofit organization created by faculty members of the MIT Media Lab, seeks to design, manufacture, and distribute $100 laptops so that every child in the world can have one (www.laptop.org). But artifacts like laptops assume other aspects of infrastructure—dust-free houses, reliable current, working telephone lines—that may not be available. And for the more than one billion people globally who live on $1 per day, even a $100 laptop may be hopelessly out of reach.

An alternative to giving people access to technologies common in the West is to develop technologies that are appropriate to different environmental and infrastructural contexts. In Sitio Malagaya, a squatter community of brick houses with tin roofs built along a seven-mile stretch of unused railroad track in the Philippines, a man named Ilac Diaz fills soda bottles with water, seals them, and installs them on rooftops, allowing the sun's rays to shine through with nearly the brightness of a sixty-watt lightbulb (http://isanglitrongliwanag.org).

Designed and developed by students from the Massachusetts Institute of Technology (MIT), the solar bottle bulb is an example of "appropriate technology"—an effort to provide simple and easily replicable technologies that address basic needs in developing communities. **Appropriate technologies** refers to the low-cost technologies using local materials to create technologies useful in specific social and environmental contexts. Bicycle-powered water pumps, self-contained solar-powered lightbulbs and streetlights, coal made from sugar cane and corn cobs, clay-pot food preservers, and many other inexpensive devices have had major impacts on people's lives, without the enormous infrastructural requirements of Western industrialization.

Microfinance

Projects in social entrepreneurship, fair trade, and appropriate technologies are sometimes funded through NGOs and philanthropies, but also often through microfinancing. **Microfinancing** involves providing small-scale financial services including loans, savings accounts, funds transfers, and insurance to low-income clients or groups, who traditionally lack access to banking services. While microfinancing is driven by ideology—efforts to alleviate poverty by enabling people to help themselves through entrepreneurship, financing educations, or facilitating savings—it is intended to be sustainable by turning a small profit on its investments.

Although microfinance can fail spectacularly, it has also provided a large number of successes. The success of microfinance seems to depend heavily on lending institutions rooted in the communities in which they provide services.

CONCLUSION

Commentators from P. J. O'Rourke to the late Steve Jobs have remarked that innovation is critical to our global future. The United States, Europe, and Japan are still leaders in research and development. To make such innovation work, however, will require more than solving of technological problems. An international studies perspective that combines geography, history, political science, anthropology, and economics (or, to phrase them in another way, population, past, power, people, and production) will be well placed to analyze and resolve these issues. International matters such as demography, information and communication technologies, war, peace, poverty, terrorism, and pollution, to name a few, demand a global integrative approach.

Our examination of the world has taken us around the globe by way of Europe, Asia, Latin America, the Middle East, and Africa. We have utilized the prisms of geography, history, political science, anthropology, and economics to scrutinize global issues such as terrorism, the persistence of war, and international tourism. We have stressed the interconnectedness of countries within regions, and regions within a global world system.

The intense cultural, economic, and political interactions among peoples and places have spread rapidly across space and time, creating ever greater levels of complexity. The last hundred years have seen incredible leaps in science and technology. Electricity lit up the Eiffel Tower at the Paris Exposition of 1900, and it still powers our computers and televisions. Electric cars may be the future of transport. Films and the escalator were also featured at the exhibition; today these technologies are ubiquitous.

People living at the beginning of the twentieth century could not have foreseen World War I, World War II, and the Cold War. Nor could they have foreseen television, computers, and the Internet. As we gaze ahead to the future from the vantage points of history, geography, political science, anthropology, and economics, we can only make educated guesses about what the world will look like in the next hundred years. As one scholar put it, "we can't predict the future, but that is not terribly significant. What is more important is that we can envision the future we want and set about making it happen" (Hammond 1999). Whatever global challenges face future generations, the interdisciplinary methodology of international studies is essential to finding solutions.

References

FTLO (Fairtrade Labeling Organizations). 2010. *Growing Stronger Together: Annual Report 2009–2010.* http://www.fairtrade.net/fileadmin/user_upload/content/2009/resources/FLO_Annual-Report-2009_komplett_double_web.pdf.

Hammond, A. 1999. Three Global Scenarios. *The Futurist* (April): 38–43.

Hayes, Mark, and Geoff Moore. 2005. *The Economics of Fair Trade: A Guide in Plain English.* Durham Business School International Workshop on the Economics of Fair Trade. http://www.udbs.dur.ac.uk/fairtraderesearch/The%20Economics%20of%20Fair%20Trade%20plain%20guide.pdf.

Kamkwamba, William, and Bryan Mealer. 2009. *The Boy Who Harnessed the Wind.* New York: William Morrow.

Mawson, Andrew. 2008. *The Social Entrepreneur: Making Communities Work.* London: Atlantic Books.

United Nations. 2007. UN Millennium Goals Indicators. www.un.org/millennium goals.

Further Reading

Arrillaga-Andreessen, Laura. 2011. *Giving 2.0: Transform Your Giving and Our World.* San Francisco: Jossey-Bass.

Bornstein, David. 2005. *How to Change the World: Social Entrepreneurs and the Power of New Ideas.* New York: Oxford University Press.

Eckaus, Richard S. 2009. *Appropriate Technologies for Developing Countries.* Washington, DC: National Academies.

Helms, Brigit. 2006. *Access for All: Building Inclusive Financial Systems.* Washington, DC: Consultative Group to Assist the Poor.

Schumacher, E. F. 1973. *Small Is Beautiful: A Study of Economics As If People Mattered*. London: Blond and Briggs.

Yunus, Muhammad. 2007. *Creating a World Without Poverty: Social Business and the Future of Capitalism*. New York: PublicAffairs.

Websites

Ashoka: Innovators for the Public. http://www.ashoka.org

AVAAZ: The World In Action. www.avaaz.org

Fair Trade International. http://www.fairtrade.net

Kiva: Empower People around the World for $25. www.kiva.org

The Schwab Foundation for Social Entrepreneurship. http://www.schwabfound .org

TED: Ideas Worth Spreading. http://www.ted.com/

Glossary

African Union (AU). Formed in 2001, the African Union was an outgrowth of the Organization of African Unity (1963). The AU has made halting steps toward creating a larger African tariff area and establishing peacekeeping forces, watchdog organizations, and political units.

aliyah. From a Hebrew word meaning "ascent," this refers to emigration by Jews from their country of residence to Palestine and, after 1948, to Israel.

allocation state. A government that does not derive its revenues from taxation but rather by selling key resources on the world market and using the proceeds to fund governmental operations like schools, roads, and hospitals. Also called a *rentier state.*

American dream. Term describing an American worldview that proposes that all people have, or should have, opportunities to achieve material prosperity through hard work.

American politics. The branch of political science that focuses on US governmental and political institutions and behavior.

anarchy. The absence of government; the global structure within which states operate.

Andes. The dominant mountain range of western South America; the Andean region includes Ecuador, Bolivia, Peru, Colombia, and Venezuela.

anti-Semitism. For centuries, Jews in Europe faced discrimination from Christians because Jews rejected New Testament claims that Jesus was the Son of God. Modern anti-Semitism added economic and racial elements, which the Nazis exploited and used as a rationale for the Holocaust.

apartheid. Apartheid was the legal system of white rule in South Africa that denied black South Africans equal rights. It was overturned in 1990, leading to black majority rule in 1994.

appropriate technology. Technologies that are appropriate to specific local needs and infrastructures.

Arab Spring. Western media term for a series of uprisings in the Middle East that began in 2010–2011. Demands of Arab Spring protestors ranged from greater representation in government, and greater responsiveness from government, to the ouster of authoritarian regimes.

Arab world. Term used to collectively describe the twenty-two Arabic-speaking countries of the world, from Morocco to Iraq, as a single geopolitical unit of some 325 million people.

arbitrary. A meaning is said to be arbitrary when it relies entirely on social convention and has no natural or essential basis. Most linguistic and cultural symbols are arbitrary.

arkaan. The Five Pillars of Islam; a set of practices concerning profession of faith, along with prayer, fasting, charity, and pilgrimage that are designed to shape faithful adherents to the practices into better Muslims.

Association of Southeast Asian Nations (ASEAN). Political-economic organization of Southeast Asia.

authoritarianism. Like fascism and Nazism, authoritarianism relies on the principle of one strong dictator to unify a country under nationalist slogans, but, unlike fascism, usually relies on support from military, business, and church elites.

balance of power. An important concept in realist theory by which self-interested powerful states achieve a stable global system through actions that offset one another's power.

Basques. Members of an ethnic group in northern Spain that has sought greater autonomy from the central government in Madrid. Their rights were suppressed under the dictatorship of Francisco Franco (1936–1975), breeding a terrorist organization (ETA) that sought an independent state.

behaviorism. A methodological approach to social science that emphasizes data collection and the scientific method.

Bolshevik Revolution. Led by Vladimir Ilyich Lenin, the Bolsheviks overthrew the Russian government in 1917, instituting nearly seventy-five years of Communist rule. Until the Soviet Union collapsed in 1991, Western liberal democracy was challenged by the Soviets.

Buddhism. Religious system based on the teachings of Gautama Buddha. Divided into Mahayana in East Asia (including Zen in Japan), Theravada in Southeast Asia, and Vajrayana (or Tibetan Buddhism) in Tibet.

burqa. Head-to-foot pleated gown with an eye screen worn by women in parts of Afghanistan and Pakistan.

caliph. Leader of the worldwide Muslim community; political successor to Muhammad.

capital. Durable goods like cash, factories, manufacturing equipment, tools, and so forth that are used to create goods and services for exchange in a market.

capital flight. The tendency for wealth to leave poor countries rather than trickle down from the wealthy to the middle classes.

carrying capacity. In environmental economics, the maximum population size an environment can sustain indefinitely, given the finite resources available in the environment, the technologies people use to exploit them, and the wastes produced as a by-product.

caudillo. Latin American military leader following independence from Spain in the early nineteenth century. The tradition of the Latin American military dictator (caudillismo) continued well into the twentieth century.

causation. Historians explain historical events in different ways depending upon their theory of causation, such as political, economic, and environmental forces, ideology, or social structure.

Central Asia. Afghanistan, Uzbekistan, and Kazakhstan are the principal countries in this region of Asia.

chaebol. A Korean megacorporation.

class struggle. Karl Marx theorized that historical change is driven by conflicts between classes; he called for the working classes to overthrow the capitalist classes to create a Communist system.

classical liberalism. Enlightenment thinker Adam Smith is most remembered for the anti-mercantilist idea that economies grow and wealth is accumulated faster when the government takes a laissez-faire approach and allows the "invisible hand" of supply and demand to operate freely.

coalition. A government or other political body that shares power among two or more political parties.

Cold War. Battle of liberal democratic and communist ideologies and geo-strategy between the United States and the Soviet Union after World War II to the end of the 1980s.

collective security. A system by which states ally to protect each other against external threat.

colonial rule. European countries established formal colonial rule over most of Africa and Asia by 1885, drawing illegitimate boundaries and exploiting human and natural resources.

colonialism. The political, economic, and cultural domination of African, American, Asian, and Middle Eastern societies by European powers.

Common Market. *See* European Economic Community.

common sense. The set of unstated assumptions we share with others in our community that we most rely on in making sense of the world around us. It is what we accept to be true without questioning or analyzing it.

communism. Karl Marx's anti-capitalist theory envisioned a classless society in which the proletariat owned the means of production, and people worked according to their ability and took according to their needs. Lenin ushered in Communism into the Soviet Union in 1917, but Marxists might claim that the Soviet system was a dictatorship of the party rather than a true dictatorship of the proletariat.

comparative advantage. This economic principle states that gains from trade follow from encouraging an economy to specialize its production. First presented by David Ricardo in 1817, if a country is *relatively* better at making one product than another, it makes sense to put more resources into that product and to use the returns from selling it to obtain those products less efficiently produced in your own economy.

comparative politics. The branch of political science that focuses on governmental and political institutions and behaviors outside the United States. It often relies on comparative methodologies.

comparison. By comparing the many different ways human communities solve the same problems, this anthropological perspective seeks to avoid mistakenly assuming that one set of practices or system of knowledge is natural or necessary.

complex interdependence. A theory or situation marked by strong connections among nations and states that make these actors mutually vulnerable and sensitive.

Confucianism. Chinese philosophical system of social order and reciprocity.

conservative nationalism. Leaders who seek to preserve their power and the socioeconomic order use pride in nation and fear of an enemy nation as a means to unify the masses and prevent domestic unrest.

constitutional monarchy. A king or queen from a royal family acts as the head of state, but the real political power rests with a democratically elected legislative branch.

criollos. Latin American–born people of European descent. During the colonial period the *criollos* dominated politics and led independence movements.

cultural and social history. The study of the history of music, food, sports, language, religion, family, gender, and other elements of culture and society.

cultural logic. The underlying mechanism that generates meaningful human action.

cultural misunderstanding. A failure of communication created by people or communities using different cultural logics to understand each other's speech and action.

cultural practices. Everyday activities of people in a particular community, as well as the artifacts they employ.

culture. A learned system of meanings by which people orient themselves in the world so that they can act in it. Culture relies on a universal human capacity to differentiate and to categorize experience.

culture shock. The unpleasant, even traumatic, feeling people get when the rules and understandings by which they have organized their lives do not apply.

Darfur. A western region of Sudan. It has experienced a civil conflict in the first decade of the twenty-first century that has taken some two hundred thousand lives. Some observers accuse the Sudanese government of condoning the genocide of non-Arab peoples.

decolonization. The end of control by imperialist powers, which leads to the independence of the countries they formerly controlled as colonies.

demand. Demand represents the amount of a good that buyers are willing to purchase at a range of prices with the assumption that all other factors remain constant. Demand is represented in a demand curve that is almost always a downwards-sloping curve demonstrating that as the price for a good decreases, consumers will buy more of the good.

demand curve. Graphic representation of the relationship between price and demand.

demand schedule. A list of goods that buyers are willing to buy at a certain price.

democide. The murder of a person or persons by the government tasked to protect them.

democracy. A form of governmental rule in which leaders are chosen by some form of electoral process.

Deng Xiaoping (1904–1997). Leader of China from 1978 to 1992.

dependency theory. An economic theory that finds Latin American poverty and stalled growth a product of the region's dependence on more advanced economies in the north.

determinism. The theoretical assumption that human intentions and efforts are largely irrelevant because all events are shaped by the events that preceded them, as well as by natural laws and conditions.

development. The process of improving the quality of human life.

dialectic. In Marxism, the dialectic refers to the continuous contest between two social classes, the capitalists and the workers, resulting in a social transformation.

diaspora. From a Greek word for "dispersal," this term is used to describe transnational communities of peoples who maintain a distinct identity in the host communities in which they settle, often through a sense of connection to a common homeland.

diffusion. The spread of cultural practices through migration or conquest, as well as through indirect contact such as trade and mass media.

East Asia. China, Japan, North Korea, and South Korea are the principal countries of this region of Asia.

ecological economics. Branch of economics rooted in the principle that realistic economic projections needed to include costs of environmental and ecological damage such as pollution and resource loss.

economic history. The study of the exchange of goods and services. Economic historians seek insight into economic trends that might inform future economic and business decisions.

economic nationalism. Economic paradigm in which economies are viewed as integrally connected to social, political, and cultural systems, and in which states should seek to intervene in markets to protect national labor, trade production, and wealth accumulation.

economics. The social science that studies, describes, models, and makes projections about flows of wealth in the process of the production, distribution, and consumption of scarce resources, by focusing on the choices made by individuals about alternative uses of scarce resources to satisfy needs and wants.

EEC. *See* European Economic Community.

embodiment. Cultural learning that shapes our bodies and unconscious behaviors, including such things as how we speak, how we move, how we eat, and our comfort level in relation to the proximity of other people.

empirical. Type of knowledge derived from direct observation and careful recording of information.

enculturation. The processes by which members of a society pass on culture to new generations.

environment. Our physical world.

environmental determinism. Simplistic belief that human events can be explained entirely as a result of the physical environment.

environmental history. A field of history devoted to people's interaction with their natural surroundings, such as water usage, farming practices, food distribution, and marine and forest preservation.

environmental possibilism. Theory that the physical environment does not determine what people attempt though it does limit what people can achieve.

equilibrium. When the demand for a good equals the supply of that good, the market for that good is said to be in equilibrium.

ETA. *See* Euskadi Ta Askatasuna.

euro. Currency of the European Union.

European Coal and Steel Community (ECSC). Created by "the Six" (West Germany, France, Italy, Belgium, Netherlands, and Luxembourg) in 1951 to regulate coal and steel production. The ECSC was so successful that its six members agreed to form the European Economic Community in 1957.

European Economic Community (EEC). A group of six European countries (France, Germany, Italy, and the Benelux countries) joined together in

1957 to lower tariffs on trade as a whole and create a common external tariff. Also called the Common Market. The European Economic Community evolved into the European Union.

European Union (EU). Formed in 1992, the European Union has eliminated most borders among its twenty-seven members and implemented currency unification (the euro). It coordinates foreign and defense policies.

Eurozone. Area in Europe in which the common European monetary unit (the euro) is the only accepted currency.

Euskadi Ta Askatasuna (ETA). Basque terrorist organization seeking independence from Spanish rule for the Basque territories.

evil eye. Widespread belief in Mediterranean cultures that a look inspired by envy or anger can cause injury or bad luck for the person at whom it is directed.

evolution. Anthropological assumption that all social and cultural systems are in a continual state of change.

exchange rate. The value of one country's currency compared to that of another.

expressive culture. Institutions through which a community articulates and elaborates its worldview in various symbolic forms, such as literature, art, drama, myth, ritual, and mass media.

failed state. A central government that has lost control of parts of the country it governs.

fair trade. A system of trading partnerships that intervenes in the market by setting a minimum price for export goods, protecting producers from severe economic shocks.

fascism. Benito Mussolini capitalized on Italy's wounded national pride and political and economic turmoil from World War I to overthrow the constitutional monarchy in 1922. Mussolini's fascism was a far-right mass movement that played on people's grievances.

Fertile Crescent. A region of river valleys, arcing from the Nile Valley of Egypt to Mesopotamia (modern Iraq), where the invention of agriculture led to the rise of some of the world's earliest cities and empires.

fieldwork. Collective term for a number of social science research methods that require periods of residence among the people studied.

formal learning. The acquisition of cultural knowledge that takes place within institutions specifically designed for this purpose, such as schools, apprenticeships, and on-the-job training.

formal region. A region defined by a uniformity of features.

functional region. A region defined by interaction among localities.

fusha. Pronounced foos-ha. Proper Arabic, that is, the classical Arabic of the Quran and of medieval literature. Today, it is primarily a literary language.

G8. *See* Group of Eight.

G20. *See* Group of Twenty.

GATT. *See* General Agreement on Tariffs and Trade.

GDP. *See* gross domestic product.

General Agreement on Tariffs and Trade (GATT). Provided a framework to gradually reduce barriers to freer trade between states. In 1995, GATT evolved into the World Trade Organization, which is dedicated to arbitrating international trade disputes and further lowering trade barriers.

generation of similarity. Function of social institutions and processes such as family, school, peer groups, and mass media to teach and reinforce common beliefs, values, orientations, and models for action among members of a community.

geographic definition. Boundaries of a continent, country, or other area defined by a geographic description of its borders.

geographic information system (GIS). A computerized mapping system that stores and analyzes many layers of data.

geography. Study of the interaction of physical and human phenomena at individual places and of how interactions among places form patterns and organize space.

globalization. The expansion of global communication and market connections, growing social and political interdependencies on a global scale, and the development of a planetary rather than national awareness among many of the world's people. The increasing interconnectedness around the world through economic, political, and cultural change.

Great Economic Crisis. A sharp downturn in the world economy that began in the United States in 2008 and has had devastating, worldwide consequences.

gross domestic product (GDP). A way of measuring the size of a country's economy; usually defined as the market value of all goods and services produced within a country in a given period of time.

Group of Eight (G8). The Group of Eight (G8) is an international forum for the governments of France, Japan, Italy, Germany, Canada, the United Kingdom, Russia, and the United States. These countries account for about 65 percent of the total global economic production as well as the largest proportion of global military power.

Group of Twenty (G20). A group of finance ministers and central bank governors from 20 major economies—19 countries and the European Union—that gathers annually in a summit to discuss the state of the worldwide economy.

hadith. Collected accounts of sayings and actions of the prophet Muhammad and his companions.

hegemon. A global or regional leader whose leadership is recognized by members of the group.

hijab. A head scarf, which covers the hair and neck, worn by some Middle Eastern Muslim women.

Hinduism. The oldest religious system in Asia and the dominant religion of India.

historical definition. A country, continent, or other area that is defined by events that occurred in its history.

historical materialism. Contrasted with philosophical idealism, historical materialism is the method for studying history and social systems advocated by Karl Marx that places the material conditions of life as primary in forming social and ideological contexts.

historiography. Summary critiques of other historians' work on a particular subject.

holism. Anthropological perspective that seeks to understand human societies as complex systems with many interwoven elements.

human determinism. Simplistic belief that people can shape the land into any form without regard to environmental consequences.

idealism/liberalism. Theory that explains political behavior as a function of moral human decisions, institutional structures, and collective interest.

identity. The feeling a person has as a member of a group or community, as well as the set of associations others may ascribe to a person as a member of a group.

ideology. The mobilization of cultural symbols to create, sustain, or resist unequal distribution of rights, responsibilities, and control over resources in a society.

IMF. *See* International Monetary Fund.

imperial borders. European imperialists finalized the borders of Africa at the Berlin Conference in 1884–1885. The borders they drew have little relation to natural boundaries or ethnic divisions.

imperialism. Political, economic, and cultural domination of a country or area by another country.

import quotas. Limitations placed on the importation of certain goods to protect a certain segment of a country's domestic industry.

import substitution industrialization (ISI). The dominant economic model in Latin America during the 1960s and 1970s, import substitution industrialization called for national industries to provide previously imported goods.

independent Africa. Beginning with Ghana in 1956 and ending with Mozambique and Angola in 1975, all of the African states gained their independence from the European imperialists.

informal economy. Economic activity that is not monitored by a government and therefore is not taxed or included in the country's gross domestic product.

informal learning. Learning that we engage in simply by watching, listening, and participating in everyday activities.

intellectual history. Historical study of the development and influence of ideologies such as religion, nationalism, liberalism, Marxism, and feminism.

intercultural relations. Flows of symbols across cultural boundaries facilitated by transnational migration, new information technologies, and global markets, which can lead to creativity and innovation but also to misunderstanding and conflict.

international economics. Focused on financial and trade relations of national economies and the effects of international trade and finance on the distribution of production, income, and wealth around the world and within nations.

International Monetary Fund (IMF). An international organization that provides financial assistance to nations with financial problems and monitors the global financial system, observing changes in currency exchange rates and national balances of payments.

international politics. Branch of political science that focuses on transnational political behavior.

international relations. A subfield of political science that studies the political relationships among nations.

IRA. *See* Irish Republican Army.

Irish Republican Army (IRA). An Irish militia originally formed to protect Irish Catholics and force the British out of Ireland. After most of Ireland gained Home Rule in 1921, the Irish Republican Army evolved into a terrorist group demanding the unification of Northern Ireland with the rest of the country.

Iron Curtain. Term used to describe the western boundary of the East European countries that fell under Soviet-friendly communist regimes after World War II (East Germany, Poland, Czechoslovakia, Hungary, Romania, and Bulgaria).

ISI. *See* import substitution industrialization.

Islam. The dominant religion in the Middle East, Islam is the second-largest and fastest-growing religion in the world.

Islamic world. The total number of the world's Muslim majority countries in Asia, Africa, the Middle East, and Europe.

janjaweed. Mostly Arab militia groups in Darfur used by the Sudanese government to massacre and intimidate the African tribes in the region.

jihad. Islamic term for spiritual struggle. The term *greater jihad* refers to the individual's internal struggle against sin; the term *lesser jihad* refers to political and military struggle.

keiretsu. A Japanese business conglomerate.

khimar. A head-to-midriff covering with an oval for the face worn by some Middle Eastern and Muslim women.

kleptocracy. A regime that loots government coffers and the national economy for the leadership's personal gain.

labor history. Subfield of economic history that focuses on the development of working-class solidarity and worker relations with management and the government.

laissez-faire. Minimal government intervention in a country's economy.

latifundia. Large plantations that dominated colonial agriculture in Latin America. After independence the latifundia persisted and established a pattern of inequitable land distribution.

law of demand. Economic theory that asserts that there is an inverse relationship between the price of a good and the quantity demanded of that good.

law of supply. Economic theory that asserts that there is a direct relationship between the price of a good and the quantity of supply of the good.

Left, the. The side of the political spectrum that espouses humanitarianism and idealism in world politics, and civil liberties and government responsibility in domestic politics.

liberal democracy. A system of government that institutionalizes majority rule, has an independent judiciary, respects the rule of law, and protects the civil rights of all citizens.

liberal economic theory. Developed during the European Enlightenment, the theory emphasizes market systems that allow individuals to trade goods and services with minimal government intervention.

liberalism. The crucial tenets of liberalism in international politics include the following: (1) Humans have a capacity for good. (2) Selfish and violent behaviors come not from human nature but from institutions that promote such behavior. (3) The primary public institution leading to war is the state, because it promotes nationalism and selfishness over global welfare. (4) Multilateral action and institutions are needed to prevent war.

life expectancy. Length of life expected at birth on average.

liquidity. The capacity of an economic unit—individual, corporation, state, etc.—to pay debts when they come due without incurring unacceptable losses.

location. Where a geographic phenomenon is. Includes absolute, relative, and nominal location.

macroeconomics. The study of the combined performance of all markets in a defined market system by gathering aggregate information about nations' economies. Macroeconomics may have nation-states or global regions as its unit of analysis.

Maghreb. Arabic term for North Africa, especially the western half.

Mandela, Nelson (1918–2013). Led the African National Congress and fought apartheid in South Africa. Released after twenty-seven years in prison, his nonviolent approach eventually brought an end to white rule in 1990. President of South Africa, 1994–1999.

Mao Zedong (1893–1976). Leader of China, 1949–1976.

map. A specialized picture of mathematical precision that expresses ideas about the world. A map is a multifaceted tool that provides a concrete understanding of the relationships that locations have with other locations.

marginal utility. Theory that the goal of business is to increase the point where consumer satisfaction is gained.

markets. Markets are a series of social arrangements for buying and selling goods. In markets, consumers gather information and participate in a voluntary exchange of goods and services, thus organizing trade.

Marshall Plan. A US-financed $13-billion aid program (1948–1952) to jumpstart the Western European economies after World War II.

Marxism. In the mid-nineteenth century, Karl Marx theorized that historical development was not a clash of ideas, as Georg Wilhelm Friedrich Hegel posited, but a struggle between classes based on their material possessions. Marx advocated violent overthrow by the working classes.

Marxism-Leninism. A form of Marxist political ideology that linked Karl Marx's economic theories to a set of political theories for the development of a communist state put forward by Vladimir Lenin.

Mau Mau rebellion. The Mau Mau were mostly Kikuyu people in Kenya who rebelled against losing their land to the British. In the 1950s, thousands of Kikuyu were killed in the rebellion.

means of production. A Marxist term that refers to the tools, knowledge, capital, and raw materials needed to produce a good.

Melanesia. Region of islands in the Pacific including Papua New Guinea, the Solomon Islands, Vanuatu, and Fiji.

mercantilism. A theory of political economy that holds that the economic well-being of a nation is directly related to its degree of control over the global volume of capital.

meritocracy. A system in which people succeed according to their own skills without regard for caste, class, religion, race, ethnicity, or kinship networks.

methodological relativism. The principle that to be comparative, anthropology must treat all social practices as data of the same type.

microeconomics. Area of economics that is concerned with studying specific market systems on a small scale, such as the economic behavior of individuals, firms, and industries, to understand the relative prices of goods and services and the alternative uses to which resources can be put in a particular market system.

microfinancing. Providing small-scale loans, savings accounts, fund transfers, and other financial services to low-income clients who normally do not have access to such services.

Micronesia. Region of islands in the Pacific including Nauru, the Marshall Islands, Guam, the Mariana Islands, and the Federated States of Micronesia.

migrant labor. Any people who travel from their homes to work elsewhere, including migratory seasonal workers within a country.

military coup. Military seizure of power through undemocratic means. Africa has been plagued by recurrent military coups that have undermined the continent's political stability, economic development, and evolution toward democracy.

Millennium Development Project. In 2002, the UN General Secretary created this long-range plan to eradicate poverty, hunger, and disease in the developing world.

Modern Standard Arabic. The language of newspapers, television news programs, schools, and contemporary literature throughout the Arabic-speaking world.

monarchy. Monarchy is an authoritarian political system in which legitimacy of the head of the government is based on royal bloodlines.

monsoon. Seasonal climate change throughout South, Southeast, and East Asia.

Muslim. "One who submits [to God]." Anyone who practices some form of Islam.

Muslim world. The worldwide community of Muslims, including Muslim enclaves in non-Muslim majority countries. See also "Islamic world."

NAFTA. *See* North American Free Trade Agreement.

nakba. "The Catastrophe." Common Arab term used to refer to the establishment of the state of Israel in 1948.

nation. A people united by some common origin and character. *See also* state.

national self-determination. The theory that every people, or nation, should have the right to determine its own political system.

nationalism. Nationalism is a constructed bond between peoples of similar language, religion, history, and culture. Nationalism breeds a sense of being different from another national group, and often feelings of superiority and chauvinism.

nationalist histories. Often glorified histories of a nation's past that serve as a unifier based on a common mission, culture, religion, language, and shared territory. Nationalist histories tend to elevate their nation's achievements and denigrate others.

nationalization. Appropriation by nation-states of the means of production—land, factories, corporations—usually in the name of "the people" of the nation.

nation-state. A Western idea that people with a common language and historical tradition should constitute a sovereign state. *See* nation *and* state.

NATO. *See* North Atlantic Treaty Organization.

Nazism. Adolf Hitler's Nazi movement borrowed from Italian fascism, adding virulent racial anti-Semitism. Hitler came to power in 1933 during the depths of the Great Depression.

neoliberalism. The dominant economic model in most parts of the world, it professes free trade and low government intervention in the economy. It is promoted by the International Monetary Fund, World Bank, and other Western lending institutions.

neo-patrimonialism. This patronage system is prevalent among some African leaders who use their political power to enrich members of their own ethnic group rather than act in the interests of the country as a whole.

New Imperialism. In the late nineteenth century, European powers divided up most of the last remaining free areas of Africa and Asia. By 1900, almost 85 percent of the earth's land surface was controlled by European peoples.

New Partnership for Africa's Development (NEPAD). An all-African organization formed in 2001 to examine failed political and economic policies and recommend new strategies for cooperation and development.

newly industrialized countries (NICs). States nearing developed-world (core) status: Singapore, South Korea, and Taiwan.

niqab. A dress that covers the entire body, accompanied by a face veil, gloves, and, in some places, an eye screen or sunglasses.

nonrenewable resources. Materials or energy that have finite amounts, whose continued use leads to exhaustion.

North American Free Trade Agreement (NAFTA). Agreement between the United States, Canada, and Mexico to encourage free trade by eliminating previously existing impediments to free trade.

North Atlantic Treaty Organization (NATO). Founded in 1949, NATO is a military and political alliance formed among West European countries and the United States and Canada, mainly to protect against Soviet attack. It has twenty-six members today.

Northeast Asia. China, Japan, and the Koreas are the main countries of this region of Asia.

OAS. *See* Organization of American States.

opportunity costs. In economics, the loss created by accepting one option over others.

Organization of African Unity (OAU). In part as a result of US and Belgian intrigue to overthrow Patrice Lumumba in Congo, thirty-two African states formed the Organization of African Unity in 1963. The OAU hoped to maintain the independence of African states in the wake of immense Soviet and American pressure to take sides in the Cold War. Now called the African Union (AU).

Organization of American States (OAS). The principal diplomatic body of the Western Hemisphere. Members include all countries in the Americas and the Caribbean, with the exception of Cuba, whose Communist government has been prevented from participation since 1962.

organization of difference. Function of social institutions and processes to regulate behavior and reward or punish deviance.

Pacific. Global region including the countries of Australia and New Zealand and the regions of Polynesia, Micronesia, and Melanesia.

paradigm. Sets of practices and the associated theories and ideas that define a scientific or scholarly discipline.

parsimony. Efficiency; a parsimonious theory is one that explains much with a few key concepts.

participant observation. Classic anthropological research method involving relatively long-term engagements with a host community in which an anthropologist enters into the everyday life of the community insofar as his or her hosts permit.

pastoralism. Economic system based on the raising of cattle. In the Middle East, transhuman pastoralism was common, involving nomadic herders who traveled with their flocks to take advantage of seasonal change.

peninsulares. Spanish- or Portuguese-born individuals living in colonial Latin America.

petrodollars. Funds deposited in mostly Western banks during the 1970s petroleum boom in the Middle East. Some of these funds eventually made their way into loans to Latin America and other parts of the developing world.

petro-states. Most of the world's oil-rich states, such as Nigeria, which have not invested petroleum profits in a sustainable economic system that benefits the population as a whole.

philosophical relativism. A position that claims, in essence, that whatever a community does is right for its members. Few, if any, anthropologists would claim to adhere wholeheartedly to this philosophy.

place. An area and the human feelings and values attached to it.

political and diplomatic history. Historical study concerned with the study of power and power relationships. The oldest historical tradition, political and diplomatic history is often characterized by biographies of great people. Politics, law, and foreign policy come under the purview of political history.

political ecology. A study utilizing politics, economy, culture, and geography to analyze environmental issues.

political economy. The interrelations of political institutions and economic systems. including markets, prices, and trade, as well as laws, governments, public opinion, and trade regulation.

political Islam. The invocation of Islam in political and economic life, both by political actors within states and by groups opposed to existing governments. Usually advocates a political system based on some interpretation of Sharia.

political liberalism. The philosophy concerned with civil liberty, political equality, and individual freedom to control one's own property and destiny.

political theory. The branch of political science that focuses on philosophies of political behavior and organization.

politics. Conflict between groups vying for power to make decisions and take action.

Polynesia. Region of islands in the Pacific including Hawaii, Tonga, Samoa, and French Polynesia.

popular histories. Histories written for mass consumption that compromise veracity for dramatic effect.

populism. Authoritarian leader's appeal to the masses with nationalist slogans and government spending on the lower classes.

postindustrial economy. An economy in which the tertiary (services) and quaternary (research) sectors are most common in employment and growth.

postmodernist history. Postmodernists argue that all history reveals as much about the motives of the author as it does about what happened in the past. They emphasize the subjectivity of the historical record.

primary sources. Artifacts, diaries, letters, memoirs, official documents, and other direct evidence from the past.

production state. A state whose government derives the bulk of its revenues from taxing the wealth of its citizens.

progressivism. German philosopher Georg Wilhelm Friedrich Hegel wrote that as new ideas challenged old traditions, a new synthesis would result to develop better political, economic, and social structures. In other words, through education and rising standards of living, people can rid society of past wrongs such as slavery, war, and inequality, and learn to live in peace and harmony.

projection. Systematic transformation of a three-dimensional representation of the earth (a globe) to a two-dimensional representation (a map).

protectionism. A political-economic strategy of imposing tariffs or establishing quotas on foreign imports, usually with the goal of limiting foreign industries' competition with domestic industries.

proto-state. Communities with a historical claim to land currently under the sovereignty of one or more states.

providential. The idea that meaning in life derives from the belief that a higher power is operating in the world, if not always in explicable ways.

public administration. Branch of political science that focuses on applied politics, especially by local public institutions.

Public Islam. Invocations of Islam in everyday public life, from everyday conversations to movies, blogs, and Web sites.

Quran. The written record of Muhammad's revelation.

rationality. In economics, the assumption that human beings, and the institutions they create (organizations, corporations, states, etc.), will always act in such a way as to maximize rewards and minimize losses.

realism. Theory that explains political behavior as a function of rational actions by self-interested states in a global system of anarchy.

realpolitik. Another term for realism, from the German.

recession. Any period of declining economic growth that continues beyond two consecutive quarters (i.e., six months).

refugees. People who must flee their country of origin due to persecution, war, famine, terrorism, or natural disaster and seek asylum in a foreign country.

region. A mental construct of an area.

relations of production. In Marxist thought, the social relations that are necessarily formed by the way societies produce and reproduce their material lives. The relations of production determine how incomes, products, and assets are socially distributed, and they constitute the social structure of the society.

relativism. The anthropological commitment to recognizing that humans are capable of collectively generating innumerable creative solutions to the problems that beset life, and to understanding how and why they work in a particular time and place.

renewable resource. A resource produced by nature at rates similar to those consumed by people.

resource. An item used to satisfy a need.

revisionist history. Historical accounts that use new evidence to revise generally accepted or traditional versions of the past.

Right, the. The side of the political spectrum that emphasizes national security and national interests in world politics, and individual liberties, private property, and low government involvement in domestic affairs in domestic politics.

royalties. Payments made based on a percentage of the number of goods sold.

scale. Relative sizes of an object on a map and in reality.

scarcity. Scarcity results from insufficient resources to fill limitless and subjectively defined wants in a world in which not all individual desires can be fulfilled.

secondary sources. Newspaper articles, journal articles, books, and other oral or written narratives derived from primary sources.

Sharia. Code of law derived from the Quran and hadith.

Shia. The largest minority sect in Islam. Members believe that authentic teaching and leadership after the prophet's death came to biological descendants of the prophet.

Silk Road. Trade routes linking Asia, Middle East, and Europe.

Sinn Fein. The political arm of the Irish Republican Army.

social democracy. Most Western European states developed a social welfare system after World War II that features cooperation between labor and management, generous state pension and unemployment benefits, and universal healthcare.

social entrepreneurship. The use of entrepreneurial principles to create, organize, and manage projects intended to produce social change.

socialism. A variety of political doctrines or movements that endorse a political-economic system whereby property and the distribution of wealth are controlled by the community.

South Asia. India, Pakistan, and Bangladesh are the main countries of this region of Asia.

Southeast Asia. Thailand, Indonesia, Malaysia, and Vietnam are the main countries of this region of Asia.

Southern Cone. The southernmost region of South America, including Uruguay, Argentina, Chile, and Paraguay.

sovereign debt crisis. The inability of the government of a country to pay back its debt in full. Also known as *sovereign debt default.*

space. The arrangement of geographic phenomena across the earth's surface.

spatial interaction. The movement or flows across space.

spatial organization. The delineation of territory.

Stalinism. Joseph Stalin came to power in the Soviet Union after Vladimir Ilyich Lenin's death in 1924. Through random purges of the Communist Party and forced industrialization and collectivization, he killed millions as he institutionalized totalitarian rule.

state. An international actor characterized by a defined territory, a central government, and international recognition as a legitimate sovereign entity. *See also* nation *and* nation-state.

state-sponsored terrorism. Term for situations in which a state harbors, funds, or otherwise supports the terrorist enemies of another state.

state terrorism. The contemporary use by states of retaliatory bombing, death squads, torture, and other such actions.

structural adjustment program (SAP). Part of the neoliberal economic model, SAPs include difficult economic policies such as currency devaluation; cuts in government subsidies, jobs, and services; opening to foreign investment and trade; and privatization.

subsidies. Forms of government financial assistance, such as tax breaks or capital payments, meant to encourage or discourage the production of a good.

sultan. Supreme political ruler of the Ottoman Empire.

Summit of the Americas. Established to allow the leaders of the Organization of American States to discuss the implementation of the principles of the Washington Consensus, a set of neoliberal policies aimed at instituting free markets for the entire Western Hemisphere.

Sunni. The majority of the world's Muslims. Members accept the authority of the caliphs as successors to the prophet.

supply. The amount of goods available for trade.

supply curve. A graphical depiction of the relationship between price and supply. As the price of a good increases, sellers are motivated to increase the supply of that good.

sustainability. Offered as a criticism of liberal economic ideas of unlimited growth, sustainability refers to a political-economic system that meets the needs of present communities without reducing the ability of future generations to meet their needs.

sustainable development. Economic change and growth that balances environmental protection and social equity over the long term.

symbol. Something that stands for something else according to a cultural convention, association, or resemblance.

tariff. A tax placed by governments on imported goods for the purpose of protecting national industries from foreign competition.

terrorism. A strategy by which subnational groups not recognized as legitimate by the states they oppose seek to resist those states by targeting nonstate actors, disrupting the flow of everyday life, and spreading generalized fear among the populations of those states.

theoretical relativism. An assumption much tested and held by most anthropologists that all human actions make rational sense when understood in their own contexts.

theories of history. Frameworks that historians use to understand the factors that cause historical change.

"too big to fail." A slogan that emerged during the global recession of 2008, explaining the need many governments felt to use tax monies to bail out foundering banks and corporations whose failures would have greater fiscal consequences than the economy could absorb.

tribe. Large groups of people who share a common identity based on an assumption of common ancestry.

Troubles, the. Began in the 1960s with the Irish Republican Army and the Irish Catholic Nationalist community on one side and the Protestant Loyalists and the Royal Ulster Constabulary, the British army, and several Ulster paramilitary groups on the other. Spurred on by the civil-rights movement in the United States and the French student riots in 1968, Irish Catholics in Northern Ireland demanded their own equal civil and economic rights.

totalitarianism. Theory popularized in the West during the Cold War to equate communism with fascism. Instead of sitting at the opposite ends of the political spectrum, totalitarian theory held that the dictatorial methods used by the far Right and the far Left were similar.

uniform region. A region defined by a uniformity of features.

utility. The attempt to gain the highest possible well-being.

value of labor. According to liberal economic theory, the value of a product is determined by consumer choices assigning values to commodities. Marxist economic theory, in contrast, argues that a product is worth the value of the work expended to produce it.

Warsaw Pact. Formed in 1955 as a military alliance of East European countries and the Soviet Union. It served as a counterweight to NATO but quickly fell apart after the collapse of the Communist regimes in 1989.

Washington Consensus. A phrase invented by economist John Williamson, who posited ten policy recommendations for economic reform in Latin American countries plagued by fiscal irresponsibility. These recommendations included reinstitution of market economics, openness to global trade, and macroeconomic discipline.

World Bank. An international organization responsible for providing financial assistance and advice to countries to facilitate economic development and eliminate poverty.

World Trade Organization (WTO). An international organization responsible for negotiating, monitoring, and regulating international trade agreements. Its goal is to help producers of goods and services conduct business without fear of trade restrictions and government intervention.

worldview. The most encompassing level of cultural integration, comprising organized assumptions people have about the structure of the universe. A worldview is a model of reality that people use to orient themselves in the world.

WTO. *See* World Trade Organization.

zero-sum approach. Situation in which one nation's advantage requires another nation's loss.

Zionism. The belief that Jews constitute a sovereign people and nation and that they should have the right to establish and maintain a state in their ancestral homeland.

Index